High Contrast

HIGH CONTRAST

Race and Gender in Contemporary Hollywood Film

SHARON WILLIS

Duke University Press   Durham and London 1997

Printed in the United States of America on acid-free paper ⊛
Set in Trump Mediaeval by Tseng Information Systems Inc.
Library of Congress Cataloging-in-Publication Data appear
on the last printed page of this book.
Chapter 4 has appeared in revised form as "Special Effects:
Sexual and Social Difference in *Wild at Heart*," *Camera
Obscura,* January–May 1991, pp. 275–95.
Chapter 6 appeared as "The Fathers Watch the Boys'
Room," *Camera Obscura,* September–January 1993–94, pp.
41–73; a revised version of this chapter will be reprinted in
Film Studies, ed. Linda Williams and Christine Gledhill
(London: Edward Arnold, forthcoming).
Brief sections of chapter 3 have appeared in revised form
in "Hardware and Hardbodies, What Do Women Want?:
A Reading of *Thelma and Louise*," in *Film Theory Goes to the
Movies,* ed. Jim Collins, Hilary Radner, and Ava Preacher
Collins (New York: Routledge, 1993), pp. 120–28.
A portion of the introduction appears in modified form in
"Telling Differences: Race, Gender, and Sex in *The Crying
Game*," *Boys: Masculinities in Contemporary Culture,* ed. Paul
Smith (Boulder, Colo.: Westview Press, 1996), pp. 97–112.

To my parents, George D. Willis (1921–1989)
and Constance A. Willis (1925–1995)
And in memory of Scott Sommer (1951–1993)
and Mildred Louise Barnes (1925–1994)

CONTENTS

Acknowledgments   ix

Introduction   1

PART I   Battles of the Sexes

1   Mutilated Masculinities and Their Prostheses:
Die Hards and Lethal Weapons   27

2   Insides Out: Public and Private Exchanges
from *Fatal Attraction* to *Basic Instinct*   60

3   Combative Femininity:
Thelma and Louise and *Terminator 2*   98

PART II   Ethnographies of the "White" Gaze

4   Do the Wrong Thing:
David Lynch's Perverse Style   131

5   Tell the Right Story: Spike Lee and the
Politics of Representative Style   158

6   Borrowed "Style": Quentin Tarantino's
Figures of Masculinity   189

Notes   217

Index   259

ACKNOWLEDGMENTS

Throughout its prolonged development, this project has received crucial support from numerous and varied sources. First, I thank family and friends for their unwavering confidence in the project, and for enlivening it with their readings of these films, and for not asking too often about my deadlines. Thanks to Amy Willis, Beth Willis, Christopher Willis, Meghan Willis, Lawrence Edelman, Steven Barnes, Billie Awad, and George Awad.

Generous institutional support has allowed for both time and invaluable exchanges. I began this project at the Society for the Humanities at Cornell University in 1988. I am very grateful to Mary Ahl, Agnes Sirrine, and Linda Allen for their support, and especially to Jonathan Culler, whose gracious directorship of the Society made that year so productive for me. I owe a special debt to the other fellows, and most especially to Biddy Martin and Michèle Barrett. My thanks also to Wimal Dissanayake and the East-West Center, Honolulu, for the opportunity to participate in the East-West Film Seminar, 1991. A visit to the University of Turku, Finland, through the kind invitation and hospitality of Jukka Sihvonen, Martii Lahti, and Pirjo Ahokas, provided me with a timely shift in perspective. Audiences at Wesleyan University, Princeton University School of Architecture, University of California at Irvine's Humanities Research Seminar, Cornell University, George Washington University, and the University of Colorado, Colorado Springs, offered me valuable critical challenges that have shaped this argument.

My colleagues at the University of Rochester in Modern Languages and Cultures, English, and Visual and Cultural Studies have consistently provided an animated intellectual environment that has sustained this project. I am especially indebted to the Susan B. Anthony

Institute's research seminar, which has been for me the most dynamic source of critical exchange at the University. My deep appreciation to Philip Berk, Lisa Cartwright, Douglas Crimp, Deborah Grayson, Ken Gross, Eva Guelen, Tom Hahn, Patricia Herminghouse, Michael Ann Holly, Rosemary Kegl, Anita Levy, Bette London, Joyce Middleton, David Pollack, David Rodowick, Robert ter horst, and Janet Wolff. Special thanks to Tom DiPiero and Sue Gustafson, for keeping me on track day to day.

My co-editors at *Camera Obscura* have had a profound impact on my thought, my methodology, and my style. I thank them for the most rewarding collaboration of my life: Julie D'Acci, Lynne Joyrich, Elisabeth Lyon, and Sasha Torres; finally, special thanks to Constance Penley, whose timely interventions have more than once brought things back into perspective. Many colleagues and friends provided vital support, insight, and encouragement. I am grateful to Lynn Enterline, Judith Frank, Teresa Jillson, Mandy Merck, Meaghan Morris, Timothy Murray, Jeff Nunokawa, Fred Pfeil, Andrew Ross, Kaja Silverman, Paul Smith, Rajani Sudan, Tim Walters, and David Wills. My fondest gratitude goes to my oldest and most rigorous critic, Elissa Marder. Our conversations have had a shaping impact on my work, and their traces persist throughout it. To Leonard Green, who sustained the uneasy early stages of this project: there's always history.

Duke University Press has facilitated the later stages of the project in every way. My wholehearted thanks to the two readers for their generosity, and their incisive and judicious criticism, to Ken Wissoker for his encouragement, and to Pam Morrison for her help. Credit for dramatic improvements in prose also goes to delightfully cranky copyeditor Bob Mirandon.

Finally, my thanks to John Michael. While he tends to think of himself as belated, in my experience his timing is perfect. He has helped me to stop rushing, and to punctuate stories more precisely. My debt to him is immeasurable.

INTRODUCTION

Our culture continues to be preoccupied with difference. From the most banal and everyday of practices to the most spectacular and extraordinary of representations, differences mark our cultural production. For some time, however, our contemporary investments have tended to eroticize and aestheticize rather than to neutralize, deny, or smooth out difference. Popular representations have amplified these eroticizing impulses by elaborating social differences as aesthetic or sensational effects. In the movies, dedicated as they are to spectacle, then, it is not surprising to find an intense focus on those differences that we are inclined to associate with visibility—gender and race. So powerful is our cultural wish to believe that differences give themselves to sight that the cinema is able to capitalize, both ideologically and financially, on the fascination that dazzling visual contrasts exercise upon us. At the same time, as films read our social field, they may both mobilize and contain the conflict, uneasiness, and overwrought affect that so often accompany the confrontation of differences in everyday practices. Cinema seems to borrow and channel those energies through a volatile affective range, from terror, panic, shock, and anxiety to titillation, thrills, excitement, fascination, pleasure, and comfort, while it proliferates representations of social difference as a central or peripheral spectacle.

This book aims to analyze the interactions between racial and sexual difference in contemporary popular films. These representations exercise reciprocally structuring effects, as each difference helps to determine the spaces that the other inhabits, the shapes it takes. This process works as actively in the context of the spectator positions and audience formations that popular films continually renegotiate, as it does in the representations that they produce. The aim of this study is to restore a political content to the social differences that many films exhibit as mere aesthetic contrast. Of course, political "content" is itself constructed in relation to fantasy. But this in no way diminishes its power.[1] Whether we are speaking of race, of gender, or of sexuality, fictive constructions and fantasies lend historical and material force to the matter of difference. While popular films built of sharp contrasts seem to assign a general weightlessness to social identities, this book proposes to assess the gravity of those social identities and to investigate the massive ideological work they perform.

This project necessarily bears on identity and identifications, which can be considered only as relations. It presumes that in constructing gendered identifications, films and spectators are always more or less unconsciously engaging with racial identifications as well. At the same time, the project explores the particular ways in which our culture's contemporary fetishization of differences may operate to transform *only* the rhetoric of the dominant discourses without changing their structural effects. To explore fetishized difference entails careful analysis of the political ambivalence that allows even those representations which try to respect social specificities, oppositional identities, and contentious positions to reproduce the cultural dominance that they seek to overturn. Animating much of our popular cinema, this ambivalent cultural labor reveals itself with particular force in the struggles and conflicts that it both dramatizes and thematizes around sexuality and race.

As popular films increasingly activate fantasies that bind pleasure to aggression, they frequently remain preoccupied, as the culture is, with crossings, displacements, and ruptures that defy or challenge social borders and with the definitions of identity and of "proper" place that those borders support. Representations that focus on the social boundaries of race, class, culture, and sexuality often exhibit ambivalent mixes of desire and violence that respond to collective anxieties about shifting borders. At the same time, they mobilize fantasmatic pleasure and aggression within structures that themselves displace differences. These essays explore such displacements as they unfold in everyday pleasures, terrors, fascinations, and distractions, where we may see how social struggle and antagonism get inscribed in fantasy structures.

To analyze displacements that map social conflict onto collective fantasies in our entertainments will also entail examining the political uses and functions of ambivalence, since ambivalent representations often expose our most highly contested social and cultural sites. As Kobena

Mercer puts it: "the moment of undecidability is rarely experienced as a purely textual event; rather it is the point where politics and the contestation of power are felt to be at their most intense."[2] Mercer emphasizes the importance of progressive political contests around such moments: "Indeterminacy means that multiaccentual or polyvalent signs have no necessary belonging and can be articulated and appropriated into the political discourse of the Right as easily as they can into that of the Left. Antagonistic efforts to fix the multiple connotations arising from the ambivalence of key signs of ideological struggle demonstrate what Gramsci (1971) described as a 'war of position' whose outcome is never guaranteed in advance one way or the other" (203).

We might characterize the interdeterminacy and ambivalence that shape both identity politics and the effects that they produce on the cultural field in much the same way. In popular representations, as in the world, identity politics is likely to go both ways, to become either a site for the progressive use of diversity or an opportunity for the conservative management of difference within existing power structures. And this is why we owe our attention, however ambivalent it is, to the work that popular representations responding to the pressures of identity politics thematize and perform upon differences. At one extreme, we find popular representations that strain to manage differences figured as pure threat in images and stories which mobilize social anxiety, only to reassure mainstream audiences by restoring the privilege of white heterosexuality, white masculinity, and the white middle-class family. At the other end of the spectrum, we find other representations that strive to accommodate diversity through scripts organized around specific identities and intended to capture new identity-based market segments.

These contemporary representations of "race" emerge in a culture marked by the difficulty that "whiteness" has had in seeing itself as racialized. Since this culture is thoroughly racialized, this means that whiteness has had a hard time seeing *itself* at all. Where it can juxtapose itself to "blackness," blackness becomes the bearer of racial meanings so that whiteness can emerge as free from meaning. For Toni Morrison, this juxtaposition is structurally central to the U.S. literary tradition. While "blackness" is saturated with meanings, Morrison argues, "whiteness, alone, is mute, meaningless, unfathomable, pointless, frozen, veiled, curtained, dreaded, senseless, implacable. Or so our writers seem to say."[3] "U.S. literature," Morrison contends, "historically maintains a structural dependency on such non-encounters with blackness, through which "unmeaning, unfathomable whiteness" appears (58).[4] This book, then, seeks to track modern representational embodiments of the continually missed encounter between "whiteness" and its own racial meanings.

In his study of the history of representations of African Americans in U.S. cinema, James Snead isolates "marking" as a common technique for managing racial difference to the profit of "whiteness." "Marking," he writes, "makes it visually clear that black skin is a 'natural' condition turned 'man-made sign.'"[5] Representations that obsessively mark the "obviousness" of the visible racial difference establish its iconicity over and over, reconstructing the body as aesthetic and ideological sign. Attention to the "obvious" as overmarked, or oversignified, leads us to interrogate the potency of the very cultural and representational banalities that obsessively insist on the legibility of social differences we take to be visible and obvious, and that we understand as subject to immediate appropriation at a *glance:* gender difference and racial difference. Popular cinematic representations inscribe these differences in and through each other, so that they consistently trade and borrow meanings. So, for example, as the iconic functions of the white female body diffuse and splinter in contemporary popular film, this is happening in a representational framework braced by the relatively stable requirement that blackness operate primarily as an icon.[6]

Morrison has analyzed the function of racial iconicity as follows: "race has become metaphorical—a way of referring to and disguising forces, events, classes, and expressions of social decay and economic division far more threatening to the body politic than biological 'race' ever was" (63). And she connects this metaphorical life of "race" to display: "it seems that it has a utility far beyond economy . . . and has assumed a metaphorical life so completely embedded in daily discourse that it is perhaps more necessary and more on display than ever before" (63). In fact, we might suggest that in contemporary U.S. culture, the metaphoricity of race is, precisely, sustained through its display. Display, of course, always entails a spectator, a gaze. But if the metaphoricity of race depends on display, in this historical context, it also depends on a dominant culture that works to imagine its own gaze as unseen. A gaze that forgets that it can be seen seeing, an attentive ear that forgets that its hearing presence can be felt, itself overheard. This is one way of figuring the dominant culture's attention to nondominant—or to oppositional—cultures, to the figures of "race" that seem to fascinate it since this gaze seems unable to imagine another gaze to meet its own.

As a limited but significant number of African American-authored productions have entered popular cinematic distribution over the past several years, the dominant culture continues to demand that films by and for African Americans display—and fix—some kind of "social reality" that lies beyond or beneath fantasy. Such a demand maintains its own privilege of ignorance under cover of the authority it grants to certain filmmakers. At the same time, big-budget Hollywood productions as well as television dramas more and more often introduce African American characters—redeeming, judging, or threatening—whose race is coded as incidental or contingent.[7] More often than not, these peripheral figures— Ella Shohat calls them "guests in the narrative"—emerge as accidental or incidental presences whose impact is often much more powerfully visual than verbal.[8]

An interesting symptom of this representational regime and the anxieties that haunt it is the ubiquitous African American judge or police chief.[9] A peripheral figure granted limited screen time and no point of view, this guy—and it is usually, but not always, a man—appears to organize and adjudicate the activities of the primary cast, often mostly white, but sometimes "multicultural." As the embodiment of legal authority or moral surveillance, confined to a peripheral spectator's role, this recurrent figure enlists the body of the actor to perform a lot of ideological work. To put it bluntly, this looks like a cheap market concession on the part of the dominant culture industry to its perception of an ambient "political correctness." Standing as visible markers or indexes of an extra-diegetic "real," such figures exhibit racial difference, but sideline it, so that they also help to hedge ideological bets. That is, they seem designed to counterbalance, in some fantasmatic symmetry, any depictions of African Americans as criminals, and so to inoculate crime dramas against inflection, or infection, with racist overtones.[10]

But the obsession with African American judges and law enforcement commanders also acts as a kind of compensatory gesture in its radical distortion of referentiality since this compulsive representation so patently contradicts the actual number of African Americans who occupy such positions in the justice system, a system consistently under fire for the inequalities it perpetuates. We also might suggest that this superego figure functions as the obverse twin of the threatening criminal id figure that historically has emerged so frequently in much popular entertainment. In its compulsive return, this figure also exhibits, or crystallizes, an anxiety about judgment, a fantasy that the truth of whiteness might emerge in another's gaze. But the dominant culture posits this gaze only in order to represent it consistently as internalized and ventriloquized, as a marker of difference in a scene where subjects do not engage in reciprocal exchange, but, rather, in mutual surveillance. So while such figures mark allusions to the social field, they simultaneously operate as indexes of paranoid fantasies that situate African Americans as the ones who know the truth about race, while avoiding any occasion for a reciprocated gaze that would cause the dominant culture to look at itself through another's eyes.

Such "guest" figures are sustained by a peculiar division of representational labor, whereby majority discourse expects so-called minority discourse to emerge as truth effect, as real effect, in texts whose relation to their producers and audiences is radically essentialized. This is perhaps the inevitable risk of identity politics—it is always open to regressive strategies that contain "identity" as evacuated iconic surface, or as a dense authenticity that resides elsewhere, to be called in to testify to the center, which thereby sustains its own "passion of ignorance," its own privilege *not* to know.

In films and television coded as "entertainment," these figures function as *markers* or icons of a certain social referentiality that the designation "entertainment" is meant to hold off, to keep out of frame. This effect coheres within a representational terrain structured by a certain dialectical interplay of distraction and intense attention, where the collective imagination that focuses intently for a week or so at a time on racial or sexual difference as "issues," tends to reduce these differences to "distractions" within any genre coded for entertainment.[11] These distractions are banalities raised to the level of event and then made to subside into the incidental.[12] My project is most particularly interested in those complex everyday representational moments of negotiation where one difference is made to stand in for, to do the job of, to trivialize or eclipse, the others.

Contemporary U.S. popular culture is a field where coincidences between objects whose manifestly different subject, aim, and address are built on a less obvious, but shared, dialogue with their historical moment.[13] In such coincidences we may read competing interpretations of social conflict that constitute the versions of history through which the culture understands itself. Coincidences belong to no one and to no particular order. But that does not mean we can take them or leave them. In all their specificity, coincidences may reorient us, may become productive, if we ask the right questions of them. As they become history, if they do not become our productive coincidences, they may well become our common disasters.

A coincidence between a megabudget studio production and the work of an "independent" auteur, like the coincidence I focus on here in the introduction, between *Falling Down* and *The Crying Game,* for example, may serve as an exemplary case through which to begin exploring the terrain that grounds contemporary popular representations and their public reception. Cinematic production ever more dramatically polarizes the field of its address between large-scale spectacles, blockbusters addressed to the largest, least differentiated audience possible—in other words, to everyone and *no* one—and small movies that aim at a specific segment of the audience. This polarized field constitutes one arena for a development that Timothy Corrigan characterizes as the "distracted privatization of political life across a public sphere."[14] But such a division of market address no doubt also helps to sustain our reinvigorated interest in auteurs. James Naremore has shrewdly argued that the persistence and frequent renewal of the auteur has to do with anchoring filmic production to a social location through its point of enunciation. Such an anchoring, significantly, allows for and encourages the formation of collective cultural solidarities organized around author figures.[15]

In the dialogue of big and small screens that helps produce a public sphere governed by the politics of opinion, competing discourses tend to structure social issues as "events," but specifically as events whose duration is punctual, whose shape can be calculated and measured. Issues appear to happen to us, and this way of conceptualizing public opinion makes it look like weather. Just as the economy is increasingly figured as meteorological activity whose rise and fall, whose quirks and catastrophes, are natural and unevenly predictable but not responsive to politics or social struggle, so, too, "public opinion" is represented as being as volatile and intermittent as a storm.[16]

A singularly shaping force within this public sphere is the regular media discussion around the film industry. Paul Smith specifies the function of what he calls the "tributary media": "Part of the discursive role of reviews and journalistic criticism (as opposed to the popular discourse that the industry describes as 'word of mouth') is to set parameters for cultural discussion, and one of the centrally important strategies in that task is the attempt to construct intentions for any given film—that is, the attempt to affirm or confirm that the film's meaning is not accidentally produced."[17] This project considers such discourse as a textual frame where consumption itself produces the object and situates us as an audience in positions that are politically fragile and volatile. Contemporary audiences, then, might be characterized, in Timothy Corrigan's terms as "a localized, emotional, and temporary position where the fascinating power of ideology lies in its instability and where the politics of a public sphere plays itself out within the distracted arena of private games and personal feelings" (198).

This brings me to the question of my own participation as a spectator in this public sphere. Perhaps the most haunting problem entailed in writing about one's own cultural moment appears as a persistent sense of engaging in the impossible effort to stop time. Either racing to keep up by incorporating each new object that emerges, or wishing that there be no more new objects, the critic proceeds in the nagging certainty of always missing something. Equally disturbing, for me, has been the suspicion that the harder I try to read exhaustively, the more likely I am to falsify my objects, finding too many similarities among texts, so that everything fits some large, consistent patterns, or finding too many shifts and differences, so that each specific articulation of the issues might be mistaken for a new ideological configuration.

Finally, the compelling pleasure and perhaps delusional feeling of urgency about dealing with one's own contemporary context produces some singular liabilities. And it is probably no accident that these tend to emerge thematically in my readings. That is, as I focus on a cultural fascination with borders, I do so in the face of my own anxiety that the bounded field I have constructed to study is largely artificial, and might be constructed entirely otherwise. Furthermore, as I examine the sensationalizing effects that many popular films exploit, exploring the ways they "borrow" affective energies from social conflict and displace them across the differences they represent, I become disturbingly aware that my own writing (for instance, in the analysis of Quentin Tarantino's work) may likewise borrow some force of surprise and sensational violence from the objects it reads. One might no doubt relate this anxiety about unconscious borrowing to the anxiety about "missing something." If I feel that the culture is always escaping me, I am reminded of the old cultural studies debates about whether or not consumers are cultural dupes. Tania Modleski has forcefully reframed that question, writing that "it seemed important at one historical moment to emphasize the way 'the people' resist mass culture's manipulations. Today, we are in danger of forgetting the crucial fact that like the rest of the world even the cultural analyst may sometimes be a 'cultural dupe'—which is, after all, only an ugly way of saying that we exist in ideology, that we are all victims, down to the very depths of our psyches, of cultural and political domination (even though we are never *only* victims)." [18] Working as I have on objects that I fell for in some way, I have burdened this project with the extra charge of worry about what escapes me, even as and *because* it takes me in.

In view of the cinema's reshaping of a public sphere, I have chosen for this introduction the coincidental U.S. release of *The Crying Game* and *Falling Down* in 1993 to lay out the terms of a dialogue between "big" and "small" productions, and "general" and "specific" issues, concerns, or discourses. My point here is to map out a politicized field of interests, pleasures, and anxieties by looking at two texts that may appear to operate at certain extremes, and to ask what these extremes may know about each other. If we were to imagine that *Falling Down* and *The Crying Game* might each respond to the other's way of knowing or imagining history and the social world it would be because each is preoccupied with telling differences. Where *The Crying Game* reorganizes a dazzling array of ambiguous sexual and racial differences through the central gaze of their beholder, a white heterosexual man, *Falling Down* scrambles to find differences that are telling within the field of the "same" in order to manage a certain middle-class white male anxiety about being falsely accused, falsely advertised, as the oppressor.

As the field of film reception now seems to overlap with, as much as to resemble, the world of television talk show discussion, it is perhaps not surprising that the stories which *The Crying Game* and *Falling Down* tell about the social force of race, gender, and sexuality could easily reduce to plots that fit the formats of television controversy. *The Crying Game* displays a powerful fascination with a body whose racial and sexual ambiguities trouble conventional categories; such bodies are familiarly the focus of intense scrutiny and of escalating discursive conflict on talk shows. Meanwhile, *Falling Down* offers a narrative built mostly of ideological slogans like the ones that audience members and guests alike are encouraged to broadcast under the guise of expressing an opinion. For these reasons, I take these films as an exemplary point of departure for exploring popular cinema's participation in the public sphere that reconstructs social issues as matters of opinion.

At the moment when Hollywood and its publicity machines have discovered that "difference" is bankable, the unexpected financial success of *The Crying Game* raises pointed questions about the ways in which popular reception articulates differences of gender, race, and sexuality together. Given that no small part of the film's commercial seduction depended on the media's collusion in guarding its "secret," *The Crying Game* offers an occasion to examine the role of fetishism in the film's internal economy as well as in our collective responses to it. Press complicity, in effect, becomes part of the text.[19]

But if the popular press could be so seduced by the idea of seducing audiences through the lure of secrecy, this should lead us to ask about the relationship of fetishism to knowingness, to the pleasures of being "in the know." At the same time, however, we need to interrogate the pleasures of obliviousness that the central secret's privilege entails. And this is because the film's "secret" lies elsewhere than in the visible revelation of sexual difference; it lies precisely in what we do not see, or, more properly, in the relation between what the film holds centrally in frame and what it leaves out of frame. If the film itself is preoccupied with successive framing effects in its discursive circulation, the big surprise credited with reframing the picture becomes the *whole* picture. The "secret" can only become the "whole picture," however, in a structural relay which suggests that race, sexuality, gender, and political position are all rhetorical figures, and figures of equal weight and intensity, operating autonomously.

Organizing its discourse around a failed effort to tell the difference between a man and a woman, *The Crying Game* makes other differences resistant to telling; they are obscured, unspoken, left hanging, as if they had nothing to tell. For instance, what difference does it make that Dil (Jaye Davidson), consistently figures as the benignly desirable version of feminine seductiveness, while Jude (Miranda Richardson), the IRA member, figures as its monstrously violent version? *The Crying Game* links these opposed versions of "femininity" in a complex intersection with male homoeroticism—where the erotic attraction between the sympathetic IRA comrade, Fergus, and Jody, the captured black British soldier, gets deflected through these two other bodies.

As the film plays its interracial love plot across a political narrative, it continually defers certain critical questions about the difference that social differences make. *The Crying Game*'s obsession with cutting and reframing creates collisions of abstracted, aestheticized, and eroticized differences instead of articulating them in a specific historical context. And in this universe, viewers are invited to line up in relation to Fergus, who spends the whole story trying not to know what he knows. Knowledge in this film hangs on the cut—real or imagined. An especially notable cut hides from view the act of fellatio that Dil performs on Fergus. Meanwhile, the subsequent sequence, which reveals the film's secret, unfolds without a cut. Once again, Dil's head is pushed out of frame, but this time without the cut that would allow one to maintain the belief that some technical trick is at work.[20]

Certainly the film treats this penis as some sort of "special" effect. Indeed, it fetishizes this effect to such an extent that we may lose sight of its appearance in a metaphorical relay that is centrally structured by the figure of a detail, one that changes everything—that changes the whole picture. Of course, this is the detail that the popular critical press celebrated in its complicity with Miramax, the film's distributor. Equally important, the cultural circulation of Davidson as an autonomous image reproduces the film's internal fetishism in a manner that is symptomatic of our collective ability to turn the film itself into a fetish object by reducing its story to this particular icon.

Against the background of the fellatio withheld from view, *The Crying Game*'s payoff comes in a later scene with the full disclosure of a flaccid penis. After Dil has revealed his penis, and the camera cuts back to his still "feminine" face, now disconnected from the body's sex by the cut in a move that mimics the cut from Dil's head going down on Fergus to Fergus's ecstatic face. Symmetrical substitutions—face for penis—operating on both Dil's and Fergus's bodies work to foreground their asymmetrical positions in relation to the camera, which retreats from Dil's penis, but veils or obscures Fergus's, as if there were nothing to be learned from Fergus's organ and everything to be learned from Dil's. The unseen and unmentioned white man's penis anchors the whole displacement from political narrative into private love story, and this displacement depends on that asymmetry. However, there is another image to account for: the sex act we do not see finally gives way to the picture of Jody, the black British soldier whom Fergus has held hostage and whose death has sent Fergus to England to evade pursuit and to pursue Dil.

But what does that image represent? In death, Jody is reduced to a framed picture, an image to which Fergus obsessively returns in fantasy. But Jody's death also serves to guarantee that the racial consciousness which he alone displays ("I get sent to the only place in the world where they still call you nigger to your face") and the masculine homosexuality which he embodies remain contained, framed beyond the boundaries of Fergus and Dil's relationship. Jody becomes the voice and the image of race through the same process that allows Dil's penis to replace his, by framing their shared race and sexuality in a site beyond narrative—the site of memory and of the fetish. Race, then, seems to adhere to Jody's body, while, on Dil's, color is a costume. But in producing these very different relationships of race to the body, the film does not undo racial meanings; it merely displaces them, like Jody, as it frames them apart from the story. At the same time, if the voice and the image of race coincide in pictures, these pictures relieve Fergus, the white man, of the necessity of speaking, reading, or knowing about race, just as they relieve the film of responsibility for the racialized stories and histories it might find around or behind the frozen images. But these stories nevertheless condition both their possibility and their allure.

If the film produces Jody as a still, iconic residue within its diegetic frame, the broader frame of *The Crying Game,* as consumer cultural artifact, produces Jaye Davidson/Dil as a widely circulating fetish object. As a number of critical and popular discussions foreground a fascination with Davidson's gender ambiguity, they follow the film in not recognizing his homosexuality. Equally important, however, is the tendency of popular press discussion to focus on his biraciality, as the son of a white Englishwoman and a black African man.[21] Davidson, then, becomes a figure of in-betweenness. But in-betweenness, in our contemporary context, especially when it entails race and gender, suggests comfortably undecidable ambivalence, the condensation of a number of differences at a distance. Equally compellingly, as an image in circulation Davidson speaks to a fantasy of difference aestheticized in a figure who represents a *unique* collision of differences held in suspense.

Retroactively, Dil/Jaye Davidson, the appealingly dangerous "woman," finally becomes the film's icon. He replaces Miranda Richardson, whose picture had appeared in the film's original publicity. Richardson's character, Jude, has operated as the film's bedrock, the character whose identity is straightforward and transparent. She remains static and fixed in frame, cast off early in the film's progress, only to return like the repressed to haunt and threaten Fergus, until Dil blows her away. And this, of course, is the murder that separates the lovers. So Jude operates as a deus ex machina for the film, which is stuck with a relationship it can neither sustain nor develop. But just as she has functioned as a lure for Jody, and a cover for Dil in the film's marketing, she also becomes the site on which the film deposits racism. In this regard, she shares Jody's fate, since the film has deposited "race" on him. Both characters take form only through their opposition to Dil, which is relentless. Jude is defined by the juxtaposition of her monstrous and violent femininity to Dil's, where Dil comes out the "better woman." Similarly, Jody's version of black masculinity can only be read across its opposition to Dil's.

Jody, then, becomes the absent site, perhaps even the *fantasmatic* site, where race is spoken and where it coincides with a homosexuality that is disconnected from transvestism. But in the figure of Jody the film hides and displays another central, perhaps even structuring, question—what is the difference between a black British actor playing a black Englishman and an African American actor playing one? Could it be that race and national identity come to interfere with each other for audiences on both sides of the Atlantic in such a way that this particular impersonation helps to exoticize the actor's race, on the one hand, and the character's on the other? Together, *The Crying Game*'s U.S. success and the ease of its translation from the British context suggest that this film makes more sense in the context of a U.S. version of "multiculturalism." But it is clear that its "sense" bodies forth because it has managed to cut history and the social out of its frame. It renders race as one of many differences colliding in a manageable spectacle for a dominant culture that is always looking at and speaking about, but rarely addressing, race. In this sense, "remembering" Jody in a different way than the film does, we might properly suggest that *The Crying Game* plays on two "open secrets," especially in its U.S. exhibition context, where race, too, often seems to function much like an open secret for the dominant culture.

The Crying Game gets caught up, or arrested, in its own fascination with the shimmering fetish it makes of Dil, where difference becomes the spectacle of a surplus body that overcomes social anxieties as it condenses together an array of differences that are not meant to strike us as telling. But this means that there can be no telling the story of masculinity that is neither heterosexual nor white. In the place of a masculinity structured in and through race and sexuality, we find the frozen fetish image of ambivalence.[22]

Particularly "American" investments in *The Crying Game*'s fetishized images of race and sexuality may come into fuller focus if we examine the film's coincidence with *Falling Down,* released a short time earlier in 1993. Like *The Crying Game, Falling Down* also tries to tell the story of white heterosexual masculinity as it maps the progress of a "white guy in a white shirt and tie," D-Fens (Michael Douglas), crossing a broad range of social territories in Los Angeles. We track D-Fens through fragmented perspectives. These include that of his own distorted street-level gaze, that of his terrified ex-wife, and that of another white guy in a white shirt, the policeman Prendergast (Robert Duvall), who is uncannily attuned to the logic that guides D-Fens's course.

D-Fens's journey is defined and propelled by a series of missed encounters, collisions, and misunderstandings. While the apparent model and subtext for all of his miscommunications is his relationship with his ex-wife, D-Fens's encounters with everyone else—from the Korean grocery store owner, to the Latino men in a park, to the clients and employees in a Whammy Burger, to the neo-Nazi surplus store owner—are structured by an increasing failure of language or speech as compounded misinterpretations amplify his rage and alienation.

Prendergast, by contrast, makes his way through the day of his retirement producing a similar series of missed encounters, as when he assumes a Japanese-American colleague can translate for a Korean speaker. Prendergast's misunderstandings, however, are set within the overarching framework of his understanding and anticipation of D-Fens's moves. On the one hand, his workday is organized by D-Fens's journey; on the other, it is consistently punctuated by his wife's obsessive phone calls.

Structurally motivated by a series of collisions or coincidences, this film seems driven to make coherent narrative meaning out of the random accidents that highlight these two white guys' parallel trajectories.[23] And while it writes the story of distinguishing between people who appear to be the "same" by constructing coincidences into a progression, it makes a parallel effort to render social differences meaningless and random in its obsessive focus on what differentiates D-Fens from Nick, the bigoted surplus store owner. As Carol Clover has put it, in the film's universe, "even Average White Men have trouble telling each other from the enemy, it seems."[24]

Falling Down's opening sequence inscribes the whole film in richly condensed form. Our hero's journey is marked as a set of delays and detours, originating in the traffic jam created by inevitable construction. While a fisheye lens discloses D-Fens's sweating face in extreme, claustrophobic, and distorted close-up, a standard-lensed camera nervously scans the surrounding chaos as if to supplement the view with that character's perspective. What D-Fens seems to see is a glut of signs, some amputated or broken, some unreadable, some of which turn out to mean exactly the opposite of what they say, and some of whose meanings are merely askew of what they seem to say. This is a world of signs "under construction."

That figure, of course, persists throughout *Falling Down,* culminating in its slick irony at the moment when D-Fens destroys a construction site with a rocket launcher. We remember that he tells a black child, who seems to believe that such things happen only in the movies, that he is making a film called "Under Construction."

But the film's opening sequence takes pains to establish the fact that we cannot establish where the problem of interpretation lies. Are the signs themselves fragmentary and unreliable, or is it their reader's perspective? D-Fens's personal slogan seems to be an angry interrogation, the one that structures the much-cited, and quite satisfying scene of consumer rebellion in the Whammy Burger fast food restaurant: "What's wrong with this picture?" This is the question he puts to his terrified fellow consumers in the Whammy Burger as he indicates that his rage originates in the discrepancy between the Whammy Burger as advertised and as lived/consumed.[25] But his question goes unanswered. The only response comes from a small African American boy who raises his hand as if in school. Significantly, the film does not let us hear from this boy, D-Fens's only interlocutor here. In leaving the scene upon the image of the mute boy, the film offers the possibility of another perspective, another voice, while at the same time withdrawing its offer.

In a similarly ambiguous effect, the fisheye lens that first reveals D-Fens to us suggests that his internal state may be inscribed on his face. But it also invites us to adopt his skewed perspective (as size and angle put things out of proportion) even as we look at him. A later echo of this effect occurs when D-Fens's eyeglasses have been broken; with one lens cracked, they materialize the asymmetry of his perspective. We are invited to see the world through the eyes of someone who is himself only a cipher.

At the same time that the camera explores D-Fens in the ever-narrowing cramped interior of his own car, a parallel sequence, intercut with this one, maps a panoramic view of the traffic around him. More and more restlessly, the camera returns to the beat-up, overcrowded car in front of D-Fens, to a woman putting on makeup, her face grotesquely distorted in the sideview mirror, to men shouting negotiations on car phones. Almost obsessively, it returns to a school bus filled with a multiethnic group of children making noise and throwing paper airplanes. This chaotic and suffocating environment, reinforced by the soundtrack, repeats periodically in the film, as when D-Fens is waiting for a bus, upon whose arrival he is literally pushed out of frame by the surging crowd of people of color who board it. *Falling Down*'s universe of signs that declare "under construction," then, also entails a reconstruction of what the "popular" means.

This opening sequence of impasse, with its chaotic abundance of messages, unfolds under a giant sign. As D-Fens abandons his car and starts the long walk home, marking the end of this sequence, he heads up a hill toward a huge billboard. Under the slogan, "White Is For Laundry," this billboard—an instance of the film's consistent bid for irony—proposes a different reading of whiteness and color than the one implicit in D-Fens's view of the multicultural traffic jam. In advertising a tanning product, the billboard broadcasts white people's desire to brown up, to acquire color, where color may suggest the desire to consume what bell hooks calls "a bit of the other."[26] But the whiteness this billboard figures carries a surplus. It bears the supplement of graffiti: a little man is crawling out of the bikini top from between the woman's breasts. Inscribed across the image the words "help me" make this a picture of entrapment. But if we read this image back across the sequence that it punctuates, a fear of engulfment by the feminine intersects with fears of being overrun by otherness, by aliens, by those who do not put English first, as in D-Fens's first encounters with the Korean grocery owner and the Latino guys in the park. In the image of the billboard graffiti, gender is inscribed in and under race. This intersection and displacement becomes one of the organizing frames of the film, since the billboard becomes both the point of origin, the original detour, and the point of orientation for Prendergast. This is the place where Prendergast and D-Fens intersect, even as it marks the site of D-Fens's detour onto a path of no return.

Surely nothing highlights the centrality of "surplus" so much as the fact that the film's pivotal moment, D-Fens's point of no return, takes place in a surplus store, in the claustrophobic backroom where the paraphernalia of American superpatriotism is piled in with Nazi implements and regalia. D-Fens definitively crosses over into criminality by killing Nick (Frederic Forrest), the store's owner, and this is the scene that gives the film its name. We might say, then, that this film is centrally *about* all sorts of ideological "surplus," remnants, fragments, residues, incoherent conjunctures. And these turn out to be the heart of the matter; they are not surplus at all, but central, core issues.

The surplus store scene turns on D-Fens's violent opposition to Nick's misrecognizing him as a fanatically bigoted vigilante like himself. Describing himself as "just a guy trying to get home," a guy who wants

to exercise his right to "freedom of speech" and "freedom to disagree,"
D-Fens asserts to Nick: "We are not the same. I'm an American and you're
a sick asshole." Nick picks up on the rhetoric of freedom in the rant that
locates him as a racist homophobe caught in the throes of a frenzied eroticized panic. As he pushes D-Fens against a table and stands behind him,
attempting to place handcuffs on his wrists, Nick carries on in a simula-
tion of his fantasies of interracial prison rape. When D-Fens resists, arguing that he cannot present his other hand for restraint because he will
fall down, Nick repeats with escalating intensity an intensely eroticized
sentence, "Give it to me, give it to me." This sordid simulated rape scene
plays on the cliché of a homosexual panic underlying fascistic tendencies, which invites us to imagine that this raging homophobe is haunted
and motivated by his *own* homosexual longings.

This moment turns out to be transformative. After this first murder,
D-Fens changes his clothes, trading in his white shirt and tie for para-
military gear, and acquires his biggest weapons—including the rocket
launcher. This is also the point where the fall begins. That fall that is suspended, only to be completed at the film's end when D-Fens finally falls
off Venice Pier, having traded his rocket launcher for the smallest and
most anodyne of guns, the water pistol, and having voiced the incredu-
lous question, "*I'm* the bad guy?" Of course this question constitutes a
distant but direct echo of the surplus store scene, the scene that means to
establish Nick as the "bad guy," for D-Fens and for the film, and to establish a distinct difference between the two men, "we are not the same."
As Carol Clover argues, this explains why Nick's character is so exaggerated: "He secures a position we might otherwise be inclined to ascribe to
D-Fens. . . . By locating genocidal viciousness in the neo-Nazi (and having
D-Fens kill him, moralizing about freedom of speech as he does so), the
film can define D-Fens as your average short-tempered neighbor who just
happened to break one day" (8). But Nick also represents an exaggerated
condensation of the tendencies that the film discourse wants to exploit.
And none of D-Fens's later actions—from his killing Nick to his taunting
rich golfers—can rewrite his hatred of everyone else; the "regular guy"
just finally fighting back does not exhaust the calculations of the fore-
going imagery.

Bluntly speaking, in *Falling Down* everything begins and ends in the
family, begins and ends with sexual difference, which is primarily articulated domestically. But this is disclosed to us only gradually in the back-
and-forth movement that brings D-Fens's and Prendergast's stories into a

collision—and into collusion—and substitutes one white guy in a white shirt and tie for another, allowing the film to "prove" its point: that all white men are not the same. What poses as a critique of the white male complaint is in fact a feint; the film is really more about Prendergast than D-Fens. And the differences between the two are slight and subtle.

Just as the (false) opposition between the two men is structured around their relationships to home, so it is structured by their relations to women as the problem. Prendergast's wife, Amanda (Tuesday Weld), figures as the hideous subtext of his reluctant retirement and his ruined reputation. Her fears have translated into what his colleagues read as his cowardice. So Prendergast's problems begin in the home, in the ruin of his wife, who "only had her beauty."[27] Part of the film's aggression lies in its making *her* ruin the site and source of *his* degradation and emasculation. On D-Fens's side, the parallel problem is not his ex-wife, Beth (Barbara Hershey), as much as it is his timid, paranoid, deranged mother, locked up in her house with her "glass menagerie." And Prendergast's insight, his skill as a detective, is confirmed on this ground: he can catch his suspect because he knows how to handle difficult, damaged women. In the film's equation, Prendergast's wife has made him a coward, while D-Fens's mother has made him a psycho.

As a husband, D-Fens is Prendergast's opposite. He has been irrationally abusive, whereas Prendergast becomes, in the film's terms, "rationally" abusive, as is demonstrated in the triumphant moment when he "gets his balls back." Prendergast finally tells his wife off, shouting viciously at her: "Amanda, shut up, shut up. I'll get home when I'm finished and not one second before . . . is that clear? And you have dinner ready and waiting for me." Perhaps the most powerful effect of this eruption is its split address. Prendergast is speaking both to his wife and to another woman, his Latina partner, Sandra Torres, who secures the ideological high ground for him by applauding his aggression. So Prendergast's position as the film's "good guy" takes shape around his success in securing dominance over his crazed wife and in reclaiming his *home* through this patriarchal posturing.

Preoccupied with homes though it is, *Falling Down* believes itself to have no ideological home. It offers incoherently competing positions and messages with one hand while taking them back with the other. Unlike the "heroes" who never quite make it home, this film, despite itself, brings all the urban social struggle down to a specific ideological home. Everything comes back to an individual's rights as a consumer—a consumer of goods, property, space, and speech. In the same movement, however, "home" figures doubly—all the violence, struggle, and chaos of the urban spaces that D-Fens traverses are nothing but a long detour in his journey back to the nuclear family. Or, more properly, the detour is generated in the space—which is impossible to traverse—between his mother's house and his ex-wife's.

Finally, *Falling Down* seems to be shaped entirely in relation to the "home."[28] Beneath its ruse of ideological homelessness, this film really is *about* ideologies under construction, renewing themselves in a series of trade-offs, transactions between sexual difference and every other social difference that demands attention. A film that appears to be blaring out a message that it is powerfully intent on *not* claiming is always, indeed, of significant ideological interest. D-Fens, an "equal opportunity" hater, remains apparently unconscious of the points of overlap between his position and a range of familiar regressive, reactionary, and bigoted positions that circulate collectively. And like its hero, the film seems to think it can bump into some of the ugliest available ideological positions while clinging to an aimless pluralist populism, writing these off to individual idiosyncrasy, while capitalizing on the allure of their potential for affective force and cathartic release, without getting stuck in any one of them.[29]

We may understand *Falling Down* as a kind of ideological centrifuge with respect to multicultural society; that is, it scatters all differences around the central force field emanating from the white middle-class family man, as if differences could only be positioned in relation to him and his radically individual identity. By contrast, *The Crying Game* operates centripetally, agglomerating all the force of difference around the dazzling fetish that shimmers under the straight white man's fascinated gaze. Such contrasting approaches may generate particular interest at a moment when popular culture seems increasingly preoccupied—both consciously and unconsciously—with social differences, just as the popular press generates endless discussion and debate around cultural diversity, regularly flattened out in the fuzzier notion of "multiculturalism." The project of this book is to explore these competing images and stories in their mutual embeddedness and their dialogue across the fields of Hollywood film, independent film, promotional media, and broader popular discussions.

The three chapters in Part I examine various big-budget treatments of the "battles of the sexes" in an effort to show how collective fantasies and anxieties about other forms of social difference—race, sexuality, ethnicity, and class—may be mapped onto, and embedded within, an arena that understands itself to be primarily organized by heterosexual negotiations and conflicts. Looking at these readings now, I am inclined to regard them as case studies. This means that the relative aesthetic or cultural importance and stature of the individual objects matters less to me than the part they play in identifiable general trends. For representative or exemplary cases I have chosen texts that seemed to me to be preoccupied in particularly provocative ways with contemporary social issues. In images and narratives that are sharply edged with pleasure, violence, and repulsion, these objects have provided me with especially densely woven elaborations of collective fantasy. However idiosyncratic some of these choices may seem, my point throughout has been to understand that, more or less critically, and more or less unconsciously, even the apparently eccentric or banal text reworks our everyday practices of gender, race, and sexuality.

Each chapter tracks the ways that heterosexual masculinities and femininities rework themselves by reconstructing sexual difference and its meanings in the representational field. But if in this "gender theater," masculinity and femininity are shaped in a persistent and anaclitic relation to each other, or, more specifically, in relation to fantasies and anxieties about the other gender, these representations also constitute a form of address to spectators imagined as stably masculine and stably feminine. Gender, figured as struggle with and across sexual difference, comes to center stage as it is isolated from social context and sanitized of other differences. And, as such, gender may become the venue through which other social differences are diffused.

Chapter 1, "Mutilated Masculinities and Their Prostheses," explores the fantastic popularity of the white male action hero as a figure for masculinity in crisis. In the two film serials to be discussed, the *Die Hard* and *Lethal Weapon* films, white masculinity's endlessly repeated crisis seems to concern its always failed effort to align its "significant others"—the white woman and the man of color—in a meaningful configuration that serves to stabilize its own whiteness and its "Americanness" along with its gender. This chapter analyzes the obsessively repetitive cycle of punishment and triumph, accompanied by repeated ruptures and alliances with black men and white women, that works in coincidence with contemporary social anxieties about "diversity" and "multiculturalism" in relation to both national identity and gender identity.[30]

Chapter 2 reads several generically hybrid films together. *Fatal Attraction, Someone to Watch Over Me, Sea of Love, The Hand That Rocks the Cradle,* and *Basic Instinct* all rework questions of sexual difference in frameworks that combine various elements of the police thriller, the action film, the horror film, the domestic melodrama, and film noir. In each hybrid form the narrative poses the question of how man's and woman's respective places shape each other. All of these films, however, struggle to manage the drama around sexual difference spatially as an incursion of social struggle into the domestic refuge, or as a terrifying loss of borders, a radical exposure in the collapse of the public space into a perversely private zone. In its escalating effort to manage the threat of difference coming from the outside, each film discloses a menacing difference already operating within. Ideologically speaking, the chapter argues, the figure of the physically and sexually aggresive woman, as lure and as threat, becomes the agent of boundary destruction because she is fantasmatically freighted with social differences and with the conflict and struggle that crystallize around them.

Chapter 3, "Combative Femininity," reads *Thelma and Louise* and *Terminator 2,* examining the conditions that produce the ambivalently thrilling and menacing figure of the murderous female hardbody, along with the conflicted critical responses that she evokes. Beginning with an exploration of the popular debates about *Thelma and Louise*'s violence, the chapter examines the junctures at which film reception finds violence and violent fantasies problematic, and it aims to explain why these junctures so often involve gender instability. Equally important, in both films the hypervisibility of that unstable gender formation emerges against the intermittent appearance of racial difference in the form of a black male figure whose arrival, like his disappearance, is presented as incidental. It is precisely this "accidental" quality that the chapter interrogates, arguing that the black male here may be structurally fundamental to the particular image of the white female hardbody that these films promote.

In their exploration of the gendered address structures that these films display and depend on, these three chapters argue that any analysis which bears on identity and identifications can only consider these elements as *relations*. These relations, moreover, are caught up in the reciprocal structuring of racial and sexual difference that is articulated in cultural representations and the forms of address which they construct, induce, or permit. Such an analysis aims to disrupt the ways that whiteness appears as seamlessly bonded to gender and, therefore, to have no impact upon it. Instead, these chapters see constructions of sexuality as fully embedded in this culture's intimate dependence on a racial divide for its fantasies as well as its self-definitions.

Part II, "Ethnographies of the White Gaze," explores the "smaller" films of three auteurs, David Lynch, Spike Lee, and Quentin Tarantino. Reading films that have crossed the boundary separating the fields of "independent" cinema and Hollywood's powerful mass distribution system, these chapters examine the production of authorial style in the consumer context of promotion and reception. In its examinations of our current working conceptions of an auteur and their social meanings, this section analyzes the discursive interactions that shape audiences for a given director. Closely linked to the consolidation of audiences as taste cultures, the contemporary auteur figures as an embodiment of "style." But this emphasis on style often obscures the social and cultural situation that underwrites it. These essays, however, seek to discern the social side of style by exploring the ways that "race" works for each of these directors and for his imagined audience, particularly in relation to gender identity, erotics, and fantasy. In discussing fantasy throughout this section I mean to explore the unstable and obscure intersection where collective or public fantasies remain steadfastly intertwined in reciprocally shaping relations with the private fantasies that we consider to be the product of a particular subjectivity.

Chapter 4, "Do the Wrong Thing: David Lynch's Perverse Style," examines the contexts of production and consumption in which Lynch has been able to aestheticize racial and ethnic difference as "decorative effects," or "local color." These operate in *Wild at Heart* as signposts, marking both the ex-centricity of locales outside the urban cultural centers and the culture of middle-class taste that Lynch represents both as its delegate and its adherent. While these signposts are meant to mark a kind of gritty, simple "real," for which they stand as icons, they also index the irony in the aesthetic reworking of the social that Lynch's style aims to effect. So "race" and ethnicity become aesthetic effects to the extent that they function as the *non*aesthetic "real" against which this particular representational "style" distinguishes itself. Despite the temporariness of Lynch's popularity, and despite his failure to achieve a rank in any contemporary canon of filmmakers, his case remains of some interest because it exemplifies the relationship of authorial style to the taste cultures that condition middle-class audience formations. It might be argued that this particular intersection has helped to prepare the ground for a figure like

Tarantino, whose very different commitment to aesthetics and personal style is equally powerful.

Chapter 5, "Tell the Right Story: Spike Lee and the Politics of Representative Style," argues that Lee emerges as an auteur in a critical field where mainstream cultural discourse consistently finds it difficult to allow him any aesthetic distance from his object. Unlike Lynch or Tarantino, Lee is publicly held to realist, even documentary, standards. This tendency to apply realist conventions is coherent with the intense focus on the violence that his films occasionally depict, stylized though it is, and that distinguishes discussions of his work. In sharp contrast, the reception of Tarantino's work, as of Lynch's before it, tends to treat its violence as aesthetic or even technical. This contrast in critical reception, specifically with respect to representations of violence and to violent fantasies, becomes central to an analysis that aims to study the distinct cultural positions occupied by these directors, particularly as they come to embody general notions of auteurism. Lee is often linked, in suspiciously organic metaphors, to his "race" and his "community." On the other hand, both Lynch and Tarantino, as figures, remain dramatically detached from concepts of community, or even from any social space whatsoever, as mainstream media discussions remain relatively inattentive to the ways that their authorial status is also profoundly shaped by their race.

Chapter 6, "Borrowed 'Style': Quentin Tarantino's Figures of Masculinity," reads *Pulp Fiction* against the background of *Reservoir Dogs* and *True Romance* to chart Tarantino's consistent construction of blackness, and especially of black males, as a specific cultural icon. His success in attracting diverse audiences should provoke our critical interest. We may wonder how the steadfastly oedipal quality of his dramas contributes to the diversity of his appeal, since the oedipal framing of his violent narratives and images works to evaporate social referentiality and, along with it, any historical specificity. In its relationship to social reference, Tarantino's work stands in sharp and significant contrast to both Lynch's and Lee's. Where Lynch's work appears to believe that its representations of race and of violence bear no political force at all, Tarantino's use of violence around race and racial epithets indicates that he understands that there are political stakes to representations; he just does not know what they are. On the other hand, we may compare Tarantino's near obsessive use of racial epithet to Lee's manipulation of racial and ethnic slurs. While Lee's work seems to insist that racial epithets speak the most fundamental and unconscious "truths" of any subject, Tarantino's work forgets that these epithets are anchored to an unconscious—both the subject's and the collective's. And this is why his films use racial epithets as if they could be sanitized of their historical meanings, removed from social circulation, while Lee's works use such epithets precisely to emphasize the effects of social circulation and exchange. But where Lee consistently relies on a notion of "race" as relatively stable, Tarantino's work powerfully displays its instabilities. What this work forgets, however, while Lee's remembers, is that race is not so unstable that an individual subject may shape it to his own private meanings.

These essays analyze such interactions between public and private meanings in the cinematic field and the popular discussions that help to shape it. If Hollywood and television, along with the popular press, display persistent interest in systematizing and managing social difference in their representational fields, this is because they must specialize in reading our collective fascinations and obsessions, reshaping them as entertainment for consumption, just as they participate in the shaping of consumer tastes by inviting us into specific audience formations that overlap with market segments. This may not be the cinema we dream of; it may tell us much more than we want to know. That, *High Contrast* argues, may be precisely the weight of its competing obviousnesses, the gravity of its banalities. It can tell us what we are working not to know.

PART I   Battles of the Sexes

1 Mutilated Masculinities and Their Prostheses:

Die Hards and Lethal Weapons

A battered white man collapses in the protective arms of a black man. This picture has become a familiar one in recent action films, and it is one of the strongest images shared by three 1980s blockbusters: John McTiernan's *Die Hard* (1988) and Richard Donner's *Lethal Weapon* (1987) and *Lethal Weapon 2* (1989).[1] The heroes of each film are versions of a familiar action film figure: the renegade cop who takes the law into his own hands and slaughters a series of criminals. In each case, the central characters enact the film's title: John McClane (Bruce Willis), the "die hard" New York City cop, single-handedly defeats a group of twelve terrorists who take over a high-rise office building in Los Angeles, and Martin Riggs (Mel Gibson), an unstable LAPD cop, seems unable to avoid killing any suspect he encounters. (Apparently he is also lethal to most women, by the way; until *Lethal Weapon 3,* any woman who falls in love with him seems bound to die.)[2] In each case, the hero has lost a woman, has come uncoupled. Distraught over his wife's recent death, Riggs is considered to be on the verge of psychosis—either homicidal or suicidal. *Die Hard's* McClane is spending Christmas vacation in Los Angeles, attempting to restore his relationship with his estranged wife, an ambitious executive in a Japanese-owned corporation.

Arriving in the city, McClane is chauffeured directly to his wife's office Christmas party at Nakatomi Plaza. Just after the couple's first dispute, which concerns her career and her return to her maiden name, the party and the building are invaded by a group of apparent "terrorists." McClane, who has escaped their detection, spends the rest of the film in the building's elevator shafts and ventilation system, conducting a one-man guerrilla-style battle with the terrorists. Meanwhile, the film interrupts and parallels this romance plot, which aims to restore the marriage, with a buddy plot. Throughout the film, the cop on the inside, McClane, remains in CB communication with a black street cop on the outside. Al Powell represents one of several competing voices of the law (the others include the FBI, the deputy chief of the LAPD, and, to some extent, the television newspeople) gathered outside the building and vying with each other for radio time and for McClane's ear.

From the start, we can say that both *Die Hard* and *Lethal Weapon* offer curious and excessive rewritings of a plot familiar to us from westerns: the hero is a lawman—uncontained by marriage—whose renegade force is unleashed by a woman's disappearance or the threat of her disappearance. And as in westerns, the relationship of the hero to the law is unstable—does he represent it, or does he become it?[3] But these contemporary versions of this plot both articulate new twists in the question of the law; they operate within an apparently generalized crisis of authority where the law itself is highly unstable—it vacillates between murderousness and ineffectuality. Significantly, the hero's relation to the law turns on the question of whether or not he can, or must, embody it—quite literally; that is, on whether or not his body can be the law, whether the law is written on the body.[4] Finally, in each case the crisis of authority combines with masculine sadomasochistic spectacle in the context of bonding with a black man.[5]

To return to this crucial and conditioning figure for these films: in all three cases the embrace between the white man and the black man constitutes the film's strongest form of closure.[6] In *Lethal Weapon* this scene seems nothing short of an obsession, repeated at the ends of both the original and its sequel, *Lethal Weapon 2*. Moreover, *Lethal Weapon 2* exhibits a particularly—and jocularly—anxious fascination with its own homoerotic subtext, expressed in Riggs's jokes on two occasions. When his partner, Roger Murtaugh (Danny Glover), finds himself sitting on a toilet that is wired with explosives, Riggs loyally remains with his partner for the controlled detonation that ensues. The two end up in a sexually suggestive pose, with Riggs on his back and Murtaugh on top of him. Riggs smirkingly suggests that they get out of this embrace, as he wouldn't "want anyone to find us like this." At the film's end, we find Murtaugh holding the wounded Riggs in his lap, as they wait for the police to arrive. Riggs quips, "Give us a kiss before they get here." Such wit here seems designed to diffuse and contain the overtly homoerotic charge these scenes produce—to offer and then withdraw the lure of homoeroticism. And this strategy persists, persists to the point that it becomes visibly crucial to the signature formula of the *Lethal Weapon* films.[7] Tania Modleski has characterized that formula as follows: "a feminist/psychoanalytic critic is entitled to regard the ingredients of the film's formula as a heavily condensed mixture of racism, misogyny, homoeroticism and heterosexual panic."[8] What requires our further attention, it seems to me, is the structural interdependency wherein each term of the formula serves to guarantee the others, as well as this structure's bearing upon the formula's tendency toward repetition. Repetition seems to produce shifts that most often tend toward more obviously "camp" readings, which we will explore later.

Even more interesting, the obsessions that compose this formula are shared, although more subtly articulated, by *Die Hard,* and the success of *Lethal Weapon* and *Die Hard* seems to unleash a series of films organized around reworkings of that formula and extending beyond the direct sequels—*Lethal Weapon 2* and *Lethal Weapon 3* (1992), and *Die Hard 2: Die Harder* (1990), *The Last Boy Scout* (1992), and, finally, *Die Hard with a Vengeance* (1995). When scenes of interracial embrace operate as narrative resolutions, they raise the question of what connections the films are working to establish through the figure of racial difference. Inevitably, it seems, this figure connects the mutilation of the white male body to social and erotic bonding. This is not a new question. It arises as early as 1958 in *The Defiant Ones* (Stanley Kramer), which starred Sidney Poitier and Tony Curtis as convicts who escape from a prison transport truck while handcuffed together.[9] This film ends with the wounded Tony Curtis cradled in Sidney Poitier's arms as they wait for the police to catch up with them.

James Baldwin takes up these issues in his *The Devil Finds Work,* a 1976 study of American cinema, particularly the cinema of his own youth, and its constructions of race. Baldwin characterizes *The Defiant Ones* as a rather mystified allegory of American race relations played out on the level of individual hatred and reconciliation. This film's bonding, however, is possible only by virtue of reciprocal sacrifice: the white man gives up a woman, and the black man gives up his chance for freedom. As Baldwin puts it: "A black man and a white man can come together only in the absence of women: which is, simply, the American legend of masculinity brought to its highest pressure, and revealed, as it were, in black and white."[10] Reflecting on what he calls the "rigorous choices, rigorously arrived at," that condition bonding in the several black-white buddy films he considers, Baldwin arrives at the following question.

> Why is the price of what should be, after all, a simple human connection so high? Is it really necessary to lose a woman, an arm or one's mind, in order to say hello? And let's face it, kids, men suffer from penis envy on quite another level than women do, a crucial matter if yours is black and mine is white: furthermore, no matter what St. Paul may thunder, love is where you find it. A man can fall in love with another man: incarceration, torture, fire, and death, and still more, the threat of these, have not been enough to prevent it, and never will. It became a crucial matter on the North American continent, where white power became indistinguishable from the question of sexual dominance. (*The Price of the Ticket*, 600)

What Baldwin understands as the embedded subtext in these films emerges as well in *Die Hard* and the *Lethal Weapon* films, with two significant changes. The heroes are now police, and not criminals, and race is not centrally *thematized*. This says something about changes in our culture since the 1950s. First, the black and white buddies can now uphold the law rather than threaten it; second, racial difference can appear on screen without any mention; it can be passed over in silence (despite a social world in which we are constantly, if obliquely and unproductively, talking about it).

A significant exception to this general silence about racial difference is *Die Hard with a Vengeance* (John McTiernan), which pairs John McClane this time with Zeus Carver (Samuel L. Jackson).[11] A contemporary reworking of the historical "race man," Zeus keeps the question of racial difference and McClane's assumptions about it constantly before us, referring repeatedly to "that race shit." Zeus specifies and analyzes the uncritical assumptions that seem to underlie McClane's position on racial difference and his efforts to "relate" across it.[12] His efforts to "relate," of course, have gotten off to a hyperbolically bad start, since his adversary Simon, the bomber, has coerced McClane into standing on a Harlem street corner wearing nothing but a sandwich board that proclaims hatred for blacks through the crudest racial epithet. Zeus intervenes, *not,* as in McClane's interpretation, out of motives that can be tied to the personal or to the personhood of the beneficiary; not, in other words, to save the other's life, but rather, for political reasons, to prevent the murder of a "white cop," which would bring a thousand more white cops to the neighborhood. At the level of language, this relationship is characterized by conflicting interpretation, interpretive misfires in both content and address. (Right from the beginning, Zeus emphasizes that their negotiations involve competing definitions of their very relationship: "I ain't your partner, your neighbor, your brother or your friend. I'm your total stranger." Of course, he is also calling attention to a curious compensatory gesture in which the white man claims a false intimacy that gives the lie to the social gulf he feels in his encounter with the black man.)

In a film that thematizes misrecognition and miscommunication across racial lines, Zeus's critical discourse highlights the super "ordinariness" that has constituted McClane's appeal throughout the *Die Hard* series. And it links that ordinariness to racial identity. McClane is just an ordinary white guy, whose very ordinariness—as *whiteness*—is marked by his unselfconsciousness about race. At the same time, however, like McClane himself, the film never quite admits to any of Zeus's accusations. Instead, it constructs Zeus as obsessed with race, where McClane is relaxed, and it asks us to consider if Zeus suffers from the mythical racial paranoia, or "reverse racism," so commonly evoked in dominant discussions of race prejudice.[13] If Zeus is liberated from the task of embodying race for this film, the price is that he is the one who is charged with "speaking" it for himself and for McClane.

Despite their ironic moments of sophistication about masculine display and the constructedness of masculinity, these action films bear similar versions of the subtext that Baldwin describes. That subtext, the site of enormous anxiety and resistance, concerns the destabilization of masculinity as a category. Somehow, these contemporary representations have anxiously and unconsciously recognized that masculinity never exists as such. Rather, it is constructed within relations of and to race, class, and sexuality. What these films put forward as the central figure of masculinity in crisis is really white heterosexual masculinity desperately seeking to reconstruct itself within a web of social differences, where its opposing terms include not only femininity, but black masculinity and male homosexuality.

To construct this version of masculinity, these representations must continually renegotiate and reestablish differentiations, and they must hold off homosexuality as well as interracial desire. Probably this is why the favored buddy figures are lawmen; symbolically, they both uphold and submit to these prohibitions, if not to the prohibition on murder.

What I am interested in here, however, is the specific representation of this "crisis": the ways in which black-and-white bonding takes place across and through the spectacle of the battered white male body, displacing any aggressive component into vicious combat between white men. In these contexts, such an operation needs to marginalize women, to foreground romanticized figures of class in the represented crisis of authority, and to displace residues of the enormous energy that this crisis mobilizes onto relentless destructive action.[14] The narrative, visual, spatial, and discursive relations among black and white figures propose particular readings of race, gender, and class, while pretending that these differences are no longer at issue.[15] Despite its explicit discourse about race, even *Die Hard with a Vengeance* participates in this tendency. While its heroes speak of race almost obsessively, that dialogue is contained and ironized in the framework of the banter which characteristically binds the action film buddies together as it holds off more direct erotic interaction. Finally, of course, the power of racial difference to produce division is radically diminished in the face of *Die Hard with a Vengeance*'s concluding resolution, where Zeus is presiding over McClane's effort at reconciliation across the apparently more unbridgeable gap of sexual difference as he encourages his buddy to call his wife.

Die Hard and *Lethal Weapon* have in common the central thematics of accidental partnerships between white and black policemen. These pairings articulate very particular stories about race relations and male bonding within the specific narrative framework of the action film. At one level, action films participate in the same kind of logic that Philip Brophy attributes to contemporary horror films: that their textuality is "integrally and intricately bound up in the dilemma of a saturated fiction whose primary aim in its telling is to generate suspense, shock, and terror."[16] Like the horror films that Brophy studies, these action films produce a gratification based on "tension, fear, anxiety, sadism and masochism" (5). And these characteristics must account for both the popularity of the two genres and the critical contempt that goes along with that popularity. But perhaps equally important, this gratification seems intimately bound to the repetitive quality of the action film genre. Susan Jeffords highlights "the pattern of internal amnesia" that she contends is "typical of male action film sequences of the 1980s."[17] For Jeffords, the sequentiality that emerges in these films produces a pattern of increasing externalization: emphasis on the body as spectacle, at the expense of "internal character developments" (246). But, even as these films repeat the spectacle of the male body as a machine for generating and undergoing aggressive assault, even as they repeat some fantasmatic body/mind split *as* spectacle, we might ask: what exactly do they keep forgetting in order to remember it? For, clearly, the forgetting is deliberate.

Paul Smith describes another structuring tendency for action films, one that implicitly seeks repetition as well, we might suggest. Smith contends that "the pleasure proffered in action movies can be regarded, then, not so much as the perverse pleasure of transgressing given norms, but as at bottom the pleasure of reinforcing them."[18] Fundamentally, it may be the case that these films rely as much on reinforcing norms as on transgressing them, but it seems most important that they require *both* moves. And this requisite suggests a pleasure in repeating the instability of the "law" in order to maintain it. But the "law" in this case comes to look more and more like a law that secures sexual difference and racial difference in order to secure itself through them. In the end, the objects of repetition—remembered and forgotten—are sexual and racial difference.

As each action film resolves the fantasmatic problem, it reproduces a troubled and unstable legacy—to be repeated in its sequels—both direct and indirect. So, *Lethal Weapon* generates the next two *Lethal Weapon* films, but it also reproduces the buddy formula, whose major threads— race, gender, and sexuality—are realigned in numerous subsequent biracial buddy films. *Die Hard,* on the other hand, begets direct sequels in *Die Hard 2* and *Die Hard with a Vengeance,* this latter recalling *48 Hrs.* (1982) in the resistance of the black partner to the white one's police business and in the hostility between the two. *Die Hard* also shadows *Passenger 57* (1992), where Wesley Snipes substitutes for Bruce Willis, as the renegade loner trapped in an airplane with a hijacker. And the *Die Hard* formula is rewritten in *The Last Boy Scout,* a film whose plot is organized around Willis again, metonymically attracting residues from *Die Hard. The Last Boy Scout*'s Joe Hallenbeck presents a degenerate and failed version of McClane; his wife respects him less than Holly McClane did her husband, and she betrays him sexually rather than professionally. Hallenbeck's degraded masculinity and paternity play off Damon Wayans's character, former football star Jimmy Dix, a far more active and erotically charged sidekick than the portly desk cop, Al Powell.

In their formative commitment to repetition, these action film series display a feature that also is central to the horror genre, as Brophy describes it: "you know that you've seen it before; [they] know . . . that you know what is about to happen" (5). For both the *Die Hard* and *Lethal*

Weapon series the "already known" is the saturation of action film codes. But the reassurance secured by saturation may be disrupted, at least for some viewers, by a competing form of excess, the tendency to push the limits of the plausibility upon which the genre depends. Reviewer Stanley Kauffman calls this tendency "permissive realism." "An action melodrama," he writes, "starts with the most finicky realism—of setting and detail and dialogue—and continues so for a while, then ends in a blaze of wildest fantasy" ("Stanley Kauffman on Films," *New Republic,* April 13, 1987, p. 24). Kauffman displays a sophisticate's contempt for the formula, as do many reviewers of action films.

Many reviewers seem disturbed by "permissive realism," or implausibility, particularly where racial bonding is concerned.[19] The problem seems to be that racial figurations are a false detail, an unnecessary—even a cynical—excess added to the already excessive quality of the action. Reviewers are often irritated by the films' calculatedly liberal presentation of race as a reassuringly anodyne and marketable contingency; but they are irritated primarily by the obvious calculation and the implausibility it produces. What they do not discuss is that race looks like an excess in these contexts because it cannot be reduced to a contingency; it is somehow constitutive of the films' logic, or of one of their logics. Saturating the action code, these films profit from the suspension of referentiality to treat social difference as unproblematic, as already managed. But the very force of shocks and violence offered by the films indicates that these issues remain intensely problematic and irreducible to narrative throwaways.

Racial coding in these films cannot be exhausted, contained, or fully saturated. Thus, race comes through incoherently in films that set out to remap the inadequately charted social territory of race relations. Their incoherence seems based in the radical contradictions between their abstract conceptual "maps" of race and the "territory" constituted by the actual concrete practices and power relations that structure our social experience of "race."[20] The map/territory model of racist ideology advanced by Philip Cohen produces the following effects:

> a certain image of the body politic is constructed in terms of a set of constant topological relations (enclosure, separation, connectedness) which structurally exclude and define the Other. In doing this, the racist imagination, as we here see, is highly mobile, selecting and combining "bits and pieces" and organizing them into certain fixed

chains of associations (codes). In this way, each map draws a specific picture of the terrain where racism describes its material effects. At this second level, a set of discourses and institutions fix designated subjects (races) to specific positions within a topography of power. It is here that the political geographies of class and ethnicity are formed and transformed. (*Multi-Racist Britain* [London: Macmillan, 1988], p. 57)

It is precisely the bits-and-pieces effect as it is articulated in these films that produces their ideological incoherence.

But *Die Hard* and *Lethal Weapon* handle race in very different ways. *Lethal Weapon* makes only one allusion to it, in an irrecuperably free-standing vignette. When Riggs and Murtaugh approach the house of a suspect they plan to question, they are immediately recognized as police by a group of small black children, who announce their arrival. When the suspect's house blows up as they approach it, the children make it clear that they see Riggs and Murtaugh as the magical agents of the explosion. Later, when Murtaugh tries to question one of the children about a man he has seen near the house, the child asks: "My mamma says policemen shoot black people. Is that true?" This question, and the reference it makes to the law's preferred place of inscription, the bodies of black men, is left suspended as the action races forward. However, the later *Lethal Weapon 2* is able to speak about race more directly, if obsessively and confusedly. Indeed, in one of the film's weirder moments, when Riggs raps out an inspirational ditty to Murtaugh, he captures the generative equation of both *Lethal Weapon* films: "We're back. We're bad. You're black. I'm mad." The implicit equation is generative because it encapsulates the film's characterological formula as well as the fundamental asymmetry that the film holds to and cannot surmount: blackness appears on the same level as madness, the term here operating in both senses—as uncontainable rage and as insanity. So both cops are deviants. But they are nonetheless not in the same position, since Riggs and Murtaugh together form the quintessential and generative figure for the biracial buddy plot as Ed Guerrero describes it: "It seems that with the biracial buddy formula Hollywood put the black filmic presence in the protective custody, so to speak, of a white lead or co-star and therefore in conformity with white sensibilities and expectations of what blacks, essentially, should be."[21]

In their reticence about race the *Lethal Weapon* films recast their drama around questions about the law, and around the figure of Vietnam as a haunting legacy (all the adversaries in the first film are Vietnam vets gone bad). As a couple, Riggs and Murtaugh figure the legacy of Vietnam in the split between the "good" Vietnam veterans and the "bad" ones. Constructed as the figure of urban violence and aggression unleashed, Riggs, a former Special Forces assassin, is a murderous borderline psychotic at the beginning of *Lethal Weapon*. It is ostensibly for the purpose of surveying and containing his aggression that his superiors assign him to Roger Murtaugh, the stable family man and lawful authority, who is also the good version of a Vietnam vet and the all-purpose father figure. In the film's oedipalized drama, Murtaugh literally brings Riggs "home" into his own stable nuclear family, and Riggs takes him on as a father. These operations reduce and "domesticate" the significance of the characters' difference, while implicitly proposing a return to benign paternal authority and the suburban middle-class family circle as a therapeutic solution to post-traumatic stress disorders. In a more spectacular gesture of displacement, the adversarial figures in the second film are all South Africans, controlled by the consulate and, by extension, by the South African government, so that the perpetrators of racism are located elsewhere, "outside," in a comforting counterbalance with our own U.S. racism, which is made to appear manageable by contrast.

Die Hard repeats *Lethal Weapon*'s central conflicts about the limits of the law and its agency in a narrative that "speaks" compulsively, although tacitly, about race. However, both of these narratives are centrally structured so that the action bypasses racial issues, pushes them to the periphery, as racial difference is redistributed, along with racial conflict, far from the film's erotic center. In both cases the erotic center is also the site— subject and object—of aggression: the white male star.

Die Hard systematically redistributes racial difference.[22] On every level of this masculine struggle for control, there is a representative of that difference, each of which is oddly, but firmly, both detached from the direct combat and de-eroticized. The German thieves "masquerading" as terrorists have a black American comrade who is their computer hacker, the technophile, who sits in control of the building's "brain," its central computer. Argyle, the limousine chauffeur who has conveyed McClane to Nakatomi Plaza, spends the entire film waiting patiently for McClane to call him with further instructions. Shown contendedly sitting in the limousine he has parked in the building's basement garage, Argyle, a sanitized version of black urban youth culture, both hints at and holds off a difference that is here physically contained. The music he plays on the limo tape deck marks his cultural distance: "Don't you have any Christmas music?" McClane asks. "This is Christmas music," Argyle answers, referring to the rap song whose lyrics McClane cannot decipher.

Finally, Al Powell is firmly positioned outside both action and erotics; he is assigned to a desk job, and he is a stable family man. As such, he becomes a spectator, his gaze eternally directed toward McClane.[23] Similarly, Roger Murtaugh's sexuality is firmly contained by the family; he is connected to erotics only through his anxious fatherly surveillance of the flirtations between his daughter, Rianne, and Riggs. His role, then, is a spectator's: it calls attention to Riggs as a sexual object, abetting the displacement from homoerotic bonding to heterosexual erotics. This plot displacement is massively underwritten and overdeveloped in the Riggs-Murtaugh bonding's subsequent repetitions, which present joke structures organized by obsessional oscillation and collision between hints of homoeroticism and miscegenation, trading off the threat of the *wrong* pairing between the two thematic chains.[24] In *Lethal Weapon 3* these hints or "rumors" intersect along the oedipal plot. Riggs finds Murtaugh drunk on his boat, as he struggles to cope with his grief about shooting a friend of his son's in a drug-related gang incident, and as he repeats the film cycle's motif of his perpetual efforts to follow through on his resolution to retire. Riggs takes this opportunity to bring their relationship to a new phase, declaring his love for Murtaugh and his dependence on him, but moving directly into a confidence about his erotic life, which occasions the scene's recourse to the screwball comic energy that has become the *Lethal Weapon* signature. "I think I might have just slept with the wrong person," he confides, only to be interrupted by his partner's eruption of rage—culminating in an almost slapstick physical attack—as Murtaugh assumes the "wrong" person to be his own daughter, Rianne. But they sort out the confusion by passing through another confusion when Riggs gives his lover's name: "Sergeant Cole." "Sergeant Cole from traffic?" "No, Sergeant Cole from homicide, Sergeant Cole from traffic's her uncle." This nexus of threats circulating around "inappropriate" object choices becomes a central feature of the biracial action genre, it seems, as *The Last Boy Scout* repeats *Lethal Weapon*'s miscegenation "gag" in the suggestive relationship that it poses between Jimmy Dix (Damon Wayans) and Joe Hallenbeck's daughter, Darien.[25] Again and again, jokes seem to highlight the ways that the threats of miscegenation and homoeroticism tend to slide into each other. But the joke structures end up strictly compartmentalizing and containing those threats.

We should also notice that *Die Hard* mobilizes the differences among its intradiegetic spectators to structure its action literally, so that the police assault on the Nakatomi building, for instance, is a sequence constructed by alternating close-up reaction shots in a rhythm of black characters and white characters that is reproduced in the film's final action sequence. These discrete and parallel figures help to anchor the competing zones of the film's action and to represent different versions of black masculinity. Presented in such strict symmetry, however, they act as spatial markers, and they produce a good object/bad object structure that duplicates the one that organizes the film's lawmen.

But it is precisely this structure that feeds into the film's irony. *Die Hard* plays with reaction shots, as opposed to point-of-view shots, to ironize the film's territory, and ironize it in a way that calls attention to our viewing habits in a highly televisual landscape (which may account for the film's thematized aggression toward television), but that also lets us examine our investment in an identification with "knowingness," precisely the identification that television privileges. Analyzing the relative weakness of point-of-view shots in television, John Caughie asks, "could it be that the reaction shot forms an equivalent figure for the ironic suspensiveness of television?" Reaction shots, he argues, "disperse knowledge . . . registering it on the faces of a multiplicity of characters whose function may only be to intensify the event." And this gesture is connected to a certain "ironic knowingness" that characterizes our position as spectators of television.[26]

Interestingly, however, the symmetrical, specular pair that matches McClane and Powell as a couple retroactively consolidates the meaning of that couple through class interests. Powell and McClane are practical street cops, workingmen united by their opposition to the professional managerial cops, the deputy chief of police and the FBI. The symmetrical opposing couple is the FBI agents, the black Agent Johnson and his white partner, *Special* Agent Johnson—a designation that might put us in mind of the dominant culture's ever-present focus on "special interests," a focus that admits no recognition of its own specialized interests. On introducing himself and his white partner to the deputy police chief, Agent Johnson adds the quip, "no relation." Now this is a commonplace racial joke. But what does it really mean? It pretends to draw humor from an apparently "obvious" redundancy with what the eyes can see. However, it also recalls the history of slavery and race relations in the United States. On the one hand, it appears as a disavowal of white men's rape of black women, which often produced two lineages with the same last name and a different racial alignment. On the other, it suggests the bizarre coincidence of property and patronymics articulated through the historical weight of slaveholders' surnames, whether imposed or adopted, borne by slaves and their descendants. Johnson and Johnson[27] are the combined figure of an uncomfortable and repressed racial proximity through U.S. history.

Die Hard seems to be about establishing the possibility of another relation across the racial divide—a relation of which Johnson and Johnson are one version—while explicitly denying any relation at all. However, the split that is established here is recoded as one of age and history. When a hysterical Special Agent Johnson expresses his excitement about their imminent helicopter strafing of the skyscraper's roof, it is in the following form: "This is just like fucking Saigon, ain't it?" The younger, black agent replies: "I was in junior high, dickhead, how would I know?" Even as the spectator may share the younger, hipper Johnson's contempt for the militaristic "special" agent, the historical enforced nonrelation between races is simultaneously recoded as a generational, or aesthetic, divide in this hybrid couple. Notably, however, it is recoded both at the expense of the Vietnam veteran whose relationship to that history is presented by this throwaway episode as psychotic and as a historically inaccurate version of the racial imbalance that marked U.S. forces in Vietnam.

This film offers no single message concerning race, since race is always subjected to split or competing readings. Racial difference is redistributed across other social differences, which are articulated together in a melange of filmic codes. If *Die Hard* rewrites the western, it does so in a peculiarly hybrid form—as a disaster film. A glance at reviews confirms the sense of pastiche. David Ansen calls *Die Hard* a "super slick, precision-tooled, post-modernist *Towering Inferno.*"[28] If *Lethal Weapon* is "*Mad Max* meets the Cosby show" for Richard Schickel,[29] *Die Hard* might be called "*Predator* meets 'Moonlighting'" (in reference to director John McTiernan's earlier film, and Willis's most important television credit). What is important here is the sense of pastiche and interfering codes— the implausible pairing of extremes—something which doubles the hybrid buddy relation that is central to the film's diegesis.

Another layer of interference—between the highly visible technical feats paraded by these films and their ironic commitment to a kind of postmodernist code of pastiche—allows for a systematic appeal to a layered audience, a simultaneous and highly profitable capture of varied audience segments. These films' continuous violent action and grittily humorous aggressive dialogue assure their appeal to the young male audience for action films. Meanwhile, they offer an ironic, self-conscious visual and discursive framework that is precisely what allows some reviewers to see *Die Hard* as "good trash." This means, I think, that the film is a good reader of the collective sensibilities of the professional-managerial class, which it attracts along with the youth audience, luring both with its glossy production values and obvious technical and financial expenditure—a particular postmodern gratification at seeing a kind of profligacy with both apparatus and capital.[30] This kind of gratification is no doubt related to a certain market as well, the one that allows for and even demands such layering of audiences as a prerequisite of a film's success.[31]

Hybridization is an organizing figure of *Die Hard,* applying to male bodies as well as to male buddies. The centrally foregrounded, combative male body (the cultured state of its nature emphasized in musculature) is uncanny, since it appears simultaneously as a machine of destruction and as constantly eroded and mutilated flesh; it is both hyperphallicized in its straining muscularity[32] and feminized as it is placed in the masochistic position—object of the murderous male gaze as well as of painful assaults. As the film's editing works consistently to structure an alternation between extremes—claustrophobic proximity and monumentalizing distance—the camera's parallel work alternates high and low angles that, respectively, miniaturize and monumentalize that body.

Die Hard's most persistent image, and one of its most gratifying, is the shattering of glass—computer screens, high-rise exterior windows, office windows. In a sense, the frame, as both enclosing and shattered, becomes a central figure of the film, one that is consolidated in the shot which closes the sequence in which McClane meets Al Powell, who has been sent to investigate an alarm at Nakatomi Plaza. After shots are fired at Powell's cruiser, and we watch Al clamber out of it, the film cuts to a shot of McClane above, Ramboesque, overlooking the street cop; he is photographed from a low angle that complements the high-angle long shot that miniaturizes Al. And McClane is framed by the shattered window he has shot out. This shattering image is doubled in the space of the building; it is unmappable, partitioned into tiny fragmented enclosures that are broken down by close-ups of clustered details.

Shattering effects also operate in parallel through what we might call, following Michel Chion, the film's auditory space. Chion contends that in recent American films like *Die Hard* we can see a renewal of the auditory dimension. "In these movies," he argues, "matter—glass, fire, metal, water, tar—resists, surges, lives, explodes in infinite variations, with an eloquence in which we can recognize the invigorating influence of sound on the overall vocabulary of modern-day film language. It is certainly looking as if an epic quality is returning to cinema, making its appearance in many films in the form of at least one fabulous sequence."[33] As the force of ambient sound fields helps to reorganize the screen space and to disorient us within it, the emphasis on noises also supports the action film agenda of interrupting the primacy of speech by means of another form of shattering and fragmentation.[34] Further, according to Chion, this field of sound actively reshapes cinematic space "with the new place that noises occupy, speech is no longer central to films. Speech tends to be reinscribed in a global sensory continuum that envelops it, and that occupies both kinds of space, auditory and visual" (156).

On the level of montage as well, *Die Hard* produces a shattered space composed of rapid cuts between noncontinuous locations, so that the action, too, is fragmented into self-enclosed vignettes. In Fred Pfeil's admirable phrase, the film's "action is simply taking place *here*—and *here*—and *here*—in spaces whose distance from one another is not mappable as distance so much as it is measurable in differences of attitude and intensity" (3).

Such effects force us to read the film as a drama of looks and framing, a drama intimately bound to the male body's subjection to related forms of violence and mutilation, plotted through a masculine struggle for control and authority.[35] In the parallel love plot, McClane's most intense and intimate interaction with Al occurs when he confesses his failures with his wife while pulling shards of glass from his bloody feet. Al functions as a substitute for McClane's wife, Holly, when McClane asks him to pass on to her his confession and his apology, the "I'm sorry" that he could never bring himself to say. This scene is orchestrated as a kind of narcissistic and masochistic display. Because McClane is sitting in front of a mirror, we see him both as subject of pain and as body in pain.

Lethal Weapon's most intense "love" scene echoes *Die Hard*'s: it is the moment when the film cross-cuts between shots of Riggs and Murtaugh as they are tortured, the parallel spaces linked only by the sound of their groans and screams. This sequence produces some of the greatest affect the film offers, and it is also the closest the film comes to a "love scene," producing as it does a kind of reciprocal "passion." Significantly, *The Last Boy Scout* offers a pointed intertextual reference at the moment when Joe Hallenbeck and Jimmy Dix solidify their newly established bond by going home together for a few drinks. When they enter the family living room, Hallenbeck's daughter, Darien, is avidly watching the torture sequence from *Lethal Weapon* on videotape. The daughter's rage and contempt for her father come out in her brutally vulgar taunts ("you're an asshole"; "he thinks he's fuckin' Ward Cleaver"), which play against the background sound of Riggs's grunts and groans.

Meanwhile, the mutilation of McClane's body in *Die Hard*, obviously designed to mobilize castration anxiety, is articulated through a gaze structure that organizes the action by situating point of view. This film foregrounds the shot–reverse shot formula despite the fact that almost no one is able to look at someone else. It is a structure of amputated looks. Because McClane is caught barefoot when the terrorists arrive, his feet become his most vulnerable point. The camera often focuses on this weakness, anticipating the moment when Hans, the leader of the gang, capitalizes on it by shooting out all the glass in an office in order to cripple McClane. McClane's cut and bloody feet become a central focus; the camera above follows his slithering motion and the sinuous trail of blood he leaves on white tiles. Like Oedipus, his hero barely has a leg to stand on. And the film takes up this pun. In their most personal conversation, McClane inquires whether Al has left street duty because of "flat feet." But Al has retreated to the office because he no longer is able to shoot a gun. And here is one of the film's fascinating throwaways, which will reappear to be activated at its close: Al is unable to wield a gun because he has shot and killed a young boy, a reminder of a familiar urban scenario in which very young men are shot by nervous cops. What is not mentioned is that most of these victims are black. Here, the black cop is made responsible, is made figuratively to shoot himself in the foot, to bring about his own incapacitation, as both the subject and the object of the law's violence. At the same time, Al becomes the site of the most explicit figurative castration, one that is inscribed on McClane's feet as well.

But a close look at an alternating inscription of the male body through point of view and framing tells another story also organized by sexual difference. McClane's argument with his wife sets in place a curious gaze structure that the rest of the film plays out. (Situated at the main plot's point of departure, their domestic dispute structurally takes on explosive proportions; it blows up the whole building.) This sequence shows

McClane in the bathroom washing up; the camera is situated at his waist level and behind his right elbow, capturing him from a low angle in medium close-up. In contrast, Holly is in medium long shot, framed by the doorway through which McClane is looking. As the shot–reverse shot produces the structure of their exchanges, McClane is framed from a point-of-view level with the desktop in a series of verticals that place him at the left of the frame in the doorway. As the camera moves in on him, he is squeezed to the left, filling the frame from top to bottom, but confined to that position. Literally, he is nearly pushed out of frame, off-screen, and contained visually, as if by his wife's rage. Her departure leaves him in medium close-up monologue with his own image, again from a waist-level point of view.

The displacement of point of view that is never quite even with the characters', and the splitting of space that is dramatized here, continues throughout the film, except in moments of equal intensity between men.[36] Holly, however, is not an equal adversary; she is visually and thematically constructed as a phallic career woman who cuts her husband down or out of the picture.

A contrasting sequence is one of the film's last: the love-at-first-sight recognition scene between McClane and Powell. Just after Holly and McClane upon her rescue have embraced for the first time in the film, we cut to the outside for the denouement. McClane and Holly are framed together in close-up, looking out into the crowd. Al is centered in frame in medium long shot from their shared point of view. But as we move in on Al, Holly disappears and McClane and Al come together into a close-up of their embrace; they squeeze her out of the frame. The next shot restores her; she appears behind and between them for an introduction: "This is my wife, Holly Gennaro." "Holly McClane," she corrects. Her voluntary name change signals her submission to marital law.

But the resolution here is overtaken by the erupting threat of McClane's primary physical adversary, Karl, reanimated and firing his machine gun. Rapid cross-cutting has McClane hitting the deck and henceforward framed horizontally. The camera then moves to Karl, and on to a close-up of a gun, isolated and suspended in the frame. Then it returns to McClane, to Karl, to the gun. The end of this sequence is marked by the camera's slow arc up and in from its previous low angle on the gun; this ascending arc reveals that Al is the shooter. The ensuing shots construct reciprocal riveted gazes between Al and McClane, offering the film's most intensely fascinated looks that are not murderous. And these looks establish an erotic intensity at the moment of restored phallic power.[37] Al's restoration is problematic, however. When the next shot shows Argyle's limousine bursting through the garage gate, McClane must intervene to keep Al from exercising his renewed, and already hysterical, vigor on another black man: "He's with me." So the white cop prevents another black-on-black murder in a fantasmatic reinscription of contemporary history.

Die Hard's and *Lethal Weapon*'s unrelenting rhythms of battle scenes driving toward a final vicious combat between white adversaries set up a logic wherein the hero's ability to represent the law depends on his body's becoming the site of sadomasochistic aggression. It is precisely this operation that allows that body to be displayed as spectacle. But what kind of spectacle is this? Again, the gaze structure is telling. In *Die Hard*'s constant circulation through amputated or suspended looks, looks that are not returned or are mirrored in darkened windows, the shot–reverse shot structure most commonly links adversaries. Allies are shot in the same frame, not looking at each other, and separated by subsequent shots. Most of the film's main events are shown from the noncommunicating and competing points of view of a variety of characters as well as from the unlocatable point of view of the hypermobile camera. For instance, the police assault on the building is a sequence constructed of shots alternating among black characters and white characters—cutting from Dwayne and Al to Theo in the computer room, to Hans, to McClane, back to Al, to Argyle, etc.—in a rhythm of black and white.

Before the film's end, the only sequences of shot–reverse shot structures linking characters who inhabit the same space are adversarial ones that encode specular violence. Here, the male gaze is riveted on another man, and the gaze is strongly marked with point of view, which implicates the spectator in the exchange. For instance, when McClane finally encounters Hans, we see him monumentalized from a low angle that is coded as the crouching Hans's point of view. And we see Hans from the high angle of someone standing over him as McClane is. When the figures are at eye level with each other, the frame is canted so that their bodies create strong and dizzying diagonals. McClane is tilted to the right and Hans to the left. The next shot–reverse shot sequence abruptly reverses them, switching their respective sides. Such a sequence codes specular violence and stabilizes point of view at the same time that it splits it between characters. The male body's image is as shattered as the space, which may account for the persistent mirroring effects that the film presents (Willis looking out a window into the night, looking through his own reflection), fragmented in close-ups, held in claustrophobic frame.[38] Within this structure, McClane is distinguished by his frequent looks at his own image as he tries and fails to see the outside, and by his looks into the camera. In this context, Al Powell is symmetrically coded as one long reaction shot.

But the momentary stabilization of point of view is quickly disrupted. Our gaze is most commonly situated with the camera's—in dizzying mobility, sweeping across action scenes, or following the characters' motion, or pulling away to scrutinize the body from extreme and implausible angles directly above or below it, zooming in to fragment it in detail. This disrupted and disrupting gaze raises the issue of authority, the law, and the sadomasochistic fantasy implicated in the spectacle of the male body.

All of this eroticized aggressive tension culminates in the face-to-face battle between McClane and Karl. Again, the camera operates to attribute point of view and to destabilize the space (as it does in all action sequences—shooting from either above or below Willis's body, tracking wildly with the action). As it tracks the violence through the scene where McClane crawls to the bathroom to pull glass from his feet, close-ups fragment the body in combat. At the same time, the camera often sweeps effortlessly across the space, as it does when it follows McClane's and Karl's battle, which ends with the hero hanging Karl up by a chain in a kinkily self-conscious reference to the sadomasochistic flavor of this violence. This vicious battle, as well as the ironically sexual suggestiveness built into the title, *Die Hard,* and, finally, the camera's interest in Willis's body indicate something about the erotic economy of the whole film.[39] That particular combination of effects motivates Fred Pfeil to specify one of the central questions that the *Die Hard* and *Lethal Weapon* films raise. "What," Pfeil asks, "is the boundary line between the diehard assertion of rugged white male individualism and its simultaneous feminization and spectacularization?" (29). As Pfeil goes on to suggest, these films may be structured to leave such a question unanswerable. But if that is so, then its persistent, even obsessive, rearticulation is itself of some interest.

Writing about the problem of masculinity as spectacle, Steve Neale suggests that for the male body to appear as the object of another man's look in Hollywood films, "that look must be motivated in some other way, its erotic component repressed."[40] "Mutilation and sadism," he goes on to argue, may be "marks both of the repression involved and of a means by which the male body may be disqualified, so to speak, as an object of erotic contemplation and desire" (8).[41] This may be the source of our fascination with combat scenes: they manifest the force of repression of the erotic, while offering the body to the gaze, but a gaze that is mediated through the looks of other characters as long as the narrative marks those looks "not by desire, but rather by fear, or hatred, or aggression" (12). At the same time, the bodies on display are figured in highly stylized fashion in combat scenes that freeze the narrative, much as song-and-dance numbers do in musicals, and, similarly, that recognize "the pleasure of display," while "displacing it," in Neale's words, "from the male body as such and locating it more generally in the overall components of a highly ritualized scene" (12).

If the spectacle of the male body involves aggression as a means of covering up or warding off the erotic gaze, in *Die Hard* it operates within a particular context—a "crisis" of masculine authority and a crisis of the body's limits. Such a coincidence is not without reason. It is, in fact, intensely motivated if we remember that masochism can be a means of subverting the law, of becoming a law unto oneself.

As critics such as Kaja Silverman and D. N. Rodowick have suggested, any examination of the gaze in relation to authority or phallic privilege needs to explore not only the aggressive, sadistic aspect, but also "the significance of authority in the male figure from the point of view of an economy of masochism."[42] Describing male masochism as a means to "ruin" "the paternal legacy," Silverman argues that the masochist subverts the paternal authority that ordinary masculinity in some way accepts.[43] "The prototypical male subject," she argues, "oscillates endlessly between the mutually exclusive commands of the (male) ego-ideal and the super-ego, wanting both to love the father and to be the father, but prevented from doing either" (195). On the other hand, the male masochist as spectacle "acts out in an insistent and exaggerated way the basic conditions of cultural subjectivity, conditions that are normally disavowed; he loudly proclaims himself before the Gaze even as he solicits it, exhibits his castration for all to see, and revels in the sacrificial basis of the social contract." Thus, contends Silverman, "the male masochist magnifies the losses and divisions upon which cultural identity is based, refusing to be sutured or recompensed. In short, he radiates a negativity inimical to the social order" (206). But this negativity is also related to a ruse that attempts to outwit paternal law since it puts a heterosexual man in the feminine position, but without a change of object. And when that ruse is read, as Silverman reads it, through Freud's essay, "A Child Is

Being Beaten," it appears as the result of elaborate convolutions that produce the subject of the fantasy as subject, object, and spectator. And for the spectator, according to Silverman, the fantasy provides that, "masculinity, aggression and sadism are definitively elsewhere in the scene, concentrated in the figure of the punishing father surrogate. Like the child in the primal scene, the shadowy onlooker is more mastered than mastering" (204). So the spectator position is "irresolute" (205).

In an operation that is also central to *Lethal Weapon*, *Die Hard* seems to work out a sadomasochistic structure that mobilizes the fantasmatic possibility of identifying with paternal authority, or with its whipping boy, since McClane's body attains its status as law through mutilation and torment. And this fantasy is dispersed throughout the film, in struggles where authority preserves itself through a mobility between identification and desire. Spectator pleasure is split between the sadistic and the masochistic, since we are able to identify with authority while seeing it punished in the person of the hero.[44] This fantasy is abetted by the unstable authority of the camera, placing us, alternately, within the action, with the aggressor or victim, or outside the action, overseeing the whole scene.[45] Here, the dominant white culture's violent fantasies are *not* projected onto black men as though returning to that culture from the outside. Rather, figuratively, they are directed recursively back onto the subject's own body.

This motivated relation between sadomasochistic fantasy and the law is connected to the necessity of figuring a "crisis" of masculinity through embodiment. Traditionally in Hollywood cinema, it has been representations of women of any race, and men of color that have done the work of embodiment, that have stood for the body.[46] And significantly, in films like *Die Hard* and *Lethal Weapon* the spectacle of the mutilated white male body emerges in a context where a white woman and black men are posited as the ambiguously threatening equals of the white male, as well as the primary spectators for this combat. This context suggests that the spectacle of white men blowing each other away before a black male onlooker acts to displace aggressive impulses back from the Other onto the same: onto white men who are specular adversaries.

Die Hard's very particular version of the anxieties generated by the fantasmatic threat of racial and sexual equality obscures their source by saturating its entire textual field with anxious fantasies about bodily and structural demolition, redistributing the anxiety through the disaster motif. Even while working to manage this "crisis," the film overestimates it by projecting it to the scale of the building. And this overestimation is one of the film's characteristic moments of hysteria, which produces a certain hilarity. Figured as the double of McClane's body, the building offers a hysterically phallic gigantism that offsets his dwarfing or miniaturization as a "bug" in its internal system. Once the building's infrastructure has been disabled, crippled (as McClane's feet have been crippled), it becomes a hostile landscape. Consequently, it is also a figure for the maternal body, terrifyingly overwhelming to the human body, and subsequently punished from the inside, internally demolished by McClane's explosive rage. And the film's tension is built and channeled through anxiety about seeing and being seen as the camera follows McClane's progress through hidden channels in the building—exploring an unmappable interior. No doubt this is another inscription of the good object/bad object fantasy structure that we have seen elsewhere.[47]

The limitations of sight here give rise to an entire economy of prosthetics within a nightmare of complete technological dysfunction, where an ordinary office building becomes a terrifying prison since it is virtually unmanageable for the scale of the human body without electronic prosthetic devices—elevators, computers, telephones, television, and video technologies. In this landscape McClane is thrown back on the lowly CB radio (which has been consistently associated with working-class culture in the movies), the remaining operative technology of the film, a technology that sustains a network of contacts between men, where they are all partially blinded, anxious spectators, propped on the prosthetic of sound, and thereby caught up in a highly charged, eroticized circuit that both brings them together and holds them apart.

The struggle for authority here overlaps with a continual struggle for control of available technologies, situated within the context of a fantasy that "terrorists" with enough weapons technology could hold off the police, who effectively just throw arms technology (tanks and helicopters) at the problem, turning it into a war games exercise. In short, this is an anxious fantasy about mismanagement, about the failure to arrive at the appropriate measure of technology. Parodically rewriting details from its two predecessors, *Die Hard with a Vengeance* locates technological anxiety in New York City's public telephones through the characters' desperate struggles to gain access to them and the constant uncertainty about their working.

Technological anxiety reaches a peak near the end of *Die Hard*, when McClane crosses the building's main lobby, now nearly destroyed by explosions. Its sprinklers are operating at full force. Together with the plantation in the fountain areas, these sprinklers and the several small fires burning nearby create a scene that resembles a jungle where McClane is a Rambo-like guerrilla. In this ironic image of the cultural dissolving into the natural, the building becomes a jungle landscape, or at least a Vietnam War movie set. And here, as at so many points, one can laugh at the film's excess; indeed, the film's relentless jokes produce a series of shocks, bursts of laughter, that compete with its fearful ones.

These shocks participate in a general structure that systematically undercuts all positions, and all images, that are available for spectator identification in the film. Importantly, here the film rehearses a collective mythology of mourning for the decline of American masculinity, linked to the failure of U.S. will and heroism through the Vietnam War. At the same time, the film undercuts this nostalgia by highlighting its artificial and mediated quality, reminding us of the ways that war was experienced as spectacle, as televisual event.

Mass media and communications technology remain central to *Die Hard*'s ironies. The film has opened with a celebration of leisure technologies, as Argyle, the chauffeur, points out to McClane the special features of the limo they are riding in, "CD, CB, TV, telephone, VHS . . . ." For all that, Argyle remains completely oblivious to what is going on in the building above him until he sees it repeated on television news. So he must watch TV to find out what is going on in the space he inhabits. Television has been powerfully present from the beginning here, in the icon of Bruce Willis, already strongly coded by his television role as the wise-cracking David Addison from "Moonlighting."[48] Further, Willis's straight-on gaze at the camera and his monologues set him up as a kind of parodic anchorman.[49] But the figure of television is charged with ambivalence: television is action, not just information. It intervenes in the events, since a television news reporter invades McClane's domestic space to interview his kids and thereby allows Hans to identify him and his wife. This subplot ends the film, with the same reporter approaching McClane after the end of the crisis. We watch on video as the newly realigned Holly McClane—whose class alliance with her husband has been reaffirmed in the loss of her Rolex watch—shows her solidarity with him by punching the reporter, thereby intervening directly in television.

Television in *Die Hard* also emblematizes popular discourse, the already spoken, that circulates in the cultural field and that this film consumes and recycles. For instance, McClane chooses the name "Roy Rogers" as his radio handle. In a conversation about McClane's identity, established through television references such as "Mr. Mystery Guest," Hans suggests that McClane is "just another American who saw too many movies as a kid, an orphan of a bankrupt culture who thinks he's John Wayne, Rambo. . . ." Later, Hans will return to these allusions in their final confrontation: "This time John Wayne doesn't walk off into the sunset with Grace Kelly." "It was Gary Cooper, asshole," McClane retorts.

Now this last scene replicates the one it refers to in *High Noon* (Fred Zinneman, 1952), a film that is written into *Die Hard* on a number of levels in a tight, intertextual correspondence that works up a pastiche of the western hero.[50] But the intertextuality also contributes to a narrative structure in which the film's foreign terrorists trash American culture, just as they, and McClane, trash the Nakatomi corporate headquarters. And the in-joke here is brilliant: the building in which the film was made is Fox's new headquarters in Century City. Hollywood trashes itself? Perhaps, but the context is very particular.

One of the complications of this context involves the film's obsession with television. The television subplot is related to the question of the camera's authority throughout since, ultimately, this fragmented, partitioned space is stitched together only by editing. The camera empowers our gaze to go anywhere, to penetrate all the recesses of the building. Within this structure, the gaze is strongly attributed to the building itself, and diegetically figured in the emphasis on the video surveillance apparatus of its security system—another television.[51] The mobility and omnipresence of our look, then, is linked to both television and to the building. Such a mobility from compartment to compartment, replicating the familiar television talking-heads coverage of disasters, produces the camera, and our look along with it, as figures of authority. But these figures are themselves completely unstable. And what emerges is an emphasis on your own eyes, your own reading—a reading that must be individual and renegade like McClane's.

The unstable authority that *Die Hard* inscribes in the gaze structures and the mobility provided by its camera reappears in the struggle for authority over popular culture and the national identity it imagines, but this authority also is implicated in the film's play between proximity and distance. In its radio representation, the voice is closer, truer than the eye; the radio has the greater authority. Image and voice continually cut each other up or off—to resist the construction of continuous action or shared space.[52] If the office building is effectively disabled and sealed up by the interrupted flow of power—the violent cutting of wires and circuits—the visual space is slashed and shattered by radio communication—the voice substituting for the gaze to link spaces and characters through affection and aggression. Radio links contribute to a destructuring and restructuring of space, an allegory for the destructuration of the social body. This allegory seems to construct race relations so as to recode intimately linked histories as long-distance, remote-controlled relations, as if people who do not look at, or see, each other in the concrete world of everyday practice become more real for each other on radio or television.

Considering *Die Hard,* we might be moved to ask in a rewriting of Baldwin: is it really necessary to blow up a building, to immolate a series of adversaries as well as a whole arsenal of technologies, just to apologize to your wife and say hello to a black man? Something else must be at work to bring to bear all this affect on such banalities. And *much* else is at work. For one thing, this gleeful fantasy of corporate and technological destruction rehearses populist anticorporate sentiments alongside technophobic ones in the context of international trade conflicts, with the Germans and the Japanese as competing foreign interests.

Die Hard is fundamentally organized by a multiculturalist fantasy. This is a film that takes as one of its questions the following: what does a multicultural society look like? It is significant that it, like *Lethal Weapon,* is set in Los Angeles, a city that, together with New York, stands for the "alien nation" within the United States. These are places that are fantasmatically produced as sites where "anything can happen," where difference is the rule, and where difference always appears as novelty. But Los Angeles and New York are sites of containment as well, precisely to the extent that those fantasies persist, even in the minds of people who live there.

Die Hard produces yet a closer containment; after all, the conflict and reconciliation of realigned differences take place in a universe that is contained within a skyscraper, one building. But *Die Hard's* multiculturalism is another problem altogether; its discourse is aware of this irony and so pushes the action to this extreme since, effectively, the film says that postmodern urban multiculturalism consists in a perpetual recoding and realignment of differences of gender, race, ethnicity, and class, all of which are both equal and autonomous. The film establishes no relations among these differences. Instead, they are made to appear as equally weighted or charged and nonintersecting, or as intersecting only coincidentally, as in the pairing of FBI agents Johnson and Johnson.

Significantly, *Die Hard with a Vengeance* takes a different approach to social conflict, as it does to social space. This is the first film of the series to launch its plot into urban public space, by contrast to the strictly contained interiors of the first two films, which confine McClane to sealed spaces. As a consequence, this film is able to articulate race and space in such a way that the visual aspects of the narrative sometimes directly contradict the discursive level. Initially, the film takes pains to construct Zeus as overly preoccupied with race, as racializing everything. He explains his reluctance to have anything to do with McClane's struggle against Simon: "That's a white man with white problems. You deal with him. Call me when he crosses 110th." McClane's position insists that "race" must be dismissed, overridden, or transcended in the face of a common threat: "This guy doesn't care about skin color, even if you do." But McClane's suggestion that Zeus shares his option to put race matters aside is directly contradicted at the visual level in the public space. Zeus's subsequent adventures in the urban space undermine that position and prove him the shrewder analyst of the thoroughly racial coding of urban geography. His movements are consistently disrupted and often blocked by bizarrely racialized encounters with white people. These encounters seem to depend on the mere *sight* of him, as when a transit cop pulls a gun to prevent him from making a phone call, or when a Wall Street professional accuses him of disliking whites because he does not want him as a fare in the cab that he and McClane have commandeered. Zeus's progress through the city and the narrative is thus marked in a way that contrasts strictly with his white partner's. McClane, we remember, has had only one public encounter that appears racially charged, and that one has been staged by Simon's orders to wear the offensive sign that interpellates the black community. For Zeus, however, each meeting that involves difference is racially charged. Yet this happens in a filmic universe that still fantasmatically "charges" him with the weight of race.

Die Hard's fantasies about social difference, however, are diffused as they are mapped onto figures of international cultural difference, where the central opposition is American/foreign. This opposition bears upon the question of what it means to be an American. But uncertainty about the nature of "Americanness" seems linked to gender as well. McClane's wife, Holly, who has gone back to her maiden name on taking this job, explains her choice by arguing that the Japanese corporation does not deal well with married women. The character of the Nakatomi corporation, embodied in Joe Takata, Holly's boss, comes across when McClane comments at the office Christmas party: "I didn't know the Japanese celebrated Christmas." Takata's response is, "Hey, we're flexible. Pearl Harbor didn't work out, so we conquered you with electronics."

Anxieties about career-minded women are here linked to anxieties about the "flexibility" of Japanese capital, fantasized as a protean and often disguised invader of U.S. corporate interests. But this conflict is written into a plot that pits fake "terrorist" politics against corporate interests and that succeeds in displaying as "contingent" the face-off between the two main rivals of the United States on the level of economics, trade, and technology, Germany and Japan. The Germans' victory effectively eliminates the Japanese presence in the film and within the literal corporate structure as figured by the skyscraper. Within this framework, then, to be American is to be a *bricoleur*, a behind-the-scenes guerrilla. The film offers the cliché of American individual initiative and inventiveness and plays it against the extratextual fantasies it relies on: German precision and bloodlessness, and Japanese regimentation and conformity.[53] These oppositions, like all oppositions in the film, are caught up in *Die Hard*'s persistent ironies.

The German "terrorist" gang itself stands for a kind of hybridism; it includes an Asian man, a group of blond Aryan types (including the Russian dancer turned actor, Alexander Gudanov), and a black American. Hans, played by the British actor Alan Rickman, is so saturated with despised American culture that he can perfectly imitate an American accent. Finally, while the gang behaves like terrorists, employs "terrorist" discourse and tactics, and musters an arsenal of technology to that end, its motives turn out to be purely economic. But there is a further ironic undercutting here; the money that the gang is after is not cash, but bearer bonds, the most rapidly and freely circulating form of capital—its protean postmodern incarnation.[54]

Interestingly, within the logic of having things both ways, Hans once *was* a terrorist who has been expelled from his group. So the fantasy here involves seeing terrorism tip over into lust for capital, retroactively calling into question political motives for action. Thus, these events and images may be contained once again within the framework of a struggle between the authentic will and motives of the rebellious individual, which are opposed to the inauthentic slipperiness of capital in circulation.[55]

But for all the pleasure we may take in seeing corporate capital, high technology, and masculinity, or, for that matter, terrorism, put into crisis, the spectacle is most interesting for the context in which it locates that crisis. In the end, this film's pleasurable effects—its narrative and visual destabilization of authority, the spectacular excesses of its demolitions, its ambivalent combination of violent affect with a seamlessly ironic wise-cracking dialogue, its frame of sophisticated self-consciousness—still work toward resolution in a figure of restored white male authority, a figure valorized by his feminist wife and his black buddy.[56]

Certain issues are necessarily occluded or mystified in this process. As if by accident, the film has negotiated threats that are presented as split between white women and black men—between feminism and racial equality, foregrounding the former and repressing the latter, "hiding" it in the best place, in plain sight. And it has negotiated these threats precisely by mapping them into competing plots, as if they had nothing to do with each other, as if social differences were autonomous and never intersected. But the excessive, hysterical pitch of the film's action belies the amount of anxiety that these differences produce, while it safely locates its discharge in a place where it is undisturbed by real historical and political considerations, in the process guaranteeing that its real anxieties appear to be peripheral because they are represented as already managed. Anxieties about racial and sexual difference are also recoded in anxieties about technology and its management, about the security of the divide between body and machine. All of these elements are mobilized in colliding or parallel plots, as if they were not fully politicized and overdetermined in relation both to each other and to a particular historical moment. Through its apparent commitment to ambivalence, the film erases overdetermination.[57]

But the crisis of white, heterosexual masculinity represented here remains—socially as well as cinematically—overdetermined by social differences. Otherwise, that crisis would not emerge in narrative and visual frames that are so referentially bound to contemporary social and cultural conflicts. *Die Hard*'s peripheral negotiation of race within a dystopian fantasy seems completely coherent with liberal discourses of pluralism and multiculturalism: failing to specify the power relations that are mapped onto differences, it depicts difference as a state of permanent emergency. Despite its happy ending, we cannot forget that its picture of a multicultural society looks like a disaster, one that brings down the house, quite literally. Within this film's escalating spectacle of disaster, difference becomes yet another special effect, as the question of multiculturalism is written into another question that buries the issue of race in culture and ethnicity: what does it mean to be American? In this context, the answer is, it seems, that being American means being a *bricoleur* and a good manager, a manager of crisis, in a culture depicted as in a constant state of emergency. And the best manager wins; he is the familiar renegade individualist.

Now, if films consume, transform, and shape popular discourses, they inevitably do so ambivalently, offering up possibly progressive impulses and indicating points of resistance as well as managing resistance and anxiety. Whatever meanings they put forward, these are structured into a context that includes a market, in this case an audience for action films, and that conditions their reading, primarily by framing the images and narratives in such a way as to suggest that they require little reading. And these films' tendency toward serial repetition may be intimately related to the ways that they deemphasize, or even discourage, reading.[58]

If we ask what pleasures are involved here, and more generally in popular culture, we have to ask about the status of trash, both in the sense of a film's throwaways, what it codes as insignificant, and in the sense of texts that offer themselves as trash, that reflect on their own trashiness and commitment to the market. They read our desires within an explicit enunciative framework that says, "this doesn't mean very much." And if, as readers of our fantasies, these objects present them ambivalently, consequently satisfying more of us, that does not mean that as critics we can afford to remain cheerfully content with our own ambivalence. While film's meanings are always negotiated and negotiable, we cannot overlook the pressures of their internal negotiations: their trade-offs, exchanges, and intersections as well as their structuring contradictions.

Hollywood has been able to rework the massively successful blackwhite buddy plot relentlessly, with only minor adjustments. But the formula has its limits. For one thing, the white guy cannot be the "buddy," cannot be remanded, in Ed Guerrero's phrase, to "the protective custody" of a black male lead. And this may have to do with the ways in which "the black body . . . becomes . . . a representational sign for the democratizing process of U.S. culture itself," as Robyn Wiegman has it.[59] Here, we might want to add that this sign functions in this way only when viewed from a particular perspective—that of the dominant white middle class, of course. But the political and representational landscape that sustains Hollywood's reworking of the biracial buddy plot also generates colossal failures, like *Ricochet* (Russell Mulcahy, 1991), a film designed for the blockbuster frame, but whose central subjects were apparently incompatible with its format. While it examined the fictional production and destruction of a black professional's public media image, this film's ironic take on the blockbuster form itself also tried to mobilize collective anxieties about "media manipulation." However, it remains unclear in what interest the film undertook its critique, what exactly it meant to subject to ironic scrutiny: its hero, played by Denzel Washington, its own discourse, or a media discourse from which it seeks to differentiate itself.[60]

By contrast, *The Last Boy Scout* exaggerates the action film's commitment to surface—where any pretext for wildly implausible and prolonged violence suffices and where dialogue consistently reduces to ironic patter, a steady rhythm of aggressive jokes bouncing back and forth. Willis's slickly impenetrable patter is balanced by Wayans's appearance as body/ image/prop in a structure that arranges them as symmetrical across a certain rhythm of look exchanges. This film replays *Lethal Weapon*'s successful formula of overlaying a black-white buddy plot on a father-son dynamic that is powerfully eroticized. But now we are dealing with the white father and with his abject degeneracy, which his daughter characterizes as she ventriloquizes her mother's contempt in her vulgar references: he is a fuck-up, an alcoholic, all but unemployed. This story repeats *Die Hard*'s paternal redemption plot, but the antihero has to come back from much farther away—he is the paternal abject. Consequently, his family cannot serve as a refuge for Dix. Rather, Dix's interventions must reconstitute the white family, salvage it from its deterioration.

As in *Die Hard,* the main character in *The Last Boy Scout* drives circuitously toward a reconciliation with his wife. And again, Willis's character ends by saying what his wife "wants" to hear. In this case his wife has told him what he should be saying to gain the respect he has lost by tolerating her infidelities: "fuck you Sarah. You're a fucking bitch and if the cops weren't here I'd spit in your face." Unlike *Die Hard,* this film balances Willis's irony and patter with that of Damon Wayans, who comes bearing the iconic baggage of his television roles on the sitcom, "In Living Color," which were noted for their outrageous jokes about race and homosexuality.[61] But Wayans is a prop, as Darien keeps pointing out; she wants to exhibit him to her friends.

Ricochet, on the other hand, invites us to focus on the black male body, drawing and sustaining our gaze across the hostile looks of white psychotics. Both films are Joel Silver and Michael Levy productions from 1991. (*Ricochet* was released in September, while *The Last Boy Scout* appeared in December; the tie-in between them persisted in the videocassette market, where Silver's *The Last Boy Scout* is previewed on the

Ricochet tape.) *Ricochet* suspends our gaze on Nick Styles (Denzel Washington), a policeman turned district attorney, in an elaborate relay of public looks: the look of the television, of Styles's boss, of the woman district attorney, of the police. At another level, Styles is framed for the gaze of his high school buddy, Odessa (Ice T), who represents the view "from the street" and voices a contempt for the mass-mediatized, middle-class black man, alienated from the community that must finally rescue him. Finally, he is framed for Blake, his primary adversary, in the glare of the hateful and stalking gaze of psychotic white supremacy, with its overtly erotic edge. In short, a lot of things are ricocheting here. *Ricochet* is a borderline film—savage and vicious. And the most vicious of its over-the-top ironies concerns the production of the African American middle-class male as an image that it posits for everyone to criticize and condemn.[62]

In its ironic zeal the film pushes the action film blockbuster formula over the top, as it plays the homoerotics embedded in the male adversaries' struggle, along with the mutilation of the male body that has become so central to the genre, to a near camp extreme. In what may have been meant as an aggressively critical challenge to its audience, the film gleefully punishes its hero, delivering him up helpless to an antagonist who drugs him, strips him, and has him sexually assaulted by a white prostitute in a process that Elizabeth Alexander aptly describes as "pornographizing" Styles ("We're Gonna Deconstruct Your Life!," p. 159). Where *Passenger 57* remains a relatively neutral, moderately successful vehicle for Wesley Snipes, *Ricochet* seems to have become an occasion for the mainstream market to respond negatively to the question: can you build a blockbuster around a black male star? But it does so by violating the action genre's terms through its excessive punishment of the hero whose embodiment it highlights. This "aberrant" film, a commercial failure, even as it fails to rework the formula in a manageable form may be the exception that teaches something about the rule. That is, it reshuffles the familiar elements in a manner that does not "take" commercially, perhaps because the transparency of its ideological lures constitutes their ruin.[63]

In the case of *Die Hard,* on the other hand, internal negotiations among competing plots allow for a false symmetry among sexual, racial, and cultural difference, and for the containment of the first two as marginal and contingent to the third. The competing plots consistently work through reciprocal undercuttings, where, for example, the threat of corporate and technological power undercuts the threat of racial and sexual equality, and the lust for money is shown to undercut not only the political motives of terrorism, but just about any other motives at all, and where, finally, McClane's wisecracking irony about the whole situation undercuts all other positions. Within a structure of such constant undercutting, we are left with an ideological paralysis, a paralysis that the film fantasmatically "cures" by a return to "individual will," specifically, a parody of manly heroic will at that.

And this is where we end up, if we accept the ironic posture that the narrative offers: laughing hysterically with McClane, but laughing nonetheless. Even if we consider that we are laughing at ourselves, we need to ask where we think we are in all of this, for such a position is a strikingly postmodern one, coherent with prevailing academic theoretical and critical discourses. And these discourses are at risk, argues Fred Pfeil, of maintaining a radical retreat from the arena of political change. He suggests that we need to take critical positions on the objects that address us, to study that address itself—since we can find ourselves both at its point of enunciation and its point of reception—in the following way. "With a properly historical and materialist understanding of the social origins of postmodernism and poststructuralism within late capitalism and consumer society, and of our own place within it, and our equivocal, complicitous fascination/revulsion with both this structure of feeling and the particular social universe which is our own—we might be able to move on to the real strategic task of constructing new political subjectivities and wills."[64]

Because popular films read, consume, and even offer partial analyses of fantasies and anxieties circulating in the social field, they are always ambivalent, and their address to us is ambivalent. If we recognize that films may tell us what we are really thinking about—are really anxious about, collectively—then we have to assume that we do not automatically understand these anxieties any more than the films do, because surely the unconscious is at work in the social field as well. Strategically, then, we cannot settle for the satisfactions of just identifying ambivalences. Rather, we need critical reading strategies that remain alert to our own seductions. If cultural studies wants to continue privileging ambivalence and negotiation, we need to be specific about what is being negotiated and what is presented as not up for negotiation, as having been already negotiated. Specific cinematic stagings of fantasies and anxieties allow particular conflicts to emerge together in ways that the film does not analyze, or even admit, but rather offers as coincidence. What is most interesting to me is not how films try to supply answers or resolutions, but how they formulate the questions, and how those formulations close off other questions. By substituting coincidence for overdetermination as the articulation among differences, then, popular cinema works to cut its own meanings, as well as our readings, adrift from the social conflicts that obsess it. Only if we critically rework these films' internal overdeterminations can we begin to see how they might formulate our questions otherwise, how they might answer differently to social fantasies.

As the circulation of male buddy action films seemed to escalate in the late 1980s, their ironies and their market success may have helped open the terrain for the female action heroes who emerged explosively in *Thelma and Louise, Terminator 2,* and the *Alien* films. At the same time, however, there is good reason to ask how the female action figure relates to other female protagonists, particularly to those who appear in markedly hybrid genres that seem to address both masculine and feminine spectators, whose pleasures and fears they align. Specifically, I mean to explore the shared configurations of desire and aggression, sex and violence that link some recent reworkings of melodramatic form with police and detective thrillers. If the recent history of a new kind of "women's film" is shot through with anxiety about the price of women's power, preoccupied with women's aggression and violence, then similar anxieties seem to circulate in films addressed to a more masculine market that includes police thrillers and action films.

In an exemplary fashion, *Fatal Attraction* (Adrian Lyne, 1987) explicitly plays with the conventions of melodrama to produce a perversely double-edged fantasy, mobilizing masculine anxiety and feminine aggression or guilt. Such a fantasy figures in many representations where women's power—always registered as erotic as well as physical, social, and economic—is consistently accompanied by diminution of masculine force or competence. Contemporary popular film continues almost compulsively to display men who are physically or psychically disabled in the face of women's force and aggression.[1] From *Fatal Attraction* to *Someone to Watch Over Me* (Ridley Scott, 1987), through *The Hand That Rocks the Cradle* (Curtis Hanson, 1992), we watch along with the sidelined man as the climactic battle between women unfolds. Such representations seem to mobilize women's anxieties about vulnerability and punishment, wrought through an intolerable trade-off where feminine force seems to arise at the direct expense of masculine power and bodily integrity. This is a universe where the good men are crippled or incompetent, and only the bastards remain empowered. But it all seems to go back to the women,[2] in a pattern we might see as reaching a zenith in *Basic Instinct* (Paul Verhoeven, 1993), a film that so privileges the murderous identificatory aggression between women that the investigating male protagonist becomes reduced to little more than their prop.

While *Fatal Attraction* introduces action film conventions into melodrama, other films inject melodrama into the police force, as the workplace and the family increasingly interpenetrate or merge. Some strikingly explicit instances that take this dissolving of borders as their central conflict include *Someone to Watch Over Me* and *Sea of Love* (Harold Becker, 1989).[3] This last film figures here because its closely woven plot emphatically links traditional film noir concerns to more contemporary versions of the detective as the embodiment of gender anxiety. *Sea of Love* revolves around this premise. Discovering a pattern of sexually related serial killings that may be linked to personal ads, two New York police detectives, Frank Keller (Al Pacino) and Sherman Touhey (John Goodman), go undercover, posing as men in search of dates. Because all of the victims are presumptively heterosexual men, Frank and Sherman assume that their suspect is a woman. As the plot unfolds, rehearsing a familiar and literal paranoia about the femme fatale, Frank, an angry, lonely alcoholic who is faltering in his job, becomes increasingly obsessed with one of the women he has met and begun dating. At the same time, he encounters more and more difficulty in distinguishing his pose from his "real life." His performance, in other words, becomes his reality, and he is unable to stop pursuing the suspect both romantically and professionally. In the end, he narrowly misses joining the series of victims, as it is finally disclosed that the killer is not the woman, but her psychotically jealous ex-husband.

Each of these films is organized by the cop's fears about his inability to keep work and private life separate, either because the criminals are literally breaking into his house or seducing his wife, or because, as in *Basic Instinct,* he himself is seduced by a feminine criminal suspect.[4] In any case, he has problems with boundaries. And these are not unrelated to larger social conflicts. As Stanley Aronowitz has pointed out, the police have become just about the last frequently seen representation of the working class in contemporary films.[5] Of course, the police force is also the site where images of intense and conflicted racial interaction consistently proliferate. Perhaps because of the ambiguous, not to say ambivalent, nature of this fictional police agency—a working class patrolling the border of the middle class, holding off a threat that is figured as an urban underclass—this is the ideal representational node for accumulating a variety of fantasies about borders and their stability.[6]

Anxieties about fragile social borders often seem to merge with images of masculine vulnerability exposed to feminine force in films that mix generic conventions in a variety of ways. These condensations make sexual difference, and the management of its meaning, the central mystery under investigation. To the extent that such films consistently link fatality to desire and to the effects of sexual difference(s), they recall and rework the conventions associated with film noir, even as they repeat certain historical exchanges between that genre and hard-boiled detective fictions. Given that noir names what are perhaps the most unstable and tenuous of generic categories, it makes some sense that contemporary films interested in hybridity would quote it or rewrite it. But perhaps an emphasis on shifting generic boundaries coheres as well with obsessions about gender boundaries.

In an article bluntly titled "Dumb Lugs and Femmes Fatales," B. Ruby Rich links neo-noir's interest in the crossing of generic boundaries, expressed through citation and appropriation, to ideological issues. "The vacuum of authority," she writes, "is a key component for Neo Noir, signifying as it does membership in postmodernism. Thus the reliance on quotation, homage, and appropriation, all elements that fuel the audience's pleasure and undermine the characters' claims to meaning."[7] She goes on to describe the men and women who seem to be structurally characteristic of contemporary rewrites of the noir genre: "The women of Neo Noir may be inexplicably evil, but that's what audiences love about them . . . the new noir films trot out smart, treacherous femmes fatales, but the male patsies who seem to be no match for them at all turn out to be the sole repositories of authenticity" (9).[8] In a sense, one might productively ask if these new noir films are not reinterpreting the symptomalogy of the classic noir films, since it has often been argued that they embrace and demonstrate a particular theory that woman is man's symptom. Slavoj Žižek, in *Enjoy Your Symptom!*, suggests that we understand the meaning of the "symptom" in a densely complicated way: "namely, as a particular signifying formation which confers on the subject its very ontological consistency, enabling it to structure its basic, constitutive relationship to enjoyment (jouissance)."[9] To understand the symptom in this manner, he continues, is to reverse the relationship of the subject to it: "If the symptom is dissolved, the subject itself loses the ground under its feet, disintegrates. In this sense, 'woman is a symptom of man' means that man himself exists only through woman qua his symptom: all his ontological consistency hangs on, is suspended from his symptom, is 'externalized' in his symptom" (155). "In other words," Žižek concludes, "man literally ex-sists; his entire being lies 'out there,' in woman" (155). What of woman now? we might ask. "Woman," Žižek contends, "does not ex-sist, she insists, which is why she does not come to be through man only—there is something in her that escapes the relation to man, the reference to the phallic signifier" (156).

Read through this schema, a film like *Basic Instinct* might appear to stage a masculine anxiety about becoming *woman's* symptom. But if in this analysis "woman" remains an "out there," might she not also be represented as the embodiment of another "outside"—the social? While Joan Copjec has suggested that it is characteristic of classic noir to unfold in an evacuated or depopulated universe,[10] films that in many recent examples incorporate noir patterns present privatized professional worlds and domestic spaces edged by an intermittently encroaching social context. While these films often try to repress it, the social seeps into their spatial organization and visual preoccupation with borders in narratives obsessed with the destabilizing effects of feminine agency.

Distinguishing new noir films from the classic genre, Rich contends that while their predecessors were "bent on capturing the instability of masculinity," contemporary versions seem "equally determined to reinstate masculinity" (10). For her, "the valorisation of stupidity is just a small part of that agenda. Neo Noir is a genre where a man is always a man, even if a woman isn't always exactly a woman. . . . The destiny of these dumb men with sex-addled brains is to be set up by the greedy women whose paths they're fated to cross" (10). While these male characters are not necessarily meant to defeat the women, they do support this "assignment": "to hold fast in a post-modern world of shifting significances, to reject dispersal and masquerade and therefore corruption, to be 'themselves' in the absence of any other comprehensible rules" (10). In identifying a central equation between masculine stupidity, or obtuseness, and "authenticity," Rich contributes a significant interpretation of the symptomatic qualities of these films. If we understand these obtuse men as figures of authenticity, meant to represent nothing but themselves and who operate as subjects of transparency without depth, then authenticity becomes an effect of the failure to read or interpret. The men lose because they fail to read. What the new noir films expose along with their protagonists' refusals of meaning, however, is that all versions of masculinity, as of femininity, operate through their failure to coincide with the abstract ideal of gender. Masculinity for these films, then, cannot simply "be" itself.

The films explored here have in common intensely symptomatic figurations of gendered relations to and across sexual difference. Each highlights the instability of the sexual divide in a hybrid format that borrows, cites, and reworks conventions from various genres and blurs the boundaries distinguishing them. Finally, and perhaps most important, the symptomatic quality of the sexual relation is articulated most forcefully through identification and the relays that identification generates. If the classic noir model is obsessional—the man is pulled along by the repetition compulsion, the death drive embedded in his desire for the woman—contemporary versions seem to hystericize the relations among characters. Identification mixes with desire in intrigues where the angry, terrified, and dazzled man does not know if he wants to make love to the woman or kill her, join with her or compete with her, have her or *be* her. These confusions are as common to *Fatal Attraction, Someone to Watch Over Me, The Hand That Rocks the Cradle,* all in some degree domestic melodramas, as they are to *Sea of Love* and *Basic Instinct,* both neo-noir narratives of the collapse of personal and public spaces. More important, the dramas of identification and doubling that these films share are articulated through relays of specular aggression and violence, where the reversibility of the gaze structure constitutes the central threat to the gendered subject's integrity (or the subject's gender integrity) as well as to the borders of public and private.

Loading anxieties onto the question of sexual difference and sexuality, these films figure a private war of the sexes that foregrounds masculine anxieties about incompetence, weakness, and failure in a universe where the boundaries between the private and the public or professional are constantly shifting. As such, they distill and crystallize the workings of displacement that condition a variety of representations of gender conflict staged as independent of a larger social context.

Policing the Family

Fatal Attraction may offer a paradigmatic case of the reduction of the social horizon of difference to gendered conflict. The film's male protagonist, Dan Gallagher (Michael Douglas), begins the closing argument that is supposed to end his weekend affair with Alex Forrest (Glenn Close) with the suggestion, "Let's be reasonable." Arising abruptly from her bed on the pretense of having a lot of work to do, Dan sets about justifying his decision, "I thought we'd have a good time." "No, you didn't," Alex contradicts him, "You thought *you*'d have a good time. You didn't stop for a second to think about me." "That's crazy," Dan argues, "*You* knew the rules." "What *rules?*" Alex retorts. At this response, Dan offers a laughably feeble summation: "Look, Alex, I like you and if I weren't with someone else I'd probably be with you. But I am." This weak stab at closure provokes a feminine rage whose escalation organizes the narrative: "Don't justify yourself, it's pathetic. If you'd tell me to fuck off, I'd have more respect for you." So he does: "All right, fuck off." In answer, Alex erupts in violence, kicking him furiously.

If the man's anger maintains a logic and an argument, the woman's rage argues by sheer assertion. If anger may remain within the discursive register, rage is all mixed up with the bodily. From this moment, Dan, the family man, a lawyer who worries that he does not "know anything about family law," will spend the rest of the film paying for having broken rules that are obscure to Alex, or, let us say, he will spend it learning the law of the family. Alex, an embodiment of uncontainable feminine rage that she is, will spend the film battering away at the boundaries that family law is supposed to keep secure. *Fatal Attraction* wants to play this conflict out as a contradiction between men's and women's economies. As it rehearses a larger cultural effort to map separate gendered logics into an archaic division between public and private, the film mobilizes generalized tensions about social conflicts invading the private interior. At the same time, it wishfully treats such conflicts as if they could be managed in some interior space—in the domestic space of the family, on the one hand, or in negotiations *between women* over commitments to private or public life, on the other.

One of the film's more bluntly conventional points is that rage is ambivalent in aim and effect, as likely to boomerang on its agent as it is to hit the wrong target or entirely miss it. Just whose attraction to whom ignites a fatal rage is the question that the film holds in suspense to structure its basic ambivalence. The fatality could go in any one of three ways here. That is what keeps us watching: to figure out whose rage is going to culminate in a murder, and who will be its victim, Dan, Alex, or Dan's wife, Beth. Ambivalence also characterized feminist reaction to this film. As Mandy Merck has pointed out, a *Village Voice* readers' poll at the time demonstrated reactions explicitly according to identifications: "among [them] feminists . . . disputed the film's meaning from within a stated identification with Alex, Amy Taubin finding a sickening pathologization of the demands of the rejected woman, Karen Durbin celebrating a powerful representation of female rebellion and rage." [11]

Finally, perhaps Alex's most enduring power and appeal may be her ability to support multiple and ambivalent identifications. We may feel ourselves to be on her side, which is not the *woman*'s side so much as the *out*side. Yet it is difficult to sustain a single and fixed identification. If our identifications with Alex seem to disintegrate from time to time, it may be because the film tends to oscillate between subjectivizing and desubjectivizing her; in the process, it provides no consistent alignment of our look with the space we imagine to be occupied by her point of view.[12]

This narrative presents competing arguments or points of view that are consistently punctuated by moments of perverse satisfaction, of gleeful aggression or irony for some feminist viewers, as, for instance, when we watch acid consuming that emblem of the middle-class professional family's security—the Volvo station wagon. But these brief pleasures erupt in a film that invites us to treat it as symptomatic in a larger context of particular social anxieties about sexual difference and of specific feminist anxieties about rage, power, and violence. To read our public cultural representations, "rage" belongs to and marks nondominant groups; those who inhabit stable positions of power do not need rage. Again and again, the characterization of rage serves the interests of a dominant order that sees it as noise interfering with the clear expression of a resistant or contentious message. But an underlying and more subtle anxiety may have to do with the haunted and unstable division between public and private, a division that is destabilized when spectacles of rage touch private anxieties. Indeed, rage may gain political force precisely to the extent that it is able to touch the dominant culture's worst fears, to embody its anxiety in spectacle, as *Thelma and Louise* did. In a feminist context, however, rage seems to threaten our fantasies of a stable and safe space, an interior constituted over and against an "outside" toward which rage might be more "properly" directed.

But just what makes *Fatal Attraction*'s particular image of rage so compelling? Its power has something to do with its ability to provide a mixture of anxiety and satisfaction, as well as a comfortable recourse to irony for both feminine and masculine spectators. And this irony may be reassuring, especially in the face of the excessive affect that this cartoonishly escalated melodrama borrows from anxieties about the borders that guarantee differences of a sexual nature. Finally, we might read *Fatal Attraction* as an allegory of the instability of more than one sexual difference: not only what is the difference between men and women, but also, what is the difference between *women* and women, women inside and outside the family?

Dan Gallagher, however, is also implicated in the identificatory delirium. As *Fatal Attraction* sees it, Dan's problem is that he is not sure if he can tell the difference between these two women, or, for that matter, between himself and the women. So the whole film focuses on an urgent effort to reinscribe the border of sexual difference at exactly the divide between domestic interior and public space. Dan struggles to secure the domestic interior as a way of deciding once and for all about sex and about women and of establishing differences: between good sex and bad, between good mothers and bad ones, between sex and violence, and between men's rules and women's, men's jobs and women's. At the climax, when a fearful Dan has locked the murderous woman *in* rather than out, we must read the film as a concerted effort to mobilize masculine anxiety about protecting the middle-class interior.

Although *Fatal Attraction* figures the threat to domesticity as coming from the outside through the agency of an urban career woman, the way domesticity is mapped visually demonstrates that the interior is already destabilized, that violence is already internalized. This is an effect that *Falling Down* exploits in the specular relation it establishes between D-Fens and Prendergast. As D-Fens fights his way to his wife's house, struggling to return to a "home" that never looked anything like his fantasy of the past he wants to restore, the film gradually demonstrates that Prendergast's real problem—his psychic handicap—really comes from his home life. What holds him back is his agoraphobic wife, who seals up the domestic space around them like a prison.

Dilated to the point of unfamiliarity as objects of the camera's anxious and obsessive gaze, familiar domestic implements in the Gallagher house encode the menace, the disruption within.[13] For instance, the ordinary sound of water boiling or a tea kettle heating up are tightly embedded within the structures of suspense. Likewise, as Alex tells Dan after he has threatened to kill her: "It only takes a phone call"—to ruin his life.[14] Male paranoia is figured in fear of the telephone as an opening that one cannot seal off. Paradoxically, domesticity is disrupted in proportion to the drama's progressive retreat into the innermost recesses of privacy: the kitchen and the bathroom. Dan and Alex's first sex scene erupts in her kitchen, mixing registers as she sits on the sink. The penultimate combat of the film also takes place in Alex's kitchen in a scene that matches in remarkable detail with the sex scene, down to the exhausted heavy panting of both partners after Dan has tried to strangle Alex.

Meanwhile, the film maps Dan's incompetent relation to the object world. Because he cannot even open a recalcitrant umbrella, Alex must rescue him from the rain, just as Beth finally rescues him from Alex. One of the film's primary ambivalences and ironies is surely this one. Its portrayal of Alex Forrest as a monster depends on its contempt for Dan Gallagher. That view is strikingly clear at the moment when we see him stumbling along, clad in his white jockey shorts, black socks, and shoes, tripping over the trousers that flap around his ankles as he struggles to carry Alex to the bedroom after the first hot sex scene in the kitchen. Dan is a man who cannot do his job. Curiously, Michael Douglas, the actor, seems to have made a career of playing such men in recent years. His haplessness is the narrative motor for *Disclosure* (Barry Levinson, 1994), and *Basic Instinct* emphasizes an obtuseness, lack of vigilance, and bumbling that make Nick Curran no match for Catherine Trammel, or Beth Garner.

Finally, Dan is as incapable of protecting his family as he is of getting a waiter's attention in a restaurant. But if he cannot do his job, he cannot do a woman's job either. He is so absorbed in the process of making a cup of tea while Alex and Beth fight it out above his head in the bathroom that he fails to notice the sign that would alert him to the battle. This is another mark of the film's irony. That sign is a proper homeowner's disaster: water from the tub's overflow drips through the kitchen ceiling.

Alex's enormous kitchen knife provides an almost laughable literalization of the double-edgedness that characterizes *Fatal Attraction*'s ironies. While she threatens Beth, Alex also is drawing the knife back and forth across her own thigh—as if she could not quite differentiate herself from Beth, to whom she addresses the tense question: what are *you* doing here? Pathological though this question is supposed to be, it stresses the film's irony. If Alex is unable to see the difference between herself and Beth, between her own bathroom and Beth's, it is because the film is about establishing those differences. And, of course, this is one reason why it has to be Beth who kills Alex. But what, finally, is the difference between these women? It seems to come down to this: Beth has an image of herself, and Alex does not. Erotically, of course, an image is all Beth has. Dan has sex with Alex, but he *looks* at Beth; the image of Dan looking over Beth's shoulder at their reflection in the mirror explicitly constitutes their erotic interaction, since, whenever they try to have sex, they are interrupted.

These women are ciphers—Beth of serenity, Alex of rage. Indeed, Beth is reduced to the image of serenity—at her dressing table, in her bathroom, always at the mirror, framed by its borders, her narcissism supported by her husband's gaze over her shoulder. Alex, we notice, never looks in the mirror. And she is repeatedly framed in head shots that emphasize her as a Medusa figure. Her head and body are not coordinated; she loses her head in rage. Beth, by contrast, is poised and posed as an image, held in frame. Alex is the one with the power to break the frame, as she breaks the rules, in frenzied, flailing activity. Beth's life is a picture, just as her family is a greeting card photograph, an image that *Fatal Attraction* confirms with brutal irony in the end when its frame melts into that of the family photograph as narrative space reduces to that frozen moment. We already have seen this family group rendered in white, framed by a picture window, an image that makes Alex violently ill. Her vomiting registers for us the internal violence that attends the policing of the border that frames the family as picture-perfect. This moment also invites us to ask what remains out of frame here, particularly since the inside is obsessively depicted in white, which seems to be the overwhelmingly dominant color of this film on all registers.

Where is the social world of *Fatal Attraction?* Cutting back and forth between the country and the city, the film fails to establish the distance that separates them, the route that connects them. This spatial vagueness works to suppress any concrete social coordinates, for the nuclear family here represents not only an escape from the city, but a fantasmatic escape from class and from all social difference and conflict, so that this battle between career woman and family woman operates in isolation from all other social negotiations. Thus, the film conveniently sets sexual difference and the internal conflicts of feminism apart from the social and material realities in which they are embedded. I want to suggest that the artificial whiteout of this film, where all women start to look the same, framed in antagonistic specular isolation, may relate to a set of fantasies and anxieties that continue to provoke feminist debate. At the same time, on another front these anxieties emerge within the dominant culture's efforts to manage social conflict in its representations of gender.

These efforts continue to figure feminism as the origin of such conflicts and to imagine a struggle whose primary antagonists are women, as those "on the outside" assail the borders of the nuclear family. This is where *The Hand That Rocks the Cradle*, because it introduces race into the domestic battle it restages, may offer an ironic rereading of the social representation that *Fatal Attraction*'s own ironies repress. What *Fatal Attraction* works to keep out of frame, *The Hand That Rocks the Cradle* forces into the picture, but in a manner that, for its very excess, calls attention to the instability and uneasiness of the connections which dominant popular culture can establish between race and gender. *Basic Instinct,* by further contrast, explores anxieties about dissolving borders in the context of women invading and manipulating, as if by remote control, the police detective's private life, his personal and psychic history, and his professional performance. Playing on images of women's desires and identifications as threatening, particularly when the man cannot *read* them, this film figures that broader threat in Catherine Trammel and Beth Garner, characters whose sexuality is not fully determined.[15]

Fatal Attraction's presentation of the middle-class family's social context reduces it to a ghostly television image obtruding in Alex's domestic isolation. We hear Mayor Ed Koch promising to investigate allegations of stun-gun torture of suspects in a Bronx precinct house, as Alex weeps, in a scene that is intercut with images of Beth and Dan enjoying an evening of bowling with friends. This emphasis on the Gallaghers' domestic insulation is ultimately connected to one of the film's most maddening effects: the way it consistently makes Alex's anger tip over into rage, so that her point dissolves in explosive affect. She does have a real argument, but the source and the goal of her rage are increasingly obscured as she becomes a figure of pathology, so that her critique is submerged in private psychotic reaction. But what happens if we set that "private" rage in a social texture, one that includes a context of contemporary representations?[16] Alex, then, is aligned with the outside, the conflict that constitutes the social world, which occasionally seeps into the frame. Intermittent though it is, the visual and spatial inscriptions of this outside (or elsewhere) reveal it as a constitutive pressure on the narrative. In *Someone to Watch Over Me,* by contrast, these pressures are more obtrusive and more densely inscribed as the film maps spatial shifts that Mike Kegan's desires and mobility produce.

The Policing Family: *Someone to Watch Over Me*

While it explores the law of the family in terms similar to those of *Fatal Attraction, Someone to Watch Over Me* presents a drama of triangulation that involves three characters who are all coded as "good" and thrown into conflict by the competing logics that they observe. Just as in *Fatal Attraction,* the single, independent, "other woman" poses an external threat to the family; however, in this case the film's rather forced resolution places her on the side of the reconstituted family of the policeman, over and against the criminal who threatens her life as well as theirs. The two women, the hero's wife, Ellie (Lorraine Bracco), and his lover, Claire (Mimi Rogers), respectively, represent the contradictory demands upon Mike Kegan (Tom Berenger) of his family and his work, and behind that, of the state. And the women "do their jobs" unerringly: Ellie is charged with preserving the family, while Claire must act as a "good citizen" and testify as an eyewitness at a murder trial. In his incompetence, indecision, and undisciplined desire, Mike, the detective husband, bears the weight of the contradiction between the competing logics of family and civil order and competing familial and social duties.

Like *Fatal Attraction, Someone to Watch Over Me* maps a spatial intrigue between opposing interiors. This intrigue appears to be governed by a paranoid gaze vigilantly watching for the murderous threat that may break in at any moment, or worse, that remains concealed within domestic space. Through the camera's gaze the film inscribes a paranoically reversible look structure into the space itself. Mike Kegan is constantly anxious about being watched by someone else, even as he watches over Claire Gregory, the witness. He worries about being seen with Claire, either by her friends or his colleagues; he worries about being seen by the murderer without seeing him first. Finally, he is the object of both Claire's and his wife's scrutiny. While his wife seems to read the incriminating signs of his affair, Claire scrutinizes him for the telltale signs of his class position, reflected in his taste and demeanor. Despite the fact that Mike is the bearer of the policing and surveying look, both women are endowed with a power of surveillance and detection that is closely aligned with the shakiness of Mike's hold on his authority and his proper place.

Observing a spatial logic as rigorous as *Fatal Attraction*'s, *Someone to Watch Over Me* juxtaposes strictly partitioned and autonomous domestic spaces between which there is no middle ground. These are spaces connected only by Mike's guard duty and by the murderer, Joey Venza, who eventually takes Mike's family hostage in order to make him exchange Claire for them. At the same time, structurally, it is both Mike's fascination with Claire and his sexual transgression that bring about this threat to his family. His desire for another domestic space destabilizes his own and opens it to violation. But this scenario unfolds only in a universe where the police and the family have already become confused. The police are familialized and the family is insufficiently policed because it has become, under the broken law of the father, indistinguishable from the police. As Ellie puts it: "My father told me. 'Never go out with a cop.' So whaddo I do? I get a job with the cops, I marry a cop, and I've probably given birth to a cop." Disregarding the paternal admonition, Ellie has replicated both her father's and her mother's positions: she has become a cop *and* married one.[17] This repetition, the film suggests, results in a confused ménage where inside and outside are unstable, where the place of the family is uncertain in much the same measure as are the gendered places of its members.[18]

But if the family is projected onto the police force, the police force is figured only in its private side and not as a social agency. This film's social universe is rigorously privatized. It is projected onto the terrain of the interior as a struggle between the genders—and between women—in a landscape that figures these conflicts as wars of taste.[19] Examining the articulation of heterosexual familial identity that organizes 1950s melodramas, D. N. Rodowick makes the claim: "The form which the problem of identity takes is one of the crucial, defining characteristics of the domestic melodrama. The forward thrust of the narrative is not accomplished through external conflict and the accumulation of significant actions, but rather through the internalization of conflict in a crisis of identification: the difficulty which individual characters find in their attempts to accept or conform to the set of symbolic positions around which the network of social relations adhere and where they can both be 'themselves' and 'at home.' "[20] Residually inhabited by these conventions, *Someone to Watch Over Me* draws them into a kind of marriage with the conventions of the thriller and film noir genres[21] in a kind of formal *mésalliance* that replicates the class mismatch at the disruptive center of its narrative. In its particular projection of domestic conflict—as sexual and class conflict—onto urban domestic space, *Someone to Watch Over Me* reworks these conventions in a drama of masculine identity as much threatened by feminine initiative, agency, and aggression as it is by the instability of an interior that is vulnerable to the encroachments of the "street."

Like most melodramatic males, or men in melodrama, Mike Kegan is uncertain of his place in the family. But this uncertainty is enhanced by his wobbly position in a convoluted network of social borders. Similarly, Mike's home is situated at a shaky urban location. Like *Sea of Love*'s Frank Keller, this working-class Irish-American has a coveted Manhattan assignment, which places him in an awkward position. He protects a neighborhood where he could never live, and he lives in a place that he cannot protect. "The neighborhood is turnin' to shit. It's a cesspool," Mike declares, establishing his anxiety about violence as connected to a social underclass, confused with an underworld, and about the possibility of the family's social descent reflected in the neighborhood's decline. The film figures this underworld threat in the person of Joey Venza, Italian-American metonym for the ethnic and racial antagonisms and anxiety that saturate the social imaginary of class. *Someone to Watch Over Me* cleverly plays this anxiety out on a double track, however, since the opposition between Mike's Italian-American wife, Ellie, small, dark, violent, and "vulgar," and his lover, WASP Claire Gregory, tall, blonde, refined, and educated, almost parodically foregrounds the class fantasies that are projected onto and embodied in these competing women and the spaces that they dominate.

If the women are anchored in class, as they are anchored in opposing interiors, Mike, for his part, is erratically mobile. He is the only figure who can move between the claustrophobic museumlike splendor of Claire's Upper East Side apartment and social world and Ellie's fragile and isolated frame house in Queens.[22] Significantly, the one domestic project that Ellie and Mike share is house-hunting; the desire for social mobility is emblematized in leaving the neighborhood for a bigger, safer house — which they do not buy. The family, then, does not move, and the husband's mobility reads as a distinct threat to it. But his mobility comes at considerable cost, which is calculated at the divide of sexual difference in terms of gendering. Moving between these spaces, Mike is objectified by women's looks, and he is subjected to their aggression. He risks the destabilization of his authority and his sexuality within a narrative logic that links mobility to passivity, loss, and incapacity. To cross the borders of urban spaces requires belonging properly to none, and concomitantly it seems to require losing a hold on one's rightful gendered place.

The men in *Someone to Watch Over Me* are perpetually out of place; they have no homes, a situation graphically figured in the cops' relation to Claire Gregory's apartment. From the beginning, they are allowed in only three areas of her domestic space: the kitchen, the bathroom, and the large vestibule between the elevator and the entrance to the apartment proper. Relegated to the borders of this space of wealth and cultivation, they are, in short, confined to spaces traditionally reserved for servants, and they are treated as such, even by Claire's cook, who declares them incompetent to use any domestic appliance except for the toaster oven. Mike's increasing intimacy with Claire is encoded as access to deeper recesses of domestic space. Significantly, his entry into her boudoir is prepared for by his first eavesdropping, as a child might, on her having sex with Neil, her lawyer boyfriend. Symptomatically, this shift puts the professional surveyor himself in a position to be taken by surprise, to become the object of another's surveillance or eavesdropping.

In the film's spatial logic, however, the innermost sanctuary is not the bedroom but the dressing room, a disorienting space completely constructed of mirrors, and whose lethal potential is realized when Mike shoots down the man who has come to assassinate Claire. Mike has been drawn to the dressing room on his first explorations of Claire's space, an encroachment that has enraged her. And this space remains more secret and private than the bedroom. Figuratively, however, it emblematizes the claustrophobic paranoia that haunts Claire's space, as seen through Mike's eyes. Mapped as it is by Mike's curious (rather than surveying) gaze, this space is eminently reversible. Everything he looks at also looks at him. The reversibility of sight that is often central to filmic paranoia saturates this interior.[23] Through its gaze structure, however, this film links the paranoia specifically to gender, and more properly, to the plight of the man subjected to women's looks. Furthermore, the woman's dressing room also acts as a figure for the secrets of upper-class femininity that Mike is so curious about. "Dressing" is intimately related to the dynamics of sexual difference as it is linked to class and economic power.

Strictly arranged in an alternation between competing interiors, the film leaves to the male figures only the station house and the spaces of transit—the street and the subway system. These are not spaces of freedom, however, but of menace and constraint. Mike's arrival home is signaled by repeated shots of his head framed under the elevated tracks as the subway looms over the neighborhood. Similarly, in interior subway shots Mike's face is seen through the handholds affixed to the ceiling of the car; visually, he is fixed, manacled in frame. Besides the station house and the transit space, there is only one other place for a man outside the family—the desolate and cramped former "splash pad" that has become home to Mike's divorced colleague, Scott, whose apartment is coded as the space of regression, since Scott's room looks like that of his son, little Scottie. The anxiety encoded here is simple: if they wander, they could end up back in bunk beds.

Concerned as it is with crossing borders, it is not surprising that this film should be obsessed with what crosses over the frame to disrupt or reinforce visual space. From the opening sequence the film's musical track partitions spaces. Its repeated theme song, "Someone to Watch Over Me," will propel the intrigue, punctuating the narrative through successive versions that register moods and, more important, distinguish spaces, as does the music in the early sequence that moves from Mike's and Ellie's party in Queens to the toney uptown Manhattan reception where we first see Claire Gregory. Mike and Ellie's dance music—Sting and Fine Young Cannibals—contrasts sharply with the black-tie party's 1970s Motown selection that suggests, with some irony, collecting and connoisseurship, a curatorial relationship to music that matches the house's relation to objects. Music establishes the primary opposition by setting up the boundary that haunts the film: class, as inscribed in urban space, clothes, taste, music—and women. In this social world, transitions are all abrupt leaps; there is no passage between spaces. Graphically, then, *Someone to Watch Over Me* figures increased class polarization in which the workingman with middle-class values finds his place and his family threatened simultaneously by an underclass and by the very rich. And those two forces are brought together in the drug partnership of Joey Venza and Claire's friend Win, which leads to the murder that Claire witnesses, the source of the narrative problem.

This first party sequence at Mike's house also crosses boundaries by using voice-over to project a space outside the frame from which the speakers dominate the space in-frame. Voice-over here first establishes the discourse of women's aggression against women. We see Mike's best friend, TJ, dancing with another man's younger wife; simultaneously, we hear women's voices from the kitchen: "He left Elaine for *that?*" "I'd like to tie her boobs together." The wives' network closes ranks in an adversarial relation to the "other woman." Women's voices dominate the scene from outside, as their looks capture the other woman. This structure sets the stage for Mike's own domination by women's looks and by the wives' network.[24]

Although women's aggression initially targets other women, when it aims at men its full force is figured as vicious and lethal, and most graphically so at the end of the film when Ellie performs in Mike's place, killing Joey Venza. But Ellie's feminine rage has previously appeared as explicitly castrating when she is practicing her shooting skills in order to protect her family in her husband's absence. Firing rapidly and with intense concentration, Ellie provides the film's only "crotch shots," filling her target with bullet holes, all concentrated at the groin area. The castration anxiety attached to images of women's active self-defense, or their access to rage and violence, touches a cultural imaginary organized as a zero-sum game, where women's gain is men's direct loss. It is also significant that both of the central women characters punish Mike physically. Claire strikes him when he is unable to protect her from the would-be assassin at a reception; Ellie expresses her rage at Mike's affair by punching him out, leaving him collapsed on a car hood, his nose bloodied.

This film foregrounds feminine aggression, using it to frame the opening sequence that cuts from Mike's and Ellie's party to the reception where Claire's friend is murdered. But women's aggression runs through the upper-class spaces as well, where it clearly expresses both class conflict and class prerogative. When Claire forces Mike to accompany her to a reception, she first alters his outfit, stopping to buy him a more appropriate tie. That she has placed him in the position of a gigolo is confirmed upon their arrival at the museum. A policeman outside the entrance recognizes Mike: "Jesus Christ, Kegan!" When Mike retorts that he is "on duty," his colleague inquires: "What kinda duty? Gigolo?" Inside the reception, Claire's female friends take the same attitude. As the camera presents Mike in close-up, one woman reduces him to a third-person object, telling Claire: "Such nice eyes for a gentleman. Oh look, he's blushing. I like that." His sensitivity, his intimidation, and his class exoticism all become part of a joke permitted only by the discrepancy in their relative social power. Another woman who scrutinizes Mike makes clear the sexual charge that is caught up in this kind of speech: "Did you ever shoot anyone? Does that make you hard? Erect? Does that give you a boner? I think it's good if a man's work gives him a boner." This is the same woman who distracts Mike at the bar while Claire is in the bathroom, where she is assaulted by Venza. Mike's failure to perform his job at this crucial point sets in motion the rest of the drama. Indirectly, it leads to his affair, since he and Claire first kiss after she has vented her rage on him for not protecting her. And the first night they spend in bed together coincides with the first threat to Mike's unprotected family home.

Structurally, however, Mike's objectification as the "butt" of women's sexual jokes marks his inability to do his job. When he subsequently trades job performance for sexual pleasure, this renders him subject to men's jokes as well. As Mike and Claire return to her apartment after having gone out for an "unsafe" drink together (in a displacement of risk from sexual intercourse to the danger of being *seen* in public; to be seen *at all* is the risk for Claire, and for Mike the risk is to be seen with *her*), her boyfriend meets them in the vestibule and reprimands them. While the camera focuses on Claire, her boyfriend's speech is immediately followed by the sound of men laughing, as if to mock the woman caught cheating on her boyfriend. But as the camera catches up with these voices, we realize that we have cut away to the precinct house, where news of Mike's transgression has already arrived. "Rough night." "This won't be the first time the taxpayers pay for a blowjob." A locker room discourse that renders Claire a prostitute also places Mike in the position of the woman who is the object of this kind of exchange or of the traditional smutty joke. Rather quickly, then, Mike's position has slipped from official police escort, to servant, to gigolo, and to lover, which serves to code him, in an intersection of the aggressive discourses of upper-class women and of his male colleagues alike, as "feminized." Unlike *Fatal Attraction, Someone to Watch Over Me* intermittently discloses its connection to a social context. Its battle of the sexes sits in an uneasy relationship of reciprocal overdetermination with at least one other explicitly inscribed difference, since part of the anxious fantasy at play here is that Mike's masculinity can be secured only if he remains in his proper class and family position.

An examination of the film's ending confirms the significance of this fantasy and its particular shape. To rescue the family from the killer that Claire has inadvertently unleashed upon them, Mike must pretend to deliver her to him. This requires a policeman to masquerade in Claire's clothes. The only way the police can successfully negotiate this situation and redeem Mike, then, is in drag. And this female impersonator's arrival is first marked on the soundtrack by the sound of his high heels on the pavement, long before the watchful camera, placed inside the family house, can catch sight of him. Female impersonation is, of course, a different kind of "woman's look," one that acts as an ironic figure for the persistence of dominating feminine looks—looks that frame this final sequence.

Equally important, the cop's cross-dressing coincides with the image of feminine vengeance as Ellie blows the killer away with the family gun. We see her framed from Mike's point of view, looking very much as Beth Gallagher looks at the end of *Fatal Attraction,* heroicized in the most conventional fashion, framed in medium long shot, on her feet, while her husband is prone. But, as with Beth Gallagher, she is heroicized as a figure of *maternal* rage. A threat is posed and domesticated, as the woman's motivation is anchored in a defense of her child.[25] What might have been a cathartic image of a woman's rage and competence instead acts here to redo the earlier scene of Ellie's violence against Mike, a scene that poses the threat of masculine disability, bringing it into the reassuring closure of a familial discourse that links feminine violence to maternal protectiveness.

With this last fatal blast, the broken family is reconstituted, as Mike moves into the frame to form a pyramid with Ellie and Tommie. We see this familial image from Claire's point of view in the film's penultimate shot. The last one again frames the Kegan family, watching as Claire is taken away in a police cruiser. Her departure in the manner of an arrest constitutes a kind of deus ex machina resolution to the family problem; the police are required to take her "into custody." Meanwhile, the family is awkwardly framed in a gesture that highlights the ambivalences and contradictions which the film has worked through all along. If Claire frames the family with her look, she is "framed," in turn, as she is carried off in the police car. Uncomfortably inscribing a reciprocal framing, the film parodically replays the standard film noir gesture of punishing—policing, and arresting, if not killing—the active feminine gaze. But the ironic subversiveness is not fully successful in overcoming the film's residual logic: women look actively and aggressively only at the risk of prevailing over and incapacitating, if not "blinding," the male look.

Outsides In: The Shattered Interior

Perhaps one of the more striking examples of the apparently persistent fascination with an obtuse father-husband figure occurs in *The Hand That Rocks the Cradle.* This film also reaches a new extreme in its staging of racial difference as a detail in a family melodrama. Covering almost

exactly the same terrain as did *Fatal Attraction,* this film offers a spectacular battle between women that more overtly displays the multiple social
anxieties that the earlier film embedded more obscurely.

Where *Fatal Attraction* begins by establishing an intimate middle-class
interior, with Beth and Dan before the mirrors in their bedroom as they
dress for an evening out, *The Hand That Rocks the Cradle* opens with a
sequence coded for suspense based on our expectations that the morning stillness of the suburban interior will be ruptured by some outside
intrusion. This opening sequence gradually penetrates the still interior,
following the flow of morning light across the empty rooms, from entry-
way to dining room, up the stairs to the nursery, where an empty rocking
chair signals the expectation of a new baby. In conventional suspense
coding, this sequence is intercut with footage of a man riding a bicycle
through empty streets and saturated with the banally cheerful soundtrack that often accompanies horror film setups. With its camera placed
at knee level, the film withholds from view the body and the face of the
cyclist who relentlessly progresses toward the interior to which the parallel editing continually returns us. The sheer length of this sequence—
six minutes—creates mounting suspense about the man's arrival and the
revelation of his identity and intentions.

Drawing to a close with the symmetrical disclosure of the house's
inhabitants and the visitor's face, the sequence continues to promote
anxiety through its painful slowness and the hesitation it inscribes in parallel sequences. These produce our impression that the visitor is closing
in on the family as it pursues its morning rituals, the pregnant wife
making orange juice in the huge, sunny kitchen, the father shaving in the
bathroom while the little girl watches. Their unguardedness is marked by
the father's and daughter's singing a Gilbert and Sullivan song together
as the stranger approaches. Finally, fully revealed and embodied in the
same camera motion, which sweeps slowly up his body from the knees
to the head, to magnify his stature from its low angle, the stranger turns
out to be a mentally disabled African American who will become the
family's handyman. We watch as he knocks on the door, unheard by the
wife over the whir of the blender, and as he moves around the porch to
the kitchen window. In classic horror film coding, Solomon's image, rendered ghostly as it casts a reflection in the kitchen window behind the
woman's head, floats menacingly—in a menace that the soundtrack encodes—until she sees him, and, startled, drops the pitcher she is holding.
A quick cut brings the husband clumsily to the top of the stairs in the first

of his delayed and bungled rescues. Thus, this film has set up the mere presence of an African American man as the explosive rupture in the seamless texture of this family interior. His mere presence or, more properly, his mere image in the window constitutes a narrative event, encodes menace and violent disruption of the flow that the film has established as it painstakingly mapped this interior.

Given the care it has taken to knit together a framework of classic suspense around this invading figure, a close examination of *The Hand That Rocks the Cradle* may shed some light on the crucial function of social differences within narratives about threats to white middle-class heterosexuality and the nuclear family, even when those narratives go out of their way to foreclose those differences. The blonde outsider figure that this film shares with *Fatal Attraction* is a governess this time, and her primary desire is to supplant the dark earth mother in her own home. Working up middle-class anxieties about exposing the family to a threat while Mommy is at work, on the one hand, and renewing collective anxieties that women are the real danger to the family anyway, this film gleefully redoubles the perverse possibilities of domestic melodrama, and redoubles them around a point of near hysteria in the media and in popular discourse—sexual abuse.

In this film the governess, Peyton (Rebecca De Mornay), operates as a figure for monstrous maternal desire as her psychological and physical battle with the wife, Claire (Annabella Sciorra), for the central place in the family begins with the seduction of both husband and children, a seduction that extends even to nursing the baby. As Peyton becomes a secret wet nurse, the perverse suggestiveness of too close contact links up with the central event that motivates the plot: Peyton's husband, once Claire's obstetrician, has sexually molested his patient during an examination. Her subsequent complaint to authorities has set off a series of similar accusations from women who had remained silent about similar experiences with him, and this publicity has precipitated his suicide. His death, in turn, causes the beleaguered Peyton to miscarry and sets her on the path of a revenge that will instrumentalize the threat of sexual abuse within the domestic interior.

This is the point at which the threat to the nuclear family's integrity is split between Peyton, the white mother's double, and the family's other domestic helper: the developmentally disabled Solomon (Ernie Hudson), whose sexuality is figured as almost utterly castrated. However, he is still sexual enough to be a threat to the child, Emma, at least in the minds of her parents, as they are manipulated by Peyton's suggestions along these lines. Peyton has immediately identified the watchful, innocent Solomon as her adversary, for he is as loyal to the family as she is treacherous. As the drama's fool figure, Solomon inhabits the position of the family dog, the good alien within, and, conventionally, animals are not fooled by deceivers like Peyton. Narratively, Peyton sets out to punish Solomon and drive him from the family because he has accidentally seen her nursing the baby. Structurally, however, the black man is struck down for looking at the white woman's breasts.

The Hand That Rocks the Cradle's final sequence makes it clear that Solomon exists as a character only to be punished, bullied, humiliated, beaten, and, finally, to save this white family despite the way that they mistrust and abuse him. In the film's last confrontation, as the two women battle it out, Solomon, who has returned to rescue the family, protects the baby, whom he has never been trusted to hold, from Peyton's blows with a fireplace poker. Thus, the film has made Solomon into a silent shield, a mute resistant body, violently punished as it protects a child.

How do we account for this? Even before Peyton's arrival, Solomon has ruptured the initial harmony of the family's suburban pastoral. And he has done so by the mere act of appearing at the kitchen window and terrifying the pregnant Claire. It is as if the entire film's project were to allay that initial anxiety about the threatening black male intruder. So the film seems to punish that figure himself for the cultural memory he evokes, for the fantasmatic crimes of his image, just as the family displaces the sexual threat that Peyton poses to the domestic economy onto Solomon's relationship with the little girl, as if trading one "dirty secret" for another. However, the film cannot so easily distance itself from the family that mistakes the source of danger, since its economy of suspense draws some of its intensity from the parallel anxiety that it rehearses at the very beginning and then refuses to take responsibility for.

This film offers a near parodic re-presentation of some of Euro-American culture's oldest clichés of black masculinity's place with respect to the white family—the site of a proximate sexual menace, a menace to be preempted by constant humiliation, continued rehearsals of castration or its threat. Alongside our pleasure in Peyton's uncanny capacity to exploit the faultlines of the yuppie nuclear family, the film exhibits an anxious strain in connection with the other figure that parallels her.

Despite its concerted attempt to keep its competing threats strictly separated, the film cannot prevent a certain leakage and contamination that pulls Peyton and Solomon together, even when it definitively locates the threat in Peyton and thereby exonerates Solomon through the very process that marks him as the first to see through her. Even as the film strives to concentrate on the conflict between white middle-class women —mothers against non-mothers, biological mothers against surrogates, women who work inside the home against women who work outside it— Solomon continually interrupts that spectacle. A figure generated by the dominant culture's oldest racist fantasies, Solomon haunts the film like history, the history of black-and-white intimacy, an often forced intimacy, in domestic orders of master and servant. As the threat circulates between Peyton and Solomon, so that one figure borrows anxieties mobilized around the other, the film exhibits, as if by accident, the intertwining of racial difference and sexuality as threats in collective fantasy.

The Hand That Rocks the Cradle pretends for all the world that Solomon's racial difference is a mere distraction, a detail. And while some critics took the figure of Solomon as racist and demeaning, they tended to dismiss this as a flaw, an oversight, and not as centrally embedded in the plot's rehearsal of collective anxieties. It is as if the dominant culture, in its obsessive focus on racial and sexual difference as "issues" in the framework of the news or of relentless talk show examinations, wants to reduce these differences to "distraction" within any genre that is coded for entertainment. But *The Hand That Rocks the Cradle* exposes how intimately it depends on this difference, capitalizing on it to enhance the threat to the suburban (white) nuclear family. So, as the film activates and puts to rest a set of anxieties about women's capacity to destabilize family borders, in the process it also absorbs and plays upon anxious fantasies about keeping other social boundaries in order.

Double Exposure: The Public Private Space

In recent years other police genre films have examined sexual difference with an anxiety intensified to a near psychotic level, an excess that suggests that what is presented as localized anxiety must be multiply determined. It is symptomatic that these films play upon rage, since rage increasingly appears as an inevitable, if not a logical, response to social conflict, in the absence of any consistent public political discourse. But an equally powerful force within the worlds that these films project is identification. Cops, criminals, and suspects rapidly change positions in a specular universe where identifications run rampant. In *Basic Instinct,* as in *Sea of Love* before it, the cop is both murderous and frightened; his anxiety, desire, and aggression are all wound around the axes of identification that keep him uneasy about his ability to establish and maintain differences, and most especially sexual differences.

Strikingly, however, violence in these films seems to accumulate around sexual difference through a fantasy of a female serial killer coupled with the spectacle of male fear and incompetence. *Sea of Love* figures this connection dramatically in Frank Keller, the dazed, lonely cop who is seduced by the suspected serial killer who finds her victims through newspaper personals ads. Here, at the very origin of its investigation, *Sea of Love* carves out much the same terrain that *Basic Instinct* will later explore. Briefly, Nick Curran (Michael Douglas) in *Basic Instinct* is also something of a failed cop, looking back at the ruin of both his relationships and his career, and early on he is coded as a renegade and possibly a murderer. In any case, he is out of control in terms of his drinking, his desire, and his violence. And like Frank Keller, only more literally so in this case, Nick fears that he is playing out an erotic and investigative script that has been written by the killer woman. *Basic Instinct*'s object of erotic and policing curiosity, Catherine Tramell (Sharon Stone), writes thriller novels about murders that she may in fact commit, and it is precisely the threat of her capacity for violence, as well as her capacity to outwit him, that seems to attract the unstable Nick.[26]

Basic Instinct's Curran is even more dissolute than Keller, for he struggles with both cocaine and alcohol abuse. His lack of control extends to his professional performance; he appears to have killed innocent bystanders on two occasions. But these two degenerate cops have an even more striking feature in common: neither has a private life. The nearly complete merging of private space with work space in each case is coherent with the protagonist's general sense of being exposed. He cannot hide from the other's scrutiny, and, more important, he figures a man who has nothing more to hide. This effect is consistent with the paranoid features of the film noir universe, as Joan Copjec describes it: "while this paranoia is usually assumed to indicate an erosion of privacy that permits the Other to read one's innermost thoughts, film noir helps us to see that the opposite is true. It is on the public level that the erosion has taken place. No social distance separates individuals, no social 'clothing' protects their innermost being" (190). But this ambient sense of exposure consistently mobilizes anxiety, and even terror, around questions of sexual difference in films that compulsively return to fragile and unstable intersections of gender and sexuality.

As the question of the killer's sex becomes a central part of the mystery in *Sea of Love,* even its resolution does not quite contain the threat of the independent woman prowling the singles scene, since it cannot erase the deliberate attentiveness that the narrative has paid to the terror she inspires in the hero. Given the strength of this image in the film and its almost direct citation in *Basic Instinct* when Beth Garner, wearing a blonde wig and police raincoat, slashes Nick's partner Gus (George Dzundza) to death in an elevator, we may read both films into a line of descent from *Dressed to Kill* (Brian De Palma, 1980). In many ways more perverse than its successors, *Dressed to Kill* made sexual difference a violent mystery, not only for the investigators, but even for the serial killer him/herself.

Significantly, as *Sea of Love* and *Basic Instinct* repeat the fascinating fantasy of the woman serial killer, the abject terror that this image inspires is elaborately staged through breathtaking spectacles of masculine terror in the midst of a seduction scene and of the policing male body out of control, trembling and scrambling. These spectacles intertwine with a dazzling variety of fantasies. In the range of obsessive representations focusing on the ambiguity of the sexual divide, the drive of the narrative to decide it, to decide the killer's sex and sexuality, is posed as of the most compelling urgency. This urgency serves to displace, if not to repress, conflicts around other social differences, even as it may borrow some of its traumatic energy from anxieties that those conflicts generate.

Basic Instinct, however, takes a cool, ironic distance on Curran's loss of both personal and professional control. At the level of tone and atmosphere, it systematically reproduces the coolness that its discourse obviously shares with Catherine Tramell's. This tone is reflected in the icy blue light of interrogation rooms, the stark color schemes of interiors, and, somewhat parodically, in the prominent place of ice. Indeed, in its adherence to surfaces and reflections *Basic Instinct* stresses the specularity and nonconcealment that haunts Nick Curran as he confronts the women suspects, Tramell and her double, Beth Garner (Jeanne Tripplehorn), whose sexuality, like their criminal guilt, remains undecided.

Sea of Love, on the other hand, opens with an alarmingly tense spectacle of masculine anxiety and fragility. As the camera moves across a darkened interior to find a man's undulating buttocks, the sounds of sexual panting give way to a more and more desperately anxious voice:

"Is this OK? Is this OK?" Just as we might begin to settle on a situational interpretation, that he is a man begging for sexual confirmation, we see the man's terrified face from back over his shoulder. While we see the gun he sees, we never see the face of the person who pulls the trigger and shoots him in the back. We never see it, that is, until near the end of the film, and consequently we do not know if this anxious, pleading question has been addressed to a man or a woman. All we know is that the addressee is a spectator watching the man's performance. Despite, or perhaps because, its addressee is absent, unknown, this question seems to dominate the film's thematics, shaping its investigation, its intrigue, and its resolution. Indeed, the whole film might seem to be about the desperate effort to get a woman to answer a man's anxious "Is this OK?" in the affirmative.

Sea of Love is organized by the anxious question of performance that persists throughout detective Frank Keller's murder investigation. This investigation refracts into several levels of inquiry: his official investigation of the sexualized serial killings of men who have all placed similar personals ads, his investigation of the woman suspect, Helen Kruger (Ellen Barkin), with whom he falls in love, and, finally, his investigation of his own masculinity. Relying on film history and on the popular memory attached to the actor Al Pacino, *Sea of Love* can mobilize resonances with *Cruising* (William Friedkin, 1980), the last major film he made before an extended hiatus in his career. *Cruising,* marked by Friedkin's tendency to mobilize sexual anxieties much more provocatively than does *Sea of Love,* features a detective who goes undercover in the gay leather cruising scene in order to entrap a killer who savagely murdered a series of men after having sex with them. (Interestingly enough, one key murder scene bears a striking resemblance to *Sea of Love*'s opening murder.)

Like Frank Keller, *Cruising*'s Steve Burns is haunted by fantasmatic over-identifications, in this case, with both the victims and the killer(s). And like Keller, Burns can play this out only because the investigation implicates his own sexuality so that the film can suggestively leave open the possibility that he finally winds up reenacting the crimes.[27] *Cruising* offers a densely complex, ambiguous, and somewhat ironic analysis of its protagonist's anxious identifications. Not the least of its ironies is its presentation of a world where he cannot be sure how he differs from the killer or killers, just as he cannot distinguish potential victims from potential murderers. The force of this effect persists through the film's last sequence, where Burns has returned "home" to his girlfriend. As he shaves, we see his girlfriend trying on his leather gear, while the sound-track directly echoes the music that has accompanied the killer's cruising. No one can stay immune from the identificatory relay of masquerade. By contrast, *Sea of Love* seems to try to take its protagonists' problems "straight," while sustaining homoerotophobic anxiety, the repressed subtext that continually returns to haunt the plot.

Along with the demand for a woman's confirmation, *Sea of Love* repeats another figure. The butt, or ass, is displayed literally in the first murder scene, where it indicates vulnerability, and then it is endlessly recalled in the policemen's complaints, jokes, and arguments. By delaying the introduction of any female characters, the film constructs Frank's world as a masculine collectivity of coworkers and buddies, which is sewn together by a running stream of affectionate, competitive, and aggressive banter through which Frank relentlessly affirms that he is "getting his ass kicked," that he "is being fucked" by the world at large and by women in particular.[28] In their excessive fascination with scatological references, the guys in this same-sex community parodically rehearse a familiar commonplace concerning men's anxiety about themselves: they continually regress from the genital to the anal-sadistic stage of libidinal organization as a consequence of their sense of ineffectual—castrated—masculinity.[29]

As it discloses the sadism and homophobia that tinge explicit masculine rivalry, jealousy, and anxiety, this relay of tropes underscores the multiple threats under which Frank and his buddies imagine that they negotiate their masculine positions: they must hold off homosexuality and "feminization" as well as defective masculinity. They read their inevitable failure to coincide with an ideal version of masculine integrity not as a sign of the impossibility of such integrity, but rather as a local and personal failure, a failure that they reprocess as an external pressure.[30] Consequently, in their desperate attempts to shore up masculine identity, they act out a failure to see or apprehend sexual difference as difference, and they focus instead on the impossible task of fixing gendered identities as a means of stabilizing that difference.

Frank's trouble, about which the film is extremely self-conscious, is that for him all of these threats are figures for one another; they are often indistinguishable. Therefore, he continually strives to distinguish heterosexuality from homosexuality and masculinity from femininity. This trouble is systematically related to identification in an investigation that constantly threatens to tip over into reenactment, where Frank places himself in both the victim's position and the murderer's. In the film's tight specularity, the victims appear as exaggerated versions of the cops' own fantasies of their castrated or masochistic relations to women, while the killer, who turns out to be Helen's jealous ex-husband, Terry, offers the deformed image of their sadism taken to its extreme.

In its careful analysis of masculine crisis and failure, *Sea of Love* sets male anxiety in the context of work and gender relations in an urban setting, and it proposes that these arenas are coimplicated rather than autonomous.[31] As Frank urgently seeks to pin Helen down—will she or won't she? is she or isn't she?—the film explores his tormented relation to his own sexuality through the implicit questions embedded in his investigation of the woman—am I or aren't I? can I or can't I? In contrast to traditional film noir scenarios, the woman in this case eventually responds with her own penetrating question, which coheres with a narrative and visual structure that suggests a reciprocity of looks, fears, and epistemological drives between the man and the woman.

What Frank is looking for is a stable identity—the woman's and his own—and what he finds is difference, a difference around which the film develops a paranoid reversibility. A disturbing specular reciprocity structures *Sea of Love* from its very beginning. The first murder and the early stages of the investigation are cross-cut with scenes that reveal the immediate difficulties of Frank's personal and professional life. A scene in which Frank sits alone listening to old records as he gets drunk and finally telephones his ex-wife quickly establishes the resemblance between Frank's lifestyle and that of the murder victim, Jim Mackey. This parallel prepares the scenario of reenactment that Frank undertakes as a strategy for catching the perpetrator and that draws him into an affair with a suspect. The motor of the intrigue, then, will be Frank's uncertainty about what, if any, difference there is between himself and the murder victims. In this context, the film loads anxieties onto the question of sexuality. But figured in the repeated image of a man's ass, these anxieties seem to concern exposure and fear of being taken by surprise, from behind, by either the woman or the man behind the woman.

The development of Frank's discourse on the war of the sexes culminates at a colleague's retirement party where he first meets Sherman Touhey, who will become his partner in the investigation as well as his buddy and the contrasting male character against whom Frank comes into relief.[32] Once he and Sherman put their heads together to solve the crime, Frank's private discourse about women dovetails with their speculations about the murderer's sex and his/her motives. By the end of the

party Frank indulges in a drunken fantasy about the murderer as a representative woman. "I admire this woman, whoever she is, for her directness," he asserts. "Guy falls asleep, she pops him." Moving metonymically from the murderer to his ex-wife, to rivalry with her current husband, Gruber, a fellow policeman also investigating this series of crimes,
Frank completely confuses his role as policeman with his role as hus-
band/lover, as he imagines a perfect reciprocity of sexualized violence,
based on his confusion of women's agency with their domination.[33] This
kind of confusion, finally operating as a form of hysterical identification,
prevails in his investigation, and it eventually puts Frank in a position to
become one of the killer's victims. Like the investigation, the narrative
must not only solve the crime, but it must resolve Frank's confusions,
must establish a difference between "equality" and a failure of sexual difference, as well as between "lethal" or dangerous and "healthy" sex and
love, and between a cop and *both* a killer and a victim.[34] In figuring problems of differentiation at these pivotal sites, *Sea of Love* anticipates the
overcharged nodes that organize *Basic Instinct*.

The troubling questions that the investigation in *Sea of Love* raises,
however, are the central ones in Frank's private life: how to distinguish
the sexual mystery "out there"—in women—from the sexual mystery "in
here"—in his own masculinity. These ambiguities cause Frank's epistemological researches to take the form of reenactment. Because the narrative resolves the enigma of the violent woman's sexuality by revealing
a deranged man—masculinity run amok—behind her, it ultimately subverts Frank's project, revealing the feebleness of its gesture of containment and foregrounding its residual effects. While *Sea of Love* exposes
masculine anxiety that feminine sexuality is violent by showing its roots
in projection, when it accepts Frank's answer to the question of what lies
behind this feminine aggression, it closes down some other questions. A
man is not all that is behind this woman. We might, for instance, see behind her the oddly unspoken threat of feminism, for which Helen clearly
stands in, but which the film never once mentions. We may further consider that a series of threats to white heterosexual masculine privilege
posed by other social differences—race and sexuality, for instance—are
condensed behind the figure of the potentially homicidal woman. This,
of course, is also *Falling Down*'s basic formula. That film's specular structure allows for an equation between D-Fens's adversaries—anyone and
everyone across a wide spectrum of social differences—and Prendergast's
ultimate opponent, the one beyond D-Fens: his own crazy wife.

Here, we might remember that *Basic Instinct* displays a similarly insidious and perhaps more vicious condensation, since it takes pains to establish a metonymic relay of women who either are, or who are suspected of being, murderers. In this relay there is finally no difference between committing a crime and coming under suspicion. At the same time, the film asks us to suspect them sexually as well, so that their sexuality and their criminality appear as intertwined mysteries. Each of these women is also somewhat mysteriously and erotically connected to Catherine Tramell, so that the relay of women seems to invite our investigation of her sexual identity through theirs—is she bisexual, is she a lesbian? In view of all the controversy generated by these depictions, we might observe that the film is equally gleeful in insinuating that the policemen whom we are to presume to be heterosexual have their own sexual secrets. Gus's apparent jealousy about Nick's affair with Catherine, and his frequent unannounced visits to Nick's apartment, are broadly suggestive of an attraction. Rather than understand this as part of a systematic effort to demonize homosexuality, however, we might see the film as striving to destabilize any smug certainty about our ability to determine any character's sexuality, any easy presumption that we can align them along a hetero-/homo- sexual divide.[35]

Confusions of boundary and register are compellingly played out in *Sea of Love*'s dating sequences, where Frank and Sherman "go undercover," placing an advertisement and arranging dates so that they can obtain the fingerprints of a number of women habituées of the personals, any one of whom might be the killer. This sequence lays out in detail the often hilarious, but ultimately very disturbing, variety of anxieties that both men and women attach to contemporary courtship among urban heterosexuals over thirty. But it also lays bare the utter impossibility of keeping public and private lives separate. Since both Frank and Sherman become sexually involved with some of the women, they *are* exactly what they are pretending to be, men looking for women to go out with. They are, then, no more undercover than the women they investigate. And the film is clear about the reciprocity; from Frank's point of view the central drama of his relationship with Helen turns on the merger of seduction and policing, of sexual and detective economies, where he struggles to determine who is stalking whom.

In taking Frank's rampant identifications as one of its central tropes, the film links him to Helen's ex-husband, Terry, who is driven to *take* the other's place, as he reenacts his ex-wife's sexual encounters. Both characters are caught between voyeurism-surveillance and rampant identification. And Frank's identifications also bear the intertextual charge that recalls *Cruising* and revises Pacino's previous role. The homoerotic anxiety that *Sea of Love* works up through its intertextuality coheres, on the one hand, with the cops' own confused localization of threats to their masculinity. On the other hand, through the brutal and deranged figure of Helen's ex-husband, it mobilizes an anxiety that exceeds this narrative containment.

As the detectives establish that the central clue to the killer's identity is her fascination with ads written as poems, poetry displaces the oldie song, "Sea of Love," as the identifying mark. When the police gather at Frank's house to collectively compose a verse for the ad that will be planted to attract the killer, this exercise generates a series of hilariously inept poems, shot through with adolescent sexual humor, but it finally reveals the utter inarticulateness of these men in terms of sexuality and emotion. This scene presents them as a bunch of wrecks: lonely, aging, and drinking heavily. Finally, as the poems begin to move from the obscene to the hopelessly maudlin, we hear another voice from across the room, beginning to recite. The camera reveals Frank's father, drunk and slumped in a chair. He offers a poem, written by Frank's mother in 1934, and this is the one they publish. Going undercover as a man looking for dates, then, also entails Frank's disguising his voice as a woman's. At the literal level here, the film links its gender destabilization with the masochistic ruin of patriarchy in the figure of the impotent, infantilized father who is so drunk that his son must put him to bed.

Frank's and Sherman's entry into the dating scene produces a structure of tight reciprocity between male and female characters, a structure that is at its most complex when it comes to Frank's relationship with Helen. Throughout, reading and interpretation seem to structure this reciprocity. The difference under scrutiny—that between men and women—is coded as the difference between competing forms of knowledge. Men and women examine each other, in encounters structured by a reciprocal look exchange where each tries to read the other without, in turn, being read. This specular adversarial relationship, then, is saturated with paranoia in both its defensive and its speculative modes.[36] In this adversarial context, Frank is the loser; he makes no claims to being a subtle reader. Significantly, women's knowledge emerges as superior. Better readers, women have greater access to the truth. Theirs is the privileged gaze, the one that *sees* the truth in the men.

For example, one woman abruptly cuts their conversation short, announcing that she has a "weird feeling" he is not who he says he is, because he has "cop's eyes." This interview lays the groundwork for the confusion of being and having—figured in competing interpretations of his gaze, his "cop's eyes"—that haunts both the detective and his investigation. Frank's "truth," it seems, is legible in his eyes. This sequence goes on to encode an equation between the gaze and the penis, when a woman registers her suspicion by telling Frank that if he is telling the truth, then she has "a dick." Sherman's response to the incident is even more interesting: "you think you could go for a babe with a dick?" Confronted with a series of women who literally advertise their sexual desire, these cops find themselves in a universe where the phallus is out of place, where they are continually asking: Who is it? Who has it? All identities are unstable: anyone might have a "dick" or a gun, and Frank's investigation plays out the reversibility of positions, since he winds up becoming prey, stalked by a woman who is stalked by a man. If a woman can be in a man's place, then a man can be in a woman's place. His anxiety relates to the reversibility of the look where the power of the policing gaze is haunted by its exposure to other gazes that may not only read and misread it, but that may capture, dominate, or annihilate it.

Basic Instinct stages the reversible gaze even more spectacularly in relation to sexuality. Initially, it inscribes the force of Catherine Tramell's gaze as it presides over the police who take her to her interrogation. She is framed in the rearview mirror, suspended above and behind Nick and Gus as she speaks. Her isolated, almost disembodied look, and her voice, split between on-screen image and off-screen location, produce her authority over them. The later interrogation sequence, however, mobilizes the force of her gaze differently. Structured as a series of shot–reverse shots that inscribe her as an equal adversary for the police, this sequence inscribes her dominance as it pans from one investigator to the next, linking them in a relay of reaction shots, all of which respond to Catherine. Cinematically constructed as the central gaze, hers is the one from which the others seem to emanate. Still more stunningly, this famous sequence connects Catherine's verbal and visual authority to her sex, if not to her sexuality. Her riveting gaze works in perfect symmetry with her genitals, as she casually flashes her interrogators. Voice, gaze, and sex, then, are completely coordinated in this "medusifying" moment. At this point, the film produces a formation to which it will return. In its pure inauthenticity, feminine sexuality is completely in charge of itself because it is coincident with itself: the "pussy" talks. Later, Gus will repeatedly reply to Nick's justifications for his affair with Catherine by asserting, "that's her pussy talking. It's not your brain." Masculine sexuality, by contrast, appears to be unstable and fragmented by virtue of its sheer, brute, or "dumb" (to cite Ruby Rich) authenticity.[37]

Like Catherine Tramell, Helen in *Sea of Love* is a most incisive and confident reader, much more so than Frank is. She knows he is not who he says he is, just as she knows his poem is stolen: "It's a lady's poem, or a girl's." Frank, in turn, admires Helen's directness, coding it as a kind of masculine athleticism. As the plot proceeds, it takes to an ironic extreme the commonly circulating fantasy that in becoming "sensitive," the "new man" risks being overwhelmed by some feminist or, in this case, of being literally murdered by her. This potentially progressive image of the mutability of gendered attributes in relation to sexuality will become one of the anxieties that haunts this relationship. And this is related to anxiety about identity, as Frank and Helen recognize that sexual difference is not stable, but continuously reinvented socially.[38] Whatever satisfactions are offered to feminist viewers by this perspective are finally limited, however, since the couple and the narrative confront two competing logics: that of sexual difference as continually negotiated and unstable, and that of sexual difference as stabilized by securing gendered identities. Because the narrative resolution of the mystery coincides with the couple's stabilization by the law of marriage, the film finally associates sexual difference as constant negotiation with the circuit of hysterical identifications that it mobilizes and then shuts down.

Symmetrical masculine and feminine anxieties escalate to a hysterical frenzy as Helen and Frank's first erotic encounter localizes the general sexual paranoia that saturates the film. The threat of violence in this scene comes directly from the woman, as Frank's furtive look into the privacy of her purse uncovers a gun, just where we would expect to see a different means of protection—such as a diaphragm. Frank frantically grabs his own gun and locks Helen in the bathroom, where she has gone to undress. In his panic he steps into the place of the assailant, a shift that mobilizes feminine fears. But the frenzied ensuing battle foregrounds the perfect reciprocity between the man and the woman, since Frank flails as desperately as Helen does.

Frank thus takes up a position that he imagines, as does the film, to be typically feminine within a circuit of identifications depicted as "hysterical." Not only does he identify *with* the victim, but he identifies victimization with feminization. And structurally, the film brings its critical pressure to bear on the possibility of uncontrollable identification across sexual difference. The rest of this scene, and of the courtship, suggests that Frank's fears about the woman killer are completely bound up with his fear-desire for a certain degree of gender inversion. Helen initiates the actual seduction by pushing him up against the wall, questioning him aggressively, replicating a policeman's approach to a suspect. In this manner the film discloses that a part of the anxiety which Frank locates in women is rooted in his own sadomasochistic fantasy. Once again the boundary between "interior" and "exterior" is unstable, as the film explores common anxieties about the relation between fantasy and actual agency where the violent or sadomasochistic traces embedded in erotic desire may be projected outside onto the other.

This anxious tension, however, is accompanied by an ironic thrust since the unfolding intrigue presents itself as allegorical of heterosexual relations. *Sea of Love* offers the spectacle of a divorced man and woman attempting to negotiate a new relationship, their anxieties played out in an affective register that ranges from the overwrought to the downright hysterical, where each urgently seeks to determine whether or not the other is a homicidal maniac. While Frank's more and more urgent project involves reinterpreting the details of Helen's life as clues to establish her guilt or innocence, increasingly the real object of inquiry for both characters becomes Frank's masculinity. And it is the question of compatibility between Frank's public and private "place" that they must finally resolve as a couple, but not, of course, before they resolve the question of Frank's resemblance to Helen's ex-husband, who really is a homicidal maniac.

More important, Helen's fears about Frank's resemblance to her ex-husband will be confirmed in their last encounter before he confronts the real killer. Questioning her brutally and relentlessly about her sexual relations with each of her "victims," Frank suggests that she preserves her independence by murdering anyone who tries to possess her. Here his behavior repeats that of her former husband. Symmetrically, the film's very next sequence reenacts the interrogation, this time putting Frank in the woman's place. Bursting into Frank's apartment, Terry, the ex-husband, repeats the scenario he has played with all of his victims: to make them undress and reenact their sex with Helen. "Show me how you did it to her," he bellows as he holds a gun to Frank's head. In Frank's case, this violent voyeurism is supplemented by a sadistic homoeroticism, as Terry climbs on Frank's back while demanding that he simulate sex. Both their positions in this truly hysterical sadomasochistic scene are multiple. Frank is made to simulate both the man's and the woman's position; he is placed in the victim's position, which is made to look like a masochistic one. As his body and Terry's together present an image of anal rape, the film reveals itself as sharing Frank's homoerotophobia, which projects its own aggressive homophobia onto gay men in violent fantasies of anal rape.[39] Though Frank succeeds in overcoming his assailant, this resolution hardly recuperates the scene's suggestiveness. The psychotic ex-husband figure has become a sort of metonym for the violent projective fantasies that the film seems to mobilize and repress.

Structurally, the residual effects of this sequence are not easily eliminated. On the one hand, by establishing Terry as the cop's deranged double, the sequence offers the satisfaction of exposing the violently homophobic potential that underlies Frank's male community and the anxieties it sustains. And one might see a progressive reading here, as the film shows the anxious and aggressive heterosexual as victim of the very violence he fosters and threatens to release. On the other hand, however, the film's ambivalence too easily associates Terry's murderous sadism with homoeroticism, and thus the source of violence is displaced from Frank and his buddies to homosexuality itself. This scene is finally undecidable; both readings coexist in a kind of mutual challenge.

Finally, the disclosure of the man behind the woman permits the film's resolution in a restored relationship between Frank and Helen. But this, too, is more complex. First, it critically deconstructs certain masculine anxieties that are projected onto women. Much of the violence, aggression, and danger attributed to women, the film concludes, is really a displacement of violence between men, an often eroticized violence that is contained through the woman, who is set up as a conduit for it. Then, however, in a film shot and narrated almost entirely from Frank's point of view, this resolution serves to redeem Helen by the most conventional of means. If she is not guilty, she is innocent, and she is innocent because she is a victim. And if Helen is a victim, Frank cannot be her victim. Finally, Helen's instrumentalization by another man redeems Frank from victimization—from the anxiety of becoming a woman's victim. Feminine agency evaporates in a process that stabilizes sexual difference through marriage and a move away from the city. But it may be precisely the exaggerated respect of a highly conventional formula here that produces this ending as forced and that highlights certain contradictions.

In this respect, *Sea of Love,* like most of the films discussed in this chapter, participates in a tendency that Paul Smith ascribes to *Tightrope* (Richard Tuggle, 1984), a film that is "tendentious" in its effort to "offer a critique of one of the most crucial and unthought elements of its own and its audience's personal, cinematic, and finally, cultural experiences—heterosexual masculinity as it is constructed to be obstinate, violent, and unreflexively vapid in this culture."[40] Smith argues, however, that this effort at criticism is all but undermined in the "generic confection of an ending," which is required by the commodity "qualities" that Hollywood commercial film "lives by and needs to reproduce in order to be successful" (138). These commodity qualities, he contends, "are achieved only by a negation or invalidation of exactly the critique that [the film] allows itself to embark upon" (138).

The invalidated or negated critique, then, may persist only as a sort of remainder or residue. While *Basic Instinct* capitalizes on precisely the destabilizing effects of nonresolution, of maintaining a permanent residue of doubt, *Sea of Love* leaves other kinds of residue beyond the reach of its generic closure. We can see some of these residual effects operating around Terry, the film's abject, onto whom it displaces a series of savage impulses, like the cops' homoerotophobia. In an early interrogation by the police he manages to deflect suspicion onto a black teenager who has delivered groceries to the building where the murder was committed. Terry describes the boy as having "black militant hair, you know, corn hoes? or corn rows?" Frank and Sherman will repeat that description to another informant, asking about a man with "Stevie Wonder hair." "Wonderhair?" asks the informant, whose accent codes him as an immigrant. This relay, a mere comic parenthesis it would seem, establishes a shared "white" discourse that exoticizes the black man, reifying his difference in the detail of his hair at the same time that it indicates the ease with which that discourse in a racist context casts suspicion on those outside it.

By attributing the source of suspicion to Terry, the film freights him with its only allusions to race. But little details like these pile up. It is striking that a film shot in New York City produces racial difference as a kind of footnote to the underside of this intrigue, and it seems to do so in order to displace racist impulses from the police onto Terry. But this is a footnote that gathers a certain force from its emergence at the margin, as an element that remains undisciplined by the narrative, another of the residues that the revelation of the killer's identity, and his deviancy, does not resolve. In a later articulation of a similar move, *The Hand That Rocks the*

Cradle offers the "marginal" element as a central spectacle within the suburban white family, forcing it into complex interpretive transactions with the murderous female. Solomon operates in a specular symmetry with the feminine figure who activates a range of anxieties about women's capacity to destabilize family borders so that the film may finally allay them. But, in the process, the family borders absorb and manage anxious fantasies about keeping other social boundaries in place. This is a strategy that this film shares, at least in part, with all of the films under discussion here. It is one that leads us to ask: where does it leave a feminist viewer?

These narratives seem to pose a question addressed to women, and specifically to feminism, that comes across through the independent, dangerous, possibly lethal woman in *Sea of Love;* as in *Fatal Attraction, Someone to Watch Over Me,* and *Basic Instinct,* and the definitively murderous one in *The Hand That Rocks the Cradle,* this challenging question reformulates the demand for women's confirmation as an ambivalent rhetorical confrontation with feminism, one that offers up a provocation in the guise of an effort at response. Equally important, these representations tend to display and explore masculinity and femininity "in crisis," but this undefined state of crisis appears independent of any social context. Consequently, it forecloses other questions. For example, how do these obsessive and fascinating "crises," restaging a "battle of the sexes," relate to race and to sexuality?

In this fragile framework, part of the violence that emerges is no doubt related to the work that gender is made to do. First of all, in the discourses of these films, gender is only manageable if it can be made to coincide exactly with sexuality. But second, as a stand-in for all the other social differences that are cast off the map, gender has too much work to do. Because it is charged with representing other differences, sexual difference must appear to be intensely turbulent, and it must be foregrounded as the primary difference from whose regulation the management of other differences might follow, as though the culture had to imagine that if people could only get their "private" homes and their domestic lives in order, then they could organize their social spaces of work, politics, and community on the same model. Meanwhile, by foregrounding and conflating the issues of sexual difference and gender identity, these films pose cross-gendered identifications in a context of simple reversibility where it is possible to trade one stable identity for another—masculine or feminine. Because they cannot fully accommodate the identifications that they propose, the films tell the story of sexual difference as extremely volatile, and that volatility both unleashes violence and expresses itself through it.

Since these films steadfastly bypass the public discourse of feminism, speaking to it but not of it, feminism may appear to be the unnamed source of all this violence. A feminist viewer, then, is thrown back on the image that erupts in the narrative, the deviant moments that act as resistance to the narratives' conventions and the regulated closure they effect. These moments, often quite gratifying, but just as often appallingly blunt in their racism or homophobia, perform ambivalently, and often they reveal the structuring ambivalences and anxieties proper to the particular film's logic. Such moments are elements of deviance that belong to the film's system; they are the sites where the film shows its seams without bursting them. Such resistant moments indicate the pressing anxieties that are incompletely resolved in dominant representations. If these are the resistances that the dominant representational regime both depends on and holds off, then they remain just as susceptible to repression or neutralization by dominant readings as they are to hijacking or appropriation by subcultural or deviant readings.

3   Combative Femininity:

Thelma and Louise and *Terminator 2*

"Rage + Women = Power." So announces the Barbara Kruger cover for the January 1992 issue of *Ms.* Set on Kruger's distinctive red-block background, this aggressive and no doubt overly optimistic message blazes across a black-and-white photograph that shows legions of women marching. In its almost celebratory aggression, the *Ms.* cover refers to a special dossier on the Thomas-Hill hearings, a spectacle that renewed the "battle of the sexes" that had so captivated the media since debates about women's rage, aggression, and violence erupted around *Thelma and Louise.*[1]

In such a context, where popular formats—from self-defined conservative to politically ambiguous to explicitly feminist—display and manipulate images and stories of feminine rage, feminism struggles with ambivalence. Rage produces compelling images precisely because of our ambivalence about it. And this ambivalence is actively at work in entertainment where popular representations of women's rage often combine frightening or ludicrous excesses with a certain gleeful, celebratory edge. That edge has to do, I think, with the fantasy of playing on the culture's anxieties about women and feminism by making them come true, of staging someone else's worst nightmares about us. As either jubilant fantasies or nightmares, figures of feminine rage have attracted considerable media attention in the wake of Hollywood's recent investments in angry women.

If we think of ourselves as feminist spectators, we take on this ambivalence to the extent that we invest in it and recognize that we are invested by it. But our ambivalence resides uneasily within the dominant culture's ambivalence, and it foregrounds the ways that fantasy may destabilize the boundaries of inside and outside, particularly for feminism as both a political movement and a cultural sign. Whose fantasies are these? What does it mean to use a possessive term here in relation to fantasy structures? How does the uneasy possessive relate to the troubling effects of linking women to violence? These investments have become more distinctly visible since *Fatal Attraction*'s runaway success called attention to the culture's increasingly obsessional effort to construct social struggle as a battle of the sexes, as if the primary divide in U.S. culture emerged within middle-class white heterosexual couples, locked together in troubled domestic economies that are neither internally stable nor safe from external disruptions.

In this context in 1991, a modest female buddy film, *Thelma and Louise,* claimed a sizable share of intense media attention alongside what was then the most expensive blockbuster in Hollywood history, *Terminator 2.* If the smaller film produced an explosive spectacle, one that overflowed its frame in the popular press, it is because it neatly intersected with popularity circulating fantasies about women and aggression. Like *Fatal Attraction, Thelma and Louise* plugged into ambient anxieties about sexual difference and about how the "battle of the sexes" aligned men's and women's places. And like *Fatal Attraction, Thelma and Louise* troubled borderlines that popular critical discourse continues to code as fragile: those between art and life, between fantasy and agency, and between cinematic fiction and the ways that we imagine and narrate our daily lives.

Public debates around the film all turned on the question of its status as a feminist statement. Within this framework, objections emerging from feminist and antifeminist quarters took several forms. A range of critics took issue with the film's depiction of men. In a rhetoric clearly borrowed from feminism, but crudely reduced, they found the film guilty of male-bashing. Richard Johnson, of the *New York Daily News* called it: "degrading to men, with pathetic stereotypes of testosterone crazed behavior" (quoted in Richard Schickel, "Gender Bender," *Time,* June 24, 1991, p. 52). Focusing on the film's women as negative and dangerous models of feminist assertiveness, critics writing from diverse positions called the film everything from "a PMS movie, plain and simple" (Ellen Goodman, also quoted in Schickel, p. 52), to "basically a recruiting film for the NRA" (Richard Johnson, quoted in *People,* July 24, 1991, p. 94), to "a fascist version of feminism" (John Leo in *U.S. News and World Report,* also quoted in Johnson, p. 94). All of these claims depend firmly on an overestimation of the film's few moments of violence and on a conviction that the film should be read as a political tract whose exemplary characters are representative of and for feminism. From another perspective, some feminists criticized the film, as Margaret Carlson did, for pessimism because it drives its heroines off a cliff at the end. "As a bulletin from the front in the battle of the sexes," she writes, "*Thelma and Louise* sends the message that little ground has been won. . . . They become free but only wildly, self-destructively so—free to drive off the ends of the earth" ("Is This What Feminism Is All About?" *Time,* June 24, 1991, p. 57). This anxiety about self-destructiveness as a political dead end was widely shared, and John Simon's is only one exemplary comment: "the filmmakers think that . . . feminist liberation, even if hurtling into destructive excess, is somehow glorious, which is surely the way benighted moviegoers are encouraged to view it" ("Movie of the Moment," *National Review,* July 8, 1991, p. 48).[2]

Violent responses to the film's "violence" are related to a common anxious fascination with the increasingly visible "battle of the sexes" in popular culture, a fascination that, in the case at hand, often produces ironic coincidences between feminist and antifeminist positions. But these responses also imply that the image maintains the power to shape spectator consciousness more or less directly through the identifications it encourages. Such positions depend, in turn, on implicit theories of the work of fantasy in general, and cinematic fantasy in particular, and on specific fantasies about female spectators and audiences as perhaps especially susceptible to identification.

Anxious interpretations of spectator identification that expect women's viewing pleasures to translate directly into aggressive attitudes and behavior toward men in daily life may themselves have their source in fantasy. Moreover, such interpretations highlight the very cultural pressures that they work to foreclose. These readings activate and seek to manage the fantasies of women's rage and autonomy coming together in figures of dangerous feminine power that seem to preoccupy the culture. Simultaneously related to women's impact as consumers and to the impact of feminism on mass marketing, these fantasies are beginning to shape images that work to produce a feminine audience whose anxieties and desires they speak in ways that remind us that the question "what do women want?" is still wide open. In men's and women's discourse, and feminist and nonfeminist discourse alike, this feminine audience itself is figured as out of control, as Thelma and Louise are.

Analyzing such critical perspectives in *Lost Angels: Psychoanalysis and*

Cinema, Vicky Lebeau argues that they depend implicitly on a figure of the "dazzled or occupied spectator." [3] This figure emerges from and reproduces an axis between "the mass/youth and the feminine spectator," which, for Lebeau, "represents a crucial link between recent feminist analyses of the dilemmas of the female spectator and a critique of cinema as a mass cultural form seducing its spectators into degraded types of collective identification" (22). [4] Thus, Lebeau contends, "the mass and the feminine, the social and the sexual, come together in film theory in a spectator associated both with a legacy of cultural pessimism attaching to mass cultural forms and a feminist analysis of, and discontent with, the masochistic, masculine or marginalized identifications available to the female spectator" (22). Reading this theoretical position back into the contemporary social context as it is addressed by the film industry, Lebeau elsewhere examines the question of feminine audience at the intersection of the representational field and the market, where young men (18–24) have become "the privileged objects of cinema," a status that depends on differentiating masculinity "from the infantile, from the familial and from the feminine" ("Daddy's Cinema," p. 253). [5] "The corollary of a young and violent masculinity," she argues, "is the passive, and possibly familial, woman, dispossessed of cinema and of fantasies of omnipotence, a dispossession that closes down a question about feminine identifications with, or pleasure in, representations of violence" (254). And this is, of course, the question that opened up around *Thelma and Louise.*

Men critics frequently expressed a certain fear and anxiety about feminist identifications with female subjects of violence and rage, while women critics, whether they defended or attacked the film, always seemed compelled to address the crude question of role models and always at some point fell back on personal anecdote, on their private temptations to identify. For example, women seemed obsessed with the most cartoonishly piggish male, the driver whose truck Thelma and Louise blow up in the film's central and monumentally spectacular image of feminine rage. Thus, Margaret Carlson claims this fantasy as her own in *Time:* "The movie may not have the impact of *Fatal Attraction,* but the next time a woman passes an 18-wheeler and points her finger like a pistol at the tires, the driver might just put his tongue back in his mouth where it belongs" (57). And *Newsweek*'s Laura Shapiro savors an anecdote that foregrounds the fantasy's enactment in daily life: "Last week four women who had seen the film were walking down a Chicago street when a truck driver shouted an obscenity at them. Instantly, all four seized imaginary pistols and aimed them at his head. 'Thelma and Louise hit Chicago,' yelled one" ("Women Who Kill Too Much," *Newsweek,* June 17, 1991, p. 63).

What allowed so many women critics to take this film so personally? The answer must lie in the film's openness to the fantasmatic scenarios one can bring to it. And discomfort with these proliferating scenarios may be what leads to critical discourses and debates in which, to cite Jacqueline Rose's brilliant formulation, "diagnosis slides into symptom."[6] Rose's examination of the mechanism of projection may account for the apparent paradox of critical discourse and popular media discussion symptomatically participating in the very "crisis" that they sought to diagnose, inadvertently reproducing a "battle of the sexes." Projection, she writes, produces a repetition "that works by exclusion—a structural incapacity . . . to recognize your relation to something which seems to assail you from the outside." In this process, "the subject expels what he or she cannot bear to acknowledge as his or her own reality, only to have it return even larger, or more grotesquely, than reality itself" (14). Thus, critics would find what they cannot bear to own coming to them in an exaggeratedly threatening form from the representation "outside." Such a scenario would of course pertain equally to masculine anxieties about women's violence directed toward men, and to feminine anxieties about a "bad object" within feminism.

However, only an oversimplified assessment of the complex processes of identification, one that imagines it to flow seamlessly into imitation, allows us to elide the question of fantasy in readings that implicitly rely on a notion of "politically correct" images and stories. We cannot analyze a film's political effects as direct statements transparently conveyed, nor can we fix its meanings in an image or plot. Nor can any wishfulness on our part, however well-intentioned, sanitize cultural representations of the unconscious fantasies that they mobilize.[7]

An analysis equal to the complexity of the psychic operations involved in identification has to acknowledge, first of all, that identification is not a state, but a process, and that as such it is likely to be mobile and intermittent rather than consistent. We will do better to think of viewer identifications as scenarios rather than as fixations. Hardly confined to identifications with characters, then, these scenarios may equally well fasten on situations, objects, and places, or the cinematic apparatus itself. A more complicated analysis would not imagine that fantasmatic identifications forged at the movies are acted out, and acted out as directly imitative behavior. However, identification is not necessarily mimesis, nor must identifications be based on consciously perceived or desired resemblances; indeed, they may come as surprises, as disruptive moments whose effects are partial, provisional, and unpredictable. Any consideration of identification as one of the primary forms of spectator experience, then, inevitably brushes up against questions of mimesis and its pleasures or displeasures. But it also secures the viewing subjectivity as individual and bounded in ways that may be misleading. For as we bind pleasure to the private and individual rather than to the social, so do we tend to affiliate fantasy structures with a discrete subject beholding— both upholding and being upheld by fantasy.[8]

Oddly enough, the implicit theory of fantasy that underlies criticisms of cinema's irresponsible presentation of "dangerous" images may actually enhance and fortify the power of fantasy through its investment in prohibition. Judith Butler argues that "the effort to enforce a limit on fantasy can only and always fail, in part because limits are, in a sense, what fantasy loves most, what it incessantly thematizes and subordinates to its own aims. They fail because the very rhetoric by which certain erotic acts or relations are prohibited invariably eroticizes that prohibition in the service of fantasy. These prohibitions of the erotic are always at the same time, and despite themselves, the eroticization of prohibition."[9]

More important, as Butler contends, the assumption of a "mimetic relation between the real, fantasy and representation that presumes the priority of the real fails the ways in which fantasy operates as the constitutive 'outside' that helps to shape the 'real'" (106). In this case, fantasy, understood as what is absent from the real, becomes the "unreal," the very "unreal" that functions as the real's boundary. If we regard fantasy as "a constitutive exclusion" in "the construction of the real," we find ourselves faced with a question like this: "In what sense is the phantasmatic most successful precisely in that determination in which its own phantasmatic status is eclipsed and renamed as the real?" (106).

Interestingly, the public critical recourse to real-life performance consistently recognizes the fantasmatic drive of *Thelma and Louise*'s pyrotechnic spectacle only to shut it down immediately, fixating instead on a stable, if imaginary, antagonism between men's anxieties and women's vicarious pleasures. But, to accomplish this recognition, criticism must eschew irony and forget the difference between fantasy and agency that is at the heart of the film. In doing so, such readings touch on a commonly shared critical anxiety about the film's implausibilities. Framing the film as generically realist, Stanley Kauffmann exemplifies that response, arguing that the script is "burdened with contrivances" ("Stanley Kauffmann on Films," *New Republic,* July 1, 1991, p. 28). For him, "the wild ride of *Thelma and Louise* was meant to be a vicarious release for all women who feel anger at the world of men. But, though there are bull's-eyes along the way, the film's artifices clutter up its original honest intent" (29). Such a drive to regulate the film according to plausibility suggests that the desire for it to work as a feminist parable or prescription also serves an agenda of containment. For this drive depends on forgetting that the film's spectacle is made of the play between plausibility and fantasy, a play organized around the figure of a body, but a body catapulting across the landscape in a car, indissociable from motion, from the drive forward into loss.

While this play gathers around the women's driving bodies, monumentally clothed in the car that is iconic of automotive and consumer history, it also saturates the landscape around them. This is a landscape in which a woman's gaze becomes panoramic and volatile. Emphatically fantasmatic, the film reminds us that one of the effects of driving is to render landscape as image, as cinematic flow, across the frame of a windshield. In this landscape a woman's gaze can become the avid consumer of the male body, as the film's most intensely eroticized spectacles capture the hitchhiker J.D.'s buttocks for Thelma's gaze, and through it, for the spectator's gaze that is going along for the ride, so to speak. Saturated with unreal color, this landscape is marked as a screen for special effects. Frequently veiled by uninterrupted sheets of even rain—Ridley Scott's signature—this geography bears numerous cultural markers. Not only does it recall the special effects landscape of Scott's *Blade Runner* (1982), but its artificial rain calls up the deliberately whimsical atmospherics of commercials. If the film seems to revel in its own production of artifice, then the critical detour through identifications and personal stories must implicitly rehearse the subject's pleasure in constructing herself as an image staged and performed. Indeed, such a detour should remind us of the ways in which we mimic Louise's implausible route to circumvent Texas on the journey from Arkansas to Mexico, the detour that circumscribes the "heart of the matter," the personal history that is at once obscure, empty, and structuring.[10]

At every turn, the film displaces its energy from narrative justification and explanation to other, less comfortable seductions—those of the road, of traveling, of speed, and those of the image. Readings of the film that are determined to decide its political meaning depend upon stubborn forgetfulness that its fantasmatic machinery produces displacements that overthrow any and all resolutions and explanations. For example, the overdiscussed violence that turns a simple weekend vacation into a journey of no return is Louise's murder of the man who attempts to rape Thelma in the parking lot of the Silver Bullet bar.[11] But we consistently forget that Louise shoots him, not in the heat of rage when she intervenes to prevent the rape, but rather in a calm pause afterward, when he insists upon having the last word with his verbal challenge, "Suck my cock!" She kills him, then, not for what he does, but for what he *says,* a far thinner pretext.

In its very thinness, we might recall, this pretext is altogether in keeping with *Thelma and Louise*'s predecessors—road movies and crime spree films ranging from *Gun Crazy* (Joseph H. Lewis, 1949) to *Butch Cassidy and the Sundance Kid* (George Roy Hill, 1969). In this context, arguments that are riveted on the film's "violence," and on linking it to cinema's social function radically reduce the complexity of films as social texts. In suggesting that *Thelma and Louise* advocates or encourages violence, such arguments implicitly propose that representations of violence logically conclude with violent or aggressive behavior in the world. What if violent fantasy does not translate simply into violent real-life agency, what if, in fact, it aims as much to deflect or contain violence? Or, what if it works to master our ever-growing anxieties as a culture about becoming the *objects,* not the *subjects,* of violence in everyday life?[12]

Perhaps more significant, however, is the urgency with which critical responses to the film consistently falsify Louise's fragile pretext, by bolstering it with the denser narrative justification of an earlier moment of being a sexual victim, betrays other anxieties. The steadfastly fantasmatic quality of the "debate" about women's violence emerges forcefully at the point where all positions seem to get stuck in an accord over the necessity of justifying Louise's homicidal rage. This sticking point may put us in mind of the ways that fantasy remains highly volatile and mobile, or, more precisely, of the ways it is in the nature of fantasy to keep coming *unstuck.* That is, if we consider the slippage and unstoppable oscillation that characterize identificatory relays within fantasy, that slippage may become particularly discomfiting and sharp when it comes to violent fantasies or images. So both feminist and nonfeminist anxieties could get snagged here. A feminist spectator runs into the discomforts of acknowledging violence and rage—or victimization—at the fantasy level and responds with a "No, that's not mine, that's someone else's." This anxiety might intersect with anxious discourses that project onto feminism a rage that has its source in the subject who casts feminism as an outside force threatening sexual relations or even sexual difference itself.

Of course, beyond the question of feminism, there is the question of femininity, or of sexual difference itself: a spectator might experience the identificatory relays that open around this act of violent "revenge" as an invitation, or a demand, to take up a stable gender position aligned on the victim-aggressor axis. Indeed, as Judith Butler suggests, much of the energy devoted to the condemnation of images may be related to the fantasmatic collapse of identification with gender identifications. As she puts it, "the postulation of a single identificatory access to the representation is precisely what stabilizes gender identity" (114). Thus, attacks on violence within representation often combine anxieties about gender identification with desires to deflect the discomfort of identifying with the victim. However, that anxiety itself might well mask or embed another powerful anxiety about identifying with the aggressor: "the insistence that the picture enforces an identification with victimization might be understood not only as a refusal to identify—even in fantasy—with aggression, but further, as a displacement of that refused aggression onto the picture which then—as a transferential object of sorts—takes on a personified status as an active agent and abuses its passive viewer (or which stands in for the phantasmatic figure of 'patriarchy' itself)" (114).[13]

Such an impulse seems to underlie discussions of the film that have insisted tenaciously on giving Thelma and Louise this narrative reason for winding up on the lam: they have been sexually victimized. And the film's retroactive production of an originary "motive" provides a kind of compromise formation that, on the superficial level, at least, leaves room for this easy resolution of the problem of feminine violence. So *Thelma and Louise* constitutes a somewhat ambivalent object. While it allows and perhaps even encourages our forgetfulness of the ambiguity and fragility of the motive, the film continually highlights the shakiness of this excuse for a headlong flight with no destination beyond the going (as the heroines insist, "Let's not get caught, let's keep going").

Meanwhile, we also often forget the displacement embedded in the plot turn that definitively precipitates Thelma and Louise over the edge of no return, the armed robbery that cannot be fully explained by a logic of sexual abuse. Thelma becomes a robber because the hitchhiker with whom she has spent the night has stolen all the money that the two women have to their names. Here is another incident of victimization: seduction and abandonment compounded by the theft. Except that Thelma reads the event as a fortunate one: she has had her first good sexual experience.[14] If we read this moment within historically conventional Hollywood terms, women who have been catapulted out of domesticity by the acts of sexual violence they endure, or by giving in to the violence of their own desire, are punished for their lust and pleasure. But Thelma does not read it that way. The punishment seems lost on her. Instead, this moment becomes her occasion for incorporating J.D.'s theatrically scripted robbery routine. Later, we watch Thelma perform as J.D., repeating this routine exactly as he had demonstrated it for her. And all of this is mediated through a cut to the store's video surveillance camera; Thelma becomes an image before our eyes and through the explicit theft of a man's posture, words, and persona.

The film's most compelling fantasies keep emerging through this kind of cross-gender identification. These are the fantasies that are thrown off, that escape a narrative logic of cause and effect. *Thelma and Louise* is about a long, erratic drive, alternately wandering and speeding toward an impossible destination along the arc of a detour. And the detour becomes the whole trip. This trip traverses the space between two images—the snapshot Louise takes at the beginning of the trip and the final still that permanently suspends the women over the abyss in their Thunderbird. The snapshot memorializes a "before" image, women dressed up and made up for an outing. This is the image that the film's journey undoes, as the women strip down to T-shirts, cast off all the accoutrements of glamour, of conventional feminine masquerade. Ending with a still image that answers to the first one as its "after," the film puts an ironic spin on the use of "before" and "after" pictures that advertise diets and beauty makeovers to the female consumer.[15] Finally, this is a film about the motion between two still moments, the route from image to image, and it all seems to come down to Thelma's lusty appreciation of J.D.'s buttocks as he walks away from their car. "That's him goin'," she tells Louise, "I luuuuve watchin' him go." This film seems to want us to say the same: we love watching it go, not watching it get somewhere.

To participate in the drive to decide, once and for all, for or against *Thelma and Louise,* to push the journey to its conclusion, or to freeze and fix the volatility of the fantasies it generates, all will lead us to repeat Louise's motto, which the film comes to take as a refrain—"get what you settle for." Rather, I would like to preserve this volatility by locating *Thelma and Louise* in a larger cultural matrix, one that has something to do with women and cars.[16] For, finally, this is a story about women and cars. What happens when women drive cars, instead of adorning men's cars, instead of sitting, fixed and still, draped across them? What happens when women wear cars instead of clothes? What happens when women strip down for a purpose that exceeds, bypasses, or falls short of sexual display?[17]

If our readings understand the film's conclusion, or its heroines' destination, as a final decision about its meaning, then we repress the partiality and disruption that make its journey so compelling. Readings that pronounce the film dangerous and wrongheaded because it invites women to take on wholesale the tired clichés of masculinity and male bonding that prevail in the history of westerns, road movies, and action films depend on certain foreclosures. Such readings argue that for women to embrace and celebrate feminine versions of the very clichés that men increasingly reject, advances nothing and merely inverts the current gender imbalance in representation. But this argument skips over the process by which the film explicitly parades the takeover of these clichés. Such exaggerated display may signal a more general popular cultural rewriting of familiar stories. Women are raised on the same cinematic and televisual images and stories as men, images and stories that offer and invite identifications as part of spectator response. And women are identifying, perhaps with more resistance, or more intermittence, but perhaps—and this is less easy to contemplate and less commonly discussed—identifying all the more forcefully and avidly with the same male figures and "masculine" scenarios as their male contemporaries. Within this framework, images of women raiding those nearly worn-out stories, trying on those clichéd postures, might have the effect of "newness" and might challenge our readings of those postures themselves. Consequently, such images may challenge our analysis of the process and the effects of identification in our histories as consumers of popular culture.

Thelma and Louise's takeover of such clichés foregrounds the posturing involved in that occupation. This posturing has several effects. It mobilizes the pleasures of fantasmatic identifications with embodied agents of travel, speed, force, and aggression that we have historically enjoyed in a cross-gender framework. But this film's female agents offer a different possibility for mixing desire with identification. At the same time, the spectacle of women acting like men works to disrupt the apparent naturalness of certain postures when performed by a male body. But it is equally important to understand this spectacle in terms of sexuality.

Exploring the "cultural hysteria the film has elicited," Lynda Hart argues that "the mechanism of [gender] reversal alone" cannot entirely account for it. "When we examine the 'logic' of the reception of *Thelma and Louise,*" she contends, "another possibility begins to emerge that is more subversive than appropriation of the 'other's' territory" (73). That possibility is this: "If Thelma and Louise are circling around the absent spaces where woman is located in the discourse of men's desire, response to this film is hovering anxiously around the threat of the lesbian as an unspeakable sign" (74). Of course, the threat also operates to titillate. It is significant that these "butch" figures should become a site both of contest and of compelling pleasures across audience formations. If butch figures are coming into cinematic prominence, this may have to do with visibility and invisibility around sexual identity as well as gender. So the butch or butch-femme couple visually announces the possibility of a lesbianism that is discursively repressed. At the same time, such figures respond to cultural fantasies organized by the wish that identity might be and might remain readily visible.[18]

These images also intersect a consumer-cultural obsession with managing and transforming the body through exercise, constructing it as sculpture and as fashion. Inscribing the subject's will to mastery on the body, exercise also reinscribes the sexual difference that we continually restage in our private and public lives. By foregrounding and exaggerating these everyday practices, cinematic images of women "transformers" produce bodily spectacles that are as much about doing as they are about showing. In this context, gender identity is not simply what we *are,* or something we *possess,* but something we *do.*[19]

In contemporary popular culture our viewing pleasures may not only tolerate, but they may even partially depend on, gender posturings that challenge conventional mythologies of sexual difference, as they do in both *Thelma and Louise* and *Terminator 2.* Julie Baumgold's cover story for the July 29, 1991, issue of the weekly magazine, *New York:* "Killer Women: Here Come the Hardbodies," explores the sites of fascination that are common to these films: the female body and its potential for violence. Baumgold's analysis epitomizes a certain ambivalent feminine fascination. In a self-consciously hard-boiled style, Baumgold describes Linda Hamilton's body in almost obsessive detail: "She is sleeveless the whole movie to show her arms. The arms have rivers of veins rising above the bulging muscle. The arms, even at rest, show their muscle. The arms are polished weapons. They show scars. They show hair" (28).

In the end, Baumgold must capitulate to popular critical convention by deciding the meanings of these bodies within a strict logic of narrative verisimilitude: "The appeal of these bone-cracker movies is the same: immediate justice and punishment of wrongs. Where does such exist in life? Where else are right and wrong so clearly defined? And of course the violence is taken as fake violence . . ." (29). However, the article's own overarching logic declares the political force of these images to be ambivalent in the following terms: "In part, the male-mogul motive is commercial. To appeal to women repulsed or bored by male action movies, they have created these warrior women. . . . What is important is that these women, created from male fantasies, have been released. Where can they go?" (29).

This article's obvious uneasy skepticism about the pleasures of viewing the female hardbody foregrounds the structuring ambivalence of these images, an ambivalence that seems central to popular culture's increasing fascination with lethal women. That fascination must have multiple sources as well as multiple uses and expressions. What does it mean, for instance, to say that these images have been "created from male fantasies"? Jacqueline Rose reminds us that "because an image of femininity can be identified as male fantasy," this does not mean that "it is any the less intensely lived by women." "Conversely," she continues, "the fact that the woman discovers something as a component of her own self-imagining does not mean that it cannot also be the object, or even the product, of the wildest male projection, repulsion or desire. Who owns what? Who gives what to whom?" (128–29).

Suppose we imagine that these figures recall the question "what do women want?" and answer it this way: "Hardbodies." Are these bodies products of a masculine imagination, its deep anxieties, and perhaps its masochistic desires? If so, are women's fantasies meeting those anxieties in sadistic pleasures at seeing masculine fears fulfilled in the image? And while these films eroticize women's physical power and force, they do so around a body whose appeals to us spectators are more directly inscribed as pose. Whose hardbodies do we want? Men's, other women's, or our own? Is women's fascination narcissistic or anaclitic, playful or aggressive? Is its source desire or identification?

Part of this fascination arises, no doubt, from the dialectic of being and having that operates in such images. We may fantasize being such bodies, having them, or both. Such a mix of desire and identification is what keeps *Thelma and Louise* available to lesbian readings or viewing positions, even before the final kiss.[20] And yet, discussions that focused on the fantasmatically escalated "battle of the sexes" seem to have done so at the cost of—or perhaps in the interest of—repressing the lesbian eroticism. According to Lynda Hart's reading of *Thelma and Louise,* such repression is coherent with the film's own efforts. "Summoned through negation in both the film's action and the critical responses is a history of identification between the female criminal and the lesbian," she writes. "Given this history, the expectation for lesbianism between women who violate the law is so strong that the film works overtime to disavow it. If the lesbian has been constructed as the manifest figure of women's 'latent' criminality, we can expect that representations of violent women will be haunted by her absent presence" (75).

If many readings bypassed the lesbian possibilities offered up by the text, this may have to do with the drive to decide, to "fix," the meaning of images by binding them into a narrative consistency that is itself bound to a stable conclusion, a drive that coheres with the desire to fix and stabilize sexuality. This drive denies the film's own resistance to decidability, since the text leaves Thelma's and Louise's sexuality undecided, leaves the question suspended, and leaves it suspended not only in the lure of the last image, but also in its failure to determine the exact relations of butch and femme, masculine and feminine. As Cathy Griggers argues in "*Thelma and Louise* and the Cultural Generation of the New Butch-Femme," these effects are not disconnected. More important, the residual last image threatens to complicate, if not to undo, the entire narrative trajectory. For Griggers, "the erotic subtext surrounding Thelma and Louise, for example, is disengaged at the end of the film from the plot's death sentence by both the freeze frame and the replay of earlier clips from the film appearing immediately after the freeze frame and running for the duration of the credits (creating a loop in time, a return to the moment before loss—the emotive function of the fetish sign)."[21]

Since the film refuses an image or narrative structure that would allow a clear alignment of gender, sexuality, and posture—butch or femme— any obsession with the film's contribution to a "battle of the sexes" appears as an urgency to reclaim the film for a heterosexual universe, in the process reclaiming sexual difference as heterosexual difference, and not as the difference, unstable though it might be, between heterosexuality and homosexuality.[22] As Griggers has it, the film is resisting precisely that

move: "In placing sexuality (signed by the kiss) after its cultural production, *Thelma and Louise* reminds its audiences that identity in the body is
the outcome of the social production of identity as a body of signs, constructed out of the real, material options one has at hand" (140). Sexuality, in short, is not simply a narrative production.

In this respect, the film suspends its spectators in indecision about
sexuality. But sexual undecidability may be a more or less obscure feature of all cultural productions. According to Alexander Doty, "within
cultural production and reception, queer erotics are part of the culture's
erotic center, both as a necessary construct by which to define the heterosexual and the straight (as 'not queer'), and as a position that can be
and is occupied in various ways by otherwise heterosexual and straight-
identifying people." [23] Doty goes on to explain that, while the culture acknowledges that homosexuals can "operate from within straight cultural
spaces and positions," it has much greater difficulty coping with queer
textuality. Just as "basically heterocentrist texts can contain queer elements," Doty argues, "basically heterosexual straight-identifying people
can experience queer moments." For him, these moments should be acknowledged as "queer," and "not as moments of 'homosexual panic,'
or temporary confusion, or as unfortunate, shameful, sinful lapses in
judgment or taste to be ignored, repressed, condemned, or somehow explained away within and by straight cultural politics—or even within
gay or lesbian discourses" (3).[24] Understood this way, the erotic positions
that texts offer would operate much as do erotic identities themselves.
As Eve Sedgwick contends, "erotic identity, of all things, is never to be
circumscribed simply as itself, can never not be relational, is never to be
perceived or known by anyone outside of a structure of transference and
countertransference" (*Epistemology of the Closet,* 81).

By introducing a third term into the dyad of gender and sexuality,
Doty and Sedgwick help to complicate the meanings we may affix to their
relationship, as well as to images and identities. Tamsin Wilton seems
to be suggesting something similar when she argues that "since the binary paradigm of gender (either being masculine or feminine) and that
of sexuality (either being queer or straight) are codependent and interca-
late, we need also to pay attention to how gender is regulated through the
policing and shaping of sexuality." [25] For Wilton, " 'lesbian' is a contested
sign and a privileged site of enquiry within discourses of both gender and
sexuality. This is largely due to the elision of gender and sexual orientation in mainstream thinking, an elision which has been challenged by
and within both feminism and queer theory, and which continues to de-

mand both careful scrutiny and a critical praxis that takes account of the ideological and political codependency of gender and the erotic" (3). Because the "erotic" names a process rather than a state, it may become a shaping term in an analysis that is not bound to imagine that sexualities can be mapped onto gender in a stable formation.

Like the erotic, fantasy designates a process. Thelma and Louise's impossible suspension as an image hanging over the abyss, monumentalized in their last kiss, stresses the film's demand to be read as fantasy, and as fantasy that reworks elements of a vast image repertoire embedded in a history and continually marked by effects of cultural circulation, among them, the postures of gender and sexuality.[26] If so much discussion of *Thelma and Louise* pivoted on violence, it is because the film stages a violence that is neither thematized nor represented on the screen. This is the violence of representational struggle both in private fantasy and in public discussion. *Thelma and Louise*'s dramatic and exhilarating transformation of women's body language—posture, gesture, gait—does not read, however, as a revelation of the "natural" body underneath the feminine masquerade of the housewife or service worker. Rather, the prominence of this bodily transformation sets the film in a network of recent images of women clearly "reconstructed" on or for the screen, like Sigourney Weaver's Ripley in the *Alien* series—*Alien* (Ridley Scott, 1979), *Aliens* (James Cameron, 1986), *Alien 3* (David Fincher, 1992)—and Linda Hamilton's Sarah Connor in *Terminator 2*.

At the fantasmatic level the film pries gender away from sexuality, pries feminine masquerade loose from effects of glamour and sexual seduction, in order to stress the body's constructed character as costume, a costume that asks us to read it both as machine and as masculinity.[27] This is perhaps the most powerful effect of cinematic representations of women who no more actively *want* than, say, Rambo or the Terminator, or Mel Gibson's Martin Riggs in *Lethal Weapon,* all of whose smoothly muscled carapaces make their very bodily presence a mute thrust of demand. In destabilizing contrast to their male precursors, these new presentations of the muscled female body stage a form of drag based on a masculinity that aggressively displays its difference from an anatomical base.[28] They thus parade an interruption: where we expect them to exhibit the mark of sexuality for consumption, instead we see the body itself as masquerade. Equally important, however, we need to ask: In what context do these images become meaningful as cultural sites, what kind of cultural space do they inhabit?

But there is another image suspended "over an abyss." This is the bicyclist whose dreadlocks might code him in specific ways—if we ever heard him speak. In this instance, we are faced with an abyss of nonmeaning or incoherence, but one which also suggests the broader cultural terrain that produces the film. As it is, the cyclist arrives as a mysterious and silent "guest," who rides into the narrative after Thelma and Louise have locked a terrified state trooper in the trunk of his car and tossed away his keys. The cyclist responds to the trooper's muffled pleas by calmly blowing some smoke from his reefer into the trunk, then rides away. He remains, then, a mute, resistant image.[29]

Griggers registers this image narratively: "the only non-negative image of a man in *Thelma and Louise* is the young black bicyclist who appears out of nowhere smoking reefer (the nomad)—a man who has his own reasons for being out on the road" (138). But this seems to be a wishful reading, one that the film encourages, to be sure, but a wishful one nonetheless. Finally, the looping effect that Griggers describes—whereby the still image/freeze frame of *Thelma and Louise* is pulled from the narrative and linked to the serial presentation that memorializes the figures in images culled from the journey that we have just followed—bypasses the cyclist, failing to gather that image into its fabric. No narrative gathering absorbs this image's residue into a sequence that fixes its meaning.[30] As such, it cannot be captured or claimed, even for the "aberrant" reading that Griggers supplies.

To align the cyclist with Thelma and Louise as an ally, as someone with "his own reasons for being on the road," and to presume that those reasons place him, like them, running askirt of, if not afoul, of the law, is to make the same gesture of narrative recuperation that characterizes readings of the film that insist upon locating rape as the motivating source of Thelma and Louise's adventures. Such a recuperation of the black cyclist aligns him with Thelma and Louise in a binary universe where the man of color operates in a renegade or disabled relation to the law. This imaginary alignment takes place under the sign of the failure of patriarchal law, embodied as it is both in the terrified and blubbering trooper whom the women lock in his trunk and in the benign and inept figure of Detective Slocum (Harvey Keitel), whose efforts on Thelma and Louise's behalf have actually put them in a position to be caught. Perhaps that failure is most stunningly marked by the desperate, ineffectual, and belated paternal "No!" that hangs in the air as Slocum stands frozen, watching the women's flight over the edge. Any effort to produce stable narrative boundaries within the terms that the film provides for the image of the cyclist is likewise failed in advance.

That image remains as a residue on the order of the anamorphic blot on the screen that Slavoj Žižek characterizes as a "surplus," "a detail of a picture" that when "looked at straightforwardly appears as a blurred spot," but that "assumes clear distinguished shapes once we've looked at it 'awry,' at an angle."[31] But the film offers us no "angle" from which to resolve the image in the first place. Indeed, we might see this figure as fetishized, to the extent that he marks a site of anxiety or intervention—the obtrusiveness of difference in the wider cultural field—but he also acts to fascinate our gaze, to stop us looking further. This figure can operate only as an *effect* here, a sort of shadow cast against the paleness of the desert landscape, the whiteness of the universe in which the film performs its interrogations of gender construction. What is disturbing is that, having taken the trouble to introduce this figure, the film presents it as a limit. But this is not a limit that reshapes our understanding of the gender drama as powerfully inflected by social differences. Rather, it becomes an absolute limit to sense. Its unreadability seems to function only to secure the deracialized status of the white femininity that plays with gender here. In this respect, the image operates as does the "thunderous, theatrical presence of black surrogacy," that Toni Morrison finds so common in the American literary tradition, a presence that that tradition works tirelessly to ignore, to render meaning-less, as it renders itself "race-free."[32] Read this way, we might see this gratuitous figure as functioning, finally, in a familiar way; its muteness helps to reinforce the even greater "non sequitur," to borrow Morrison's term (33), that is whiteness in the dominant cultural imagination.

Difficult as it is to pin down a reading for this fragile and unaccountable trace in *Thelma and Louise,* we find that the trace emerges all the more powerfully from the film's texture when we read *Thelma and Louise* alongside *Terminator 2*, its blockbuster contemporary. Both films shared a certain replay of the road movie plot, along with the spectacle of a violent and aggressive "butch" female character, as well as the apparently gratuitous introduction of an African American character at a crucial moment. Yet the status of violence in *T2* never comes under scrutiny in public discussion, and this may be because of the film's steadfast generic framing as fantasy.

In addition to its widely publicized technological innovations—the computer morphing through which it produced its special effects—*T2* was able to claim historic significance at the box office, since 42 percent of its opening weekend audience was made up of women, as against the more standard "action film draw" of 20 to 30 percent.[33] Strikingly enough, *T2*'s rewriting of its antecedent, *The Terminator* (James Cameron, 1984), seems to recast and displace the terms of the previous film, even at the level of its audience address. In this respect, *T2* performs "the pattern of internal amnesia," which Susan Jeffords contends is "typical of male action film sequences of the 1980s,"[34] in such a way as to contradict the general tendency of action film cycles, where "repetition" operates as "re-production" (247). *T2*'s parodic replay of action masculinity "as externalization" (246), however, produces displacements, since the film is much more about action femininity and the ways that it operates as externalization: the terminator itself is busy with *in*ternalizations.[35] And this is only one of the many inversions that the film exhibits.

The kinder, gentler *Terminator 2* organizes its rewrite of *The Terminator* through a parade of astonishing images that body forth what the film thematizes: transformations. That is, its very material format emphasizes feats of technological wizardry—morphing—at the same time that Sarah Connor's dramatic reconstruction as a female hardbody emerges as a spectacle that interrupts or suspends the narrative of heroic maternity functioning within a couple.[36] A nonlethal, negotiating version of the terminator joins forces with the newly pumped-up Linda Hamilton, whose muscular physique looks like a carapace, visibly inscribing her psychic and emotional hardness. This initially implausible alliance between the human mother, remote and robotic in her devotion to her mission, and the cyborg who was her mortal enemy in the first *Terminator* film generates a particular narrative logic. As she hardens—her surface closed like a shell, her eyes concealed by aviator sunglasses, her body draped with weapons—he softens, becoming increasingly obsessed with the human emotions that he lacks.

Some of the transactions that this spectacular odd couple enact appear to be grounded in an ironically overdone bodily masquerade that organizes the human-cyborg difference in a gender theater that continues to play with the fantasy of a visible phallus. If we connect the image of Sarah Connor to that of female bodybuilders as well as to the various incarnations that make up the icon of "Schwarzenegger," we may read the text's commitment to hypervisibility in connection with a destabilization of gender at the point where masculinized female bodies, along with hyper-masculinized male ones, both trouble the relationship of masculinity to the phallus. As Jonathan Goldberg argues: "The spectacle of body building, in which female body builders bring to a crisis patriarchal definitions of femininity, points too to the fact that hypermasculinity always transgresses, refuses, exceeds the phallic measure. The excesses on both sites defuse the heterosexual imperative even as an attempt is made to install it—forever. If these bodies are the phallus, the phallus has been so dispersed that it is the proper name of nothing but a scandal . . ." (179).

But *T2* maintains competing logics around this couple: its oedipalizing plot reinforces the economy of the human-cyborg couple, claiming it for a determinedly heterosexual universe of gender difference. While the film struggles to make those developments perfectly coincident with its newly central "humanist discourse," that humanist—and humanizing—discourse depends intimately on our memory of the previous film, whose gleeful pleasure in the terminator's over-the-top violations of social rules was central to its appeal. Moreover, the previous terminator's lawlessness distinctly targeted the middle-class world of nuclear families, a world that *T2* seems intent on celebrating.[37]

If *T2* violates—even explodes—the compelling narrative logic of time travel that organized the first terminator film, and violates it precisely by producing a future that grants centrality to human agency and, specifically, to female agency, it does so through a nexus of ideological lures. As Forest Pyle argues, the central opposition between human and cyborg continually dissolves in *T2:* "however much the film may want to extricate itself from the logic of machines," he writes, "the knotting of human and cyborg is inextricable: in *Terminator 2,* the triumph of humans and humanism is made dependent on the humanizing of cyborgs."[38] We should note here that "the triumph of humanism" is intimately linked to vision as well, since the technology of the camera consistently humanizes the T101 by assigning it a point of view, while the new terminator, the T1000, seems beyond point of view. Its gaze is a mobile, mimetic, but sightless one, completely disconnected from our own, which is intermittently aligned with the T101's.

This humanizing process is crucial to the narrative resolution. If Sarah Connor has a future, it is a function of that process, which her controlling voice-over makes explicit at the end of the film. "The unknown future rolls toward us. I face it for the first time with a sense of hope, because if a machine, a terminator, can learn the value of human life, then maybe we can too." What we have here in the coupling of humanist and superficially "pro-life" discourses is a fragile clump of ideological lures that dissolves readily.[39] While the terminator's acquisition of a human interior, an emotional life, gives Sarah Connor a new future, the film produces an ironic swerve here as it simultaneously transfers the oedipal dream of being one's own father from John Connor to the terminator himself. Consequently, *T2* bypasses the woman once again, since this film reveals that Skynet has originated from the debris the terminator left behind on his first visit. Thus, the "good" terminator is revealed to be a literal *"chip off the old block,"* sent back in time to expiate the father's crimes, to repeat the mission of the original *Terminator*'s visitor from the future as a form of mechanical reproduction.[40] So, *T2* plays back in reverse—and ironizes—the problem posed by *The Terminator:* that of distinguishing the terminator from the father.

Equally important, close attention to the terminator's last appearance in *T2* discloses that, once again, he has deposited a residue in the present. This time it is his amputated hand, a potentially regenerative member, and one that replicates the mechanical hand that has been preserved along with the fatal chip. Ironically enough, in a film that rewrites its predecessor by rendering as comic the previously terrifying figure of the T101 by emphasizing his "primitive" nature in comparison to the T1000, the residue he leaves is iconically the most primitive prototype of technology: the extension of the hand, a tool that registers as purely mimetic.

Meanwhile, the film's relentless campiness, and the radical inconsistencies of its time-travel plot, in concert with a series of spectacular images, work to interrupt, to disarticulate, those other logics. In the process, the film throws off a set of irreconcilable, residual images that, when read back into the film's narrative resolution, undermine it. If we read it through its uncontainable residues, *T2* appears more and more as an ideologically incoherent text, whose effort to imaginatively exploit contradictions only forces them into collisions that throw them into relief.

T2 throws off other residual effects, however, that continually interrupt the already ironic reconstitution of the nuclear family.[41] As it works to redeem Sarah Connor from the status of "bad mother" that is conferred upon her by psychotically single-minded combativeness, it does so in a discursive universe that is fragilely and ironically secured by the shifting poles of "good" object and "bad" object, embodied in a series of doublings. The "original" bad terminator returns to us as the good one, to be distinguished from the new model, the T1000, in relation to which he is literally junk, salvage. That model, more a replicator than a cyborg, threatens to become indistinguishable from its objects, to take their place, an effect that reminds us that the person of Arnold Schwarzenegger makes it difficult to distinguish the actor from what he impersonates. The film's frame, then, is entirely ironic, and its irony means to offer the doubt that the mimetic effects produce as a kind of ideological refuge.[42]

In this universe *T2* aligns Sarah Connor with the terminator, who qualifies as the best possible father, in order to reconstitute a relatively functional family unit. At one of the film's most strikingly ironic moments Sarah Connor's voice-over explains this lure: "Watching John with the machine, it was suddenly so clear. The machine would never stop, never leave him, never hurt him, shout, get drunk and hit him or say it was too busy. . . . Of all the would-be fathers, this thing, this machine was the only one . . . who measured up. In an insane world, it was the sanest choice." Here, the film offers a knot of ideological lures. While it seems to trumpet the privilege of the nuclear family unit headed by some version of a heterosexual couple, producing this image within a discourse whose key word is "choice," it also radically undercuts the ideological binding together of biology, paternity, masculinity, and phallic authority.[43] The best father, the father who "knows best," parades an externalization of conventional phallic attributes whose infrastructure is a machine, an interior whose hollow is only mapped as it incorporates its "master's voice," the voice of the "son," supplying the words, the fixed phrases (like "no problema"), that act as a stand-in for consciousness. In the end, however, the best father will wind up at best a relic, at worst a piece of junk, recycled in a vat of molten liquid metal.

Sarah Connor's physical and emotional resemblance to the terminator and the militaristic discipline she applies to her affective relationship with her son, along with her obsession with weapons technology, code her as a threat to conventional maternity and establish her as a figure who mobilizes various anxieties. On the one hand, she suggests a brutal incarnation of women's reproductive autonomy, and her mastery of destructive technologies may operate as a metaphor for women's continued, if increasingly limited, access to technologies necessary to maintain choice about reproduction (technologies of "termination"). And this is why, I want to argue, that the film needs to stress that Sarah Connor really is the "good mother," ever ready to give her life to preserve her child's. *T2* wants to have it both ways, so to speak, and this may represent the culture's most powerful wishes and fears around the issue of women's reproductive rights. At the same time, in the context of the earlier terminator film's obsessive focus on the uncanniness of exteriorizing the body's interior, we may read a parallel anxiety about the increasing capacity of medical technology to penetrate and modify bodily interiority, to produce hybrids of biotechnology by intervening in organic processes.

Collective anxieties about new reproductive technologies fit coherently within the science fiction frame, preoccupied as it is with technology's own "reproduction," or proliferation, and with the breakdown of distinctions between the human and the machine. In this regard we may be as anxious about technology's capacity to prolong life as about its ability to end it. *T2* reminds us of this explicitly when John Connor uncomfortably asks the terminator: "How long do you live? . . . Uh, last?" *T2*'s last scene confirms that this is an underlying preoccupation as the terminator reveals what may be the most powerful difference between this cyborg and his human companions: he is constitutionally unable to end his own life. In his words, he cannot "self-terminate." So Sarah Connor must become his "terminator."[44] Thus, specific issues of women's autonomy and rights over their bodies are subsumed into more general anxieties bearing on technology's impact on individual self-determination and the status of the body.[45]

That the specific social struggle over abortion, which has become a near phobic, apotropaic site in Hollywood films and on television, haunts recent representations of female hardbodies is acutely evident in *Alien 3*, the sequel that finally wastes its action hero, Ripley, the "mother," so to speak, of all these hardbodies. Once the Cameron film of 1986, *Aliens*, had equipped Ripley with a certain nurturing impulse, as it equipped her with a foster daughter, the orphaned Newt, the third film was able to play the memory of that development into a plot that fulfills the anxiety generated in the logic which has sustained the series—that Ripley herself would be occupied by larvae, that she would be the final surrogate body in which the alien seeks to incubate. Of course, as the series has evolved, it has overdetermined the image of pregnancy embedded in this forced incubation by plugging into collective fears about HIV attacking the body with its rampant replicating capacities.

Alien 3, like *T2*, gets to have it both ways, since Ripley—aggressively combative to the end—"aborts" the alien through her own suicide, which almost parodically repeats the demise of both terminators, the good object and the bad object alike, in a vat of molten ore. That is, if the film highlights a refusal to bear this monstrous offspring, it sets that refusal in a frame where this choice really is no choice. (On the other hand, if we read this conclusion in the framework of images of AIDS, its wishfulness becomes much more complicated, suggesting a fantasy that there could be some consolidated sacrifice capable of putting an end to transmission.)[46]

As in the previous films, *Alien 3* sets this choice within the frame of a battle between two females—the hyperreproductive alien, the "bitch," and the nonreproductive, androgynous Ripley. The trailer for *Alien 3* concludes with the punchline slogan, "the bitch is back." But the "bitch" here is also clearly the "butch." And the trailer seeks to capture our interest in precisely these terms. First framing Ripley alone in close-up, her head spectacularly shaved, the trailer moves across the words, "the bitch is back" which, thus ironically, refers to Ripley. Then, the alien's head we have been anticipating is brought into a tightly framed two-shot with hers. So the real "bitch" is back, and Ripley is, if less bitchy in her complete terror, considerably more "butchy" than in the first two films. But the promise here is coherent with the organizing image of the *Alien* series: that of a cosmic catfight where social anxieties are thrown off onto battles between females on opposite sides of the law and the family, battles thinly veiled in the figure of the human-nonhuman divide.[47]

By foregrounding gender in and as performance, *T2* plays on the familiar social anxieties about women's autonomy that are sharply evident in newly escalated abortion debates, but it does so in the context of other anxieties about unstable identity, about the erasure of difference, and of our ability to "tell" the difference. The film sets Sarah Connor's resemblance to the Schwarzenegger terminator against its dystopian fascination with the figure of the T1000, the "bad" terminator, a protean cyborg that can assume a variety of forms, composed as it is of "a mimetic polyalloy." T1000 is a figure for proliferating mimesis powered by metonymy (he needs only a momentary contact with his object to reproduce it). Thus, the T1000 literalizes fantasies about identification as a kind of contamination.[48] Equally intense fantasies about women's autonomy and about the failure of difference emerge in the conjunction of the combative female body and out-of-control technologies. In this case, these technologies have come to look like technologies of identity.

T2's "bitch," then, operates at the intersection of several obscurely related logics. One of the film's most breathtaking spectacles—despite or perhaps precisely *because* of its lack of pyrotechnic effects—occurs when the film sends its female action hero, rigged out in full Rambo combat gear, catapulting into the suburban living room of scientist Miles Dyson, and frames her menacing the terrified family as they cower together on the floor. The film casts this moment as pivotal, since it is only through

Dyson that Sarah Connor and the terminator gain access to Cyberdyne headquarters to destroy the incipient autonomous computer network and thus change the future. For many reasons, this scene highlights the political instability and ambivalence that makes the film engaging.

While this ambivalence is equally powerful in relation to sexual and racial difference, the narrative consistently focuses our epistemological curiosity on the difference between the human and the cyborg. From the beginning, the film exhibits an overarching drive to link that distinction to sexuality and sexual difference, as an early scene that powerfully stresses vision and point of view demonstrates. Our first sight of the terminator, as in the first film, finds him crouching naked in a parking lot. When he rises, the camera follows behind Schwarzenegger until he enters a local bar. It then allows us to take up his point of view. We see the reactions of the patrons of this bar through the terminator's "eyes," a video screen that also registers various data across our view of these spectators as they examine Arnold. Comically enough, we follow their looks, which inscribe the trajectory of gazes to his crotch and then register as reaction shots the impressiveness of the member that the film coyly and ironically withholds from our view. This comic curiosity about the actor's anatomy coincides with an implicit narrative interest in cyborg sexuality and enhances the epistemological and erotic fascinations that the film weaves into its spectacles of the phallic female body alongside the machine phallus that the terminator represents.

In the film's final sequences that spectacular coupling emerges at Dyson's direct expense. Because Dyson, wounded by the police, agrees to stay behind with the detonator that will blow up Cyberdyne and him along with it, Sarah Connor can go on into the now uncertain future, a future that is not yet written, that has not yet been staged on the screen of her internal cinema. At Dyson's direct expense, she gains access to her own historical agency, newly unbound from its previous determinants, in a future where her only fate is "the one she makes." The utopian dimension here concerns not only the fantasy of an individual's punctual intervention changing history, but also the fantasy of being certain about the effects of your own agency. Concomitantly, however, Dyson's sacrifice lines up with the terminator's as the necessary condition of Connor's reunion with her son in a "functional" family, her return to her maternal place, and her effectiveness as an agent.

If *T2* literally immolates these two characters on the altar of a future conditioned by humanist values, as Sarah Connor makes plain at the film's conclusion, it also equates them structurally through their parallel ends. But the film consistently skews this equation. Miles Dyson can self-consciously facilitate his own death; the terminator, on the other hand, has no illusion of or ambition to self-possession. On the contrary, his dispossession is complete. Not only must he ask Connor to terminate him, but, we remember, he does not even own something as intimate as his own pain, he only "senses injuries." "The data," in his words, "could be called pain."

In the film's universe the troubling questions get mobilized around the terminators, beginning with the basic question uttered by one shocked bystander: "What the fuck is it?" This central question easily transmutes into the question, "what's the difference between 'it' and us/me?"— a question treated through the alliance between Connor and the terminator. And that alliance generates related questions: what difference brings them together, and what difference keeps them from uniting as a sexual couple? Relentlessly foregrounding and eroticizing their difference as the central focus of a fascination articulated on and through spectacular special effects, the film displaces sexual and racial difference onto this cyborg-human divide. This continually renewable displacement offers the possibility of depoliticizing those differences as it attenuates their historical references to social conflict beyond the fantasmatic frame of the screen.

Using its generic science fiction frame to present a utopian vision of the multicultural future in which sexual difference, however destabilized, remains sharply visible, the film attaches no particular significance to Miles Dyson's race. There is no doubt some progressive potential in this. But this film is centrally preoccupied with radical visibility. For example, at the moment when Dyson sees the terminator cut open his own "flesh" to expose the mechanical workings it covers, he immediately identifies his common interests with Sarah Connor. He makes his decision at a glance, for all intents and purposes. In the context of this preoccupation with visibility, even the narrative justification for Sarah Connor's murderous rage—that Dyson's single-minded scientific commitments will lead indirectly to nuclear apocalypse as a computer network takes over the world —cannot contain the political resonances of the image before us: an enraged white woman and her black victims. Finally, this scene condenses a variety of competing fantasies: the combative force of the woman warrior is directed at a middle-class African American man, who, just by the way, is ultimately responsible for the destruction of the world. Perhaps more important, this scene moves from the spectacle of the black man cowering in abject terror on his living room floor to a moment of alliance that unites him with Sarah Connor, her son, and the terminator. That is, the story that emerges within the utopian science fiction fantasy here rehearses several figures of contemporary identity politics as it aligns the white feminist with the black male professional.

T2 maps the negotiation toward this alliance in striking visual terms. After John Connor and the terminator have arrived to disrupt the stalemate between Connor and the family, where they are all immobilized in a tableau, the film cuts away to a different scene. In the kitchen, speech replaces physical violence. Connor presents her discursive version of the conflict that they must overcome to form an alliance. "Men like you," she begins, "built the hydrogen bomb." As Connor lays out her accusations, the camera moves in on Dyson's face, reinforcing her controlling position. Coming from out of frame, behind Dyson, her voice takes on the authority of a judge, or an analyst. But the cinematic gesture that establishes her authority also inscribes Dyson's wife's disappearance, as she is literally pushed out of frame while Dyson's face increasingly fills the screen in a prolonged reaction shot that writes the meaning of Connor's accusation on his face.

"Men like you . . . you think you're so creative," Connor continues. "You don't know what it's like to really create something, to feel it growing inside you. All you know how to create is death and destruction." At this point, her more sanguine and stable twelve-year-old son intervenes to mediate the conflict with a hilariously therapeutic comment: "Mom, Mom, we need to be a little more constructive here." The sharp edge of this comic intervention comes in its aggressive undercutting of the white woman's feminist speech, rendered ironic as this cyborg mother claims a "natural" female superiority based on reproductive power, which opposes the black man's apolitical technophilia, his scientific "disinterest."

"Men like you." This phrase ironically highlights Dyson's exceptional position. By certain visible and commonplace criteria, there are no men like him in this film. This may lead us to ask, as Lisa Kennedy does, why is this particular character black? Kennedy records her reaction to watching T2 with a predominantly black audience in an essay that concerns African American responses to mainstream popular culture: "who couldn't be thrown by the sight of an African-American scientist . . . being chastised . . . and not scream 'whoa!' ('Who? Black men?'), and then wonder why the collective body continued to root and respond after that moment. Is there some more compelling (though perhaps unconscious) logic than the simple, 'that's entertainment'?"[49] That more compelling logic, I want to speculate, has to do with the way racial difference and specificity get elided under a global gender conflict in Sarah Connor's speech. While the film forcefully attributes this elision to *her* obsessions, while it constructs her "feminist" moment in a speech we can find only laughable, it cannot so easily write off the meanings of racial difference. Despite this film's emphasis on its generic frame as science fiction fantasy, its image of a world in which racial difference *makes* no difference emerges in a field of contemporary cultural struggles where race is centrally embedded, if erratically acknowledged.

If we look at the *Alien* films alongside *T2*, an uncannily repetitive pattern begins to emerge. It begins to look like a prerequisite of science fiction films featuring female heroes that they form alliances with a self-sacrificing African American man. In *Alien 3*, Charles S. Dutton's character—clear-headed, disciplined, and unambiguously Sigourney Weaver's ally—directly echoes the Yaphet Kotto character in *Alien*. As Ripley's staunchest allies, and the only men to win her full trust and to sacrifice themselves for the collective good, these black characters most closely resemble the android ally, Bishop, who is spectacularly disabled in *Aliens* when the lower portion of his body is ripped off and cast into space, leaving him as nothing more than a talking torso that advises Ripley on her last battle.

At the same time, if Miles Dyson gets to be the embodiment of scientific arrogance, we cannot forget that he redeems himself precisely through his body's devastation as he sacrifices himself to allow the white nuclear family to escape intact. But *Terminator 2* quickly outruns this scenario, leaves it behind as a subplot, just as Connor and company leave Dyson behind at Cyberdyne headquarters. In a striking parallel, popular discussions of the film left racial difference behind in their fascination with the couple that Connor and the terminator form, a couple that condenses sexual difference into the cyborg-human divide. And here we might remember the paradox that Jonathan Goldberg observes about Miles Dyson's death: that his "destruction . . . also happens to mean that the future on which the films have built . . . no longer obtains" (196). So the film effectively grants Dyson the status of a key element, a centrally necessary component of the future threat that guarantees and generates the narrative. But the moment of his generative centrality is also the moment of his elimination. In a sense, then, the *Terminator* films outlive their own logic and shed the black male presence—whose necessity signs his death—leaving it behind as a shadowy residue.

Racial difference seems to make little difference in the film or in its reception. Miles Dyson's race is framed out of most critical discussions in favor, precisely, of a fuller focus on Linda Hamilton's bodily transformation. In favor, that is, of the spectacle of the combative female hardbody, the *white* female hardbody. No doubt such discussion succeeds in sanitizing the film of racial significance by assuming that its science fiction frame guarantees a pure and disinterested fantasy which generates and fixes the stable meanings of both bodies. At the same time, *T2* is also framed by its market position as a blockbuster, a category that increasingly defines itself through its address to "everyone," over against the "small," or independent, film that presumes a specific and differentiated segment of the audience.

This is the context in which some apparently unrelated questions come together, at the point where two such apparently dissimilar films as *T2* and *Thelma and Louise* begin to display some striking commonalities. What the violence of the debates about *Thelma and Louise*'s violence suggests is that our popular representations are themselves consumers of our collective wishes, anxieties, and fantasies. And, as consumers, they work upon ambivalence: the fear and exhilaration of fractured identifications, failures of difference and failures of identity alike, where pleasures are bound to aggression and threat. If violence and fantasy structures become such crucial popular categories of critical response to *Thelma and Louise,* but remain vacant categories with respect to *T2,* this must be because, by contrast, *Thelma and Louise*'s audience appears to be specified, anchored to a particular social location that remains a source of anxiety.

Equally important, why do white women's hardbodies seem to be propped on the "ghosts" of African American men? And why is such a connection so hard to register in critical response? This kind of propping depends on the filmwork's potential to evaporate social and historical referentiality in the displacement of one difference onto another, which is cast structurally as the "key" difference. This displacement should alert us to the mixed and ambiguous political effects of our popular representations, where figures of social and sexual ambivalence, of mixing or nondifferentiation, of misplaced, unstable, or "undecidable" identity, are all sites of erotic or eroticized intensity. In part because the culture continues to feel "race" as its greatest conditioning social divide, some of the aggressive intensity that charges this divide may be reassuringly siphoned off onto the sexual one.

In the context of popular debates that implicitly focus on the status of the psychical processes like identification and fantasy in representations which explore social differences, it is significant that feminism becomes a central object of discussion as well as the dominant culture's privileged interlocutor about these issues. Consequently, it becomes a matter of more than passing interest that such debates around fantasy in relation to material behaviors and practices, and around the relationship of identification to identity, are strikingly similar to ongoing feminist debates that are increasingly preoccupied with the issue of "feminist identity." At the very moments when we experience serious challenges—from diverse positions—to the political efficacy of gender identity as an organizing category, "feminist identity" emerges as the often implicit, and occasionally explicit, stake of both political and theoretical debate. On the progressive side, recent identity politics questions whether gender is ever really a sufficient ground for solidarity, since it is never independent of racial, ethnic, and sexual identity. But feminism's struggles to construct viable collective political identities while respecting the specific differences among them also find strong parallels in broader dominant cultural efforts to construct clearly bounded identities that manage antagonistic social differences by recoding them to bodies, making them fully visible and consolidated at recognizable sites.

Cultural struggle increasingly plays out as struggle over, and within, representations and their audiences, and it specifically plays out over objects that can "go both ways." [50] In a public context where the question of social representation has begun to overlap in the popular press with questions of access to cultural representation, as well as with the recent visibility of audience formations linked to community identity, feminist discussions of internal identity politics may entertain an indirect dialogue with the attention to spectatorship and audience that fascinates both the popular media and the entertainment industries that aim to profit from new audiences. In this context, feminist theory may well greet with a mixture of celebration and wariness the recent focus on female audiences and female spectators, because contemporary media attention to female audiences, as to feminism, tends to immobilize the volatile field of identity politics.

Feminist analyses, then, must respond by reconceiving and renegotiating questions of identification with the understanding that gendered identifications always entail racial ones as well. We can analyze these effects only by acknowledging the conflicts and contradictions that inhabit even our apparently resistant fantasies, just as we need to recognize the aggressive and violent components of our identifications. As we take pleasure in the recent visibility of fantasies about women's agency that move us, and that we can imagine authoring, we also begin to glimpse the costs, burdens, and pains that are bound up with that pleasure. As feminine subjects of fantasy begin more and more to produce representations for popular consumption, women are emerging in our collective imagination as the agents of culture and of fantasy and not just as their objects. Since these fantasies are complex and contradictory, and since they are embedded in a specific moment in a cultural history, this greater access to representational production will no doubt continue to expose the anxious and negative side of even our most exciting, progressive, or jubilant visions.

PART II   Ethnographies of the "White" Gaze

plores the ways that various incarnations of the auteur have rewritten the relationship of high art to popular culture in critical strategies characterized by sometimes "baffling mixture[s] of elitism and populism."[3] In this connection, "Lynch," despite his ultimately failed status as an auteur, nonetheless displays certain features that seem paradigmatic of auteurism's historical tendency to cut both ways. As Naremore has it: "auteurism always had two faces. It mounted an invigorating attack on convention, but it also formed canons and fixed the names of people we should study" (21).

Differing from previous moments in the history of auteurship in its more intense emphasis on style and its apparently diminished focus on history, tradition, and canon construction, the current interest in auteurs has nonetheless laid the groundwork for a certain filiation that can be traced from Lynch to Tarantino. No doubt this filiation, or legacy, extends to audience formations as well, especially in view of the ways that fandom tends to accompany contemporary production of the auteur. Equally important, however, the aesthetic and cultural effects that we find associated with Lynch's success may have constituted a definition of the auteur and of "style" itself that other independent filmmakers—the case represented here is Spike Lee's—might react against.

It seems to me that we cannot begin to examine—or even to watch— *Wild at Heart*, like *Blue Velvet* before it, without exploring the common terms of discussion that elide questions of race, class, and gender under a series of fascinations: with the auteur himself, with psychoanalytic resonances, with film-historical references, with urban ethnographic impulses, with collective nostalgia, and with cinematic special effects. Not coincidentally, I think, these fascinations, lures, and distractions are precisely the means by which *Blue Velvet* deflects attention from its misogyny, and *Wild at Heart* redirects our focus away from the combination of racism and misogyny that structures it. In other words, *Wild at Heart* seeks and imagines an audience that may accept its own unconsciously racist and sexist terms.[4]

Most of the critical response I examine rests on the assumption that "Lynch" is *representing* racism and misogyny rather than *enunciating* them himself. But this view depends on a confidence that we can establish a clear separation in this case between the film's point of view and that of its characters. This separation is problematic, since it is a central strategy in *Wild at Heart* to make those points of view alternately slip into coincidence and slide apart. Moreover, such a critical position also would imply that in our historical and cultural moment it could ever be possible to "represent" the discourse of racism or misogyny without, from time to time, speaking them directly. This would suggest, in turn, that there is a clearly defined "outside" to these discourses and that we can identify and occupy that outside. The response to Lynch, I want to argue, was symptomatic of our difficulty in analyzing such discursive problems. Part of Lynch's popularity might have depended on precisely the reassurance that he seems to offer about our individual ability to get outside racism or sexism. *Wild at Heart,* specifically, secures its reassurance that representing and enunciating racism are distinct by invoking categories of "fantasy," "style," and the "avant-garde." Consequently, I will treat the film as a center of circulation, both of the collective fantasies and anxieties it mobilizes and works over, and of the discourse of reception and audience formation that read it. A look at a few critical responses may suffice to make my point that the "Lynch-effect" involved the distraction of our gaze, and our investments, away from the referential and the analytical to fasten them on effects of style and on affective shock.

Movieline's Virginia Campbell begins her article on *Wild at Heart* by recounting an anecdote told her by a friend about a screening of *Blue Velvet* in New York City, where the auditorium began to fill with smoke. "But up on the screen," she writes, "Dennis Hopper, inhaling god knows what gas from his clear plastic mask, was in the middle of terrorizing Isabella Rossellini, screaming, 'Mommy! Baby wants to fuck!' with Kyle MacLachlan watching from the closet in Oedipal thrall." "Instead of stampeding for the doors like responsible New Yorkers," she continues, "the people in this audience were just sort of half-heartedly backing their way up the aisles, eyes fixed on the screen. And when no actual flames seemed to materialize, they all sat back down again."[5] In conclusion, this author asserts, "If you ask me, that's entertainment" (34). But I think we need to ask what "entertainment" means here, while bearing in mind that we are "entertained" by objects that are also "entertaining"—in the sense of maintaining, and inviting in—certain discourses and images that operate in wider social circulation. Furthermore, in some sense, while the film entertains us, we also "entertain" it, temporarily entering into its discourse in some fashion, taking up its images, its speech, and its fantasies in complex ways. In this case, the description of audience fascination reproduces Kyle MacLachlan's "Oedipal thrall," as if the author imagined that the audience "*entertained*" his fantasy structure, and the film's, as its own for a moment. But what if this "Oedipal thrall" is, finally, very comfortable because it offers an already known and commonly available framework, or dramatic structure, through which we may channel a whole set of other fantasies to be contained, or even exhausted, by it? A structural feature of all of Lynch's work, this "Oedipal thrall" seems to present one of the strongest points of fascination for critics and audiences.

Village Voice critic Georgia Brown's response to this enthralling effect is telling: "(Lynch shows he's stuck back in the 50s by making all his minorities into terrorizers.)," she writes parenthetically, and then goes on as follows: "It takes a psychoanalytic virgin like Lynch to place Oedipal desire and castration anxiety right up front. . . . *Wild at Heart* joins the boy's anxiety to a girl's by tapping into both the Gifford novel and that classic American on-the-road text, *The Wizard of Oz*." [6] Rhetorically, Brown's turn toward the superficial psychoanalytic fascinations of this film relegates its consistent use of black men as figures of menace, and specifically sexual menace, to the status of a mere manifestation of his regressive, not to say infantile, sensibilities.

Consequently, a 1950s nostalgia that must include a desire for a simpler time, a time when racial separation and hierarchy held fast, might appear almost as an oversight, an insignificant, though unfortunate, feature of a general and *aestheticized* infantilism. But the consistency of this conflation within *Wild at Heart* permits a sexual fascination/obsession to defuse or erase a racial one. At the same time, "psychoanalysis" here really refers only to personal and subjective anxieties (the boy's fears about castration, and, most certainly, adult female sexuality), and thus it absorbs all analytical energies at the expense of the social and political register. "Psychoanalysis" here becomes a marker of consumer style and taste. In other words, you have to know its basic terms to see how transparent the film is, how artificial and artful is its "innocence." The film functions, then, to differentiate audiences into insiders and outsiders, the "hip" readers and the "uncool" ones. In Brown's reading, the transparent psychoanalytic interpretation also contributes to, and perhaps guarantees, the film's sophistication, as expressed in its ironic distance from its characters, its "content," and its context. It is the "psychoanalytically" sophisticated posture that allows the film discourse, and the audience in the know, to register the "perversity" of the ordinary, as the film parades its own manufactured "guilty" pleasures, which are already read, interpreted, and accounted for.

However, the surface veneer of psychoanalytic thematics looks quite different if we read those thematics through the filmic details. In at least three powerful sequences *Wild at Heart* rehearses a structuring oedipal triangulation. In each case, however, specific details emerge to complicate, if not to overturn, that oedipalized account of the scene. The film's opening sequence, its first scene, presents a horrifying murder that comes to act as the film's "primal scene." This scene, coded as the prehistory to the romance plot, and which launches the film as a road movie, begins with a shot of the elaborate vaulted ceiling of a ballroom or public hall. The music, diegetically set up as dance music, and the clothes of the assembled crowd at the top of the stairs fail to provide us with any temporal cues.[7] As the music in this first sequence places us in a kind of timeless, generalized prehistory, this seems to become the film's prevailing temporality.[8] A similarly striking auditory effect characterizes Quentin Tarantino's *Pulp Fiction,* whose cinematic universe unfolds in a temporality determined by a soundtrack that weaves a complex musical web overlaying sound from the 1950s to the 1990s, almost as if to produce the present as a memory of itself, beyond history, in the film's projected temporal utopia.

Bob Ray Lemon, the one black person in this crowd, approaches Sailor Ripley (Nicholas Cage) and threatens him with a knife. The rest of the sequence consists of Sailor's brutal assault on the man, first smashing his face repeatedly on the bannister, and then bashing his skull on the marble floor until it gives way and his brain spills out.[9] This murder, which figures as *spectacle* rather than event, because it falls before any narrative, is structured in such a way as to make Bob Ray someone else's agent; he has been sent by Marietta Pace (Diane Ladd), the mother of Lula Pace (Laura Dern), Sailor's girlfriend.

Marietta presides over the murder; her look controls it as much as any look does. Camera work here dictates that "no one" is supposed to really see this scene, since the camera and editing apparently construct a movement across points of view—from Lula's in the middle of the staircase looking down on Sailor and Lemon below her, back to Marietta's at the top of the stairs. However, this movement, which catches all of the figures in medium long shot, finally produces a detachment from subjective point of view. Lula's and Marietta's looks are coded as reactions because the camera is riveted in fascination on the action from a point of view that does not correspond at all to either woman's. So sharply does it diverge from them, in fact, that the reaction shots are the only artifice holding all figures in the same space. But this is a space in which their relation to each other is completely uncertain until the end when Marietta is established as "on top of the situation."[10]

Marietta's centrality sets up the film's explicitly central drama—that of the alternately menacing and abject mother who relentlessly and brutally attempts to separate the lovers. Although Lemon threatens Lula on his way to kill Sailor (he fondles her on his way down the stairs), the cinematic inscription and subsequent narrative interpretation of the scene produce a different triangulation, one that is presented as a *discovery* of the secret "truth" underlying the events. It is Marietta's gaze, and her anxious, aroused facial expression, to which the camera continually returns our suspended point of view (with occasional shifts to views of Lula's anguished face). But finally, when Sailor looks up from the foot of the staircase to point a bloodied, accusing finger, it is clear that Marietta has been positioned as the controlling gaze, the determining force of the scene, since she watches from above.

Compositionally, the film inscribes a triangle with Marietta at its pinnacle—as the central focus of Sailor's and Lula's looks. Her own gaze bifurcates the scene as it cuts between these figures. We watch the murder from a point of view independent of hers as well as of Sailor's and of Lula's. And this is the space of spectator anxiety in several registers. Our gaze is unanchored to any point of view but the camera's agitated, disorienting mobility. At the same time, we experience the discomfort of being brought in too close and from an uncomfortable angle. We watch, with a camera placed nearly at floor level, as Sailor smashes Lemon's head on the marble. Any anxiety about how much we will witness as Lemon's head repeatedly descends out of view is quickly dispelled in revulsion when the camera pulls back to show us more than we "should" see—his exposed brain. But it is precisely this shock—our affective, bodily reaction to the abject body—that forces our look away. Such a forcing of the look, however, also forcibly deflects our attention; we can easily forget the terms at work here.

Our revulsion from this abject body echoes throughout the film. Most strikingly, it is repeated with an almost justificatory, legitimating, and aestheticizing symmetry when Bobby Peru's head is blown off. (The film renders this sight ridiculous through excess: the head flies several feet high, and its flight is intercut with the spectacle of the two feed-store employees slipping on a bloody floor as they search for the severed hand that a dog carries away). Such a symmetry produces a pattern that helps to "aestheticize" the opening scene, to qualify it within the Lynch aesthetics, which is characterized by disgust, coupled with pseudotransgression. Georgia Brown describes these aesthetic effects: "From scene to scene, in that candid, child-like way of his, Lynch amazes us with how *far* he's will-

ing to go. But he just seems like a kid" (58). Whether she is being ironic or
not, Brown seems willing to accept that the simplest of "Freudian nightmares," in her words, produces significant transgressiveness, but without
making it clear what transgressiveness means, what value we assign it.
As it turns out, most of these "transgressions," "goings too far," seem to
be red herrings that distract us from other references and from the overdetermining elements and context.

Besides acting as a Lynch signature, "shock" here short-circuits analysis, which may account for the general silence about this scene in critical
response. Before going on to examine the function of shock itself, however, it is worth examining the readings that the film smuggles in, and the
ones it occludes, through its pattern of shocks. Bob Ray Lemon's murder
is "motivated" retrospectively. He is Marietta's sexual emissary, as well as
her homicidal one, we later learn. Apparently, Marietta's murderous rage
is unleashed when Sailor refuses to, in her words, "fuck Lula's Mama"
in the bathroom at the dance. But Marietta has rewritten the event so
that Lemon can claim he has been asked to kill Sailor for trying to "fuck
Lula's Mama" rather than for refusing to do so. While constructing the
mother as the most conventional figure of woman as a sexual menace,
the film adds an additional charge. A white man is forced to kill the black
male agent of "Mama's" murderous sexual lust. This merely reverses a
historically conventional figure in the dominant culture's collective fantasy structure in which white men struggle with black men over white
women. So another fantasy is imbricated with the oedipal one. Yet this
sequence, along with the flashbacks that "read" and interpret it for us, ac-
complishes a complete erasure of the racial dimension under the oedipal
or sexual one. This erasure has a remainder, however: the brutal murder
of a black man by a white man is surreptitiously charged to the white
woman's account.

In the first flashback to the bathroom scene, a flashback coded as Marietta's, we learn that Sailor has seen something—perhaps something that
he should not have seen—between Lula's parents. As it will turn out, this
is a reference to Marietta's and Santos's murder of Marietta's husband.
Indeed, this is the transgression that Sailor will pay for, along with the
competing transgression of not "fucking" mama. Interestingly, the scene
between Marietta and Sailor in the bathroom—the generative incident—
is repeated in a series of flashbacks alternately attributed to each of them,
but always from the same point of view (that of a third party watching
them), as if their memories were identical. The prevailing subjectivity

established here belongs to the film's discourse itself. But the cinematic violence unleashed is filmically attributed to the sexuality of the phallic mother. Within this narrative logic that woman, who acts to punish Sailor, is herself punished cinematically—her body is progressively rendered more abject.

More significantly, the way that the film articulates this murder sequence as its own antecedent tells us a good deal about its overall structure. The opening sequence is separated from the succeeding ones by one of the film's many references to *The Wizard of Oz* (Victor Fleming, 1939), one of its competing subtexts. We see a shot of a hand, its fingernails painted bloody black, passing over a crystal ball. Subsequent fetishistic attentiveness to Marietta's fingernails, along with her repeated figuration as the Wicked Witch, will encode this as an image of her hand.

This break in the film, preceding Sailor and Lula's reunion and the beginning of the road trip that structures the narrative, casts the first sequence as a primal scene, the generative event. And this event is motivated, as will be seen throughout, by Sailor's having seen what he should not see. But his doing so must lead us to ask about the symmetry between his position and ours, since we, too, have just seen something that we should not have seen. This parallel, however, is embedded in the film's general tendency to link sex and violence in a particular erotics of shock.

Repeated rhymes, some of which amount to fetishes, will inscribe that complex structure at the expense of other content, draining all attention and investment into it. For example, the characteristically overloud and parodically intrusive musical soundtrack that augments the visual tension of the opening sequence and repeats in the first love scene between Lula and Sailor serves to bind the two scenes together. According to Michel Chion, music has a significant spatio-temporal mobility: "All music in a film can function like the spatiotemporal equivalent of a railroad switch. This is to say that music enjoys the status of being a little freer of barriers of time and space than the other sound and visual elements. . . . Another way to put it is that music is cinema's *passe-muraille,* capable of instantly communicating with the other elements of the action" (81).

In a startling match of sex and violence as one scene musically bleeds over into another, the film erases or evaporates the racial determinant in the opening murder before we even get to ask about the status of this gratuitous detail. Consequently, we need to step back from the narrative to ask: why should Bob Ray Lemon be black?[11] What is the meaning of his race for the scene and for the film? In other words, we need to invert the problem of the primal scene, of seeing what one should not see, in order to ask what we have not seen that we should have. And this question will emerge again and again, alongside the eroticized violence and the problem of sexual difference in the film. But it will emerge to one side, in the narrative logic, as well as in the critical response.

In his *New York Times* review, Vincent Canby passes over the first scene, telling us only that "Sailor Ripley is a gentle young man who has just served 22 months and 18 days for manslaughter, having killed a man who attacked him with a knife."[12] Instead, Canby emphasizes, as most critics do, the striking Lynch style: "David Lynch's work is all a matter of disorienting scale, of emphases that are out of kilter. . . . It's the old fun-house principle. Nightmares are made real. Without moving, one seems to plummet through pitch darkness. The response in a fun house is a pleasurably scary physical sensation. The Lynch films go several steps farther: nothing in life is fixed. All reality is relative." Here again is the rhetoric of daring and risk, of "going too far." Equally important, a general sense that "all reality is relative" seems to exhaust the meaning of the scene. Somehow the wacky, out-of-scale formal and technical articulation of the film expunges all referentiality. But is this a formal issue? Why might we be so taken with the "out-of-scale," unless it acts as a means of framing the most vicious fantasies in a manageable form? If we crave disorienting perspectives, these perspectives seem to be political as well as visual.

It may be part of the "Lynch-effect," dependent as it is on a certain "uncanniness," that much of the discourse surrounding the film mimes its diegetic mood and moves. The homicidal outburst is reduced to pure narrative motivation, or pure spectacle, whose overdetermining fantasies disappear. Writing in *Time,* Richard Corliss describes another version of primarily affective response to *Wild at Heart:* "Heads splatter, skulls explode, biker punks torture folks for the sheer heck of it, and a pair of loopy innocents find excitement in a side trip to hell. Pretty much like *Blue Velvet.* Yes, it's different, but the same kind of different; Lynch could no longer shock by being shocking."[13] Claiming for Lynch and vicariously for the spectator a kind of immunity to "shock" through its mastery, Corliss locates these violent fantasies under the category of the bizarre. The prevailing impulse of the film and its viewer, then, is a kind of aestheticized perversity, but without context. It is as if by reading *Wild at Heart* within an auteurist circuit, we could reduce the "shocks" to mere aesthetic and technical effects toward which one would maintain a cool connoisseurship in such a way that these effects become signatures—signatures that refer only to the artistic process.

Even as politicized a critic as the *Nation*'s Stuart Klawans passes over the racial character of the opening violence: "The proceedings get started with a bang. Immediately after the credits, there's an uncommonly bloody killing, which lands Sailor in jail." [14] Somehow, the uncommon bloodiness of the murder comes to blot out all other features. Perhaps this is because our popular cinema has been glutted with bloody murders of black men? Klawans, however, makes a point of his uneasiness about Lynch, but in reference to the later "rape" scene between Bobby Peru and Lula. He describes his own viewing at the end of the excruciatingly long shot, where the camera roves along Lula's body in close-up, as Bobby Peru demands that she say the words he repeats, "Fuck me": "Then Bobby left. He had shown his power over Lula; and Lynch had demonstrated much the same thing to me. Once more, he had proved he could push my buttons, and once more he'd turned out to have no good reason for pushing them" (286). Taking a less than "cool" position, this critic identifies a major source of resistance. A spectator who feels assailed by the film's vicious images may not read them as empty and may instead question the ideological function of such forcefully violent effects.

Where Canby is seduced by "disorienting perspectives," and Corliss by the shocks that do not touch him, Virginia Campbell celebrates the oedipal lure: "Most important, Lynch gave *Wild at Heart* his signature psychosexual kick. He transformed Lula's mother, Marietta, into a character who parallels Dennis Hopper's Frank Booth in *Blue Velvet*" (38). Stressing the film's obsession with sexual difference, Campbell continues: "*Wild at Heart* plays as a kind of Pink Velvet. . . . It's the feminine side of the great, horrible adventure of facing one's sexual nature and winning liberation from the parents inside one's head" (38). Campbell's response is revealing. She is certainly on to something in noting that one of Lynch's signatures is a "psychosexual kick." That signature is related to the one that Georgia Brown emphasizes in saying that "he just seems like a kid"—a kind of regressive infantilism that is related more obscurely to the signature which Canby picks out, "the out-of-scale" world of Lynch's images.

Lynch's fascinating and often astonishing scale, which exaggeratedly amplifies and reduces the objects it treats with obsessive attention, operates to oedipalize even visual perspective. Cinematic perspective—the timing and relation of image to frame—is one strategy for oedipalizing the visual field along with the narrative, offering the spectator an uneasily and unevenly infantile point of view. At the same time, part of that strategy's appeal is its combination of a familiar scenario—the family romance, which contains the violent excesses, at particular remove, in a ready-made fantasy—with a deliberate and exhaustive fetishization of image and technique.

When we read *Wild at Heart* against *Blue Velvet,* as Campbell does, however, it becomes hard to remain fixated, as these films themselves are, on the formal organization of narrative and image around an adolescent replay of an oedipal drama of sexual differentiation and separation, because their violent force draws on much more than adolescent fantasy. Indeed, the adolescent fantasy structure, reinfantilized, is a container for a more vicious subtext. Part of the thrill of Lynch's films, it seems, depends on our accepting the films' proposition that this oedipal structure is the frame, the container, and the content. To accept this proposition, however, is to risk foreclosing any sociohistorical referentiality, any reading of the specific competing fantasies articulated within that structure.

In fact, the ruse of these films is to present what is already manifest as if it were latent. Discussing Lynch's films, Sean French contends: "In each case, the force and challenge of the film has come from Lynch's ability to probe beneath the surface, to expose the dark irrational passions above which the mundane world is just a facade." [15] On the contrary, I think, one might say that *Wild at Heart* works to present the manifest as the revealed latent content (the oedipal scenario), while simultaneously obscuring, as a kind of latency, something that should be more evident: the racial overdeterminations of its violence, the connection between race and gender that is played out in its "primal scenes."

At first glance, I think, the "psychosexual kick" of *Blue Velvet* and *Wild at Heart* rehearses anxieties about the breakdown of the paternal metaphor in contemporary culture (by which I mean Lynch's lifetime, the fifties through the eighties). But on a closer look,[16] the parallel between Marietta and Frank Booth breaks down in a couple of ways. Booth is the negative, nightmare father-baby within a network of fathers, "good" and "bad." The Lynch "signature" ambivalence, the good object/bad object structure, in *Wild at Heart* provides no figure to counter Marietta. There is no good mother here.[17] So the ambivalence breaks down, as the mother becomes the agent of destruction of the paternal metaphor.[18]

Furthermore, as we will see, the repeated figures of the primal scene that structure this film produce a development firmly bound to the child's point of view and, more properly, the son's. After all, the central and deadly conflict there is between Marietta and *Sailor,* not Marietta and Lula. The apparent parallel with *Blue Velvet* breaks down because the earlier film's array of father figures educate, coincide with, and align with Jeffrey's perspective such that he becomes a figure for split perspective and internalized ambivalence, where the paternal voice enters into dialogue with the son's. In contrast, Marietta is a figure who incorporates both the battered mother and the bad father of *Blue Velvet.* That thoroughly and monstrously negative figure, product of infantile fantasies, she is both the abject victim (abjected by the camera, just as is Isabella Rossellini's Dorothy Valens in *Blue Velvet*), and the violent, devouring mother (absorbing the frightening energies of Frank Booth). We view her, moreover, from a spectator position inscribed as infantilized. We often see Marietta from below, as in the first scene with Johnny Farragut in her living room, where she crawls across the floor, parodically catlike, and into Johnny's lap. Later, when she vomits in the bathroom, the camera is placed very low, by her feet, as if we had just crawled to the door to spy on her. When Marietta talks on the phone with Johnny, or with Lula, her hysterical outbursts are shot in close-up, and the camera alternates between low angles and straight frontal shots. Her face is frightening in part because this framing casts it as monumentally huge: she is dilated, enlarged to monstrous proportions. At the same time, this gesture is ambivalent; even as it constructs Marietta as a menacing figure, its overclose scrutiny of her face and body does a kind of violence to her.

Significantly, Campbell's description of the film as offering "the feminine side of the great, horrible adventure of facing one's sexual nature and winning liberation from the parents inside one's head" seems to be way off the mark. This is exactly what the film is not about. First, Laura Dern's character functions the same way in both *Blue Velvet* and *Wild at Heart,* as a support for the hero, the son who is locked in combat with one parent figure; this is not about her struggle at all. But, second, while Lynch's films are all about struggles with "the parents inside one's head," they are about protecting and preserving those internal imagoes, internal censorships. Consequently, they offer the lure of protection from history and politics by imagining that everything comes down to a private psychosexual adventure, or drama. It is all in our heads.

If we take *Wild at Heart* at its word—that the oedipal drama determines the narrative development, providing both its source and its resolution in the answer to its mystery—then we need to focus on the primal scene structure that holds the film together. These scenes and the connections among them are the net that gathers and contains the film's random forces, that articulates together a series of repetitions of apparently arbitrary details, which then do not require an account, into a kind of resolution. This is not, in fact, the secret. The film's lure is to promise a secret center, but this center is only the one that it pretends to uncover. Our work, on the contrary, begins where the film leaves off, when we try to unpack some of the baggage loaded into this oedipal valise.

At the exact temporal center of *Wild at Heart,* and consequently at the heart of the matter—of its matter—is a scene that resonates with the opening sequence. This segment offers the film's second homicide, the murder of Johnny Farragut. Its psychological tension, built on sadism and suspense, about how much we will actually have to witness, as well as its specific details, reproduces certain fantasies from the opening sequence. Thus, these two sequences become propped on one another. This scene's location, its thematics, and its unaccountable collision of details make it emerge as one of the film's "dirty secrets," which links it, in turn, to a series of primal scenes.

In a film that insists on lining its characters up along a brutally simple and clear dividing line between the "good," though wayward but ultimately innocent, and the "perverts," those whose violence is always sexual and whose sex is always violent, Johnny Farragut (Harry Dean Stanton) is Marietta's "good" suitor, and gangsterish Santos, Mr. Reindeer's associate, is her "bad" boyfriend. But the agents of Johnny's death are a black man and a white woman with an artificial leg (played by Grace Zabriskie, who also played Laura Palmer's mother in "Twin Peaks"). This mutilated white woman, incoherently presented as a figure somehow connected to voodoo, encourages her black lover, Reggie, to kill Johnny quickly so that they can make love. Indeed, the eerily claustrophobic scene incorporates Johnny's murder as a kind of foreplay, making him a sacrificial victim in their lovemaking ritual.

Since the scene culminates with Johnny's being made to see evidence of Marietta's sexual betrayal with Marcello Santos, this murder recalls the explicit primal triangulation of the story, the one that has caused the murder of Lula's father, which Sailor has accidently witnessed: Marietta, her husband, Clay, and Santos. Johnny's murder is orchestrated by the woman who commands the two men (Reggie and a white voyeur, who remains behind Johnny, looking over his shoulder the whole time), so that the scene's tension, like the murder itself, appears to be controlled by the woman's voice, keeping time and repeating the phrase, "Fuck me now,

Reggie." That phrase comes to coincide with the command to kill. This scene, which contains some of the most extreme close-ups of film, holds Reggie and Juana (who is overcoded, or, one might say, overloaded with "difference," given her Cajun-Creole accent and Latina name) tightly framed as they passionately kiss.

This sequence opens with a close-up of Juana's face, established from Johnny's point of view, as she leans in to kiss him on his taped-over mouth. The trace of her lipstick on this white tape heightens the resonance of this image of the mouth as wound (an image that is obsessively repeated throughout the film), and the scene's emphasis on orality, sucking, and consuming. We then see a close-up of Reggie and Juana kissing; their faces are smeared with makeup, hers with dark makeup, his with white, as if each of them had rubbed off some of the other's color.

Choreographed by cross-cutting between close-ups of Johnny, Juana, and Reggie, where the frame gradually closes in on Johnny's face and maps Juana's distance from the action by framing her in medium shot, then in medium long shot, this sequence inscribes Johnny's face—and his gaze—between the bodies of the lovers. Meanwhile, it establishes Juana as the terrifying phallic dominatrix: we see her framed with her cane between her legs. Her cries, "Fuck me now, Reggie," control Johnny's execution by a gunshot to the head, and they seem to produce the temporal and spatial rhythms of the scene. In these respects, hers is a near-perfect double of Marietta's position in the opening scene. It is the film's pretense, then, that she is Marietta's stand-in. But since this scene opens up the central fantasy structure of the film, I want to suggest that Marietta may be the stand-in or screen for Juana—the excessive and ambivalent figure of the phallic woman, the mutilated woman, who is also a figure of ethnic and racial exoticism and difference.

Our spectator position moves into alignment with Johnny's as he watches Juana work herself into an obscene erotic frenzy: "I'm too fucking hot now. I'll kill him myself. Fuck me now." At this point, we see Reggie's face, monumentalized by a low angle, as he moves behind Johnny and puts the gun to his head. Johnny, in close-up, gazes sightlessly directly into the camera. Then, just before the shot ends, bringing on a fadeout, we see Juana again. We are lined up with Johnny as witnesses to this bizarre foreplay, witnesses not to his death, but to his last sight—the sadistic, lust-crazed woman who dominates the violent force of the black man and the entire scene. Once more, the black man is the agent of violence that is charged to the account of a white woman.

The parallel between Johnny and Sailor is explicit, since each has witnessed an illicit act committed by an outlaw couple. In Sailor's case, this is Marietta and Santos murdering Lula's father, and in Johnny's case, it is the lovemaking of the interracial couple. At the same time, this equation of the two establishes one of the film's controlling equations in which sex and murder (murder of the "good father" and the little boy) are linked. It is the "good father" who is supposed to protect the little boy by keeping such outlaw couples apart, and his failure unleashes all of the film's violence (we remember that Sailor has had little "parental guidance," which accounts for his light sentence for the murder of Bob Ray Lemon). At the same time, this primal scene produces a corollary effect that sets Johnny up as the voyeuristic little boy catching his parents making love and paying for it with his life.

But it is also this scene and its resonances with the beginning and end of the film that focus our attention on the film's regressive center. *The Wizard of Oz* references, one might say, are a kind of distracting marker, signifying nostalgia and regression but as a false trail. If the second "primal scene" retroactively reads the first one and emphasizes its link between white women's lust and black men's violent power, the third image of a "primal scene," the film's closing sequence, seems designed to recast the first two in a more reassuring fantasy.

In this last sequence we watch Sailor and Lula on the car hood as he serenades her, but we watch from the point of view of their six-year-old son, Pace, through the windshield, or wind*screen*. One of the things this scene does is reinstantiate the "screen," the windscreen, through which we have watched Sailor and Lula throughout this road trip; this is both a screen and a shield. When the couple is finally reunited, our point of view seems to be matched with that of little Pace, who is now positioned to look up the mother's dress. But the camera's height is subtly displaced. In the shot-reverse shot structure here, we first look at Pace from above, from Sailor and Lula's point of view, and then we see the three of them from a low angle. But they are framed in a medium shot, from the waist up. Another cut immediately frames them in medium close-up. In keeping with the film's fetishistic economy, we do not get caught looking up the good mama's skirt. Sexuality is displaced upward, to the singing mouth; the parental couple's erotic connection is discreetly sublimated in song. The camera averts our glance, cuts the mother's sex out of frame, and provides this subtle dislocation as an escape hatch that we share with the six-year-old boy, whose point of view oversees the film's narrative closure. In some way, this six-year-old's point of view is the symbolic home that we finally reach; it is the home base of our gaze, the home of the film's gaze, and, figuratively, the source of these fantasies. Consequently, the whole film discourse may be retroactively and ironically attributed to this child, its infantile fantasies accounted for by him.

As unaccountably as in the two previous sequences, and in a way that tightens their connection, men of color make a cameo appearance as the final threat to the central couple, but with this difference. In the final sequence, men of color do not operate as the violent agents of a woman's sexual desire. Instead, the sexual desire of the *good* woman and mother provides Sailor with a refuge from struggle, violence, and possibly death. When Sailor abandons the reconstituted family, leaving Lula and Pace in the car, he is quickly surrounded by a large group of young men, carefully selected, it seems, to provide a vast range of "nonwhite" figures—black, Latino, and Asian. He reacts to their presence by demanding: "What do you faggots want?" This provokes a beating that ends abruptly with the intervention of the "good" witch. *Wizard of Oz* references thus intervene again to help wrap up the film, to recast its fantasies as benign and comic, since Sailor wakes from unconsciousness sporting a cartoonishly grotesque broken nose, a ludicrous phallic reference that will lend irony to his final song, "Love Me Tender," since it undercuts the Elvis allusion by deforming Sailor's face.

In its own ironic way, the film has provided us with the perfect alibi in Pace, because our temporary acceptance of his point of view must function to ironize our attitude toward all of the identificatory postures that the film offers us, to give our gaze a certain distance. This last scene reverses a central organizing principle of the film, which seems to be working on the question of what infantile fantasies would look like if they could be acted out with adult agency.[19] Ultimately, this fantasy seems to be the source of the film's egregious violence, as well as its justification. This principle is reversed, and symbolically disclaimed or disavowed, in the last scene where all these adult fantasies are finally given back to the child, cinematically attributed to him. This is the payoff, our reward for previous punishments directed to our guilty gaze, which has watched the rape-seduction of Lula, the murder of Bob Ray Lemon, and the love-making that has led to Johnny's death. But what fantasies are domesticated and defused as they are placed in the safe container of infantile fantasy and desire? And why are these fantasies consistently associated with race, with black men's connection to white women's "perverted" desires?

Why does it seem that black men have become the father that the boy wants to kill to get to mom, or the failed father who, instead of protecting the little boy from mom's monstrous desire, abets her attacks on the son? This is what the film tries to screen.

In the choreography of violence that characterizes *Wild at Heart,* the scene of Johnny Farragut's murder is fraught with eroticized tension that is produced not only thematically, but cinematically, by the structure of interruption—cross-cutting that suspends the action, freezes it, holds us up in anxiety. The scene is built of internal cross-cuttings among close-ups and parallel editing that links it with a sequence of Sailor and Lula's progress through Texas. Violence is displaced back and forth between this closed room and the open road, where Sailor and Lula come upon an accident whose one survivor (Sherilyn Fenn, from "Twin Peaks") dies after an incoherent conversation with them. Like so many of the apparently peripheral images that litter the roadside of this story, this battered young woman is one that most critics cite as memorable for the uneasiness it creates. The dying woman's frantic scratching at her bloody hair and scalp (typically magnified by the amplified soundtrack here) works effectively to make viewers' skin crawl. Like a series of other uneasy images that stand forth for their "weirdness" or "repulsiveness," this one takes on an autonomy from the narrative; it emerges as free-standing. Autonomous though it is, this image resonates with other, equally creepy ones. Part of the capacity of these images to unnerve comes from Lynch's characteristic exploitation of sound, amplifying particular details, what would normally register as background noises, to saturate the ambience. In this sense, he treats noise as he does music, like the Elvis songs.[20] Since it occurs in a sequence that intervenes to interrupt the narrative of Johnny's death, this spectacular scene becomes frozen as an image fragment; it performs like a fetish. And the film's narrative stutters along in uneasy parallel with a network of fetish-images that operate the way obscene roadside billboards might, or, to keep within the film's metaphorics, like hideous accidents, to interrupt, punctuate, or even produce a detour in the trips of passing motorists.

So much for the form of such images. What of their content? Many of them, especially the ones generated in this scene, link up with one or more of the film's subtexts, those "random" details that most critics read as contributing to the ambient "weirdness" while producing no pertinent meanings. This failure of analysis, of course, seems itself to be fetishistic in its refusal to *look further,* to look beyond the surface.

For instance, we can reconstruct a subtext around the scene where Sailor and Lula attempt to help the female accident victim as she stumbles around insisting that "her mother is going to kill her" and demanding that they find her purse, her comb, her lipstick. This scene offers an ironic invocation of a murderous mother, like Marietta, who may kill the children, and it concludes with a special Lynch smirk. As blood gurgles out of her mouth, the dying woman murmurs, "Get my lipstick. It's in my purse." The blood trickling out of a mouth painted blood-red produces an obscene visual and verbal pun that connects to a series of image fetishes—Johnny's taped mouth, Lula's and Marietta's ever-changing lipstick colors. Most pertinent perhaps, the scene echoes Marietta's mouth and nails, objects to which the film pays as much obsessive attention as this viciously parodied southern suburban matron pays to coordinating her lip and nail color. The verbal echo here is based on Marietta's interdiction on Johnny Farragut's kiss: "No tongue. My lipstick." The visual one is related to the scene of Marietta's greatest abjection. Having smeared her face and hands with blood-red lipstick, Marietta dissolves into a hysterical attack after a phone call to Farragut. This sequence ends with Marietta lying on the bathroom floor, wearing Wicked Witch shoes, and vomiting. As a final gesture of feminine abjection, the film presents a medium close-up of Marietta's blood-red lips dripping with vomit.

This image resonates with a whole series of sullied, bruised Lynch women—like Dorothy Valens battered and naked on the lawn in *Blue Velvet; Twin Peaks'* hysterical, screaming mother; and the catatonic, battered girl coming out of the woods naked the day after Laura Palmer's body is found.[21] It should be amply clear by now that Lynch hates women's bodies; his camera is kindest to the dead female body and most vicious to the maternal one. The female bodies most admired by the camera are those of dead young women, like Laura Palmer, or the accident victim in *Wild at Heart.* And it always admires them from a distance that allows the gaze to study an unmarked, unflawed carapace of a surface, where blood appears as an explicitly decorative, aestheticizing effect. By contrast, Laura's mother, Marietta, and Dorothy Valens are abject.

It would be convenient to imagine Lula as a corrective, or counterweight, to Marietta in *Wild at Heart,* as innocently sexual, as embodying healthy desire and nondestructive passion. But the film's strict binarism dictates that women are bound to body and therefore to a menace that needs to be sadistically mastered, punished, and contained. Lula's body is treated as sadistically as Marietta's, but in a more sanitized manner. She is the exhibitionist, parading in lingerie, or pinned down for the camera's lingeringly excessive scrutiny of her body. This movement culminates in her rape-seduction by Bobby Peru, where Peru becomes the camera's stand-in, takes the rap for the camera's gaze, so to speak. The female body's presentation as abject or adored object in this film admits no in-between. The space between here is disembodied—occupied by men, and dead women.[22]

The roadside accident scene is structurally pivotal to the film, for it signals an acceleration of the film's progressively intensifying fetishism, organized around women. Women are constructed as both subjects and objects of fetishism (as in the scene before the accident), and the camera's fetishism increasingly takes on a degrading, punishing function as the female body is treated as object of disgust and aggression. Every detail seems to contribute to this economy, from the chorus line of three excessively obese women who appear gratuitously to dance in revealing lingerie at the motel in Big Tuna, to the clever verbal match that joins narrative segments when the film fades out on Johnny's murder to pick up Sailor and Lula entering Big Tuna.

On the back of the fish-shaped sign that welcomes visitors to Big Tuna, the words "Fuck You" have been scratched.[23] First, we see this sign from Sailor and Lula's point of view, but a few shots later it returns to center frame, with no mediating gaze. This is another Lynch signature—an aside as direct address. That strange, dilated image, one which the camera arrests in a characteristic Lynch pause, matches directly with Juana's injunction to "Fuck me." This match must be taken together with the other obvious echo, Lula's humiliation by Bobby Peru in the rape-seduction scene. Bobby and the camera avidly examine Lula's body—he tactilely; the camera, and spectators, visually. Bobby's offer, it should be remembered, is that he will leave Lula alone if she will just say, "Fuck me." This uncomfortably long scene is marked by a particularly loud soundtrack: Bobby's voice ventriloquizing the demand he wants to hear: "Fuck me." In a particular twist of obscenity, he wants to make her say his words. Figuratively, saying his words, Lula is made to eat his words. The metaphor of consumption is not out of place here. The camera repeatedly returns to close-ups of their open mouths, to her panting, and to Bobby's decaying teeth—a spectacularly revolting detail that reads as both a special effect and a prosthesis.

In this case, the demand "Fuck me, fuck me," is really a verbal gesture of aggression and deflection that should be read: "Fuck you." Coupled with what we have seen written on the screen, framed and held up for us, we can read a powerful subtext of aggression toward the audience in all of these actions. That is, the audience is aligned with Lula in a masochistic position. This alliance is true of the opening scene as well, where we read our own horror expressed on Lula's face. And it may be precisely this masochistic posture that offers another alibi to the spectator. If we are punished for what we see *by* what we see, if we are victims, too, of disgust and revulsion, then we *pay* for our sight.[24] But there is more to this viewing cost, because we experience our bodies at these moments. We start, or shudder, avert our eyes, gasp involuntarily—all symptoms of helplessness, loss of control, and of the body and its affective responses prevailing over the intellectual, analytical, and discursive responses that we might have. One is allowed, then, temporarily, to fall away from the film's discourse, to refuse any identification, any address. These moments offer themselves as eroticized thrills because they are experienced as powerful *bodily* reactions.[25] The pretense of "eroticism," then, in some way excuses the image. Cheap thrills, these are, because we feel that we have paid for them on delivery.

This is part of the effect that allows Stuart Klawans to argue that Lynch's films are both empty and cynical. "*Wild at Heart* . . . is not only lopsided and brilliant but utterly cynical as well. That's a striking conjunction, given the way Lynch's work has been received. . . . So why don't people just say that "Twin Peaks," *Wild at Heart,* and *Blue Velvet* are cheap thrills in expensive wrappers? . . . Whenever you hear the words *disturbing, transgressive,* and *subversive* tossed around, whenever rules are supposedly broken and authorities challenged, you may assume you're in avant-garde territory. You're among the institutional avant-garde when the transgressors have MFA degrees from good schools and are on a first-name basis with at least three arts administrators" (286). What we need to ask here, I think, is exactly how and why this works and what audience the film addresses and constructs. What does it mean to be seduced by these fantasies that are clearly dependent on a sense of distance rather than identification?

The transactions that Lynch's films offer us are organized by a set of internal mechanisms for mobilizing shock effects and then containing them; they offer clearly manufactured traumas. These mechanisms are twofold: a kind of internal censorship entails the preservation of a superego figure, paternal authority instantiated by the punishment, and an explicit overinvestment in "style" and technique. The camera's overseeing eye oversees us, too, and reprimands us. In this way, masochistic charges exacted from the audience from time to time are amply rewarded by containment. This structure—part of Lynch's "signature"—indicates that the auteur, in some powerful way, loves and needs censorship. (This is why "Twin Peaks" works so much better than the films, because, unlike them, it cannot show it all.)[26] Not only is the shock, the trauma, produced *for* the screen, and contained within the screen, but it is literally "screened" for us, held at a distance.[27] If there is an identifiable audience craving for shock in a manageable form, for shock as entertainment, we need to ask why people go to the movies for "uneasiness," as if one could not be uneasy enough in the world in general. But this is precisely the point, I think: uneasiness, to be manageable, must be transferred into a narcissistic circuit of affect and fantasy. Along with an aestheticization of social conflict, then, we have the political recoded as individual neurosis—Lynch's and/or our own—and managed as such.

Breaking away from conventional structures of address that tend to channel our investment into alignment with the gaze of characters, or with the central lines of narrative, *Wild at Heart* relentlessly forces us into subjective points of view only to rupture those attachments and cast us into a disjuncture. This movement corresponds to a kind of internal censorship that relies on the "coolness" or "hipness" of attitude performed in the film's controlling discourse and gaze. It is cool irony that regulates the hot, affective shocks we give in to, and we can give in to them *because* we can count on the ironic cool of the film's discourse to manage our reaction, to catch us up and bring us back laughing. But in the process, we find ourselves detached from any productive engagement; we end up following the film's refusal of historical engagement.

Built as a structure of "effects"—shock effects, special effects, and "weird" effects—*Wild at Heart* encodes them as elements of style representing a kind of personal signature. Again and again, what permits our disengagement is the film's emphasis on pyrotechnics. Every shock of horrific physical violence is cushioned by the explicit obtrusiveness of "style," based on the ironic discourse that manages the film (visual puns, verbal jokes, repetitions that link the horrific to the comic): technical finesse. Since most of the shock to these violent images has to do with their verisimilitude, we are again lured by a structure of disavowal: "I know this isn't real, but nevertheless . . . ." Ultimately, then, we invest in the manufacture of perfect illusions. In the verisimilitude of brains spilled on the floor is a larger disavowal. Race, racial conflict, and white anxiety and rage are foreclosed as the film transfers disavowal from the specific image and scene to the referential level, counting on the lure of first illusion to cancel our interest in any external reference. Similarly, Bobby Peru's mouth, as the center of the rape-seduction scene, fascinates and disgusts us, but at the same time it foregrounds the technical manufacture of such "real" effects and, precisely at the expense of narrative content here, the humiliation of the woman. The pleasure of such images, then, has to do with our fascination with "real" effects, and their ability to cancel, to grant "relief" from referentiality. Lynch's films seduce because they not only stage fantasies, but emphasize the technical staging of fantasy. Verisimilitude, and special effects, in short, are themselves the site of investment.

But there is another important series of effects that the film codes as minor. This series captures our investment, just as it implicitly structures the film as a road movie while relieving us of the referential stakes. These effects are almost "decorative": they present themselves as "local color"—literally. But at the same time, they structurally stand out as pure image, pure spectacle, foregrounded as a kind of punctuation, a transitional pause in the narration, around which narrative slowly gathers in a retrospective, and often forced contextualization of the image. There are several striking examples of this effect, some coded as threatening, some as benign. Among the threatening images, of course, are Bob Ray Lemon and Juana; but another is the interracial gang that attacks Sailor. What does it mean to offer such figures as devoid of specific and historical racial content but to choose them so carefully for color? These selections encode an obscure subtext that plays with white racist fantasy, but, perhaps more important, this subtext inscribes the film's address to an audience imagined and constructed as "white." One of the more benign images is the elderly black man at the gas station. The musical soundtrack is rendered diegetic across this figure who comes into view as we listen. Tapping his foot, swaying, and smiling and pointing his finger at Lula, he becomes both an index of "local color" and an internal admiring spectator for Lula's parade in a red teddy. Without voice, without place, this character is, like the music, an index of the local, the ordinary life of a particular site.

Two other images are similarly linked to music. They feature Koko Taylor singing in a New Orleans nightclub, and a Creole woman dancer in the French restaurant where Marietta and Johnny dine. These figures are place markers, punctuation that facilitates the change of scene, acting as music does to cue a change of sequence. At the same time, they function as an index of the "authentic," the "real," of a site and a culture taken to be elsewhere, outside the culture inhabited by the film. In this sense, *Wild at Heart*'s images of people of color register a contemporary phenomenon that Cameron Bailey finds in certain "avant-garde filmmaking" associated with Lynch, Demme, Sayles, Byrne, Jarmusch, which couples a critique of popular culture with another tendency. According to Bailey, "Marginal cultures in these films work as repositories of the real, the only place left to look for authentic experience" (29–30). But, as Bailey suggests, this kind of exoticism and "xenophilia" is ambivalent; its other side is an aggressive desire to possess and contain its "others" and to reassure the cultural producers and consumers that their own positions are not threatened. In this respect, the Creole woman dancer and Juana emerge as dense with meanings, as does New Orleans itself. All of these figures signify the "exoticism" of racial mixture that is socially and mythically associated with New Orleans, known for its specific Creole culture, a site where prevailing U.S. definitions of "white" and "black," of race and color, and the dividing lines that hold them in place, breaks down completely—a place where the dominant cultural outsiders do not know the codes.

But in this film most of these codes can stand only for "difference," acting as a kind of fetish of difference, since they are presented as index or punctuation and not as meaningful in themselves. Presenting such figures as punctuation, rather than as meaning, the film erases their overdetermining impact on the fantasies that it stages. The referential charge of these figures is also diffused because they are inserted in a network of cameos, featuring actors from "Twin Peaks" as well as such figures as John Lurie, an "insider," an intertextual figure who is a regular in Jim Jarmusch's films, and who has a similar cameo function in Jonathan Demme's *Something Wild* (1986). Thus, they help to construct an audience of insiders who understand the intertextual references, while at the same time they contribute to the film's atmospherics, which are composed of weird takes on an "ordinary life" that is presumed to be somewhere out *there*.

If we accept this position, then, the figures of racial mixing in this film function to code an authenticity that is somewhere else but that is nevertheless available, accessible to those with the proper measure of cultural capital. But this cultural capital is connected to a sense of in-group hipness or coolness, one that distinguishes itself from Middle America by its appreciation of exotic and campy details.

Wild at Heart, then, depends for its legibility on certain specific forms of reading competence and knowledges. These emerge again and again in critical discussions that consistently elide questions of race, class, and gender under a series of fascinations. These fascinations fix on the auteur himself, on "psychosexual kicks," on film-historical references, on urban ethnographic impulses, on collective nostalgia, and on cinematic special effects. Not coincidentally, these fascinations and lures are precisely the means by which *Wild at Heart* directs attention away from the combination of racism and misogyny that structures it. In other words, *Wild at Heart* is aiming for an audience that might accept its strategies for neutralizing its own racist and sexist fantasies as ironic. To imagine that this film always knows the difference between *representing* racism and misogyny and *enunciating* them is to presume that we can establish a clear separation between the film's point of view and the larger cultural discourses incorporated and represented within it. Part of Lynch's appeal, then, may reside in his work's attempt to parade the rhetoric of racism and sexism in a framework that allowed us to feel ironically distant, inoculated from these pathologies, as it were, as the films emphasized instead "fantasy," "style," and the "avant-garde."

The "cool" associated with Lynch has to do with an appreciation of style and technique, but equally important it has to do with the ways that his apparently contingent figures become central to the production of "distinction" (in Bourdieu's sense) for the audience. *Wild at Heart,* like all of Lynch's work, aims to capture the fascination of the professional middle class, whose consuming activities always aim to produce distinction, to maintain its ragged and uneven differentiation from the middle class and lower-middle class that generated it.[28]

David Lynch turns out to be the perfect emblem for this professional middle class. He has been constructed as a figure both for the avant-garde and for "authenticity." This ambivalence may be central to his appeal. Most media stories about Lynch seem fascinated by an ambivalence. Campbell, for instance, finds the work to be resolutely continuous with Lynch's subjectivity: "you . . . have an obviously sophisticated person who intermittently affects extremely unsophisticated enthusiasms, all without a trace of irony." She sees the author's posture perfectly reflected in "Kyle MacLachlan's Agent Cooper in 'Twin Peaks,'" who is "reportedly a deliberate, affectionate portrait of Lynch" (34).[29]

Such a reading turns on questions of class, taste, and the complete identification of the man with his work as well as with a whole class of urban professional cultural consumers. Lynch is one of his own characters, at his best when offering an "affectionate portrait" of himself. Lynch's appeal depends substantially on the irony that he invites his viewers to apply to his deadpan lack of it. As a figure, then, Lynch is the perfect compromise formation. He is an authentic Middle American who shares his chosen audience's contempt for the people whom they imagine inhabit that zone unselfconsciously. He reviles the middle class that he comes from, but this gesture is justified by his continuity with it. The Lynch-effect, then, is coherent with the effort of a particular professional middle class to position itself as "hip" by projecting its own violent and rebellious fantasies onto the ground of the "ordinary life" of another class (and race), projecting those fantasies in order to consume them as the perverse, kinky side of that life.

The posture of sophistication that helps to obscure the referential level, as well as the politics of representation in *Wild at Heart,* is also bound to the thematics of nostalgia that pervades it. A familiar nostalgia for the fifties and sixties is almost ambient, and it serves to overdetermine both images and narrative. This is now a common enough feature of postmodern popular culture, but Lynch makes explicit the overlay of childhood oedipal memories onto historical nostalgia. And this would be a very interesting gesture were it not for the film's persistent figuration of the oedipal drama as definitively cut off from social and historical context. We read the fifties and sixties rewritten as *The Wizard of Oz* and in Sailor's fetishism of Elvis—in short, in the cultural consumption of Lynch's youth and our own. Such a subtext is compatible with the film's ethnographic fetishism of "ordinary life."

At the same time, some of the horror of a fantasmatically conceived ordinary life is expressed and channeled into the film's horrific imagery —its bad or "sick" taste, which is structurally correlated with the camp posture it assumes toward its nostalgic subtexts.[30] But, in this case, good taste and bad taste amount to the same thing—the anxious inscription of a dividing line between the professional middle class and its parent class, that is, the class of its parents. More important, as class and cultural struggles are increasingly represented in and through consumer products, such gleeful, aggressive spectacles of bad taste represent these struggles as nothing more than domestic, generational rebellions, waged on the terrain of private tastes, figured as individual choices.

Meanwhile, the film enacts its nostalgia through an oedipal subtext that constructs the 1950s and 1960s as periods whose central conflicts and crises were familial, whose struggles were rebellions against paternal authority, waged by white middle-class sons and daughters. Read this way, the celebrated regressiveness that Lynch fans find so appealing is thrown into relief. For *The Wizard of Oz,* the subtext designed to parade a gleeful nostalgia for the images of our own past, was itself an allegory about the paternal function, popularized by annual network television showings throughout many viewers' childhoods (and Lynch's). Such a retroactive allegory thus serves a compensatory function; it produces the dream of an unassailable paternal figure whose integrity is revealed and reinforced by the son's unsuccessful rebellions.[31] Lynch's own successful assimilation by Hollywood and television testified to this function and its satisfactions for a certain group of consumers. This is the upshot of the allegory: it is a story of rebellion as adolescent adjustment, and rebellion that functions as a sure means to ward off any radical political gestures that not only could *not* be contained within a family drama but that might overturn its foundations. Completely consistent with this allegory, *Wild at Heart* projects social conflict onto the ultimately more manageable terrain of a family that, even when riven by murderous maternal psychosis, is still steadfastly conceived as *private,* so that social difference is treated as external, as a byproduct or a decorative frame to the "real picture."

Perhaps inadvertently, *Wild at Heart* exposed the real dark side of the ordinary life of our middle-class culture. It is not our perverse subjective fantasies, our particular personal rewritings of the oedipal drama, but the ease with which these fantasies are imbricated with the dominant white middle class's collective social anxieties about sexual and racial difference. What was perverse in this context was that those fantasies were not so shocking, but rather that they were too banal to attract much more than passing notice; they receded into the ambient weirdness that became Lynch's primary selling point. Despite its pyrotechnic efforts to shock, what was really wild about *Wild at Heart* was that it exhibited the political side of our collective fantasies without comment.

5 Tell the Right Story: Spike Lee and the

Politics of Representative Style

As more and more Hollywood films and television series feature "accidental" pairings of black characters with white ones, we can hardly see their emergence as incidental. Since these couplings often function structurally either to write race out of consideration, in narratives that rarely really speak of it, or to provide a site of containment, where "race" becomes pertinent only in this punctual location, they implicitly suggest that the rest of the narrative, and its viewing context, are empty of racialized meanings. We might profitably examine the specific ideological work that these "innocuous" figures have been doing in the dominant representational field by reading them across the striking image of an interracial couple formed by Wesley Snipes and Annabella Sciorra in Spike Lee's 1991 *Jungle Fever*. Hardly innocuous in its context, this couple constitutes the motive force for the film's narrative unfolding.

This couple, who produce an overt emergency for the various communities represented in the film, had a brief afterlife of aestheticized immobility as an icon of vexed social relations displayed at the center of media discussions about interracial sex. This afterlife raises some questions. How does that film get reduced to an icon, like the one offered on *Newsweek*'s cover (June 10, 1991)? This staged image posed Snipes and Sciorra (and, significantly, *not* John Turturro and Tyra Ferrell, the actors who played the film's other interracial couple) in a highly theatrical embrace. What we have here is a retroactive icon, untethered from the film's narrative, produced in response to its box office draw. But how does this iconicity abet the magazine in making that film the occasion for a discussion of interracial love and sex, as it did in articles titled "Tackling a

Taboo: Spike Lee's Take on Interracial Romance" and "Mixed Couples on Love and Prejudice"?

The popular press and television rewrite films as events, to be treated like news, and they rewrite them, to be sure, within the same discursive machineries that frame historical events as spectacles or images and that replace political debate or analysis with opinion polls generated around "controversies." Certainly a key aspect of such controversies is how stunningly short their lives turn out to be. When staged as punctual spectacles, it often seems, social issues take on a dramatic—or melodramatic—shape that is designed to suggest swift and effective resolution. Perhaps the closest analogue to this "dramatic" structure is that of the television situation comedy, which returns serially (weekly) to another version of the same "family" or community problems.

The shape that "public discussion" takes seems especially crucial to understanding the particular and specific forms taken by the dominant culture's "passion of ignorance" about "race." Indeed, the subject of *race*, figured as an *issue* involving interracial love, desire, and sex, may be one of the most volatile examples of the striking intermittence of public attention that produces conflict and struggle in the form of *events* to be resolved in their telling. From time to time, this borderline case in the field of "race relations" emerges, or perhaps erupts, as a point of fascination and urgency, but it seems to be repressed just as suddenly. It is as if the dominant culture needed to maintain interracial sexuality as its "repressed," permanently ready to return, however briefly.

In interrogating this particular moment in the recent history of film reception, my point is to analyze the ways it is both limited by and dependent on the "passion of ignorance" that allows dominant cultural representations to continue encouraging many people, in Baldwin's words, to "think of themselves as white,"[1] and to think, consequently, that racial meanings are located in or generated by people of color. This thinking continues to shape a dominant representational field that is more or less unconsciously obsessed with "race." No longer obsessed with repressing race so much as with consuming it, contemporary representations often reinvest the racial divide as they try to rework it.[2] If we start with Wahneema Lubiano's question—"what is race in the United States if not an attempt to make 'real' a set of social assumptions about biology?"[3]—it should not surprise us that the dominant cinema and media's efforts to accommodate the challenges of identity politics anxiously rework the boundary between fantasy and reality, a boundary that constantly exhibits its fragility.

Our investment in the stability of this boundary has a variety of effects, not the least of which may be an insistence on the difference between documentary effects and images that are taken to have no relation to the referential. As the culture continues to organize its political discussions around imaginary poles of "majority" and "minority" discourses, so-called majority discourse persists in ignoring the ways that it is shaped in relation to so-called minority discourses. These latter, then, bear the burden of accounting for, and containing, what majority discourse constitutively represses: its own constructedness in and through racial and sexual identities.

Within interdependent representational frames, where public discussions take cinematic figures as representative of social groups, these discussions increasingly focus on identification as the principle process that structures both audience formation and spectator response. But such discussions tend to collapse identification with identity and representativeness with representation, thus generating what Kobena Mercer has called "the burden of representation" borne by nondominant producers and productions. By locating "social problems" in identities and not in political struggles, these discussions propose that feminism—not sexism—and race—not racism—are the central issues for debate. In 1991 this representational context of public discussion reinvested Spike Lee as an icon, while it briefly circulated the image of *Jungle Fever*'s central couple as an occasion for testimonies and debates about interracial desire and sex.[4]

About the same time, the *New York Times Magazine* (July 17, 1991) carried a cover article on "Hollywood's Black Directors," whose title seductively ventriloquizes these directors as a speaking commodity in an echo of Spike Lee: "They've Gotta Have Us." The article repeats the contemporary narrative conventions that govern Hollywood's "discovery" of this group of cultural producers along with an audience for them. And not unexpectedly, these conventions are similar to the ones that structure contemporary discussions of "affirmative action" and "multiculturalism," organized as they are by a contradictory vocabulary of "representativeness" and "native informants," where the figures selected as cultural "authorities" are simultaneously constructed as *exceptional*.[5]

In its quest to market what it calls "black product," Hollywood publicity continues to rely on the crudest forms of auteurism, stressing the continuity between a director's life and his work as a direct expression of personal experience. Valerie Smith characterizes that effect as the "documentary impulse," where "directors, studios, and their marketing experts collude in shrinking the distance between referent and representation in films such as . . . *New Jack City, Do the Right Thing, Boyz N the Hood, Straight Outta Brooklyn,* thereby delimiting what counts, or sells, as black film." Smith argues that "the marketing of these films provides one way in which they are constructed as 'real life,' " since "in short, most reviews of or feature articles on these films assure us that the directors are in positions of authority relative to their material."[6] These directors emerge as exceptions against the backdrop formed by two other figures of African American masculinity that the dominant culture industry currently capitalizes on: icons of rap music, like Ice T and Ice Cube, who get transposed directly to the screen in films like *New Jack City* (1991) and *Trespass* (1993), and the threatening "mass" of nonexceptional, regular guys who appear only as violent menace.

This very marketability has its own symptomatology, one that African American women critics have criticized forcefully, since it both depends on and perpetuates the representational marginalization of black women. In a 1991 article, "The New Ghetto Aesthetic," Jacquie Jones predicts the release of a "battery of films which 'illuminate' the life of the young Black male, the nation's most recent sociological curiosity." Jones suggests that the appeal of this sociological curiosity is suspiciously linked to the kinds of narrative it can support: "this new homeboy cinema does not threaten existing conventions. Instead, it exists as a modification of sensationalist Hollywood formulae."[7] In another essay, "The Accusatory Space," Jones develops her critique, exploring the easy "fit" between this new black male-authored cinema and U.S. popular culture's prevailing trends toward "a unified credo espousing racial solidarity (nationalism), an appropriated Americanism (vigilantism), and a uniform sexual politics (male-dominated heterosexism)."[8] In the process of providing a certain mass appeal (something for *almost* "everyone," with the telling and symptomatic absences that that suggests), she argues, these films offered narratives familiar to us from television news, as "the news became a factory for Black mass media imagery in cautious, conservative times. The boys, of course, were in the forefront, but always behind them, just inside the frame, was the corps of silent girls, standing on the curb or sitting on a couch" (96). Around the question of sexual difference, the films share with the media what Jones calls "the accusatory space from which representation . . . can continually be reprogrammed along gender lines" (96). Specifically, this means that the girls and women are not just marginalized in the frame, but their marginal space is as structured as that of the symptomatic cause underlying the narrative. "Somehow," she writes, "these girls seemed to me to exist in the space of the accused. After all, according to the news of the early eighties, it was those teenage, female-headed households that produced these boys" (96).

Like many other African American women critics, Lisa Kennedy focuses on this gender imbalance, writing: "Where are the women?!? From *House Party* to *To Sleep with Anger* to *Mo' Better Blues* to *Boyz N the Hood,* the sons are working overtime to secure the place of the father and, in doing so, themselves. If ever there was a symbolic effort to counteract a sociological assertion—that of paternal abandonment—it has been these films, which depict a world of fathers and sons."[9] Similarly, as Michele Wallace puts it in her analysis of *Boyz N the Hood,* the condition of women and girls is made to seem "somehow marginal and derivative" in a cinematic vehicle that offers an "opaque cultural analysis," whose "formula is simple and straightforward. The boys who don't have fathers fail. The boys who do have fathers succeed."[10] While recent male-authored African American films may marginalize women as a byproduct of the intensity with which the films pursue an oedipal plot, the limitations of their capacity to represent black women, their tendency to represent them as symptoms, is itself a structural problem and one that gets in the way of a more systemic analysis. Consequently, the symptomatic quality of their competing narratives and the displacements they effect fit rather neatly with certain of the dominant culture's representational agendas.

One need only glance at the most recent mainstream media reinventions of the narratives that are supposed to account for a ghetto "culture of poverty" to see the way that these films intersect with the dominant culture's familiar stories. Consistently seeking a punctual site of "pathology" to be treated, and avoiding a systemic analysis, such narratives more and more focus on the "problematic" black family, one symptomatically characterized as fatherless and female-headed.[11] In this respect, then, the strongest arguments about this masculinist privilege in African American film insist that the background or subsidiary position of African American women is culturally and ideologically advantageous for the dominant culture. Paul Gilroy, for instance, explores this problem by looking at the ideological work that "the trope of the family" performs in some contemporary African American cultural productions as well as in the critical discourse about them.

Gilroy criticizes a tendency within which "authenticity" is "disproportionately defined by ideas about nurturance, about family, about fixed gender roles, about generational responsibilities." "This authenticity," he argues, "is inseparable from talk about the conduct of bitter gender-based conflicts, which is now recognized as essential to familial, racial and communal health. Each of these—the familial, the racial, the communal—leads seamlessly into the next." [12] If one fails to recognize and explore the articulations among these levels, instead imagining something as complex as a community to be analogous with a family, according to Gilroy, one risks either reducing the social to the psychic, or reducing the psychic to the social.[13] Such an analogy obscures the conflicts and contradictions within community, and it neglects their relationship to political struggles in and with the dominant culture.

But if the familial trope and the oedipal narrative function in some African American male directors' work as signs of "authenticity," mainstream public discourses are organized around another problematic trope or figure for authenticity—the native informant. At the same time, this obsessive focus on the native informant betrays enormous anxiety about the border between art and life on another front: that of reception. When it comes to spectators, the audience that Hollywood and the media imagine for these films hypothetically resembles the directors: it is young, black, and male. Like the new director figures, these spectators are imagined to bridge the gap between fantasy and real life. Newly constructed in popular discourse as a market segment, these spectators appear as the impressionable agents of fantasy, whose cinematic consumption may turn into acting out; hence, the figure of the volatile urban black male audience, the audience for whom a range of critics in the mainstream press believed that Spike Lee's *Do the Right Thing* (1989) might be "incendiary," and the audience that provoked such anxiety in those theater owners who withdrew *New Jack City* from exhibition after its opening weekend.[14]

In the weeks following *Do the Right Thing*'s release, the film's "message" became a site of struggle as journal after journal set up the debate for us in terms like these from *U.S. News and World Report:* "Doing the Controversial Thing: A provocative discussion of race relations in the 1980s or a racist incitement to riot?" (June 6, 1991, p. 51). Even as it trivializes controversy, this caption exploits it, and it does so in a move that locates racism on the side of African American resistance. Strikingly enough, this "symmetrical" structure relies on conflations between violence against persons and violence against property on one level, and between the cinematic staging of fantasy and the advocacy of daily life violence on the other. In its insistent focus on the burning of Sal's pizzeria, the debates around *Do the Right Thing* regularly read the film's climactic action as steadily building violence that developed from the moment when Sal smashes Radio Raheem's boombox to Raheem's murder by a police chokehold, to the moment when the neighborhood crowd trashes and then torches the restaurant. By setting up an evolutionary framework of fantasmatically escalating violence here, the discussion obscured the distinction between property crimes and murder and between police brutality and the crowd's spontaneous but displaced reprisals, which targeted property.

In a typical fashion, *Newsweek* staged the debate under this heading: "How Hot Is Too Hot?": "Spike Lee has always provoked discord—but not like this. Is his new movie irresponsible or vitally important? *Newsweek*'s critics disagree." Jack Kroll, representing the negative side of this debate, leads off: "Spike Lee's *Do the Right Thing* is the most controversial movie in many years. To put it bluntly: in this long hot summer, how will young urban audiences—black and white—react to the film's climactic explosion of interracial violence? This incendiary subject, coupled with the brilliance of Lee's filmmaking talent, makes this question inescapable. People are going to argue about this film for a long time. That's fine, as long as things stay on the arguing level. But this movie is dynamite under every seat. Sadly, the fuse has been lit by a filmmaker tripped up by muddled motives" (July 3, 1989, p. 64). And what is the source of this muddle? Ambivalence. An ambivalence that leads Lee, in Kroll's words, "to substitute pizza politics for the hard realities of urban racial conflict" in an "evasion of the issues." And Kroll finds that ambivalence reflected in the famous juxtaposed quotations about violence—one from Malcolm X and one from Martin Luther King—that conclude the film. Paradoxically enough, Kroll has to advance this position in a framework that replicates the same kind of ambivalence since his article is designed to face-off with David Ansen's positive position on the film.

As this debate carried on in the same rigid either/or terms, the language of much of the popular critiques of the film took on a suspicious resemblance to descriptions of the filmmaker himself. More often than not, the film appeared as an organic extension of the director's person as well as his personal style. Take Jeanne McDowell, writing in *Time:* "Lee is serious and taciturn. . . . But press the right button, and he engages like an assault rifle, his words ricocheting off familiar targets (like Mayor Koch). . . .

beneath the arrogance he wears like a badge of honor is the deeper, pro-found racial anger that fueled *Do the Right Thing*" ("He's Got to Have It His Way," July 17, 1989, p. 92). Or, take Richard Corliss: "He holds the film like a can of beer in a paper bag—the cool sip of salvation on a blistering day—until it is revealed as a Molotov cocktail" (*Time*, July 3, 1989, p. 62). In a bizarre turn that interweaves an anxiety about the film's effects in the real with a fantasy about Lee himself, such comments remind us that one of the stunning aspects of the "Lee" phenomenon in dominant popular discourse is its compulsive focus on the director as a public figure and its utter neglect of his screen persona. Lee always emerges in his films as both a slippery, ambivalent, and slightly shady character, who is often the object of implicit critique, and as an extradiegetic resistance inter-rupting the narrative texture.[15] As a textual figure, then, Lee circulates his own body and image through his films as he does those of many of his regular actors, whose roles from film to film vary dramatically. Such an effect interrupts any easy correlation between on-screen and off-screen realities.[16]

Dominant media discussions, however, continue to relate certain rep-resentations—those whose audience address is regarded as socially spe-cific—to reality by imagining that stable identification shapes the spec-tator's relationship both to images and to fantasy. Interdependent with a notion of spectator identification that sees it as originating in recog-nizable resemblances and as sliding into imitation is an equally impover-ished theory of fantasy's relationship to agency in the real. Judith Butler analyzes this implicit understanding of fantasy and its consequences in "The Force of Fantasy: Feminism, Mapplethorpe, and Discursive Excess," arguing that this theory understands fantasy as "that which both pro-duces and is produced by representations and which, then, makes pos-sible and enacts precisely the referent of that representation. . . . Accord-ing to this implicit theory, the real is positioned both before and after its representation; and representation becomes a moment of the reproduc-tion and consolidation of the real."[17] Such a version of fantasy's relation-ship to the real, Butler contends, collapses the signified into the referent and consequently ignores the ways that the very concepts of the "real" and the "fantasmatic" are mutually constituting. Equally important, by imagining what Butler calls "a single identificatory access to the repre-sentation," this understanding of fantasy disallows the ways in which our access to it is multiple, mobile, and intermittent, fixing on moments and letting them go. Certainly in the case of cinema we invest our fantasmatic identifications in places, in space, in scenes, in gestures and movements, and in the technical apparatus itself, as well as in characters and stories. A theory of fantasy that cannot take this complexity into account assumes a stabilized psychic identity that either comes into possession of, or takes on, a stably bounded fantasy, or one that is acted on, taken over by a fantasy whose meaning can be determined.

In the case of the dominant popular discourse's superegoic relation to young, urban, black male audiences, its discourse assumes a stable identity, passively acted upon, whose pleasure translates directly into acting out. But surely it is important to be able to think as well that identifications need not always issue in—or from—pleasure. They may equally well generate displeasure or anxiety; they may have their source in fear and may operate defensively. Particularly in the case of the representation of violence, we need to entertain the uncomfortable proposition that at the simplest level we can never definitively separate our identifications with the aggressor from our identifications with the victim or, for that matter, our pleasure from our displeasure. Finally, a belief that representations directly motivate acting-out ignores the crucial function of fantasy as Butler describes it: "the view that fantasy motivates action rules out the possibility that fantasy is the very scene which suspends action and which, in its suspension, provides for a critical investigation of what it is that constitutes action" (113).

Obsessed with the capacity of cinematic fantasy to break the frame of spectacle—to incite an unruly audience—public discussions betray their own anxious fantasies about an audience whose oppositional interests might be moved to consolidate into a real world force that might work to destabilize the dominant order. These discussions also attempt to contain films whose address is *specific* within a coherent narrative structure of argument that reduces cinematic representations to plots organized around exemplary characters. Striving to shape ambivalent meanings into the form of two-sided controversy, this structure works to preclude recognition that that very ambivalence marks sites of central political contest in the culture. Addressing African American audiences as critical consumers, Wahneema Lubiano has argued trenchantly against a collective tendency to read these films exclusively on "their own" internal terms, insisting that, instead, they must be understood in a broader representational context. On the other hand, we might suggest that the dominant popular Euro-American discourse went in the opposite direction, tending precisely to *overlook* the film's own terms in its urge to find a sociological argument that would "get it right."[18]

But if mainstream and liberal white culture seeks to acclaim or reject *Jungle Fever,* like *Do the Right Thing* before it, in terms of the correctness of its "argument," the roots of this impulse lie in a collapse of "real effects" with social reality, and in the corollary impulse to construct Lee, its privileged interlocutor, as a delegate speaking for a whole population. This question of the "real effect" may be the site of some overlap with African American audiences, at least as certain critics characterize this reception. Analyzing the "documentary" effect in the receptions of recent fiction films, Valerie Smith argues that this effect works to conceal the films' "status as mediations" and to "suggest that they occupy an intimate, if not contiguous, relation to an externally verifiable reality" (59–60). Lubiano describes a certain pressure in African American film reception that at times constructs the "realist" film as continuous with referential reality and, concomitantly, constructs its producer as a delegate for a community. "Realism," she writes, "suggests a disclosure of the truth (and then the closure of the representation); realism invites the readers/audience to accept what is offered as a slice of life because the narrative contains elements of 'fact'" (182). Those are the very paradigms of reception, she goes on to argue, that operate within the dominant representational regime to confine African American film production to an arena of competing claims for realist authority, an authority construed as access to sociological "truth." Such paradigms, of course, foreclose consideration of reality as constructed through representations produced within a historical context constituted by competing political interests. Thus, Lubiano argues that we cannot address the "construction of reality" by "more claims to realism without considering how and why both hegemonic realism and resistance to or subversion of the realism are constructed" (184). Understanding realism as a strategy within a politicized representational context further leads Lubiano to frame the problem in reference to the critical consciousness of audiences: "what happens in the shadow behind the 'real' of Spike Lee—once it becomes hegemonic for African-Americans? . . . What happens to the construction of 'Blackness' in the public discourse?" (184).

In exploring realist representations, these critics argue that the failure to see documentary effects as precisely representational strategies in various contemporary debates eradicates the tensions within "black representation," tensions between "representation as a practice of depiction and representation as a practice of delegation." [19] Flattening this tension by conflating realism with "reality," or truth, not only contributes to the construction of African American cultural producers as the voice of "reality" for the mainstream, but it forecloses the complexities of audience response: the critical and analytical side of people's response to everyday entertainment; the distinctions within audiences, both mainstream and African American; and the significant divergences between resistant, negotiated, and dominant readings within and between audiences. Finally, failure to acknowledge this tension facilitates the reduction of a cinematic text to an argument, which does not allow us room to think through any relationship to fantasy structures or to the ways that hegemonic representation may be challenged at the level of the cinematic apparatus—the material level of production—as well as through representational strategies.

Organized by collisions among competing discourses, Lee's films present contradictions that are highly resistant to resolution as a clear assertion or statement—precisely the form required by a dominant discourse that seeks to place them as examples in its ongoing story of contemporary race relations. By framing in advance the questions that his films may raise, this story reduces their contradictions to the size and shape of the political debate as it is carried on in the mainstream media. And these films seem intent on raising questions that do not fit easily within this format, questions that might, if taken seriously, change the terms of debate.

Thus, dominant public discourse about *Jungle Fever* wound up thematizing its own inability to accommodate questions that are framed differently. Of course, the film itself thematizes precisely that failure as well, since it confronts one possible intersection between race and sexuality in a narrative organized by "opinions" in collision. David Denby is representative of critics who responded negatively to the film's competing discourses: "The movie is words, words, words . . . *Jungle Fever* is raucous, tendentious, shallow, self-canceling. . . . Lee carefully sets up an interracial love affair and then buries it in the predictably enraged opinions everyone has about it" ("Skin Deep," *New York,* June 17, 1991, p. 76). A corollary of this criticism is the familiar one that the characters we expect to act as protagonists come off as ciphers, lacking psychological depth, or interiority.[20] But suppose we try to understand this lack of depth as part of the film's effort to map cultural contradictions and fantasies around the category of race. In a dominant cultural field that privileges visibility, that struggles with anxieties about the noncoincidence of the visible and the essential, *Jungle Fever* seems to play as much with the question of how people *look* — in both senses of the word — as it does with a discursive war of positions about the meaning of race and of miscegenation.

If Flipper and Angie are ciphers, their status as such is visually inscribed. More looked at than *looking,* their individual points of view are gradually submerged in the figure they make together as a couple that is the object of other people's looks. The film initially attributes a point of view to these characters, granting them a gaze of eroticized interest that it later defines as curiosity when Flipper tells Angie that the meaning of their relationship is exhausted once that curiosity has been satisfied. Their seduction operates in a rhythm of shot–reverse shots that quickly gives way to an almost obsessive two-shot structure, where the obvious artifice of lens filters and lighting effects heighten or subdue the contrast in skin tones between Wesley Snipes and Annabella Sciorra. Once they are coupled in two-shot, however, these characters rarely support point-of-view shots that would allow our gaze to coincide with theirs. This is the cinematic mechanism that evacuates their interiority, but it also puts us in a position to observe how they function as signs that the other characters continually interpret.

So even while these characters continue to talk about the clichés and fantasies of racial difference that bring them together and hold them apart, we see them as one figure, and this means that the reciprocity of gazes between them tends to evaporate. Within the film's syntactic unfolding, this effect establishes an asymmetrical echo with the other interracial coupling that the film suggests — that between Paulie (John Turturro) and Orin (Tyra Ferrell). This second couple is structured through reciprocated gazes across spatial boundaries; these are characters who have to work their way to a meeting that is motivated by analysis and decision.

Inscribing the contrast between its parallel couples through shot composition and editing, the film registers Paulie's and Orin's desire in relation to place, because Orin repeatedly enters the paranoically closed space of the news store, while at the film's end Paulie crosses his neighborhood — literally and figuratively — to meet Orin where she lives.[21] And the film charts this crossing carefully, tracking with Paulie as he walks rapidly toward Orin's house, pursued, taunted, and physically impeded by his cohort from the news store. Never shown in close two-shot, Paulie and Orin are mapped into a space where their mobility and agency are foregrounded, whereas Flipper and Angie, by contrast, are often immobilized in an aestheticized relation to surroundings that flatten into a background. Narratively as well, they are out of relation to place, since they choose an apartment at a geographic middle ground between their respective neighborhoods, a limbo: downtown. As a couple, they are neither here nor there, halfway between Harlem and Bensonhurst.

Yet it is the figure of difference fetishized as high contrast in skin tone between Flipper and Angie that comes untethered from the film as its iconic residue in media and advertising. And this is where Ed Guerrero finds that, even as the film exposes whiteness as construction, it also gets itself into a bind. "Considering the way that any film's most powerful ideological argument is usually embedded in the visual . . . it would seem that Lee's enticing depiction of black/white sex and affection between Flipper and Angie, visually undercuts the argument and outcome of the film's separatist narrative. In a subtle, ironic manner, then, Lee is perhaps spreading the 'fever' that he wishes to critique if not cure."[22]

If we follow out this logic, we might find that the contradictions between discursive and visual levels in this film also entail interdependencies between separation or prohibition and the fetishism of difference. So while it is true that the film must to some extent perform this fetishistic eroticism of a racial divide that is presented, framing effects—both cinematic and discursive—may interrupt this performance. Where Guerrero contends that *Jungle Fever*'s "argument" ultimately takes place at the visual level, I want to suggest that the trouble here is that the visual cannot argue very effectively. It argues, so to speak, only by assertion. Perhaps most like the unconscious in its final inability to admit negation, the visual makes assertions that often exceed containment by narrative or argument to persist as residue. That is, what the visual offers is never fully erased or withdrawn by subsequent narrative accountings. What the visual does do, however, is interfere with, interrupt, throw into question, and even overturn what a film asserts at the discursive level. This is part of what Lee's films play on, the work of contradiction that goes on between the visible and the arguable or discursive, work that seems particularly important in a film intent on displaying the contradictions embedded in radical visibility.

If we read *Jungle Fever* in its social and historical context, the film seems to be predicated on a critical challenge to fantasies about race as *visible*, a challenge that works at the borderlines where some things become

visible at the expense of others. Looking at "race" as contact and collision, *Jungle Fever* explores the differences among specific perspectives on
the ways in which U.S. culture, in its diversity and its power distributions,
continues to reconstruct, reinvent, and reinvest "race." In the process,
it foregrounds contradictions within the dominant as well as in oppositional discourses. While this film may at times succeed in setting out
"whiteness" as a sign, like "blackness," it also produces uneasiness around
this question: who reads off the meaning of the sign?

Amid the difficult and vexed trade-offs that *Jungle Fever* asks us to entertain, there is always the work of Ernest Dickerson's camera: obtrusive, intrusive, interfering with effects of naturalism or "reality" through canted
angles and filtered lenses. No position, no scene, escapes collision with
others. No scene stands on its own "ground," so to speak, without the
intervention of a situated gaze, without the pull of cinematic syntax,
forcing it into relation with other scenes or moments. In its visual unfolding, the film forces us to acknowledge that the camera is withholding
from sight as much as it is giving. Examples include the following Lee
"signature" techniques. Lee frequently tracks the characters along with
the camera, so that instead of an ordinary tracking shot, we have the
characters rolling along on a track as well, often shot from a low angle,
as when Cyrus and Flipper are walking the streets while their wives con-
fer about Flipper's affair. In this sequence the two glide off in an impossible space somewhere above the sidewalk, moving both too quickly
and too smoothly for any verisimilitude, silhouetted in two-shot against
the nighttime city horizon.[23] Another technique isolates characters one
after the other at canted angles within the frame, so that each is held at
a stylized diagonal to the frame, especially in sequences where the dialogue emphasizes divergent perspectives. Yet another is the movement of
the camera in a continuous elliptical arc around a space, as when Flipper
argues with his bosses about his promotion and their attitude toward affirmative action. In this case, the camera's unbroken arc clashes with the
brutal back-and-forth rhythm of the argument in a scene that stresses
disjuncture, or noncontinuity, in broken communication.

Equally obtrusive visually is the mise-en-scène in any number of sequences. To take one example, we witness an intense dispute between
Flipper and his wife, Drew (Lonette McKee), about his affair in the self-
consciously stagey environment produced by Drew's office in the backroom of the sales floor where she works. The characters are framed, as if
on a stage, between curtains of yellow fabric, just at the moment when

Drew is running through the litany of epithets that she has endured because of her color: "high yellow." This scene follows a sequence that moves across the sales floor to focus on Drew; because of the predominance of reds in the clothing on display, the whole sequence is coded in glaring primary colors, thus literalizing its emphasis on the imaginary primacy of color here.

At the level of abstraction, then, this sequence reminds us of the film's frequent return to questions of "color." It is significant that, even as Drew is set up as the analyst of the meanings that are socially assigned to color, the film inscribes the complexity of color across her body and Angie's. Through its play with lighting effects, the film highlights the similarity of skin tones between the two women who are separated by the social "color" line, thereby emphasizing the imaginary and constructed nature of what passes for "biological" difference and for *visible* difference.[24]

Because the film tries to expose the work of the imaginary, as well as the workings of power in the ways that "color" is saturated with meanings, it avoids falling into any simple representation of difference as "consumable" in the way that bell hooks argues that our culture increasingly offers social differences as fetishized consumer lures. "Currently," hooks asserts, "the commodification of difference promotes paradigms of consumption wherein whatever difference the Other inhabits is eradicated, via exchange, by a consumer cannibalism that not only displaces the Other but denies the significance of that Other's history through a process of decontextualization" (31). The process that she accurately describes characterizes the contradictions in which recent African American-produced films emerge; to some degree, they all may be marketed as themselves *marketing* differences. These, then, would be the reception conditions that *Jungle Fever* contends with and, however erratically, challenges. Here, we remember that *Jungle Fever*'s distributor marketed it through the icon of intertwined black and white hands, one of the "visual constructions" that "fetishize and manipulate the contrast of black and white skin," which Guerrero points out is central in the film and its advertising. This is the fetish (of consumable difference) that the film both offers and has to undo.

But *Jungle Fever*'s play on skin tones calls attention to a particular intersection between race, or color, and sexuality that makes the film's structuring contradiction visible. As Guerrero sees this contradiction, "the film comes off as confused on the issue of exactly how 'race' is constructed" in that it implicitly articulates the premise that Flipper makes explicit when he finally tells Angie that their affair is futile, that they cannot continue, cannot have children who would be "a bunch of mixed nuts." That premise is "that there is a biologically pure essence of 'blackness' somewhere out there in America, generally agreed upon and uniformly upheld by black people . . . longing for a pure essence of blackness in Flipper's last name, 'Purify'" (174). However, as Guerrero points out, in emphasizing the lighter skin tones of the women, the film itself exposes the contradictions within Flipper's position, and it does so through its visual obsession with "color": "Flipper and Cyrus would only have to look at their light-skinned wives to realize how contradictory and out of touch their notion of a mythic physical homogeneity really is" (175).

In a film so fascinated with how people look, it is significant that these characters are unable to look at this crucial moment. But perhaps the film leaves that looking to the spectator, at the same time that it suggests that even what is right before one's eyes is not unmediatedly legible? In the face of "Cyrus and Flipper's clearly stated preference for light-skinned wives," Guerrero suggests, "one must ask *the* critical question and, so to speak, play the child pointing out the emperor's nakedness. Where do all of these light-skinned African-American wives for the black bourgeoisie ultimately come from, if not from some form of the process of miscegenation itself?" (177). How things look, and the relation of that "look" to how *we* look, are indeed among the film's central preoccupations. Again and again, visual effects foreground the film's syntax, the artifice of editing that produces a context for meaning, but a context whose contradictions force us to struggle over meaning, much as the characters do. A single developed example should suffice here: the sequence that opens when Flipper brings Angie to dinner at his parents' house, and the subsequent scene of the couple's return to their downtown apartment. This sequence explores the gaze as a social phenomenon when it examines the construction of racialized meaning based on visibility in a development that exhibits Flipper's and Angie's obliviousness to "how they look."

In the dinner sequence, where Flipper's father takes a didactic posture in a speech whose implications far exceed the boundaries of the moment to reverberate through the film, Angie's whiteness emerges as a sign whose meanings are produced in a densely saturated historical nexus. And as her whiteness emerges as a sign, one of the things that becomes "visible" is the permeability and the shiftiness of white ethnicities. Angie's Italian-Americanness and her class position disappear beneath her white femininity here.[25] Indeed, it is her femininity that makes her whiteness visible. In the context of her relationship with Flipper, her femininity makes it visible in the liminal field that Abdul Jan Mohammed calls "racialized sexuality," a field "in which neither race nor sexuality appears as independent of the other."[26]

The Good Reverend Doctor (Ossie Davis), whose name stands as an excessive disavowal of his own past transgressions, may not be the most reliable observer that the film has to offer. But, of course, *Jungle Fever* consistently plays strong positions and strong readings off against each other in order to exhibit the partialness of the truths that they advance. Nevertheless, the intensity and force of the Good Reverend Doctor's gaze on Angie produces a powerful impact. His discourse reframes her as an icon of the inescapable resonance of historical meanings that seem to emerge at the very sight of her within this particular cultural moment.

But the father's judging gaze meets another one as the men's exchange of looks across Angie forms an asymmetrical triangle that is squared by the mother's quiet witness. She presents a gaze, most persistently in relation to Gator (Samuel L. Jackson), Flipper's crack-addicted brother, that simultaneously reinforces and undermines that of her husband.[27] However, in this sequence the mother's gaze takes on a particular gravity through its participation in the film's systemic relay of black women's gazes—gazes that witness and judge. In some ways this character anticipates *Crooklyn* (1994), a film centrally organized by the memory of the mother's gaze and her judgment, explored this time, significantly, through the daughter's eyes. To read the figure of Flipper's mother, the grieving mother who watches, waits, mediates, forgives, and mourns, we need to set her in the context of the other women who watch Flipper, who read him, criticize him, judge him, and negotiate with him.

Erasing part of Angie's social specificity, this scene frames her mutely staring at the Good Reverend Doctor as the stake of a brutal exchange between these men. And the tension between this performative level and the thematics of the father's discourse makes Angie into the emblem of historical "white Southern womanhood," calling our attention to fantasmatic investments in race as a sign. Since this sequence displays—in close-up, so to speak—the mechanisms by which one person's visible aspect, one's face, can be made into a projecting screen for collective fantasy, and since it does so at the expense of the white, Italian-American woman, it rehearses for a "white" gaze the ways that collective fantasies around race and gender can collude to bind one figure into the position of stand-in for a whole group. That group is, likewise, bound to screen the projecting gaze's worst fears and anxieties about itself.

At the same time, history emerges powerfully in this scene as weight, however fantasmatic some of the investments it attracts and reshapes may be.[28] Flipper's father interprets the couple's image in a historical frame through the history of white men's rape of black women and lynching of black men, a history sustained by eroticized racist fantasy whose brutal effects in the social world have helped to shape the look of this couple in his eyes. Speaking to his son across the mute body-as-sign of the white woman, the Good Reverend Doctor tells the story this way. "The white man said to his flower of white Southern womanhood, 'you're too holy, too pure, to be touched by any man, even me. I'm going to put you on a pedestal, so the whole world can fall down and look at you. Any nigger so much as look at it, I'll lynch his ass.' She believed him." He continues, "Her husband ran down to the slave quarters, grabbing every piece of black poontang he could get . . . the white ladies felt abandoned . . . so proud to be white and superior . . . mouths shut, legs locked together . . . late at night and alone on the hot bed of lust, they must have thought what it would be like to have one of them . . . thought about the big black bucks their husbands were so afraid of. . . ." And to his son, he asserts, "I feel sorry for you, in the nineties trying to make up for what you missed, a black man who still has to fish in the white man's cesspool."

At this point, the Good Reverend Doctor's passionate tone may momentarily reframe the content of his tirade, as it emphasizes the erotic charge of these imaginings within the moral speech. And this turn is not quite out of keeping with the shady past that the film suggests is disavowed by this character, nor is it out of keeping with the ferocious affect that many characters consistently bring to bear on the juncture of racialized sex within the film. And this affective intensity is crucial, for it reminds us of the force of repression that attends interracial sex, and of historical pressures that relegated certain interracial couplings to unspeakability and invisibility, while speaking obsessively about others, which thereby acquired a hypervisibility.[29] It might seem here that the film is on the verge of discrediting the Good Reverend Doctor, both through his own near hysteria (he did, as Flipper points out, knowingly invite his son's white girlfriend to his home), and through the striking parallel between his behavior and that of Angie's father, who beats her up when he learns that she is involved with a black man. If he were fully discredited, however, the film would not proceed, as it does in the next sequence, to escape the privatized limits of oedipal narratives and to acknowledge the weight of history as it shapes those narratives. In other words, having appeared to establish through the symmetry of paternal rebuke that the erotic "curiosity" that drives Flipper and Angie is fed by a primarily oedipal transgressiveness, the film's next sequence places the couple under a different kind of policing gaze, one that remains steadfastly nonfamilial.

Flipper's and Angie's abrupt departure and their return home opens a sequence that responds to the previous one by representing the material effects of those fantasies' continued vitality. As the couple play outside their parked car, mock-boxing while calling out the names of Italian-American and African American boxers in a parodic reprise of the discussions between Mookie and Pino over the wall of fame in Sal's pizzeria, the camera offers us two perspectives on the scene. One is located at ground level and choreographs the lovers' play into a social history of interethnic competitiveness.[30] A second gaze, anonymous and unattributed, looks down from an upstairs window. This is the gaze that seems to bring the howling siren of a police cruiser and two white officers who announce that they have received a call about an "Afro-American" man raping a white woman. Significantly, these cops are played by the same actors who played the beat patrolmen in Mookie's neighborhood in *Do the Right Thing*.

Structurally, this scene is coded as bringing Flipper to consciousness of the futility of this relationship. Breaking it off shortly thereafter, Flipper appears to embrace the policeman's pronouncement, which concludes their encounter: "What a waste." If Flipper's position paradoxically coincides with the cop's, as this sequence would suggest, it is because he has finally realized how he looks with Angie, or he has realized that his position is regulated by anonymous surveying gazes. And the arrival of the police here brutally literalizes one of the meanings of the Good Reverend Doctor's story: that the culture polices racialized borders all the more strenuously for their being imaginary. Those borders take on a certain hypervisibility when a sexual pairing calls attention to the ways that they are always already intensely eroticized—an eroticization emblematized in the policeman's contemptuous "What a waste."

This sequence also powerfully inscribes the suggestion that the interpretation of an image, or of a body, has much to do with how the gaze that sees it is situated. In the context, however, this sequence is hardly an argument for relativity, since what is dramatized narratively is precisely the violent material effects of perspective and interpretation. Part of the film's point is to make visible some of the ways that cultural meanings are constructed and used by focusing on sites that are intensely invested with both power and erotic fascination. It is crucial to remember here that *Jungle Fever*'s frame—its credit sequence—memorializes Yusef Hawkins, an African American murdered in Bensonhurst, a predominantly Italian-American neighborhood in Brooklyn. The perpetrators claimed that they had mistaken Hawkins for someone else, an African American man who was dating one of the young women from the neighborhood (by way, among other things, of implicitly blaming her for inviting men of color to a birthday party in this well-guarded territory). While of course they did not claim a "right" to kill the "right" man, their declarations remind us that in this urban context, all identity is susceptible to being "mistaken"—by some*one,* at some *time*—to the extent that it is based broadly on "visible" racial difference.

In its exploration of Bensonhurst through Angie and her community, *Jungle Fever* is able to stage moments in which white identity is "mistaken," but we will do well to bear in mind that, as penetrating as the film's analysis of this working-class Italian-American neighborhood may be at times, that analysis is unable to include an exploration of the ways that urban working-class neighborhoods in general have become—or remain—borderlands in which struggles that extend throughout the culture are fought more violently than in other sites. However, it is possible that some audiences could overlook the ways in which one Italian-American community here stands in for the dominant white culture. Not to see that community as a synecdoche, in which the dominant culture is fully implicated, would mean to read it as a rather more reassuring figure, the culture's abject.

In connection with the historical incident to which the film alludes, it is worth noting that this sequence rehearses the contemporary mappings of race into neighborhood, and the mutual structuring of surveillance and visibility that they entail, especially when these mappings are overlaid on sexuality—real or imagined. Equally important, by juxtaposing the dinner scene with the police scene, *Jungle Fever* manages to expose the workings of identity as visible sign by showing how Angie and Flipper are read differently by the father and by the police. But it also emphasizes that they are signs whose meaning is shaped by their physical interaction as a couple.

The cultural and political effects that attend our function as signs that are public and historical, but whose meanings are subject to collective imaginaries, are effects completely saturated with the workings of power. At least at this juncture it would be fair to say that *Jungle Fever* understands white privilege to be upheld in part by its "invisibility" as racially constructed. This invisibility fits into a system of effects that Hazel Carby points to when she writes on the subject of multiculturalism that "we need to recognize that we live in a society in which systems of domination and subordination are structured through processes of racialization that continuously interact with all other forces of socialization. . . . In this sense, it is as important to think about the invention of the category of whiteness as well as that of blackness, consequently, to make visible what is rendered invisible when viewed as the normative state of existence: the (white) point in space from which we tend to identify difference." [31]

What, then, are we to make of the dominant popular culture's feverish efforts to make *Jungle Fever* answer its questions about the meaning of interracial relationships in the current social landscape? Or of its inability to ask questions about the film's emergence in the context of other representations of race as *merely* a visual marker of difference, a difference that is undertheorized?

Writing in *New York*, David Denby harshly criticizes the film for its failure to restore what amounts to the confessional aspect that talk shows foreground: the inside of the love affair rather than its outside community reactions. "*Jungle Fever*, it turns out," he argues, "is not about adultery, or marriage, or sex, or even sex and race together, that most explosive of combinations. The film touches on all of these things, but it's really about what interests Lee the most, race hatred and color. Color is the only reality. But is Lee perhaps a bit . . . overwrought? I know a few interracial couples, and I see more walking around the city. They don't seem pursued by howling furies every minute of the day." [32] By constructing the film's central interests as race hatred and color, Denby's position participates in a common tendency to elide racism, a political process, under race, a category, as if the social issue were "race" and not the power relations that are mapped onto it and the meanings that the culture assigns to it. And this happens in the context of Hollywood's concerted address to a "white" gaze whose dominance depends on remaining unconscious of the ways it is inflected by racial meanings. If the dominant media kept trying to read *Jungle Fever* as a failed ethnography of interracial relationships, it overlooked the possibility that the film might perform *another* ethnography, an ethnography of the dominant white gaze.[33]

In response to this film's refusal to supply a confessional interiority as the "truth" of the relationship, Denby produces his own "native informants" and offers up his own experience in the form of vague observations. A similar tendency emerges in the loquacious popular discussion that took the shape of a general effort to "finish" Lee's film. This discussion steadfastly avoided what *Jungle Fever* foregrounds: the symptomatic public meanings of certain relationships. Instead, the discussion imagined that the truth about such relationships could be spoken only from their inside and confessed to the rest of the world. Consequently, the logical format for the film's reception became a series of talk shows that paraded native informants reporting from a newly discovered, suddenly visible social territory. A territory to which, paradoxically, no one is native.

As if by some magical osmosis, both partners in the interracial couples were popularly inscribed in the place all too often occupied by the African American native informant, "the one who is supposed to know about race." To the extent that this discursive structure prevailed, fetishizing these couples as symptoms who were asked to speak, such popular exposure helped to guarantee that the cultural and political effects of racialized sexuality would not be interrogated.[34] The central question that this kind of privatized public discourse was unable to get to was this: what are the variety of meanings of such relationships for the culture itself? How do those meanings differ for us depending on our specific location within the nexus of racial, gender, and class divides that are mapped together with power distributions?

In this connection it is, of course, interesting to note that certain film critics, among them Denby and Terrence Rafferty, have suggested that the film itself is tainted by a discourse that owes much to talk show formats. My argument remains that the film works to criticize the common rhetorics that our contemporary culture produces around "race." That means, then, that it is not so easy to identify cause and effect here and that it is possible to argue that Lee's film focuses on what is symptomatic about the language that we use for social identities. If I am right, then the film's easy appropriation by the very talk show format it implicitly criticizes is a symptomatic irony.

Complex questions about racialized sexuality that were largely repressed in popular discussions do emerge, however, in *Jungle Fever*'s famous women's "war council" scene. Texturally different from any other sequence in the film with its naturalistic lighting and documentary-style camerawork, this scene interrupts the narrative by staging an argument, in the sense that the characters offer articulated positions that do not reduce easily to opinions. As such, this scene offers a stark contrast to other moments whose central metaphor is color as well: the discussions of race and interracial eroticism pursued by Paulie's Italian-American cohort in the sealed, paranoid, and emphatically masculine world of the candy store. Here, characters address everyone and no one; their only back-and-forth exchanges consist of accusations and counteraccusations about color designed to push the buttons of white racial paranoia that these characters so prominently display; for instance, they repeatedly make reference to the mother's sexuality in relation to the son's own skin color. Significantly, we might note that the war council eventually establishes the generally metaphoric or figurative status of color, whereas the candy store scenes establish only its literal instability in relation to "blood." This significant discursive difference plays out in the divergent visual techniques that mark the contrast between these parallel moments.

Spatially, the candy store scene codes as spectacle, as highly staged and ritualistic, since all of the figures are immobilized in a heavily partitioned space, punctuated only by the door and the window on which Paulie's gaze, and our own, obsessively fix, as if awaiting intervention or seeking escape. This scene cinematically registers, on the one hand, a desperate effort to fortify the inside against imagined dangers of invasion from a threatening outside and, on the other, Paulie's longing for a liberatory space outside.

By contrast, the war council scene is filmed in quick, jumpy pans that establish a space of reciprocal exchange, where the speakers lead the camera through a space of mobility and change that promises no resolutions. Rather, this scene rehearses a series of positions, more or less imaginary, more or less affectively invested, and more or less aggressive, as the participants themselves recognize. Not so much about knowledge or truth as it is about the ways in which affect and the imaginary are mobilized in the continual redrawing of racial and ethnic boundaries, this scene acknowledges the complexity of contemporary social relations. Refusing to reduce the question of interracial relations, or of race, to simple binary opposition, this scene recognizes that the "racial" field is complicated by ethnicities, class, sexuality. To cite a few exemplary comments, the discussion includes the following claims: that the only black men who are not drug addicts, or in jail, or "homos," are married, or have "ten women"; that white women continually "throw themselves" at black men; that black men feel successful only when they have "a white woman on their arm"; that black women are looking for men in the wrong place, that they need to be able to consider men who are not professionals; and that men who are not professionals have difficulty living with women who are. Later in the discussion, one participant proposes to deemphasize "color," as she announces that she dates "the whole spectrum: Chinese, Jews, Asians" as long as the man is "nice and sweet and loves me."

In this framework Drew becomes a kind of central switchpoint for the meanings of color, owing to her ambiguous position in this imaginary spectrum as a woman of racially mixed ancestry. In this regard, her resemblance to the actress Lonette McKee, whose own biography, as well as her role in Julie Dash's 1984 film, *Illusions,* where she plays a studio executive who is passing in Hollywood of the 1940s, adds to an "effect of reality" that circulates around the body of this actress in this scene and throughout the film. We remember the moment when one of the group tells Drew that "back in the days" black men privileged women like Drew herself, "light-skinned," but that now that category of privilege has been displaced onto white women. Or, for that matter, we may recall that Drew's concluding comment suggests the ways that "color," or racial difference, is socially hyperinvested so that it becomes a convenient tool of aggression, even as she personally tries to disinvest it: "Don't matter what color she is, my man is gone."

Various critics have singled out this scene for special consideration, characterizing it as an exemplary site of presumed authenticity in some cases and of distortion in others. For Terrence Rafferty, reviewing the film in the *New Yorker,* the sequence typifies the film's concession to talk show rhetoric: "the dialogue has the tone of daytime television confessional jamborees like 'Geraldo' and 'Sally Jessy Raphael'" ("Skin Deep," p. 99). Rafferty contends that "the movie has shown us Drew and several of her women friends (most of whom have been dragged onto the screen for this sequence alone) holding forth on the issue of interracial sex: whether 'white bitches' throw themselves at black men, whether black women should ever date white men, and so on. The sequence, which goes on for quite a while, plays like a clip from an 'Oprah' show, and it is puzzling, psychologically. What does it mean that Drew has translated her personal anguish into generalities, policy statements?" (100). Here, Rafferty seems to disavow the idea that personal anguish could intersect with the social. To arrive at his own generalities, he needs to overlook the affective register of the scene, so that he can conclude, "the rhetorical barrage that Lee unleashes here gives the picture a peculiar, halting rhythm: individual scenes have force and momentum, but the movie as a whole seems stalled, inert, uncertain where it is headed" (100). One might argue with equal plausibility that the culture itself is "stalled, inert, uncertain where it is headed" when it tries to formulate "race" and sexuality into easily manageable issues and that the film performs some of these collective "stutters" or "resistances," to set them out for analysis rather than to present resolutions.

By contrast, Ed Guerrero describes the war council scene as strictly differentiated from the rest of the film, as breaking through the film's surface, holding up its contradictions in a way that exceeds any narrative resolution. In his estimation, this scene offers "a powerful articulation of the film's uncontainable excesses, those usually unspoken social truths, energies, and contradictions that in brief illuminating flashes break through the formal surface of the dominant cinema text to pose some unexpected challenge or set of questions to the 'official story'" (178–79). Given that the documentary texture of this moment interrupts the film's narrative drive to closure and distinguishes this sequence from all others, we are invited to wonder if this is a privileged intervention.[35]

Lee himself certainly seems to see it as a privileged moment, and specifically as a moment of authenticity. As he put it in an interview: "we just rolled the cameras and kept shooting and shooting and the women, man, they forgot about the script. They were just vomiting that stuff up! I think it was all from their personal experience and that's why that scene works."[36] Perhaps not surprisingly, given that his films explore the ways in which social difference becomes a site of verbal, physical, and psychic violence, Lee shares a fairly common conviction that no matter how we may resist them at the conscious level, all of us find racial and ethnic stereotypes readily available in the form of epithets, at least in moments of affective extremity. This is another way of saying that all such stereotypes remain easily available in the reservoir of the unconscious.[37] Lee credits this sequence with exposing a special psychic "truth." But to treat such discourse as truest because it is most buried, and to see its truth as ultimate, final, and fixed, is to ignore the interaction of our psychic lives with the external social world as well as our tendencies to project the former onto the latter and to leave out of account the "truths" that may be generated as conscious discourse confronts unconscious effects.

If *Jungle Fever* momentarily assigns the power to know more and to speak more truthfully to the African American women in this sequence, it also runs the risk of setting them up in the role of judges. If women are supposed to be the "ones who know," then they get to bear responsibility for the truth of the matter, a situation that leaves the males free from responsibility to do their homework. This effect echoes forcefully in Queen Latifah's cameo appearance as a waitress in the Harlem restaurant to which Flipper takes Angie. Her character scolds Flipper in scathing terms, as much for a childish flaunting of his erotic choice as for the choice itself. What is most interesting here is perhaps the accumulation of extradiegetic "real effects," the rapper and the restaurant, around another figure of black female judgment aimed at a man who seems to go out of his way to encounter it.

Because the war council scene is not addressed to the male characters, we are asked to see it as a parenthesis, an enclave whose inclusivity is built on an assumed racial and gender solidarity. An interesting contemporary contrast is to be found in *Waiting to Exhale* (Forest Whitaker, 1995). Hardly documentary in feel or effect, that film expands the private space of women's friendship, making it its central concern. Though the film was touted as offering an unprecedented and much anticipated exploration of middle-class and professional black women's emotional lives, of their psychic interiority, it wound up staging a series of superficial popular clichés about the economic and social pressures on black women's relations with black men as it reproduced a depthless and unanalyzed series of criticisms of black men. Perhaps more disappointing, the film failed to reproduce the Terry MacMillan novel's primary appeal.[38] MacMillan's novels are about nothing so much as friendship and feeling, both of which they treat in meticulous detail. That depth was lost in the film; friendship, like the criticism of black men, was loudly asserted, but nothing bore it out. Symptomatically, at the end of an evening together, one character announces that the only things which the four have in common is that they are all women without men.

It is not surprising, I think, that *Waiting to Exhale* provoked so much harsh criticism, especially from black women critics, in places ranging from the *New York Times* Op Ed page to the *Village Voice*. Significantly, the terms of critique generally avoided the simple documentary or realist ones through which the film was marketed, instead asking more complex questions about audience address. This question needs to be taken seriously, given the enthusiasm with which white female audiences seemed to greet the film. One wants to ask whether or not the crossover appeal depended on the pleasures of hearing some scathing attacks on masculinity uttered *elsewhere*. In that case, black women would be charged with telling a brutal truth about relations between the sexes, or worse, with providing the reassurance to white women that there is an even worse deal to be had across the racial divide.

In *Jungle Fever*'s rendition of black women's solidarity, the war council scene, however, because the documenter's position is not inscribed in the scene, our spectator position may even feel voyeuristic, as if we were eavesdropping on a private moment where things can be spoken that would not be spoken "publicly" in a more heterogeneous space. This framing paradoxically enhances the sense of "truth" here, but it also serves to undercut the documenter's and spectator's positions by rendering them parenthetical. What are we to make of this temporarily privileged position that emerges parenthetically in the context of the film's framing moments, those where Flipper's passage through his neighborhood is interrupted by a crack-addicted hooker offering him sex? The film's last image fixates on Flipper's protective paternity, and his morality, when it holds on him shouting, "No!" as he clings to the young hooker in an echo of an early scene where a similar woman provides him with an occasion for paternal admonition to Ming.

This effect may be what provokes Michele Wallace to conclude that what this film is really about is "the threat of a female or aberrant sexuality to traditional family values" (127). As she puts it, "Not only is Flipper deeply threatened by the prospect of dominant female sexuality—Angie's, as well as Drew's, Vivian's, and his daughter Ming's—but the yawning threat of female sexuality somehow also becomes, within the film's larger narrative, responsible for the devastation and the insularity of ghettos, both Italian and black American" (129). Certainly there is reason to ask what remains unavailable to *Jungle Fever*'s discourse since, in exploring the contradictions of racial fantasy, it produces a range of feminine characters as the sites of most visible intersections between race and sexuality.

In this connection, the parenthetical status of the women's war council scene becomes symptomatic. The war council foregrounds the social specificity of African American women's position, a position that does not allow the fantasy of separating racial and sexual identity which is available to other social positions, and one that does not allow the imaginary leap in which one cancels or overrides the other. Kimberlé Crenshaw describes this position as "intersectional" in her article, "Whose Story Is It Anyway?: Feminist and Anti-Racist Appropriations of Anita Hill." Crenshaw is very specific about what she means by this term, which, she suggests, is necessary to conceptualize "the particular experience of black women in the dominant cultural ideology of American society."[39] For Crenshaw, this social position has to do with representation, and not identity: "Intersectionality captures the way in which the particular location of black women in dominant American social relations is unique and in some sense unassimilable into the discursive paradigms of gender and race domination" (404). This formulation echoes Hortense Spillers's rendering of the position of African American women as a figure whose repression is structurally crucial to the history of American national culture as well as to its rhetoric of race and identity: "I describe a locus of confounded identities, a meeting ground of investments and privations in the national treasury of rhetorical wealth. My country needs me, and if I were not here, I would have to be invented."[40]

Crenshaw is suggesting that the ideological and political stakes of this nonassimilability are structural, and that therefore these are high stakes for everyone in the culture. Her description of the intersectional position suggests that the structure of contemporary discussions around "race"—as well as around gender—within feminism and identity politics, as well as within so-called conservative and liberal political discourses, may depend upon not representing that position, not recognizing, let alone circulating, the narratives it generates.[41] As she puts it, "the place where African-American women live" is "a political vacuum of erasure and contradiction maintained by the almost routine polarization of 'blacks and women' into separate and competing camps. Existing within the overlapping margins of race and gender discourse in the empty spaces between, it is a location whose very nature resists telling" (403). Her logic suggests that in legal discourse, political discourse, and cultural representation to admit narratives from this intersectional position would transform the conceptual structures within which we claim and sustain "identities." This is the challenge of her argument, for it demands that we begin to think seriously about the structural function of "race" and sexuality in all identity.

If *Jungle Fever* remains unable to follow through on the critical challenge posed by this intersectionality and instead chooses to frame it parenthetically, to freeze it as iconic, in much the same way that the film fixates on the immobilized figure of Flipper and Angie, we may read this inability as symptomatic of the representational regime in which it is produced and read. For the most part, *Jungle Fever* skillfully refuses to bear the "burden of representation" with which the dominant culture may wish to saddle it. Yet, if it structurally poses the women's discourse here as a "moment of truth," then it risks simply passing this burden on to African American women. And because, as many critics have pointed out, most of the women who appear in this scene appear in cameo since they are not characters anywhere else in the film, the film risks offering them as mere "figures" of the truth, an all too common gesture in contemporary discussions, perhaps most painfully, within feminism.

Hazel Carby offers trenchant criticism of the figural status assigned to African American women within feminism and to discourses of so-called multiculturalism when she argues that the burden of representation placed upon this constructed and to some extent imaginary figure works to prevent us from seeing that "everyone in this social order has been constructed in our political imagination as a racialized subject," so that "we would see that processes of racialization are determining to all our work" (193). Feminist theory, Carby argues, has frequently produced "an essential black female subject for its own consumption." And this figure has taken the place of real analysis of the racialization that conditions all of our representations, "because this black female subject has to carry the burden of representing what is otherwise significantly absent from the curriculum, issues of complexity disappear under the pressure of the demand to give meaning to blackness" (192).

To construct figures as icons—as iconic of a "truth" that they do not speak, and of a history that they cannot tell—is to repeat the preferred gestures of dominant cultural representations. In our contemporary cultural landscape, films are released into a diffuse discursive circulation, where political struggles are played out as competing voices in the arena of public opinion, to take on an afterlife as print media and talk show events that mobilize private consumer narratives. Where representativeness emerges as a primary category of popular critical response, it becomes increasingly important to analyze the symptomatic structural functions of this figurality and what it represses in cultural representations where, by and large, almost all of the women are still white and almost all of the blacks are still men.[42] Even as more films addressed to diversified audiences emerge, Hollywood remains largely unable to keep more than one difference in frame or to explore the ways in which social identities are not accidentally or occasionally inflected by each other but, instead, are mutually constituting. Rather, it tends to privilege those differences that can be made to fit into the well-worn channels of "special interests," where black women remain prominently and consistently left out of the frame.

In the years since *Jungle Fever*'s 1991 release, the narrow, marginal representational zone allotted to black women has widened considerably. However, it is not clear that the articulations of black women figures within that zone have grown much more flexible or nuanced. Lee's own *Crooklyn,* released three years later, focuses centrally on a mother-daughter drama filtered through the daughter's grief at her mother's death. But the film is peculiarly unbalanced, since it sets the mother up as the superego for the whole family, and then proceeds to treat the impact of her voice and her judgment as enormous and oppressive for the daughter and peripheral for the sons. It is as if Lee were fixated in an oedipal universe structured by father-son and mother-daughter dramas, where no real cross-gender exchange occurs.

In recent mainstream developments we see black women entering the frame with white women, but they are doing so in films that continue to construct their relationships as accidental, even as unaccounted for, in much the same manner that Lawrence Kasdan's *Grand Canyon* (1993) presented an interracial friendship between Kevin Kline's and Danny Glover's characters. Alfre Woodard, as Jane, meets Glover's character, Simon, on a blind date that has been arranged by Kline. So her appearance is an accidental byproduct of the original accident that brought the men together. A similar sense of accident, and the whimsy that goes with it, pervades John Sayles's 1992 *Passion Fish,* which showcases the growing bond between a nurse played by Woodard, and the white woman invalid who employs her (Mary McDonnell). This film falters when it comes to accounting for the sources of the bond, however. Similarly, *How to Make an American Quilt* (Jocelyn Moorhouse, 1995) features in its distinguished cast both Alfre Woodard—once again—and Maya Angelou. Both characters come across as operating in cameo roles, and not only because of the offscreen weight of Angelou's reputation. Equally important is the film's apparent inability to account for these women's interest in the quilting circle that the elderly and middle-aged white middle-class women carry on. Indeed, at times it seems as if the two black women are meant to do the work of figuring some idealized women's "tradition" that the film imagines to be somehow enfeebled or attenuated among white women.

A striking alternative to these "incidental" presences emerges in the careers of black women "stars," whose offscreen personae certain films exploit. The few cases in point would of course include Whoopi Goldberg, who seems increasingly to operate as the offbeat counterpoint to whatever is going on in the "white" center of a film, and Whitney Houston's recent film career. *The Bodyguard* (Mick Jackson, 1992) effectively builds its entire drama around the body and the persona of the star herself. Much the same might be said of Houston's role in *Waiting to Exhale,* where her character's primary function seems to be to provide imported "glamour," as if the ensemble cast might not supply it in sufficient quantities.[43] Perhaps the most striking exception to these terms is Angela Bassett's role in *Strange Days* (Kathryn Bigelow, 1995), where her character is alertly conscious of her racialized and gendered position, but she is not on account of them pinned down to additional representational work.

As the terms of popular debate inevitably drive to reduce ambivalence, so they tend to map diversity in discrete and easily separable categories, thus continuing this culture's historical obsession with keeping gender and race scrupulously distinct. This logic's fantasmatic lining is clear: it is a desire to keep race de-eroticized and sexuality de-racialized, a desire that goes back as far as *The Birth of a Nation* (D. W. Griffith, 1915) in the movies, and much farther of course in literature, and a desire that colludes in locating "social problems" in identities and not in political struggles. And this matrix of effects shapes cultural struggle as competing "special interests," without intersection, as a set of oppositions that could make sense only for a dominant culture that wants gender and race to be fixed, embodied, and spoken, *else*where. To recognize the projective functions that go into constructing this elsewhere as an absolute difference, a definite outside, entails a systematic analysis of the coimplication of inside and outside. It requires analysis of the ways that all of our representations and the identities that they sustain and depend upon engage symptomatically with power relations invested with racial and sexual meanings.

6 Borrowed "Style": Quentin Tarantino's

Figures of Masculinity

Quentin Tarantino's characters spend a lot of time in the bathroom, and because they do, the bathroom acquires a dramatic centrality in his work. The bathroom is an ambivalent site, since the activities that take place there become in these films structurally both world-making and earth-shattering. In *Pulp Fiction* (1994) and *Reservoir Dogs* (1992), as well as in *True Romance* (Tony Scott, 1993), for which Tarantino wrote the screenplay, the bathroom anchors a dense nexus that connects blood and violence to anal eroticism and smearing. It thus permits delicate intersections of aggressive soiling impulses with tense efforts to consolidate, to clean, and to retain at the literal level and with social hygienic dreams of sanitizing a word like "nigger" at the figurative level. Tarantino's bathroom links consolidation to fragmentation, and it links affective release with getting caught unawares and exposed. In the process, the bathroom also realigns cultural authority in relation to refuse, or trash, on the one hand, and to "race," on the other.

Often, like *Pulp Fiction*'s Vincent Vega (John Travolta), Tarantino's characters get caught with their pants down. We might even understand that as the film's central metaphor. Not only does Vince Vega get killed as a consequence of an untimely visit to the john, but the anal rape of Marcellus Wallace is the most deeply embedded episode in its interlocked plot structure. Wallace (Ving Rhames), Vega's boss, is the central figure who organizes all the characters diegetically and who orchestrates the narratives' intertwining. So, in some sense, the film is about catching the big boss with his pants down literally, even as the other characters strive to keep from being caught that way. Indeed, this metaphor is set up as the film's watchword from beginning to end. In the untitled opening sequence in the Hawthorne Diner, which acts as the framing story for the three titled narratives, the bungling thieves, Honey Bunny (Amanda Plummer) and Pumpkin (Tim Roth), try to rob the diner to test their theory that they should switch targets from liquor stores and gas stations to restaurants because it is much easier to "catch everyone with their pants down."

Getting caught with one's pants down seems to be the prevailing effect that these films aim to produce in the spectator as well. Tarantino addresses this effect—provocatively—in connection with his films' reputation for violence: "I actually had an epiphany about why people think *Reservoir Dogs* is so violent. . . . You're watching it, and even while the humorous scenes are going on, the threat of tragedy . . . is hovering over the movie. This is going to end horribly." [1] More specifically, the effect of catching the spectator off guard and exposed is central to *Reservoir Dogs'* most discussed scene. "The thing that I am really proud of in the torture scene in *Dogs* with Mr. Blonde, Michael Madsen," Tarantino tells Dennis Hopper in an interview, "is the fact that it's truly funny up until the point that he cuts the cop's ear off. While he's up there doing that little dance to 'Stuck in the Middle with You,' I pretty much defy anybody to watch and not enjoy it. . . . And then when he starts cutting the ear off, that's not played for laughs. . . . So now you've got his coolness and his dance, the joke of talking into the ear and the cop's pain, they're all tied up together, and that's why I think that scene caused such a sensation, because you don't know how you're supposed to feel when you see it." [2]

To be caught laughing when something horrific happens, to gasp at the mismatch between our affective state and the next image, may be to reproduce, or at least to recall the embarrassment, or even shame, of being caught with our pants down in a breach of social discipline. Tweaking our internal social censorship mechanisms as they do by the mismatches that they effect between the funny and the horrifying, the abject, or the frightening, these films leave us to manage that affective excess, which we may do by turning shock into embarrassment, or by taking satisfaction in the alibi they provide, so we can feel that we are getting away with laughing when we should not.

Curiously, the filmmaker addresses this kind of excess through references to taste, food, and consumption, a category definitively mismatched with the bathroom and its functions. "Funniness and scariness," in the words of the film geek-turned-auteur, are "two great tastes that taste great together" (Kennedy, p. 32). By appropriating a jingle this way, Tarantino mimes the discourse of *Pulp Fiction,* a film that, like *Reservoir Dogs,* self-consciously speaks and is spoken by fragments of popular culture. The films consume the soundtrack of daily life, and they recycle it, spit it back to us. Bits of discourse, figures, and fragmented texts from television, radio, and print become found objects that circulate as residues and trash in ways that may be linked to the films' metaphorics of shit, which is of course associated with the bathroom.

Part of the reason that bloodletting can be humorous in Tarantino's work is that blood really operates like feces, so that the spilling of blood is very much like smearing. But smearing, in all of its evocation of infantile activity, not only provokes laughter, but also implies violence.[3] Though this connection between blood and shit might seem at first farfetched, a look at Tarantino's signature effects suggests that it is not. While the celebratory clamor about his emergence as the American auteur for the nineties turns on his wizardry with violence and its eroticized possibilities, the filmmaker's own appearance as a figure in his films is as closely associated with shit as with violence. Tarantino's character in *Reservoir Dogs* loudly proclaims this in so many words. Complaining to his boss— in his signature whine—about his alias, Mr. Brown, he asserts: "Brown, that's a little too close to shit."

Soiling and cleaning are, of course, the central subject of "the Bonnie situation." This is *Pulp Fiction*'s central comic moment, the one that is supposed to rewrite and contain the film's violence as entirely "over the top," and thereby to retroactively ironize much of what has gone before. Vince Vega precipitates "the Bonnie situation" when he accidentally shoots Marvin, the only survivor of the opening confrontation, in the face, blowing skin, blood, skull, and brain matter all over the backseat and into his and Jules's (Samuel L. Jackson's) hair. This moment echoes the sequence that opens and anchors the action of *Reservoir Dogs,* as Orange (Roth) and White (Keitel) bond while fleeing the aborted diamond heist, with White driving and Orange screaming, whimpering, and writhing in the back, while his blood spews all over the white vinyl upholstery. As the film progresses, more and more blood drains out of Orange, until he writhes and struggles and slides around in what looks more and more like a spill of red paint. Curiously, the film's duration seems to be controlled by the amount of time it takes someone to bleed to death. This blood seems to signify something other than the violence that produces it and to refer more definitively to the shocking aesthetic effects that the smears of red on a white background produce—a violent soiling.

Tarantino's character in *Pulp Fiction,* Jimmy, who appears only in this episode, is frantic to clean up all the bloody evidence of Jules's and Vince's visit to his home. In a central and particularly hilarious moment, Jules, clearly the film's best cleaner, as well as its most articulate speaker, is infuriated by Vince's poor bathroom habits, since he leaves the wash-cloth stained with blood and looking like a "maxipad."[4] This sequence is about hygiene in an uproarious way; but its structural link between blood and the bathroom suggests that blood is Tarantino's way of "smearing." Soiling and cleaning, then, become central organizing processes for these films—at the literal and the figurative levels.

When Mia (Uma Thurman) asks Vega, "Don't you love it when you come back from the bathroom and your food is there," her remark constitutes an attenuated echo of a number of bathroom events. Of course, it anticipates a later incident in this story when Vince returns from a trip to the bathroom to find Mia comatose, drooling, and bleeding from the nose. But it also resonates with the sequence where Jules and Vince enter the apartment of some college boys who have cheated their boss on a drug deal. As they shoot two of the three young men, the film parallel-edits shots of a fourth hiding in the bathroom, where he has been interrupted with his pants down. His emergence from the bathroom produces a "miracle," at least according to Jules's later assessment. When he opens fire on the two gangsters with an automatic weapon, every shot misses them. Similarly, in the closing segment of the film's framing sequence, Vega emerges from the bathroom to find the Hawthorne Diner in the middle of a full crisis. In *Pulp Fiction,* as in *True Romance,* emerging from the bathroom sometimes has the status of an emergency in a universe where going to the bathroom has transformative effects on the *outside.* With striking frequency, people emerge from the privy to find that the world has changed in their absence, the situation has exploded or imploded.

What can happen inside the bathroom? Somebody can, for instance, consolidate his position or his image, as Vince Vega does when he spends several minutes in Mia's bathroom posing before her mirror and earnestly talking himself out of sleeping with her. Of course, when he returns to the living room, the whole situation has changed; she has overdosed on his heroin.

Someone also can use the bathroom as Mia does, "to powder her nose," as she puts it, with cocaine. So the bathroom is, metaphorically, the site where one consumes "shit" as well as where one produces it. Mr. Orange in *Reservoir Dogs* has a central moment in the bathroom as well. The film takes great pains to demonstrate that the undercover cop is an actor, and thus, in order to structure this character as the film's self-referential center, it has Roth repeatedly rehearse a number that he performs until it satisfies his black superior, his best audience. While he tells a story of a drug deal that almost went wrong because he entered a public bathroom and found cops in it telling stories of arrests, cinematically Roth's character moves from the performance into the story that he is telling. This is the moment of central embedding and self-reflexivity, and it happens in the bathroom, a leveling space where the simple equation of cops to criminals is displayed and performed.

This central bathroom, the private zone embedded in public places, the privy to which the films return obsessively, operates in densely woven communication with the particular public space of popular culture. Tarantino's bathroom users participate in constant exchanges of popular culture artifacts, both with each other and with the spectators in a public space articulated as an abstracted and disembodied community linked by television, radio, and videocassette. After all, Vince Vega is always reading *Modesty Blaise*[5] when he retreats to the bathroom. And *True Romance*'s narrative action is often motivated by Clarence's private audiences with a popular culture icon—Elvis.

True Romance also constructs the bathroom as a space for consolidating oneself. Clarence's consciousness is effectively represented only in the bathroom, where his interior monologue is exteriorized in dialogue with Elvis; it is here, too, that he retreats to repossess the image he is trying to cultivate: his "cool." Moreover, that space is finally the site of Elvis's miraculous incarnation as an image that we see, rather than simply a voice that we hear. As Clarence stands in front of the mirror, washing up, he and the audience receive the gift of Elvis's face. In this moment, Elvis coincides with the father's voice, telling Clarence how proud he is of him. So this is the gift of the father's face, and its arrival in the bathroom associates it with soiling and cleaning.[6]

The bathroom's relationship to anality and aggression is of course what underlies its connection to emergencies, to world-making and earth-shattering change. The infantile lining to the fantasies that Tarantino's films mobilize around this site discloses itself across the story, "The Gold

Watch," the middle one of *Pulp Fiction*'s three embedded narratives. From its opening, this story establishes both its pleasures and its shocks as rooted in infantile regression to anal sadism and the satisfactions of "producing" a "gift." The gift is, of course, the father's watch, the gold of the title.

This sequence opens with a cartoon image that fills the screen, later to be matched on the television in the child Butch Coolidge's living room. As spectators, then, we are watching Coolidge's childhood television of the 1960s. Coolidge becomes the character that the film links most closely to the television set; he and his girlfriend are riveted on a motorcycle gang movie on morning TV in their hotel room. And the sound of automatic weapons fire from the television is ambient when Butch wakes up there. This soundtrack recalls the opening of the story, where the child Butch receives his dead father's watch from a Vietnam war buddy, Captain Koons, played by Christopher Walken.

Walken himself operates as a certain icon of 1970s rereadings of the Vietnam War, through his performance in *The Deer Hunter* (Michael Cimino, 1978). In some sense, he reproduces the deranged voice and look of his character in the earlier film as he explains to Butch that the watch is a paternal legacy that goes back to his great-grandfather and that it passes from father to son as an amulet to protect them in war. (Of course, the watch has only functioned that way for one father, since the other two have died.) Its most recent passage from man to man has transpired in the prisoner-of-war camp where Koons and the senior Coolidge have been incarcerated. And, as Koons tells Butch with blunt force, his father hid the watch "up his ass." When the father dies of dysentery (a disease that, in the context of *Pulp Fiction,* reads as excessive production of shit, or the inability to retain anything at all), Koons installs the watch in his own rectum—for two years. So the adored fetish for which Coolidge risks his life later in this episode is a gift that issues from the father's ass. It is also, metaphorically, both a gift from the site of the father's death, and a gift that passes from man to man in an exchange forcefully coded as anal. Here, the relentless focus on the anal indicates the persistence of preoedipal impulses underlying the oedipal structures. Indeed, as *Pulp Fiction* unfolds, we might see it as producing an increasingly tense friction between oedipal organization and ferocious preoedipal impulses.[7]

As is the case with many sequences in *Pulp Fiction,* at the level of dialogue this scene is quite funny, particularly as Walken's character moves from solemn reverence about his war buddy and his own surrogacy in fulfilling the paternal legacy to a vulgar diatribe about the discomforts of carrying a watch in one's rectum. Equally ironic, the father surrogate's appearance is heralded by a television image, and a TV set continues to play throughout this sequence. Television and televised visions of the Vietnam War have come to coincide with the figure of the father. It is as if the television news and war movies of the 1970s were Butch's father, as Elvis is Clarence's, at least to the extent that television inscribes the co-incidence of the father's images endlessly rerunning with the figure of the father's gaze. That is, the child Butch has Vietnam War movies and video footage in place of the absent father. And when Captain Koons enters the living room, we see Walken in his function as an image retrieved from a repertoire of 1970s television and movie versions of ruined masculinity in search of rehabilitation.

In this sequence the gray light of the television presiding over the scene seems to inscribe the ghostly paternal gaze. Where the previous sequences have unfolded under Marsellus's absent but ambient gaze, this story substitutes a paternal gaze emerging from the concreteness of the television set, the site of a different kind of unlocalizable gaze. But even more important, this effect coheres figurally with a reading of the film's overarching project as a drive to turn shit into gold. This is one way of describing the project of redeeming and recycling popular culture, especially the popular culture of one's childhood, as is Tarantino's wont as well as his stated aim. To follow out this logic, then, Walken himself is part of the detritus that is being recycled here, as are John Travolta, Dennis Hopper in *True Romance,* and Harvey Keitel, both as Winston Wolf in this film and as Mr. White in *Reservoir Dogs.*[8]

Harvey Keitel figures an interesting link between the well-known actors of this generation who function to anchor both the ensembles of these films and the popular culture of Tarantino's own past that animates and circulates through the narratives and image repertoires.[9] Keitel, however, also figures as a father. Not only is he the coproducer of Tarantino's first film, *Reservoir Dogs,* but his character cares for Mr. Orange with a certain tenderness, as well as the authority of experience, in a way that is firmly coded as paternal, and he instructs the other criminals in a similar manner. Likewise, his character in *Pulp Fiction,* Winston Wolf, who orchestrates the cleanup in Jimmy's house, brings a certain paternal force to bear on the situation, instructing and ordering Jules and Vince to perform their tasks, reassuring Jimmy about his ability to restore order to the suburban home. He is also, of course, in this sequence a director figure, orchestrating the action, and referring to the people involved as "the principals." It is surely no accident that this kind of director figure appears to discipline and reassure the character played by Tarantino himself here, a character desperate with anxiety that he will not be able to fulfill domestic responsibilities presumably set out by his wife, Bonnie. Tarantino's person, then, figures as irresponsible in ways that have interesting resonances for the rest of the film, particularly concerning his repeated use of the word "nigger," a term that the film keeps in volatile circulation. But this sequence also evokes the director-as-auteur, his persona for the press. In an interview with Lisa Kennedy, Tarantino locates Harvey Keitel in his personal psychodrama: "the father I never had" (30).

Speaking as auteur, Tarantino shapes himself as a fan, so that Keitel's paternity constitutes a relationship of cultural adoption. Within the same metaphorics, a figure like Travolta is orphaned by Hollywood and then reclaimed or restored as he is adopted by Tarantino. Indeed, Tarantino's texts are full of adoptive fathers and father surrogates; we might see his reclamation of the French New Wave and its American B-movie predecessors as adopting fathers.[10] Recourse to Tarantino's performance in interviews here may not only be justified but necessary to the extent that the interview is increasingly part of the textual frame for his work. As Timothy Corrigan contends, "if, in conjunction with the so-called international art cinema of the sixties and seventies, the auteur had been absorbed as a phantom presence within a text, he or she has rematerialized in the eighties and nineties as a commercial performance of *the business of being an auteur*."[11] Corrigan continues: "*auteurs* have become increasingly situated along an extratextual path in which their commercial status as auteurs is their chief function as *auteurs*" (105).

What is interesting about Tarantino in this connection is that he is both the phantom presence within the film and a commercial performance extratextually—which is probably why he has emerged so spectacularly as the auteur of the nineties.[12] This ability to combine two types of authorial function is no doubt part of Tarantino's debt to the French New Wave and part of his appeal to "art" audiences.[13] In this regard, he fulfills what James Naremore describes as the "two faces" of auteurism. "Marginalized social groups," he writes, "can declare solidarity and create a collective identity by adopting authors as culture heroes—names that signify complex, coded meanings; indeed I would argue that international auteurism in its early phases had roughly that use." "Once these same culture heroes have been established and widely recognized, however," Naremore continues, "they can become icons of mass memory to touchstones in a 'great tradition' " (21). Tarantino's function as an icon of the mass memory like those he recycles is certainly worth serious attention. But this should be understood in the context of his appeal to cult and fan formations, and perhaps most particularly because he presents himself as a superfan.[14]

In this respect, the rapidity with which Tarantino has developed a huge fandom may have to do with what Corrigan describes as the increasing importance of cult viewing in relation to auteurship, where the auteur operates "as a commercial strategy for organizing audience reception, as a critical concept bound to distribution and marketing aims that identify and address the potential cult status of an *auteur*" (103). Significantly, as the case of David Lynch has shown, a cult audience may suddenly and paradoxically expand to rather huge proportions, can even become temporarily mainstream. The particular vicissitudes that may shape this process in Tarantino's career are, of course, unpredictable.

And perhaps this is why Tarantino is so intent on inscribing himself, multiply, in his films. Butch Coolidge is only one of a series of characters, like Clarence Worley, Mr. Orange, Vince Vega, Vic Vega (Mr. Blonde)—all representing some defiance of paternal authority, however indirectly— and, of course, the characters Jimmy and Mr. Brown, whose presence inscribes the author as one of the very "fanboys," film buffs drawn to a male youth collective identity, that he identifies with and seeks to attract.[15] Tarantino's auteur status is closely coincident with his cult status for the following reason: the filmmaker's persona and his films embody a nostalgia for a 1970s that is continually circulating in television, videocassettes, and radio. This is the popular culture that formed the previous generation—the parent generation—now the shapers of dominant critical discourse about popular culture. And if that generation experienced as children the formative effects of a popular culture whose nostalgia and recollection were seeking to make some sense through cultural artifacts and repetitions of the 1960s, later appropriations of the products of the 1970s recycle them as a kind of nostalgia to the second degree: nostalgia for nostalgia. Tarantino's work stresses the absolute contemporaneity— the contemporaneity of the always already "missed"—that television and radio recycling posit for these cultural artifacts. And this artifical contemporaneity operates as a kind of utopian eternal present.[16] In relying on these artifacts as central organizing devices, his films offer the perfect salvage operation, redeeming a past for the generation that inhabited it, but that also "missed" it. To redeem a previous generation's trash may be, metaphorically, to turn its shit into gold and to posit a certain reversibility of cultural authority in the process. At the same time, we need to explore how this obsessive return to oedipal narratives and images for processing a cultural history produces a powerful—even structuring—equation in Tarantino's work between African American masculinity and popular culture.

Butch circulates through episodic structures that are governed by another figure, one who also emerges under the sign of the father and the law. This is Marsellus Wallace, the "big man," the boss that Jules and Vince keep referring to in the preceding sequence, the authority whose sense of just punishment they dispute when they speculate about his motives for throwing Tony, their half-black, half-Samoan colleague, out a window. Significantly, this sequence establishes another authority at the same time: Jules is the authority on television in this pair. Explaining the term "series pilot," Jules reminds Vince that the mere fact that he never watches television by no means accounts for his ignorance, because the form is ambient.

While Marsellus is absent from all but the opening scene of this segment, he is clearly constructed as the ultimate authority in Jules and Vince's work world as well as the central narrative organizing principle to the extent that he holds all of the plot lines together. Operating as the intersection of plots, Marsellus himself is the link that connects the divergent episodes and initially unrelated characters. Having initially established him as the unseen law of this world, the film introduces his physical presence at the beginning of "Vince Vega and Marsellus Wallace's Wife," in a sequence that we will later understand to be a snippet of the "Gold Watch" segment. At first, Marsellus is only a voice instructing Butch Coolidge. When he does appear, we see only the back of his head, dilated to fill most of the frame. In place of a face, we see the blank screen of his shaved head, a surface interrupted only by the risible mark of a Band-Aid of that pinkish-beige color that white people often used to call "flesh." This puny and familiar little object, placed as it is in the middle of the back of Marsellus's skull, operates as a blemish, a mark that highlights this character's skin tone in a world that is white-bound at the level of the most banal everyday object. This scene, which turns on Marsellus's transaction with Butch, paying him to lose a boxing match, also establishes his relationship to Vince and Jules. Upon noticing Vince at the bar, Marsellus greets him jauntily as "my nigger." Where Jules, the avenging angel, is the character who first employs this term and thus links its use to his own moral/spiritual authority, Marsellus is the character with the lexical authority to displace its reference, to make it apply to Vince, a white guy.

However, to understand the many functions of Marsellus as authority or law, we must read this initially disembodied figure who is most powerful in his absence, as, for instance, a voice on the phone, and as a spectacular body, so that we may examine the resources and effects of this embodiment. It does not seem accidental that the two white "hillbillies" in the gun shop–surplus store choose Marsellus Wallace as their rape victim.[17] And it seems all the less accidental as the film establishes these characters as racist through their recitation of "eeny-meeny miney moe, catch a nigger by the toe." Intentionally or not, this moment establishes the nonaccidental character of the very chance that is invoked here.[18] And, as we will see, part of the reason that this is not an accident is that *Pulp Fiction* depends ambiguously and ambivalently on the very racism it wishes to distance itself from, to establish as its outside, its elsewhere. At the same time, in their effort to humiliate Marsellus before they rape him, these characters reduce the "big man" to "boy." And this may be the point at which the embedded symbolics of the film's most anxious and horrifying moment of suspense emerge, because the reduction of man to boy in the context of this anal aggression returns us to the problem of fathers and sons, and to the oedipal-preoedipal tonality with which the whole film, like Tarantino's work in general, is tinged.

As spectators, we are implicated in this scene's construction as a primal scene; we are required to wait anxiously, staring at the closed green door from behind which issue sounds of violence and bodily strain, which could easily be confused with sexual sounds. We might find in this position a certain analogy with a curious child outside his parents' bedroom, or waiting outside the bathroom door. Straining to see beyond the wall, at the same time that we fear the sight which we await, this is also a position that might put us in mind of the film's opening sequence, where, at a certain point, the screen goes black, and we anxiously await the return of the image. When it does, we are looking up at Vince and Jules, and we retroactively locate the camera in the trunk of the car.

This is the position that Marvin's body will soon occupy, once Vince has accidentally blown his head off.[19] So *Pulp Fiction*'s spectator position might resemble that of the victim abducted and thrown in the gangster's trunk. At the same time, the rape scene emphatically replays the familiar Tarantino effect: it catches us laughing completely inappropriately.

While Marsellus is concealed in the closed room, Butch manages to get free. In a visible, but unaccountable, "change of heart" that is a familiar move for Tarantino's characters, he goes to seek a weapon with which to rescue Marsellus. Our enjoyment of Butch's slow, deliberate choice of weapon, ending up with the least appropriate, the samurai sword, is abruptly interrupted by the revelation of the rape in progress behind the door. We get caught laughing at an anal rape—caught, figuratively, with our pants down—and at the very moment when Marsellus is literally caught with his pants down.

The violence and aggression that attend this literalization produce an affective force that is somewhat hard to localize, and this may be because of the reversibility suggested by our own position as spectators—caught off guard and rendered vulnerable.[20] In the sadomasochistic economy that drives the most gleefully violent sequences, the spectator seems subject to a constant oscillation between the position of subject and object of violence, an oscillation in which we are at constant risk of being caught out.[21] If Tarantino's films seem to smear the screen with blood, to return us over and over to anal aggression, they also ask over and over: Have you had enough? It is as if they were addressing an audience whose visual, aural appetite for knowledge—curiosity—were the unmistakable counterpart of that anal aggressivity.

Indeed, it seems that in *Pulp Fiction*'s universe, everything is reversible, another indication that its fantasies are steadfastly infantile. As soon as he is freed, Marsellus retaliates by shooting his rapist, Zed, in the crotch, and by threatening him with distinctly racialized violence: "I'll get a couple of hard pipe fitting niggers to go to work on Mr. Rapist here with a blowtorch and pliers." If the film had any ambition to sanitize the anal rape of its racial overcodings, this moment certainly reinstates the racialized edge of this homoerotic attack.

Writing about Tarantino in the *Village Voice*, Lisa Kennedy takes the risk of citing the speculations of her black woman companion about what lies behind the conjunctions of race and sexualized violence in his work. According to Kennedy, at a screening of *Pulp Fiction*, her friend blurted out: "What he wants is a big black man to fuck him up the ass!" Kennedy continues, contextualizing the remark: "Well, she's frank if nothing else and for her a guy wanting it up the ass by a brother is not necessarily a bad thing" (29). I find this remark most interesting because it seems to depend on the fundamental reversibility that structures the film's staging of the fantasy of anal sex with a black man. On the other hand, I think the image of this anal rape only comes into full legibility if we set it in the context of the obsessional patterns that emerge around the bathroom and around violence in relation to race, sexuality, paternity, and culture in Tarantino's films.

Like *Reservoir Dogs* and *True Romance, Pulp Fiction* seems to channel an ambivalent mix of desire and hostility through recourse to adolescent, "boyish," bathroom humor. And both desire and hostility seem to be directed at fathers in attacks staged to win the approval of women and black men. Notably, in many instances these figures are represented as popular culture icons. These films depend centrally on a structure that repeatedly effects a displacement and substitution of authority between an idealized absent black male peer—represented by a figure like Marsellus Wallace—and the white father, frequently associated with the popular culture industry, as either its star (Elvis) or its abject or residue (Walken). *True Romance* renders this condensed and economical oedipality quite explicitly. Its final explosive three-way shoot-out between police, drug lords, and movie director and drug buyer, Lee Donowitz (Saul Rubinek), and his personal bodyguards seems nothing more—or less—than a spectacular patricide.[22] Donowitz, the fictional producer of a well-known Vietnam film, *Coming Home in a Body Bag* (a title that alludes to *Coming Home* [Hal Ashby, 1978]), and the object of superfan Clarence's fetishistic adulation, resembles action film producer Joel Silver.[23] He may also allude to Oliver Stone, a figure of intense, nearly ecstatic, rivalry for Tarantino, at least in Tarantino's auteurist interview persona.[24] Donowitz is betrayed by his slimy assistant, Eliot Blitzer (Bronson Pinchot), a younger man who is forced by police to entrap his mentor in order to avoid prison himself.[25] The dramatically ironic oedipal tone of this final conflagration could not be more graphically established. Lee Donowitz breaks the standoff by throwing coffee on Eliot Blitzer, since Blitzer's plea to the police officer that he be allowed to leave reveals his complicity in the police entrapment scheme. Donowitz has become the voice of Hollywood—not only a Stone parody but the voice of film as a commodity in the same universe as drugs: "What the fuck . . . you little piece of shit . . . your career is over . . . you little cocksucker, I treated you like a son and you fuckin' stabbed me in the heart."

Clarence emerges from this bloodbath a lucky survivor marked permanently by the parodically unsubtle sign of its fundamentally oedipal character: the black patch that covers the eye blinded by a gunshot. The celebratory and triumphant quality of his emergence is guaranteed by the woman's adulation; the last words of the film, tracked with images of the renewed nuclear family, father, mother, and little son, Elvis, the father restored in the son's paternity. Alabama has the last word, as she has the first, since her voiceover generates and conditions the whole story. But what is the story? Basically, it is this: a man succeeds in killing the fathers—all of them—in order to father a son with the woman to whom all of his activity is addressed.[26] And his action, like his wit, takes the form primarily of posturing. Alabama determines this definitively: "All I could smell was violence in the air. I look back and I'm amazed that my thoughts were so clear. Three words went through my mind endlessly: you're so cool, you're so cool."

Certain telling Tarantino obsessions run through *True Romance* and repeat in *Reservoir Dogs* and *Pulp Fiction*. For example, in each case at some point one character asks another if a particular man "looks like a bitch." To the invariably negative answer, the characters always offer a reply along these lines: "Then why are you trying to fuck him like a bitch?" To be fucked equals to be a bitch. This equation of men and "bitches" circulates obsessively in Tarantino's work, and it operates on both sides of the law. Indeed, it may be precisely the figure that collapses the law, as police and criminals entertain an equal fascination with anal sex between men.[27]

But the obsessive rehearsal in Tarantino's films of oedipal structures—and of the preoedipal ones that underlie and break through them—intersects with suspicious frequency with ambivalent racial meanings, as it does in the figure of Marsellus Wallace. Such intersections are made of a negotiation that often flipflops between idealization and abjection, two processes that may operate in a dialectical interplay around the father and extend to other figures as well. But is Daddy black or white? We might be moved to ask about the fantasmatic father's race and its impact on the oedipal dramas that the films are playing out through their collisions of cultural artifacts. Tarantino's films seem to map social differences as competing cultures, where icons of African American culture are constructed as an intervention, a critical challenge to Daddy's culture of the 1970s. Racial difference, figured as cultural capital or expressivity, operates fantasmatically to interrupt white paternal authority, as young white men watch their white father under the intervening gaze of an imaginary black male, either alternate father or rival brother.[28]

In *Pulp Fiction* the father's watch—his gift, his excrement—is a source of obsessive fascination that reminds us of the gaze and surveillance as well; it is as if the watch, like the TV, and popular culture in general, were an instrument of the reversible gaze. In this web of reversible infantile fantasies, authority and its gaze are linked to shit. But which father is watching? It is worth recalling Mr. Orange here, the undercover cop in *Reservoir Dogs* and the character who embodies the film's most powerful references to its own production processes, as he explicitly rehearses and performs the story and the persona that will authenticate him as a drug dealer to Joe Cabot. Orange's mentor, boss, and the final addressee, director, and judge of his performance is an African American superior. This oedipalized coupling perhaps provides us with some clue about the address of the masculine posturings that emerge as the central subjects of Tarantino's films. And it might suggest that the point of address is as important as the performance itself.

Reservoir Dogs produces a pivotal instance that connects racial meanings to paternal surveillance, and one that helps to render legible the link that organizes Tarantino's narrative universes. In a sequence that immediately precedes the famous scene in which the horrifying Vick Vega, alias Mr. Blonde (Michael Madsen), tortures the captive policeman, the film provides us with a little backstory on this character. By sheer force of metonymy, the film asks us to look at the preceding sequence for a certain explanatory power. And while what we find is incoherence, flippant adolescent humor, and the titillation of eroticized racial suggestiveness, the sequence has the dizzying effect of providing a false and even delirious account of the character's psychology, his desocialization—a delirious account, but an account nonetheless that the film does nothing to displace or rewrite.

This sequence finds Vick Vega returning from prison to the office of Joe Cabot. Under the welcoming paternal gaze, Vega cavorts and banters with his buddy, Eddie Cabot (Christopher Penn), who punctuates their ritual exchange of insults by periodically invoking his father, "Daddy," as witness and judge. Their verbal tussling begins with basic homoerotic aggression, as the guys roll around on the floor, in an embrace that ends with Eddie's appeal, "Daddy, he tried to fuck me." Eddie continues: "You've been fuckin' punks up the ass, I'd think you'd appreciate a nice prime rib when you see it." To which Vega replies, upping the ante: "If I was a butt cowboy, I wouldn't even throw you to my posse. I might break you in, but I'd make you my dog's bitch." Eddie's comeback retroactively racializes this entire scene of male posturing: "All that black semen been poked up your ass backed up so far in your brain it's coming out your mouth." Turning to his father, he concludes: "It's a sad sight, Daddy, a man walkin' into prison white and comin' out talkin' like a fuckin' nigger." In this elaborate performance, race is coded as culture, through its figuration as pure linguistic expression.[29] "Race" becomes a kind of switchpoint here, lying at the center of a knot that condenses oedipal rivalry with homoerotophobic attraction-repulsion, an attraction-repulsion that is also aligned with anxieties and desires about feminization. In this vortex of the reversible infantile fantasies of anal aggression, raping the father reverts to being raped by him. At the same time, however, "race" becomes a transformative term, placed at the border where identification rubs against murderous hostility.

One of *True Romance*'s most compelling and virtuoso scenes, a moment of stunningly slick banter between two popular cultural patriarchs, Dennis Hopper and Christopher Walken, capitalizes on a different intersection between racial meanings and paternity. Where the racialized eroticism is staged for Daddy's approval in *Reservoir Dogs,* in *True Romance* the scene where Walken's character, Don Vicenzo, a mob boss of Sicilian descent, interrogates Hopper's character, Clarence Worley's father, about his son's whereabouts is meant to provide a reason to blow Daddy away. Worley's answer to Don Vicenzo's insistence that he can tell if his interlocutor is telling the truth because of Sicilian folk wisdom handed down by his father comes in the form of a story about the mulatto origins of all Sicilians. "Way back then, Sicilians were like wops from Northern Italy. Blonde hair, blue eyes. But, ah, then, the Moors moved in and . . . did so much fucking they changed the bloodline forever. . . . Sicilians still carry that nigger gene. . . . Your ancestors were niggers. Your great great great great grandmother fucked a nigger. . . . If that's a fact, tell me . . . am I lying? Cause, you, you are part eggplant." At this, the still smiling Don Vicenzo blows Worley's head off. The over-the-top hilarity and adolescent glee at merging racial slur with ethnic insult between the two smirking characters here combines the pleasure of transgressive hate speech in the safe container of highly staged artifice—performance—with the pleasure of blowing Daddy away for uttering it. And part of the power of the scene's effect is its ambiguity about what its primary point is. That ambiguity is bound to the satisfaction of seeing someone—Daddy, who in this case might be imagined as an internal imago, an inverted superego figure, that is, an id figure—punished for saying what may give a spectator pleasure for its sheer transgressiveness. This scene depends on the possibilities of pleasure in hearing spoken elsewhere what remains censored and unavailable to speech. It depends, that is, on imagining that some of us—individually or collectively—must be working to censor such speech. It imagines, in other words, something like a cultural id that functions on an analogy with individual unconscious processes.

To return to Marsellus Wallace's function as a paternal figure, and to the peculiar intersection he produces with racial meanings, we need to understand this figure in relation to *Pulp Fiction*'s other black male authority figure: Jules. Jules the avenger, quoting redemptive verses from Ezekiel to his victims, is the only character who judges the universe that these characters inhabit, and, finding it insufficient, he retreats from it. Effectively, by exiting when he does, he puts an end to the potentially endless series of episodes that might unfold here. If Jules is the ultimate judge and the would-be redeemer of Honey Bunny and Pumpkin, he also expresses the film's most consistent viewpoint and is its most consistent mouthpiece; he sees and analyzes everything. By contrast, we never directly see things from Marsellus's point of view. This effect helps to establish his perspective as omniscient and ambient—or unsituated—as the patriarchal god who commands, and judges, where Jules mediates and redeems. There is one exception to the Law of Marsellus's point of view, however, one shot that seems anchored to and governed by his gaze. This is the moment when Jimmy's absent wife, Bonnie, is given to our sight, as Marsellus, talking about the "situation" on the phone with Jules, imagines her coming home to find the disarray. This shot, assigned to Marsellus's knowledge or fantasy, establishes Bonnie as a black woman.

If Marsellus Wallace may figure the law of the film—what holds it all together—his authority is superseded by that of the black woman, Jimmy's wife, whose image, after all, he supplies for us. Where the other women in *Pulp Fiction* appear as narrative agents only to the extent that they produce accidents for the men to handle—Fabian's [*sic*] forgetting Butch's watch, for instance, or Mia's heroin overdose—the woman is the whole point of the Bonnie situation. The segment is conditioned by and addressed to her absence. When Jules and Vince retreat to Jimmy's suburban house to clean their car of Marvin's blood and brains and to dispose of his body, the situation goes into comic overdrive as Marsellus calls in a specialist, Mr. Wolf, to mobilize the bumbling group in a desperate cleaning binge—and all to forestall a woman's rage. This entire segment deals with the men's anxiety about a woman's anger, and so it is shaped by a parodic address to Mommy.

But this very address shows the father to be deficient. The figure of the black woman interrupts his authority, since even Marsellus fears Bonnie. Of course, this is part of the segment's comic effect—all these violent, aggressive males, including the most hypermasculinized, Marsellus, are intimidated by the absent, unseen nurse—the phallic Mommy. And we know this because the fantasy of Bonnie's return to catch the boys with their pants down, so to speak, is visualized from Marsellus's point of view. Hence, the black father is completed and complemented by an address to an absent black woman. But it is the phallic overtone assigned to racial inflection that is the significant symptom of the form of racial fetishization that is specific to Tarantino's filmic universe.

And we have seen this before: the men's behavior in the Bonnie situation echoes the fumbling band of boy fans in *Reservoir Dogs,* boys who are explicitly presented as popular culture fans, from the opening scene in a diner where Tarantino's character, Mr. Brown, gives a reading of Madonna's "Like a Virgin," to the moment in the car on the way to their job discussing the relative merits of white women and black women: "black women ain't the same as white; they won't put up with shit." The example of black feminine resistance is a waitress named Elois, a woman whose sexiness—"every guy who ever saw her had to jack off to her at least once," one character announces—seems related to her authority and force. These are exemplified in an attack on a man's sexuality; she takes revenge on her man by glueing his penis to his belly with Krazy Glue. This is a woman the characters adoringly describe as resembling Pam Grier, a 1970s female blaxploitation action hero.[30]

The guys in *Reservoir Dogs* fetishize Pam Grier as fans, and this might remind us that *Pulp Fiction*'s male group at Jimmy's house is like a bunch of fans. And perhaps the fans in the films, and the fans imagined outside it in the audience, are a group of boys that it is fun to hang out with, but that you would not want Mom to see? Perhaps this is why the Bonnie situation is so compellingly essential to the narrative intricacies of *Pulp Fiction,* because it discloses a central motivation for the film's excesses, playing with what you would not want Mom to see or hear: shit, genitals, and obscene language. Such a reading is consistent with the status of feminine authority in the Bonnie situation. This is consistent with the film's gendered universe, which is mapped by the divide between the schoolgirls' room and the boys' room, where all sorts of challenges to authority are marked as oedipally addressed: to Mommy or Daddy.

But there is another aspect to this authority as well. Jimmy, the character Tarantino himself plays, expresses his rage and anxiety in a characteristic riff where dialogue comes close to pure performance. He rants on and on: "What do you think this is? Dead nigger storage?" This explosive eruption, coming from the white actor, and repeated four times, is clearly meant to shock. In the context of this episode and the absent authority who presides over it, the film aims to place racist epithet at the same level as obscenities. Everything proceeds as if, by figuring Jimmy's wife as African American, the film could insulate the director's own image from the racist edge of his discourse. Bonnie functions, then, as his alibi; she is supposed to exempt him from cultural rules, from ordinary whiteness.[31] At the same time, given the way the film sets her up as the ultimate judge of the men's housekeeping operation, she both authorizes this moment of verbal smearing and spewing and symbolically cleans it up, sanitizes it. Thus, this moment emerges as contained by the female authority to whom it is addressed. Equally important, the condensation of aggression, abjection, and authority here constitutes the implosion of the oedipal narrative into the preoedipal figure that it both addresses and wards off— the phallic mother figure.

A central address to absent feminine authority might explain some of the pleasures of Tarantino's films for the young white males who largely constitute his fan audience. But it may also account for an appeal to certain female spectators as well. Tarantino's films are nothing if not symptomatic. If the absence of women in *Reservoir Dogs,* for example, or in the Bonnie situation does not put off female spectators, it may be because Tarantino's films offer a masculinity whose worst enemy is itself. Or, it may be because the film interpellates women spectators into the reassuring posture of judge, adjudicator, or evaluator. In this case, self-deconstructing adolescent white masculinity is on parade before the discerning, and perhaps satisfied feminine gaze, a gaze that can take its distance from a transgressive eruption designed precisely to provoke her.

In this particular structural sense it is worth considering that the viewing pleasures that Tarantino's films mobilize resemble pornographic ones. That is, they may draw on some of the same energies that are at play for the presumed masculine addressees of certain versions of heterosexual pornography, and specifically, on the structure of the fourth look.[32] Paul Willemen describes this fourth look and its effects: "when the scopic drive is brought into focus the viewer also runs the risk of becoming the object of the look, of being overlooked in the act of looking." "The . . . possibility of that overlooking-look," Willemen argues, "gains in force when the viewer is looking at something she or he is not supposed to look at, either according to an internalized censorship (superego) or an external, legal one (as in clandestine viewings) or, as in most cases, according to both censorships combined."[33] The fourth look, then, articulates internal psychic processes with a social dimension. Interestingly, for Willemen, there is reason to speculate that the fourth look is most often imagined as a feminine spectator overlooking the male viewer. In this sense, and for this specific form, it offers a structural analogy with the old "smutty joke" that Freud analyzes. Willemen describes that analogy as "relating not so much to the place of the fourth look in the process but to its function as a space" (180). As the joker turns his male rival for the woman's attention into his ally and stand-in at "another place of the discursive process," the woman is "relegated to the field of the other whence she, the repressed, returns as the subject of the fourth look." "This," concludes Willemen, "allows the men to function as the subjects and objects of the look at the same time: one is the object of a look, the other is the subject of an enunciation" (181). And clearly, if we are considering the uses of pornography that these structures would extend to what the viewer might be doing while he is looking, he is entertaining the fantasmatic risk of being caught with his pants down by the fourth look.

If we can explore this analogy with regard to the viewing structures that Tarantino's films offer us, the figure of the woman overlooking the scene—Bonnie, for instance—represents the social and its censoring demands. She also serves as an ultimate chastising or punishing addressee. Consequently, within the pleasurable structures of reversibility that allow the viewer to be both subject and object of the look, she might also be imagined to be the origin as well as the addressee of the fantasies. The pleasures of transgressive viewing are secured in the framework that mobilizes another judging gaze, which both threatens the spectator with exposure and also guarantees a certain containment. Equally important, this structure suggests that it is specifically in relation to the possibility of her look's catching the viewer unawares that his pleasure emerges. Certainly we might plausibly argue for the importance of such structures in *Reservoir Dogs,* where women enter only in smutty jokes—Madonna, Pam Grier, and Elois. As Manohla Dargis suggests: "The ties that bind these men in masculinity are raw and crushing in part because women, like the crime, have no present reality; both are blanks, screens for uncontradicted fantasy."[34] And one of the fantasies, perhaps the most powerful, is about the woman reprimanding and managing men. *Pulp Fiction* foregrounds this effect.[35]

At the same time, the film inscribes an address to two audiences, the one performing for the other. If the fourth look is assigned to women and African American males in particular, the specular aggressive posturing and display that animate the gang in *Reservoir Dogs,* as much as it does the group in the Bonnie situation, seems designed to capture the fascinated and transgressive identifications of white male fans. Tarantino's films imagine a fandom for "boys" that would recognize itself through an identification with a bad boy fan auteur. Both the films and the fandom, however, depend on a reinscription of sexual and racial difference to mark the border that sets this band apart.

We remember here that Tarantino's films appear under the logo "band apart" films, in a reference to Godard's *Bande à part (Band of Outsiders).*[36] Outsiders become insiders in view of a virtual gaze overlooking their specular posturing for each other and overhearing the stream of insults and obscenities with which they amuse themselves. We might ask how this circuit of specularities and identifications is linked to *Pulp Fiction*'s drive to lift the word "nigger" out of its web of social meanings, and how its ruse that this is a simple lifting of a repression, like any other, can only fail. One reason for this failure, of course, is that the pleasurable charges that the film means to mobilize as the word erupts from its characters are structurally associated with obscenity and anal aggression.

Within the rather resolute oedipality of these structures, Bonnie figures as the ultimate condensation of gendered and racialized authority, an authority that seems to preside over the circulation of racial epithets as a form of transgressiveness that is exactly equivalent to obscenity. But this analogy is false, and we need to inquire why obscenity and aggression continually accumulate at the borders of racial difference. This overcharged friction around racial difference seems to blend abjecting and idealizing impulses, just as it mingles fetishism—in the fantasy that blackness is phallic—with projective identifications. Part of what Bonnie authorizes, I want to suggest, is white male posturing in imitation of *images* of black men. Of course, Jimmy's "dead nigger storage" riff is a paradigmatic example of this posturing, as is the banter between Eddie Cabot and Vick Vega in *Reservoir Dogs.*

Even more spectacular is Gary Oldman's performance as Alabama's pimp in *True Romance.* With his dreadlocks and his gold-capped front teeth, Drexel Spivey looks the part of a white "wannabee." In his confrontation with Clarence, Drexel parades and postures in a particular version of Hollywood conventions for rendering African American "street talk" familiar to broad audiences.[37] Highlighting racial difference, he distinguishes himself from Clarence—"I know exactly where your white ass is, man"—and asserts his own belonging in the all-black context of the brothel, asking his black colleague, "Musta thought it was white boy day. It ain't white boy day, is it?" Drexel's violent encounter with Clarence ends when the latter shoots him, first in the crotch, and then in the face. But the over-the-top posturing and its connection to vicious violence might lead us to ask, what intersecting structures of identification are on offer here? Drexel's insertion in a parade of popular culture icons permits the film to attribute a generalized iconicity to black men. Like Jimmy's tirade, Drexel's posturing ventriloquizes his fantasy—a white male fantasy—of black masculinity, where racial difference is reduced to a cultural icon for the dominant culture.

Tarantino's universe seems to depend intimately on such an iconic construction of African American masculinity. This is the universe in which *Pulp Fiction* posits that the term "nigger" can be neutralized through a generalized circulation in which it designates anyone at all, of whatever race. Race plays similarly in *Reservoir Dogs*. One of the more hilarious moments in that film involves a problem of color and naming. As Joe Cabot in a space that resembles a locker room prepares his men for "the job," he speaks in the language of football coaching and police briefings familiar to us from television and movies, but inflected with a slight corporate spin toward good management. As boss, he assigns them aliases: Brown, Blonde, Blue, Orange, Pink, and White. Pink's name is the subject of much joking and of dissatisfaction to its bearer: "pink, faggot, pussy." One character demands to know why they can't pick their own names. "It doesn't work out," Cabot replies. "Put four guys in a room and let them pick their own colors, everybody wants to be Mr. Black." "Black" is the coolest name, and, for these characters, the only other "cool-sounding" name is "White." It is this boyish association of "blackness" with "cool" that forms the context in which we may examine the circulation of the word "nigger" among the interlocutors who inhabit *Pulp Fiction.*

Through white men's identifications with them, black men become icons, gestural repertoires, and cultural artifacts, as the threads of cross-racial identification are wound around a white body that remains stable. Perhaps more important, these fantasmatic identifications maintain an aggressive edge: the white subject wants to be in the other's place, without leaving its own.[38] These are identifications that still operate through a gaze that is imagined to remain stable before the volatile image it wants to imitate. What results is a reinscription of black masculinity as an image, a cultural icon, seen through white eyes. And this is why neither Bonnie nor Marsellus Wallace really has a point of view.

In a commentary for the *Chicago Tribune,* Todd Boyd examines and contests the use of "the N-word" in *Pulp Fiction.* He points out that "certain whites use the term [N-word] to assist in maintaining a certain 'hipness quotient,' which is clearly the way Tarantino sees himself using it."[39] For Boyd, in our current cultural context, "the recurrent use of the N-word has the ability to signify the ultimate level of hipness for white males who have historically used their perception of black masculinity as the embodiment of cool." "Tarantino sees his use of the N-word as proof that he is conversant in the nuances of black culture in the most sophisticated way," Boyd continues, and this use allows reference to "one's own whiteness without fear of compromise." In effect, Tarantino's films seem to reterritorialize and stabilize whiteness. In the process, however, we might speculate, they offer up for critical scrutiny explicit anxieties about race. Such anxieties clearly emerge in the fascination invested in a masculinity that expresses itself as racialized *and* as constituted by the exclusions it continually memorializes.[40] But "race" is continually resignified culturally. As Judith Butler argues, its "boundaries and meanings are constructed over time not only in the service of racism but also in the service of the contestation of racism" (18). In the context of ongoing cultural work that remakes "race" both for and against racism, we need to entertain the possibility that *Pulp Fiction* might resecure racialized representations for a racist imaginary, even as it tries to work them loose from it.

It is notable that in an interview with Lisa Kennedy, Tarantino theorizes his use of the word "nigger" as a means of defusing its power, and then links the level of violence in his films to a successful imitation of black culture. "No word should have so much power," he tells her, quoting himself. He goes on to cite someone else's account of his films in relation to race in a citation that is telling on several counts, since it slides between films and their audiences: "Someone said to me at Sundance when *Reservoir Dogs* was there, 'You know what you've done, you've given white boys the kind of movie black kids get.' You know like *Juice,* and . . . *Menace II Society.* Blacks have always had those movies. . . . Being bad, looking cool being bad, with a fuck-you attitude. The only time white guys could ever duke it out with black culture when it comes to being big and the coolness of being big is in the 50s, in the rockabilly days, when guys would walk around with big ole houndstooth coats and big ole hair. That was as big as black culture in the 70s, and it's all based on looking cool, looking like a badass" (31).

If Tarantino's films propose that they are entertaining some kind of "conversation" with African American popular culture, we might want to ask exactly what form this conversation is taking and what its subject really is, since its structure of mimicry and ventriloquism suggests more a one-sided broadcast than a dialogue. For Tarantino suggests that his commitment to violence and brutality is related to his admiration of African American spectator practices, a position that depends on imagining a homogeneous audience rigidly distinguished from other audiences and inhabiting a separate cultural space—to say nothing of projecting his own fantasies onto that imaginary audience. In an interview with Dennis Hopper, the filmmaker cites his love of "spaghetti westerns" and of their original Italian audiences, which "tend to laugh at violence," tend not to take it seriously. "Now, actually, the only people in America that take that attitude are black people. They don't let violence affect them at all" (14). Somehow, the admiring imitation of African American masculinity here becomes intertwined with the centrality of violence and brutality to Tarantino's film universe. Interestingly enough, dominant critical accounts of violence in productions authored by African Americans seem to find in it an excess of social meaning, where violence in Tarantino's films is understood to function in a deficit of meaning, as a formal issue, rather than a content.[41]

If *Pulp Fiction* from time to time displays an identificatory delirium—where white men posture as "talking black" and confuse speaking as and speaking with—the film, like its author, seems to believe that there is a certain inoculating effect to code-mixing and code repetition.[42] What the film forgets to remember is that the social force of words cannot be privatized, that it cannot cite the word "nigger" outside a context formed by its enunciative conditions, which include the author's social location as well as the word's history. Indeed, the word functions to highlight the ways that the very racism the film discourse wants to abject forms instead the border against which it takes shape. Equally important, this dream of sanitation ignores the force of the unconscious speaking through us. But what if, in a spectacular misfire, that word becomes the signifier that organizes all of the others, much as Marsellus Wallace's body seems to organize all of the other bodies? What if the word itself remembers history? It then remembers *for* the film, and it acts like the film's unconscious.

Pulp Fiction, like *Reservoir Dogs* and *True Romance,* knows that no one "owns" race or culture, either individually or collectively. But it does not quite own up to the differences in the ways that we, as specific social subjects, remain dispossessed of the very processes of racialization that nevertheless circumscribe our cultural locations. And that is why all its efforts to render "race" as performance, much as they symptomatically highlight the instability of "race" as a category, and much as they challenge any imaginary coherence between appearance and identity, cannot escape capture in a circuit of cultural meanings that strive to restablize race. More important, *Pulp Fiction* depends on the fantasy that the category of white men is meaning-free in order to cast it as the blank screen upon which racial meanings may be written—and voluntarily at that. Even in a filmic world that seeks to disarticulate meaning from appearance, white men figure as not meaning anything by themselves or to themselves or to anyone else. And what a privilege this is.

Given the public enthusiasm with which the author-persona connects his "will to be cool" with his desire to imitate his cultural fantasy of black males, Todd Boyd's analysis of the uses of "the N-word" seems all the more compelling. As Boyd indicates, this word is also in more frequent circulation in a wide variety of actions and objects of African American-authored popular culture. And this may be precisely what allows Tarantino to appropriate the term as an artifact from the culture with which his films seem to entertain a playful and admiring rivalry—rap culture. Tarantino's use of the word has as much to do with his wish to mark himself as a cultural "outsider" with the privilege of an "insider" inside the "outsider" culture he fetishizes. And the word stands precisely as the mark of that fetishization.[43] At the same time, the steadfastly oedpial nature of the author's relations to popular culture—so that he can pick up the term as found object and combine it with an address to the fantasmatic black male rival through display and impersonation—may be what allows him to continue insisting on the politically progressive possibilities in his "sanitizing" project. Similarly, his recourse to blaxploitation images, for instance, operates as a false social anchor, a mere referencing in a universe where all artifacts have equal weight. For the world of Tarantino's films is a world without history—a world where all culture is simultaneous, where movies only really watch other movies. *Pulp Fiction* is steadfast in its refusal to be assigned any specific historical moment; its very collision of styles and signs undermines any effort to stabilize it historically. A variety of details recall recent decades in a dense jumble— from the twist scene and the club in which it takes place as iconic of the 1960s, to Bruce Willis's fifties' face, to Samuel L. Jackson's incoherent hair—combining seventies' sideburns with eighties' jheri curls.[44]

Tarantino's films are cult movies *about* cult viewing. When Timothy Corrigan describes cult viewing in reference to contemporary audience formation, he does so in terms that are remarkably appropriate to the ways in which Tarantino's films seem to imagine the audience that they address: "Instead of reading movies, contemporary audiences now adopt movies, create cults around them, tour through them" (81). According to Corrigan, viewers "can now literally possess images as the ubiquitous backgrounds and ornaments of their lives," and, through this particular pattern of use, "those images are recast as social objects defined by the conditions and contexts in which they are viewed" (6). Equally important, because they are built of collisions of cultural debris, cult films reflect audience practices, that is, the "use of the film text as debris in and of itself" (83). For this reason, Corrigan contends, there are "for cult films, no first-time viewings, since these movies by definition offer themselves for endless reappropriation: their worn-out tropes become the vehicles not for original connotations but for the viewer's potentially constant re-generation of connotations, through which the audience reads and re-reads itself rather than the film" (90). But what, we might ask, does a spectator read about himself in them?

Tarantino's characters, like his films, live in no community, none but the public space that is built into television, radio, and videotapes—a community of popular culture users. In a world of equal "users" we are allowed to imagine that the meanings of a word in popular circulation can be interrupted and reshaped by a set of individual speech events. Similarly, the films that seek to disalign body from speech, names, and race forget their own dependence on the bodies of actors—familiar and often iconic faces and gestures—recycled and reprocessed. In this privatized public sphere, memory and history become entirely contemporary in the user's use. It is as if these films offered history as the screen for one's own fantasies.[45] What kind of identification does one make with this screen? *Pulp Fiction* offers its screen beyond history, since history is figured in the textures of recycled and replayed popular music, television, and movies—sound and image tracks we all share—and whose continual contemporariness functions as the mark of a nostalgia untethered from a historical moment. How should we take its aggressive figuration of a cultural legacy and history as refuse, a refuse whose emblem is surely the father's gold watch stashed in his rectum?

Corrigan understands cult mechanisms through an oedipal framework where "any sort of presiding, determining, or patriarchal relationship is displaced between audience and screen; the acquisition of those images as a material and moveable substance in their own right becomes their chief significance for the cult spectator. . . . Whether through the redefinition of the cinematic apparatus as an adult toy . . . or through the perverse materialization of the logic of an Oedipal imaginary, cult movies are the product of a viewer who acts out simultaneously the vision of child and adult" (84). It is precisely such an oedipal imaginary that seems to govern Tarantino's work's relation to the popular culture debris it gathers and redistributes. If popular culture artifacts are stepchildren to be adopted, Tarantino as auteur presents himself as a stepson, claiming fathers like Oliver Stone or Jean-Luc Godard, and seeking to be affectionately adopted by his male fans.

But we need to ask why his films map the sphere of popular culture as thoroughly oedipalized. Their steadfastly oedipal account of cultural production and exchange displaces or erases social conflicts in favor of the drama of fathers and sons. Interestingly enough, Tarantino applies the familial metaphors that Corrigan employs to talk about cult viewings, but, specifically, in relation to race. In a stunning comment, Tarantino explains his position on racialized representations to Lisa Kennedy: "I kind of refuse to deal with it as this white guy talking about black guys or a black wannabee guy or a white wannabee black guy thing. In my heart of hearts I know where I'm coming from. . . . Some comedian really hit the nail on the fucking head when he said America's like this ridiculously dysfunctional family and blacks are our stepchildren. 'You never wanted me, you never liked me, why didn't you love me?' the blacks say, and there's a little bit of white America as the parents looking back and going, 'Okay we never really did but shut the fuck up about it' " (32). So social difference and conflicts around it become a family affair, another oedipal story.

One of the things that Tarantino's hyper-oedipalized playing with popular culture artifacts does is to embed a nostalgic reading of popular culture versions of masculinity of the 1960s through the 1970s. To do so, he implicitly reads the Vietnam War protests as generational rebellion. Such a view, however, erases the political activism that preceded and intertwined with that movement. In this reading, a conflict between fathers and sons eclipses the civil rights movement, the women's movement, and pre- and post-Stonewall gay activism. Nostalgia is not history.

And history is not nostalgia, nor is it simply generational. The same cinematic moves that figure history as cultural waste, as trash to be collected and recombined, allow for the production of false social anchors in, say, images drawn from blaxploitation films, as if "race" were susceptible to private manipulations, as videotapes are to private screenings.[46] In the end, the obsession to organize history oedipally upholds the powerful and curious equation that structures Tarantino's filmic universe: the equation of African American masculinity and popular culture.

Tarantino's films seem to posit that we might read history by sifting through the father's waste. But then they do not go on to read what they find there. If they posit, likewise, that history is what catches you with your pants down, they do not examine the social context in which such an event takes on meanings. The symptomatic edge of these films extends in several directions. For better and for worse, these are white-authored films that understand masculinity as racialized and that understand their own context as multicultural. These may be the first films of their genre to play so explicitly and self-consciously on a multicultural field. We may not like them; these may not be the films we want. But, then, films are rarely about what we say we want, what we consciously want. Instead, they tend to produce what we buy, what works on us by appealing to our pleasure, our pain, our fear or anxiety, or by appealing to what we do not want to own. Or, what works by catching us out and exposed. And for these reasons it is worth exploring the stunning asymmetry of the equation that seems to underlie Tarantino's aggressive identifications with icons of African American masculinity, icons presented as exact equivalents of Elvis, for example, or seventies' music. Such an equation emerges at a moment when the dominant white culture might begin to take seriously the ongoing historical conversations with African American cultural production that have always been centrally structuring to its very fabric.[47] Tarantino's ahistorical reading of these conversations is deeply fetishistic. But other readings, respecting history, might ask what U.S. culture would look like without this conversation, saturated with struggle though it has been. Critically analyzing and contesting the work that acknowledges this conversation may be our best way of owning up to the ways in which we do not own culture. Rather, it owns us, as it lays claim to us. Tarantino's films offer something different; the symptoms they display signal certain shifts in the terrain of racialized representation. And this bears watching, since it is watching us.

NOTES

Introduction

1 Indeed, as Judith Butler has argued, to call "race a construction or an attribution in no way deprives it of its force in life; on the contrary, it becomes precisely a presiding and indispensable force within politically saturated discourses in which the term must be continually resignified *against* its racist usages." *Bodies That Matter* (New York: Routledge, 1993), pp. 247-248.

2 *Welcome to the Jungle* (New York: Routledge, 1994), p. 202.

3 *Playing in the Dark: Whiteness and the Literary Imagination* (New York: Random House, 1993), p. 59.

4 In *The Black Atlantic,* Paul Gilroy provides an argument that complements this one, exploring the fundamental contributions that the culture of the African diaspora, in collision with the dominant cultures of Europe and the Americas, has made to Western modernity. Gilroy contends that "tracing the racial signs from which the discourse of cultural value was constructed and their conditions of existence in relation to European aesthetics and philosophy as well as European science can contribute much to an ethnohistorical reading of the aspirations of Western modernity as a whole and to the critique of Enlightenment assumptions in particular." *The Black Atlantic: Modernity and Double Consciousness* (Cambridge, Mass.: Harvard University Press, 1993), p. 8. In particular, Gilroy emphasizes the dependency of white culture upon meanings that are racialized in specific historical ways for its unarticulated self-definition: "Notions of the primitive and the civilised which had been integral to a pre-modern understanding of 'ethnic' differences became fundamental cognitive and aesthetic markers in the processes which generated a constellation of subject positions in which Englishness, Christianity, and other ethnic and racialised attributes would finally give way to the dislocating dazzle of 'whiteness'" (9). Considering the case of the United States, Gilroy traces the effects of the "double consciousness" that Du Bois ascribes to African Americans upon the general culture of modernism.

5 James Snead, *White Screens, Black Images* (New York: Routledge, 1994), p. 5. On the tactic of "marking" he has this to say: "As if the blackness of black skin were not enough, we

seem to find the color black repeatedly overdetermined, marked redundantly, almost as if to force the viewer to register the image's difference from white images" (5).

6   Patricia Williams describes the experience of being someone else's cipher: "I think: my raciality is socially constructed, and I experience it as such. I feel my blackness as an eddy of conflicted meanings—and meaninglessness—in which my self can get lost, in which agency and construct are tumbled in constant motion. This sense of motion, the constant windy sound of manipulation whistling in my ears, is a reminder of society's constant construction of my blackness." *The Alchemy of Race and Rights* (Cambridge, Mass.: Harvard University Press, 1991), p. 168.

7   Notable exceptions to this trend, all of which appeared on network television in recent years, include "Homicide," "NYPD Blue," and "ER." Each of these series features black or Latino figures whose characters are as dense, conflicted, mobile, and volatile as any of their white counterparts.

8   "Ethnicities-in-Relation: Toward a Multicultural Reading of American Cinema," in *Unspeakable Images: Ethnicity and the American Cinema,* ed. Lester Friedman (Urbana: University of Illinois Press, 1991), p. 240.

9   A striking exception, however, is Lieutenant Arthur Fancy (James McDaniel) of "NYPD Blue." This character confronts racial issues directly, offering criticisms of his colleagues' racial attitudes in arguments that fully develop the complexity of the problem. Like Fancy, "Homicide" 's Lieutenant Girardelli (Yaphet Kotto) is deeply involved in his own personal and professional conflicts, some of which entail discussions of his feelings about others' appropriations of his race, and some of which are shown to dovetail with social pressures. I leave aside here "Homicide" 's most compelling character, Detective Pembleton (Andre Braugher), in order to focus exclusively on commander figures.

10 It is worth remembering here that the African American judge, or figure of the law, is a specific contemporary incarnation of that long and fundamental tradition in American literature that Morrison identifies as an "Africanist" presence or persona and the projections that it is called on to support. Morrison describes this persona as "the image of reined-in, bound, suppressed, and repressed darkness," and she argues that we need to be attentive to the ways that the "duties of that persona—duties of exorcism and reification and mirroring—are on demand and display throughout much of the literature of the country" (39).

11 Shohat suggests that we need to read in view of "ethnicity as culturally ubiquitous and textually submerged" (219), and most particularly when it comes to "Hollywood's ethnically embarrassed texts" (220)—those which insist that they are not "about" race and ethnicity at all. Such texts demand that we pay attention to what she calls "inferential ethnic presences; that is, the various ways in which ethnic cultures penetrate the screen without always literally being represented by ethnic and racial themes or even characters" (223).

12 In this instance, I use the term "banality" in the sense that Meaghan Morris, following Michel De Certeau, accords it: "the arrival at a *common* 'place,' which is not (as it may be for populism) an initial state of grace, and not . . . an indiscriminate, inchoate condition, but on the contrary, the outcome of a practice, something that 'comes into being' at the end of a trajectory . . . where the ordinary is no longer the object of analysis, but the *place* from which discourse is produced." "Banality in Cultural Studies," in *Logics of Television,* ed. Patricia Mellencamp (Bloomington: Indiana University Press, 1990), p. 35.

13 For instance, this is the way that Andrew Ross examines *Batman* and *Do the Right Thing* — two films whose relation to each other might at first glance seem to be exhausted by the coincidence of their near simultaneous release. For him, each evokes stories that are "versions, from the centre and the margin respectively, of a history that won't stand still." "Ballots, Bullets, or Batmen: Can Cultural Studies Do the Right Thing?" *Screen* 31, no. 1 (1990): 28. "The seamless mythological history that *Batman* reaffirms," Ross continues, "is the history that *Do the Right Thing* needs to know in order to challenge the mythical assumptions that support the official story of 'national culture.' By the same token, the social narrative recounted by *Batman* needs to incorporate its occluded parables about race into a constantly updated version that makes its story stick, at least for the spectators of both films . . ." (41).

14 *A Cinema Without Walls* (New Brunswick, N.J.: Rutgers University Press, 1991), p. 198.

15 See his "Authorship and the Cultural Politics of Film Criticism," *Film Quarterly,* Fall 1990, pp. 14–23.

16 Meaghan Morris has argued that, in fact, "media opinion is a matter, not of contents, precisely, but of *mood.*" "Tales of Survival and Crocodile Dundee," in Andrew Ross, ed., *Universal Abandon?* (Minneapolis: University of Minnesota Press, 1988), p. 118. She suggests that such moods operate currently in a political gap, and a gap that we need to work to transform: "the gap between the politics of production, and of regimes of consumption, or rather, since that distinction is now engulfed, between the politics of culture and the politics of politics" (124–25). "This distance," she continues, ". . . is presided over by the figure of appropriation and its subsidiaries — like the rhetorical gap between mass culture (what the industry does) and popular culture (what we do with it). How to invent — not discover or retrieve — some connections is now a major ethical and imaginative action problem for radical politics" (125).

17 *Clint Eastwood: A Cultural Production* (Minneapolis: University of Minnesota Press, 1994), p. 95.

18 *Feminism Without Women: Culture and Criticism in a "Postfeminist" Age* (New York: Routledge, 1991), p. 45.

19 Numerous review texts foregrounded the "secret" and their own silence about its context; what they also foregrounded in the process is the extraordinary direct communication between the film's producers and journalists indirectly engaged with promoting the film's distribution. See, for example, Richard Corliss, "Queuing for *The Crying Game,*" *Time,* January 25, 1993, p. 63, and "Don't Read This Story!" *Time,* March 1, 1993, p. 57; David Denby, "Art and Politics," *New York,* December 27, 1992, p. 64; Richard David Storey, "The Cult of *The Crying Game,*" *New York,* January 25, 1993, p. 38.

20 *Rolling Stone*'s Jeff Giles writes in the introduction to his interview with Jaye Davidson, interviewing this time as a man: "There are people who have seen *The Crying Game* . . . and yet persist in thinking that the penis in question is some sort of special effect." "*The Crying Game* Star Jaye Davidson Breaks the Silence," *Rolling Stone,* April 1, 1993, p. 39. The film's producers themselves seem to have counted on this effect. "Stephen Woolley, the film's producer, theorizes that perhaps a quarter of the audience knows Dil's gender at once, another quarter suspects it, and at least half are completely in the dark. 'Many,' he says, 'still insist that Jaye is a girl,'" *Time,* March 1, 1993, p. 57.

21 See, for instance, the Jeff Giles interview, "*The Crying Game* Star Jaye Davidson Breaks the

Silence," pp. 38ff. The title suggests more secrets disclosed, and the interview is manifestly fascinated by identity questions, moving from Davidson's sexuality, his relationship to cross-dressing, to inquiries about the race of both of his parents.

22   Paul Gilroy has recently examined the market status of "difference" in the following terms, which seem particularly apt in this context. "It has been suggested that the new global culture of capitalism we inhabit somehow thrives on difference, skillfully turning it into nothing more than a powerful marketing tool. I dispute that. It is not difference itself that is a seductive adjunct to the sale of soft drinks or clothes, but the safe recuperation of supposedly absolute otherness into a domesticated diversity which creates both pleasure and excitement" ("Mixing It," *Sight and Sound,* September 1993, p. 25). In the context of U.S. culture's contemporary fascination with figures of sexual and racial difference, this film's exploration of "identity," sexuality, and "difference" exemplifies the effects that Gilroy is reading.

23   In his analysis of the contradictory spectator identifications that this film invites, John Gabriel describes certain moments of D-Fens's acting out that provide for gratifying "fantasy-identifications." "The D-Fens character thus provided a rich repository for moments of recognition and identification," he writes, "a series of collisions between the film's structure (expressed through narrative, cinematography and casting) and audiences' backgrounds and experiences. Such collisions resulted in a sense of release on the part of the audience." "What do you do when minority means you? *Falling Down* and the Construction of 'Whiteness,' " *Screen,* Summer 1996, p. 134.

24   As Carol Clover has put it, in the film's universe, "even Average White Men have trouble telling each other from the enemy, it seems." "White Noise," *Sight and Sound,* May 1993, p. 9.

25   Gabriel reports that the viewers he interviewed "built their strongest attachments to D-Fens, and in particular to his role as consumer, as motorist, as customer and citizen" (134).

26   See bell hooks, *Black Looks: Race and Representation* (Boston: South End Press, 1992). hooks discusses the erotic lure of a "bit of the other" in the following terms: "Commodity culture in the United States exploits conventional thinking about race, gender, and sexual desire by 'working' both the idea that racial difference marks one as Other and the assumption that sexual agency expressed within the context of racialized sexual encounter is a conversion experience that alters one's place and participation in contemporary cultural politics" (22).

27   One of Prendergast's colleagues endorses this reading, questioning him as he leaves his own retirement party at the point when a stripper has begun to perform. "What, are you afraid of women too?" asks the colleague. Another replies, "Of course. Have you seen his wife?"

28   Gabriel suggests that the obsession with home that this film shares with D-Fens "provides a space for one of the many appeals for a return to the way things used to be, part of the universal and recurrent cinematic theme of 'going home' explored in such films as *Fatal Attraction*" (137).

29   In this respect, *Falling Down* efficiently epitomizes a process that Jim Collins describes: "Our knowledge of what constitutes 'our culture' at any given moment depends on the accumulation of views. . . . The resulting configurations do not form a planned or very well-managed pluralism, but a discontinuous, conflicted pluralism, creating tension-

filled environments that have an enormous impact on the construction of both representations and the subjects that interact with them." *Uncommon Cultures: Popular Culture
and Post-Modernism* (New York: Routledge, 1989), p. 27.

30   These essays exhibit a curious shifting between the terms "black" and "African American." I have endeavored to systematize their use as much as possible, according to the
following logic. "Black" appears in discussions of representations based in fantasies about
color and by opposition to "white." "African American" indicates a conception of race as
cultural, and it also refers to real human subjects rather than figures.

1   Mutilated Masculinities and Their Prostheses

1   This essay was written a few years before I had the opportunity to read Fred Pfeil's mas-
terful analysis of several of these films. *White Guys: Studies in Postmodern Domination and
Difference* (New York: Verso, 1995). Because Pfeil treats many of the same issues, I have registered his readings frequently, and have indicated where my reading coincides with and
diverges from his. Generally speaking, our approaches are quite similar, although, where
Pfeil contends that "these films translate racially coded actants into gender-coded ones"
(17), I have focused on the reversibility and reciprocity of this process. In the end, I think,
my analysis foregrounds this volatile system of trade-offs and highlights its overdeterminations in such a way that it is no longer a question of direction, or of destination, for
such translations. Indeed, I prefer to think of these operations more as negotiations or
transactions. Further, I have placed more emphasis on the complexities of the films' erotic
economies in the interest of avoiding the collapse of sexuality into gender. Finally, I have
set my readings of the *Die Hard* and *Lethal Weapon* films in the context of the relentless
repetition and variation on their formulas. It seems to me that the tendency to repetition
is somehow foundational to these films. Equally important, because that repeatability
has led to more and more extravagant, ironic, and perverse renderings of the black-white
buddy scenario, as in *The Last Boy Scout,* the repetition and its play on the genre itself
may be as important as any of the particular forms it takes. Two recent films present particularly challenging repetitions, however: *Die Hard with a Vengeance* (1995) makes racial
friction a central theme, and *The Long Kiss Goodnight* (Renny Harlin, 1996) pairs Geena
Davis and Samuel L. Jackson in a wildly and explicitly ironic reading of the action-buddy
genre that foregrounds race and gender.

2   *Lethal Weapon 3* will violate the formula and thus conclude with an open question: what
can happen to the buddies if Riggs is able to enter into a relationship with an adult
woman? It is important to note that this woman is Riggs's female double, herself a lethal
weapon, whose body is the site of aggressive spectacle and martial skills display; she is,
like Riggs, subjected to near fatal assault by the conclusion of the film.

3   On the question of the law and its relation to oedipal desires in the western, see the work
of Raymond Bellour, particularly Janet Bergstrom's interview with Bellour, "Alternation,
Segmentation, Hypnosis," *Camera Obscura* 3-4 (1979), esp. pp. 87–103.

4   This essay was originally written before I had seen Yvonne Tasker's fascinating volume
on the action cinema, *Spectacular Bodies: Gender, Genre and the Action Cinema* (New York:
Routledge, 1993). Tasker characterizes action cinema's treatment of the hero's body in the
following terms: "Within the action cinema, these male bodies also tell powerful stories
of subjection and resistance, so that muscles function both to give the action hero the

power to resist, at the same time as they confirm him in a position that defines him almost exclusively through the body" (79). In the framework of a monograph on action film as a genre and its social and industrial context, Tasker is able to provide a much broader synthetic analysis of the history surrounding the recent burgeoning of the genre. In the interest of studying context, consumption, and what she describes at one point as the "elusive qualities of atmosphere and tone which are crucial for an analysis of spectacle-based cinema" (60), Tasker spends somewhat less time on close textual reading than I do.

5   Tasker is also particularly interested in the ramifications of the black-white buddy pairing: "the narrative relationship between the white hero and his black informant allows for both the display of the hero's body, largely dispensing with the work of investigation, and the enactment of relations of racially defined dominance and subservience. Indeed the two are intimately bound together, so that the suggestion and demonstration, through the performance of the narrative, of the superiority of the white hero over his black infor-mant functions to allay an anxiety attendant on the sexualized display of the white male body" (40). For my own part, I am not sure which anxiety functions to allay which, and I am attempting to explore the apparent "passivity" of the figure that Tasker names "the informant" as an *active* feature of the spectacle that the buddy pair itself offers.

6   Of course, the classic study of the centrality and persistence of this bonding trope to American literature is Leslie Fiedler's *Love and Death in the American Novel* (Garden City, N.Y.: Anchor Books, 1960). Fiedler argues that race and sexuality intersect in the con-struction of gendered national identity in assertions like the following: "whatever the symbolic necessities which demand that the male *hierogamos* be inter-racial as well as homoerotic, that marriage takes on, by virtue of crossing conventional color lines, a sociological significance as well as a psychological and metaphysical one" (366).

7   In this connection it is noteworthy that the extravagantly affected comic figure of Leo, the mob accountant who becomes a protected witness and a sidekick to the buddies in *Lethal Weapon 2*, reappears in *Lethal Weapon 3*. This time, his function as a relay for homo-erotic joking is secured. Indeed, his look continually constructs Riggs and Murtaugh as a potential couple, so that the joking energy is now split between perspectives that are both internal and external to the pair. For example, in *Lethal Weapon 3*—which brings the homoerotic plot *home*—when Leo enters Murtaugh's house and finds him taking a bubble bath, his smirky inquiry, "Is Riggs under there too?" is blatantly suggestive of oral sex.

8   Tania Modleski, *Feminism Without Women: Culture and Criticism in a "Postfeminist" Age* (New York: Routledge, 1991), p. 141.

9   This is an image that *Die Hard with a Vengeance* takes up, perhaps as an occasion to satirize the earlier film's liberal discourse of racial tolerance as it ambiguously both promotes and undercuts Zeus's (Samuel L. Jackson's) criticisms of McClane's racial assumptions.

10   James Baldwin, *The Devil Finds Work,* collected in *The Price of the Ticket* (New York: Grove Press, 1976), p. 599.

11   In view of *The Long Kiss Goodnight*'s dynamic reworking of the conventions governing this seemingly inexhaustible genre, we might speculate that it is becoming a more and more critical form. Written by Shane Black, whose signature amounts to a generic marker by now, *The Long Kiss Goodnight* ironically recalls Black's earlier *Lethal Weapon* films, along with *Die Hard,* and melds them with resonances from *Thelma and Louise* by casting Geena Davis as Samantha Cain, alias Charly Baltimore, a professional assassin, and Samuel L. Jackson as Mitch Henessey, her somewhat reluctant ally.

12 In one of their first exchanges McClane addresses Zeus as "Man," evoking the quick re-tort: "Are you trying to 'relate' to me? Talk like a white man." Here the word "relate" itself becomes a code word for white posturing in encounters with African Americans. In a later moment Zeus criticizes one of McClane's typical assumptions. When McClane ex-presses surprise that he does not know how to fire a gun, Zeus admonishes him, "Look, all brothers don't know how to shoot guns, you racist motherfucker." ·

13 In an exchange that seems to quote more or less directly from *Home of the Brave* (Mark Robson, 1949), at a pivotal moment of anxiety, when the two men are arguing, McClane stops short of uttering an insult. Zeus insists that McClane was about to use a racist epi-thet. McClane, on the other hand, insists that he was about to say "asshole." And he goes on to accuse Zeus: "Just because I'm white, you don't like me. Have I oppressed you? Have I oppressed your people somehow?"

14 Yvonne Tasker suggests something similar when she argues that "in recent action cinema, problems of location and position are increasingly articulated through the body of the male hero" (77). Further, Tasker associates this articulation with the "sexualization of working class male bodies" (79).

15 Fred Pfeil formulates these relations somewhat differently, putting the emphasis on their transcodings: "these films' black-white racial code turns out to be transmitting messages that are as much about gender as they are about race, its woman-man code turns out to fuel its reactionary politics with the high octane of anti-professional, anti-corporate *res-sentiment*" (20).

16 Philip Brophy, "Horrality," *Screen* 27, no. 1 (1986): 5.

17 Susan Jeffords, "Can Masculinity Be Terminated?" in Steven Cohan and Ina Rae Hark, eds., *Screening the Male: Exploring Masculinities in Hollywood Cinema* (New York: Routledge, 1993), p. 246.

18 *Clint Eastwood: A Cultural Production* (Minneapolis: University of Minnesota Press, 1993), p. 167.

19 See John Simon, "Good Citizenship, Dubious Packaging," *National Review,* September 30, 1988, p. 59, on *Die Hard:* "So the encoded message here is interracial brotherhood, with which one cannot quarrel, except for the calculated way it is presented in this altogether cynical movie." See also Richard Schickel, on the contemporary action film genre that *Die Hard* represents: "Like that other fantasy form, the evening news, shoot-to-kill movies require the services of an anchorman, someone who can ground implausible events in an attractive, recognizable reality." "Is There Life in Shoot-to-Thrill?" *Time,* July 25, 1988, p. 65. And Terrence Rafferty, who objects to the way that *Die Hard* features "the fattest, most Teddybearish black cop congratulating the white protagonist on his guts and inde-pendence." "The Current Cinema: All Sizes," *New Yorker,* August 8, 1988, p. 78.

20 Philip Cohen describes the operation of racism within representation as follows: "What the map unconsciously represents is the desire for mastery which produced it, a desire to render the world as real and natural, by denying the existence of the Other as a locus of the unknown. From this omnipotent or Archimedean reference point the map consti-tutes a network of discrete meanings which are articulated to specific terrains of experi-ence. These territories are always and already delimited by specific contexts and conjunc-tures; they are staked out by relations of power which are themselves traversed by human intertextuality." *Multi-Racist Britain* (London: Macmillan, 1988), p. 56.

21 *Framing Blackness* (Philadelphia: Temple University Press, 1993), p. 128.

22   On this account I would argue that it participates in the "randomizing" of racial difference that Pfeil attributes more specifically only to *Die Hard 2* (*White Guys,* p. 13).

23   This organization of a set of intradiegetic viewers is a familiar one. Think of "Miami Vice,"
where the blond Sonny's radiance burns all the brighter when caught in the gaze of his
coworkers, who are all black and Latino, with the significant exception of comic foils Stan
and Larry, the ill-dressed, rumpled specialists in surveillance devices. It is no accident
that they do surveillance; their job is to stay out of view.

24   These trade-offs clearly participate in the films' tendency, as Pfeil describes it, "to translate racially coded actants into gender-coded ones," where the "perfect adequacy of this
all-male couple" renders all women superfluous (*White Guys,* pp. 16–17). Yet I want to
leave more room for the consideration of sexuality and not subsume it under gender
coding.

25   If the condensation of energies here were not clear enough, the dialogue between Dix and
Hallenbeck highlights it, as Hallenbeck responds to Dix's coy suggestion that he might
"take your daughter out," with "I'll stick an umbrella up your ass and open it."

26   John Caughie, "Playing at Being American: Games and Tactics," *Logics of Television,* ed.
Patricia Mellencamp (Bloomington: Indiana University Press, 1990), p. 54. Caughie com-
pares television and film: "the specific conditions of television produce the possibility of
more ironic forms of attention than the conditions of, say, the cinematic. Less intensely
fascinating in its hold than the cinema, television seems to insist continually on an attention to viewing as mental activity and 'knowingness' (almost a 'street-wise' smartness),
rather than to the obedience of interpellation of the affect of the 'always already' " (53).

27   No doubt one thinks of the Johnson & Johnson Company, famous for baby powder,
among other products, and at the same time the possible reference to Johnson Publications, the largest publishing corporation owned by African Americans, which is responsible for *Essence* and *Jet,* among others.

28   "Reactivating Action Heroes," *Newsweek,* July 25, 1988, p. 58.

29   *Time,* March 23, 1987, p. 87.

30   Such special effects even form part of the film's framing discourses, its advertising, and, in
the case of *Lethal Weapon,* its videocassette jacket copy: "Hot LA days and nights explode
in one show-stopping action scene after another, culminating in a no-holds-barred battle
between Riggs and his Angel-of-Death nemesis (Gary Busey)—an electrifying sequence
incorporating three martial arts styles and requiring four full nights to film." Again, this
copy stresses the important appeal of a massive technological apparatus supporting the
film and an excessive expenditure on this level. Tellingly, in this case, such expenditures
are invested in the staging of bodily combat.

31   In this connection we would do well to bear in mind Fred Pfeil's contention that the
professional-managerial class is implicated at all levels of cultural production; that is,
the critics and producers of mass culture effectively belong to the same social class and,
therefore, most mass culture in some way addresses cultural critics: "the professional-
managerial class of the West [is] . . . both author and primary target for most postmodernist work . . . mainstream and avant-garde." "Potholders and Subincisions: On the
Businessman, Fiskadoro and Postmodern Paradise," *Postmodernism and Its Discontents,* ed.
E. Ann Kaplan (London: Verso, 1988), pp. 77–78.

32   See Richard Dyer, "Don't Look Now" (*Screen* 23, no. 3–4 (1982): 71). Dyer describes the instability of the male image as related to the discrepancy between the real penis and the

imaginary phallus: "The penis can never live up to the mystique implied by the phallus. Hence the excessive, even hysterical quality of so much male imagery. The clenched fists, the bulging muscles, the hardened jaws, the proliferation of phallic symbols—they are all straining after what can hardly be achieved, the embodiment of the phallic mystique."

33 Michel Chion, *Audio-Vision: Sound on Screen*, ed. and trans. Claudia Gorbman (New York: Columbia University Press, 1994), p. 155.

34 But equally important for Chion, the impact of this kind of ambient sound on cinema also resides in its capacity to recall the silent cinema: "Noises are reintroducing an acute feeling of the materiality of things and beings, and they herald a sensory cinema that rejoins a basic tendency of . . . the silent cinema" (156).

35 As Pfeil has pointed out, we may also read in these effects a "rhyme" between "bodies and buildings" (*White Guys*, p. 29). On the question of authority in a related argument about *Predator 2*, Yvonne Tasker suggests that it may be articulated with race: "If blackness signifies, and is signified through, marginality in *Predator 2*, then whiteness signifies and is signified through, an authority that is not to be trusted" (52). Something similar obtains in *Die Hard*; indeed, we might explore suspicious authority in connection with white racial identity as a more general figure in popular culture.

36 Chion reminds us that true POV shots actually are relatively rare: "The notion of point of view in this first spatial sense rests on the possibility of inferring fairly precisely the position of an 'eye' based on the image's composition and perspective. . . . Let us recall too that point of view in the subjective sense may be a pure effect of editing" (90). For an exhaustive study of point-of-view structures, with a particular emphasis on disrupted, delayed, suspended, and misleading points of view within an overall cinematic tendency to *suggest*—but not entirely to fulfill—the strictly subjective shot, see Edward Branigan, "The Point-of-View Shot," in *Point of View in the Cinema: A Theory of Narration and Subjectivity in Classical Film* (New York: Mouton, 1984), reprinted in Bill Nichols, ed., *Movies and Methods, II* (Berkeley: University of California Press, 1985). According to Branigan, "What is important is not the camera as an absolute reference point but the relation among camera, character, object and a perceiver's hypothesis about this relation" (679).

37 Pfeil also analyzes this key moment of restoration that is common to *Die Hard* and *Lethal Weapon*. In his reading, "the black man seems to receive from the white man's hands . . . something very like virility itself" (*White Guys*, p. 13). And this, he continues, is a story whose corollary is the "proto-sexual healing of the white man by the black" (13). For Pfeil, this healing is "more accurately, *gendered* healing, *feminine* healing" (13). For my own part here, I would prefer not to specify the restorative and therapeutic codes as so stably gendered in the interest of following the free play of erotics that these films exploit.

38 On "shattering" in relation to sexuality, see Leo Bersani, "Is the Rectum a Grave?" *October* 43 (1987): 199–223.

39 I am grateful to Henry Abelove for pointing out the kinkier inflections of this sequence.

40 "Masculinity as Spectacle," *Screen* 24, no. 6 (1983): 8.

41 This protective deflection of erotic contemplation into a scene of aggression may account for the intensity of the male agonistics that structure so many films. As Neale continues: "hence both forms of voyeuristic looking, intra- and extradiegetic, are especially evident in these moments of contest and combat . . . in those moments at which the narrative outcome is determined through a fight or gun-battle, at which male struggle becomes pure spectacle" (12).

42   D. N. Rodowick, "The Difficulty of Difference," *Wide Angle* 5, no. 1 (1981): 8.

43   *Male Subjectivity at the Margins* (New York: Routledge, 1992), p. 212.

44   First of all, the anxiety and pleasure of the male body's destruction are bound in spectacular fight scenes, which depend on a number of effects, the most significant of which is probably the split between actor and character. Mel Gibson and Bruce Willis are bearers of a certain media history and iconography as figures (the former representing almost paradigmatically the male body as masochistic site, given that his career was in some sense launched by the *Mad Max* films, whose whole narrative tends toward the mutilation and erosion of the male body, toward its increasing "prostheticization"). At the same time, this iconic history guarantees their intactness as actors. Part of the charge is the play at destruction of beauty, in the context of its guaranteed reconstruction. But the charge is also lodged in our film literacy, which assures us that the actor's body is not at risk because of doubles and special effects.

45   Paul Smith specifies the effects of the tensions involved in masochism: "Masochism . . . would be a closed space where masculinity sets the terms and expounds the conditions of a kind of struggle within itself—not a struggle necessarily for closure, but a struggle to maintain in a pleasurable tension the stages of a symbolic relation to the father—a struggle in which, ironically, the body becomes forgotten" (166).

46   On this question, see Richard Dyer, *Heavenly Bodies: Film Stars and Society* (New York: St. Martin's, 1986), in particular chap. 2, "Paul Robeson: Crossing Over."

47   It would be worth examining the ways in which this effect may be related to the one that Tania Modleski finds in *Lethal Weapon:* "As much as the film is engaged in the denial of the body's vulnerability, then, it is equally engaged in disavowing the realm of the psyche—the source of desire and inward-turning aggression (masochism) capable of undermining the subject's control" (142). The "body in pain is thus turned into a manipulable machine, and in the process the films manage both to render the psyche its due (through the use of psychiatric techniques and mechanisms for controlling psychotic behavior) and to deny its force. Indeed, the films try very hard to render the body/machine and the psyche, as the realm of the irrational, into a binary pair" (143).

48   This very sort of intertextuality is what allows Richard Schickel to put his finger on the link between a crisis of authority and a crisis of masculinity when he grumbles contemptuously that "Bruce Willis has based his career on apologizing for being a man" ("Is There Life in Shoot-to-Thrill?" p. 65). This comment is especially appropriate, since the central conciliatory gesture of the film (although it is transacted between McClane and Al) is McClane's request that, should he die, Al tell his wife that he is sorry for his inability to be supportive of her career. Such apologies, we should note, seem to be marketable—Richard Schickel's view notwithstanding—only when presented in representational contexts that seek to correct, often excessively, for any erosion of masculine authority.

49   For Yvonne Tasker, Willis's reliance on voice distinguishes him from some of the hulkier action heroes: "The strong silent type finds his complement in the kind of wise-cracking action hero played by Bruce Willis in films like *Die Hard, Hudson Hawk* (1991) and *The Last Boy Scout* (1991). Whilst these are still big-budget spectacular films, Willis is known for his voice as much as his body, and his role in these films as a wise guy enacts a different kind of masculine performance to that associated with the bodybuilder. The relationship between the body and the voice is central to the action cinema's articulation of male identity" (74).

50 Interestingly, *High Noon* is written into *Die Hard* on a number of levels. The hero has lost his wife because he will not step down from his job as a law enforcer; both wives have the role of castrator, trying to disarm the man. The course of the action reunites the couple as allies against a third party. In both films someone who is against the use of guns takes one up in order to save the hero (in *High Noon,* it is the wife, Amy, here reencoded in the figure of Al). *High Noon* is also the story of a solitary hero, whose role is contested and betrayed by the townspeople who refuse to help him against a gang of outlaws, just as McClane is here betrayed, interfered with, and constantly questioned by the police. The failure of alliance is dramatized with the framework of a drama of sight. Gunfights are about the inability to see around corners. Amy's attack on her captor goes for his eyes.

51 Of course, more recently, both film and television have become virtually obsessed with this figure. Examples include *Thelma and Louise,* Carl Franklin's 1993 *One False Move,* the Hughes brothers' *Menace II Society* (1994), and television successes in the mold of "Cops," a show that has made the obsession part of its generic definition.

52 Significantly, the confusion of space here appears to be coherent with the spatial effects that Chion attributes to sound: "Spatially speaking, a sound and its source are two different entities. In a film the emphasis may fall on one or the other, and the onscreen-offscreen question will pose itself differently, according to which thing—the sound or its cause—the spectator reads as being 'in' the image or 'outside' it. For sound and cause, though distinct, are almost always confused. But surely this confusion is inscribed also at the very heart of our experience itself, like an unsettling knot of problems" (79).

53 Takata is juxtaposed to Hans in an ironic specularity—the German identifies Takata's suit: "John Philips, London. I have two of them myself." This symmetry culminates when the German blows Takata's brains out. But the symmetry also locates the two "foreign" powers on the side of fashion, leisure, and consumerism, and therefore as powers whose authority is satisfyingly challenged by the authentic will of the workingman, McClane. This image might be linked to a corollary anxiety at the time about Japanese investments in this country.

54 I am grateful to Khachig Tololyan for pointing out the significance of these bonds as well as of the structure of relentless undercutting that prevails in the film.

55 I thank Barry Cannell for offering this concise assessment of the equations that the film produces.

56 Indeed, even the tiniest of the film's details contributes to its nearly seamless proliferation of ironies. For example, Holly's Rolex watch, the symbol of her corporate success (introduced at her first reunion with her husband), nearly kills her. When McClane blows Hans out the window near the film's end, Hans grabs Holly's arm, and dangles for tense moments, gripping the watchband that neatly shackles her wrist. Only when McClane is able to unhook the despised symbol from her wrist is she saved from a plunge to her death. Hence, the fashionable terrorist drops off with the symbol of corporate fashion and achievement to which he has been clinging.

57 Such a configuration of differences, it seems to me, is only possible within the kind of multiculturalist ideology that currently prevails in U.S. institutions, primarily educational and social ones, where the term "multicultural" conflates race and ethnicity and winds up dissipating specific differences in a fantasy of ambient differentiation, a sort of infinite color spectrum, in which we are all imagined to participate in equivalent ways. Philip Cohen addresses the underpinnings of such an ideology, and its attendant dan-

gers, when he describes the British context in *Multi-Racist Britain*. The egregious error of "multiculturalism," according to him, is a conflation of race and ethnicity. "Race is the object of racist discourse and has no meaning outside it; it is an ideological construct, not an empirical social category; as such it signifies a set of imaginary properties of inheritance which fix and legitimate real positions of social domination or subordination. . . . The notion of ethnicity, in contrast, lacks any connotation of innate characteristic whether of superiority or inferiority. It is a myth of origins which does not imply a congenital destiny; unlike race, it refers to a real process of historical individuation—namely the linguistic and cultural practices through which a sense of collective identity or 'roots' is produced and transmitted from generation to generation and is changed in the process" (23-24). Unless we maintain the critical distinction between these categories, we obscure real historical power relations as well as the analyses necessary for progressive social change.

58   On the issue of reading practices and legibility in contemporary film, see Timothy Corrigan, *A Cinema Without Walls* (New Brunswick, N.J.: Rutgers University Press, 1991): "If many contemporary viewers have an increasingly distracted relationship with the images they appropriate in one way or another, today that relationship and those images seem more and more structured to resist legibility and interpretation" (52).

59   "Black Bodies/American Commodities," in *Unspeakable Images*, ed. Lester D. Friedman (Urbana: University of Illinois Press, 1991), p. 325.

60   This confusion is no doubt related to an effect that Elizabeth Alexander describes as characteristic of this film: "*Ricochet* raises some very important questions about what it means to look at black men from any number of subject positions simultaneously. Mulcahy builds this multiplicity of perspectives into the film; Styles is the object of our ocular desire throughout, no matter who we are." "We're Gonna Deconstruct Your Life!" in *Representing Black Men,* ed. Marcellus Blount and George P. Cunningham (New York: Routledge, 1996), pp. 158-59.

61   The film's use of Wayans seems to represent a variation on Hollywood's use of "black iconicity," as Ed Guerrero characterizes it: "A further implication of the narrative isolation of the black star involves the fact that they are packaged the way Hollywood has always packaged stars, as supreme icons and incarnations of the rootless, de-cultured 'individual' in industrial consumer society. Specifically, in the case of black stars, this amounts to dominant cinema's effective erasure of the star's identification with a black collective consciousness and sense of politics" (126-27). Damon Wayans, however, seems to capitalize on an ambiguous relationship to both community and politics, one that we would be hard pressed to pin down.

62   Elizabeth Alexander puts it this way: "*Ricochet* is a movie whose camera work asserts that we all want to look at black men, whether we are gay or straight, black or white, male or female. The desire to look is veiled in the trappings of bourgeois success—we 'watch' Styles's ascent—but the real reason for looking, no matter who we are, is the sex of it" (161).

63   Alexander's reading of the film is somewhat more optimistic than mine. She concludes this way: "However, perhaps the movie can lead us to an intracommunity questioning of another order: How does fear of the complexities of one's own desires, as well as conservative, upwardly mobile black family discourse, truncate imagining other forms of family and community? Where is a model of black male sexuality and self-pleasure that can

narrate itself without a concurrent narrative of dominion that mimics the very system it abhors?" (170).

64 *Another Tale to Tell* (London: Verso, 1990), pp. 77–78.

2   Insides Out

1 Other 1990s examples of this seemingly inexhaustible thematics include *Presumed Innocent* (Alan Pakula, 1990), *Final Analysis* (Phil Joanou, 1992), *The Last Seduction* (John Dahl, 1993), *Romeo Is Bleeding* (Peter Medak, 1994), *Single White Female* (Barbet Schroeder, 1992), and *Disclosure* (Barry Levinson, 1994).

2 Masculine debilitation or incompetence has become an obsessive topos in recent films. In *Pacific Heights* (John Schlesinger, 1990), Melanie Griffith's businesslike handywoman character must single-handedly defeat the psychotic tenant, while her husband lies on the couch downstairs, literally crippled by a broken shoulder, while in *Sleeping with the Enemy* (Joseph Ruben, 1991), battered wife Julia Roberts is forced to blow away her murderous ex-husband after he has flattened her current lover—the sensitive man—with one punch. More and more, these updated female gothic plots offer the woman a choice between a powerful and effective male agent, a bastard, and a sensitive but completely ineffectual man. Perhaps one of the most spectacular examples of this trend in recent cinema is *Presumed Innocent*, where the lawyer hero's investigation of his lover's murder leads him to the discovery that his wife has killed her rival across his own body, quite literally. She has staged the rape of her victim, using her husband's semen as the instrument that suggests a misleading scenario and that provides incriminating evidence against him. Implausibly enough, then, the wife's murderous rage makes her a sex criminal as well.

3 Another example would be *Internal Affairs* (Mike Figgis, 1990).

4 Perhaps the ironic culmination of this obsessive interest comes with *Unlawful Entry* (Jonathan Kaplan, 1992), where it is the cop who is the psychotic intruder violating the middle-class interior because of his violent sexual fixation on the wife.

5 Stanley Aronowitz and Henry Giroux, *Postmodern Education: Politics, Culture, and Social Criticism* (Minneapolis: University of Minnesota Press, 1991), p. 177: "From the mid-1970s, there are simply no direct representations of working-class males (much less working-class women) in television. Representations are dispersed to beer advertisements . . . ; or to cop shows in which characteristic working-class culture is displaced and recontextualized in the station house, on the streets, in the bars where cops congregate. These are displacements, so we only see the remainders—conviviality, friendship that is overdetermined by the police buddy system, the obligatory partnership. . . . In recent films, displacement of class to the police continues, but is joined by displacement of sex (gender) relations to class as well." Aronowitz's argument goes on to foreground *Someone to Watch Over Me* as paradigmatic of this trend toward displacement. However, he does not pursue in any detail the question of why the police force has become the most readily available site for such displacements. Nor, for that matter, does he examine the transactions that implicate race and ethnicity along with gender and class here.

6 Of course, many of the anxieties surrounding the police have been played out all too regularly as the media covers incidents of police brutality, perhaps the most explosive of which was the Rodney King beating and its aftermath. It may not be stretching things to

suggest that part of the appeal of Fox television's "Cops" rests on its ability not to deny a basis for such anxiety, but to confirm it—only at a distance. By contrast, "America's Most Wanted" encourages us to imagine ourselves as a vast community of citizen-cops ourselves, definitively establishing our common interests with police.

7   *Sight and Sound*, November 1995, p. 10.

8   Consider the contrast between *Body Heat* (Lawrence Kasdan, 1981) and *Double Indemnity* (Billy Wilder, 1944). In her first seductive encounter with dissolute lawyer Ned Racine (William Hurt) in *Body Heat*, Kathleen Turner's character remarks drily: "You're not too bright. I like that in a man." In allowing the femme fatale such a judgment, and then bearing her out, this stylish remake of *Double Indemnity* rather dramatically shifted the terms of the genre it was reworking. Phyllis Dietrichson, after all, would never have been so blunt and direct in her assessment of Walter Neff.

9   *Enjoy Your Symptom!: Jacques Lacan in Hollywood and Out* (New York: Routledge, 1992), p. 155.

10 See "The Phenomenal Nonphenomenal: Private Space in *Film Noir*," in *Shades of Noir*, ed. Joan Copjec (New York: Verso, 1994), esp. p. 189.

11 "The Fatal Attraction of *Intercourse*," *Perversions; Deviant Readings* (New York: Routledge, 1993), p. 198.

12 For Žižek, the passage from the desubjective position of the object to a subjectivized position "confers upon the hitherto impossible/unattainable object a body, which gives the untouchable thing a voice and makes it speak—in short, subjectivizes it" (57). This effect, he finds, is homologous to the moment when the femme fatale in the hard-boiled genre subjectivizes herself. "She is first rendered from the perspective of her (masculine) social environment and appears as a fatal object of fascination which brings perdition and leaves behind ruined lives, 'empty shells': when we are finally transposed into her point of view, it becomes manifest that she herself cannot dominate the effects of 'what is in her more than herself,' of the *object* in herself, upon her environment—no more than the men around her, she is a helpless victim of fate" (67, n. 39). We can suggest, therefore, that it is precisely the passage between these two states, emphasized in the film, that destabilizes.

13 As the camera peers out from among enormous objects, we are subject to the uncanny sensation, from time to time, that we are viewing the world from an object's perspective.

14 For a fascinating and exhaustively detailed study of early cinematic depictions of the telephone in the context of "a history of the reception of technology" (185), see Tom Gunning, "Heard Over the Phone: *The Lonely Villa* and the de Lorde Tradition of the Terrors of Technology," *Screen* 32, no. 2 (1991): 184–96. In this essay, Gunning explores the "genealogy" of *The Lonely Villa*. "With its last minute rescue; invasion of the bourgeois home; strict alternation between gender positions . . . ; and, most important for my purposes, the technological link via the telephone that propels the climax into action, *The Lonely Villa* has become recognized as an archetype of film melodrama. But if the film is often cited as an ur-form of later rescue melodramas, we need to realize that it actually retells an older story which had already undergone a number of transformations. Retracing these various versions, we uncover a grim fable of technology whose fascination for early filmmakers reveals some of the darker aspects of the dream world of instant communication and the annihilation of space and time" (188).

15 Much discussion has been devoted to precisely the question that the film refuses to

answer as insistently as Nick Curran refuses to ask it: are they lesbians? For Lynda Hart, the film is "an allegory for the 'becoming woman' according to the teleology of the instincts that begins with autoeroticism and ends with 'genital organization,' that is, heterosexuality." *Fatal Women: Lesbian Sexuality and the Mark of Aggression* (Princeton, N.J.: Princeton University Press, 1994), p. 132. In other words, she argues, the film "consummates Catherine's heterosexuality" (132).

16 Rage may produce such compelling images precisely because our ambivalence about it works actively in our spectatorship. Because *Fatal Attraction,* and films like it, offer moments for feminist identification with the woman's rage, and satisfactions and discomforts that no final narrative closure fully contains, they may remind us of feminism's difficulties in separating rage from anger, aggression from violence. Such difficulties are often related to identification, which seems to be both a structural necessity and a structural effect of political solidarities, and of feminism in particular. Because it emphasizes similarity or commonality, organized by ideal images, political identification is bound up with narcissism and aggression. To the extent that we identify with and as feminists, then, we may maintain an imaginary fantasy of feminism as a safe space, an interior whole. At the same time, the very psychic mechanisms embedded in this solidarity may trouble its "inside," to the extent that it may be hard to separate political conflict from narcissistic aggression. Equally important, a politics that emphasizes identification by neglecting difference or overlooking internal conflicts will inevitably sustain a certain return of the repressed. Only by thinking feminist practice and feminist politics *not* as grounded in a stably bounded interior, but rather as thoroughly embedded in a whole set of social conflicts, would we be able to sustain and exploit the productive political force of anger.

17 Significantly, Ellie is not a working mother. Her profession is part of her past; its traces remain in her skill with firearms. Thus, the Kegans embody the dream of an older domestic order—the one-income, middle-class, homeowning family. Alongside this reading, however, we may also suggest a nostalgia for the "paternal metaphor." For Žižek: "this is what is ultimately at stake in the noir universe: the failure of the paternal metaphor (i.e., the emergence of the obscene father who supplants the father living up to his symbolic function) renders impossible a viable, temperate relationship with a woman; as a result, the woman finds herself occupying the impossible place of the traumatic Thing. The femme fatale is nothing but a lure whose fascinating presence masks the true traumatic axis of the noir universe . . . i.e., the default of the paternal metaphor" (159–60). In this case, the fatal woman enacts the compelling law of that universe which says that she is herself entirely under the sway of this default as well. Given that this is a Ridley Scott film, we might see it as repeating some of the obsessions about the paternal and the maternal places that were so central to *Blade Runner* (1981).

18 In a sense, *Someone to Watch Over Me*'s combined police thriller and family drama plot confirms the anxiety provoked by the collapse of the illusory private-public boundary that sustained the traditional detective plot. D. A. Miller argues that such plots are implicated in a particular ideology. "If one were to speak of an ideology borne in the form of the detective story," he writes, "here would be one of its major sites: in the perception of everyday life as fundamentally 'outside' the network of policing power." *The Novel and the Police* (Berkeley: University of California Press, 1988), p. 36. It is particularly important, in this regard, to consider the coincidence involved in depicting "everyday life" both fully

inhabited by the police, and completely exceeding the policeman father's control, in a drama that simultaneously figures male authority as displaced by feminine agency.

19 Writing about the novel, Miller demonstrates the persistence of this anxiety in middle-class culture: "In the same degree that it propagates the worry and anxiety needed to maintain the family, it keeps alive the ever-present danger of its fall. The novel everywhere publishes the same fear of falling and implies the same urgency about holding one's place. The 'outside' of power regularly incurs the risk that it may be annexed—or, worse, may already have been annexed—by the 'inside'" (104).

20 D. N. Rodowick, "Madness, Authority and Ideology: The Domestic Melodrama of the 1950s," *Home Is Where the Heart Is: Studies in Melodrama and the Woman's Film,* ed. Christine Gledhill (London: British Film Institute, 1987), p. 272.

21 See Dana Polan, *Power and Paranoia: History, Narrative, and the American Cinema, 1940–1950* (New York: Columbia University Press, 1986). Discussing the particular form of horror in forties' films, Polan reminds us of the psychoanalytic connections that the form maintains with film noir. "If, as Robin Wood has suggested, the formula of classic horror is 'Normalcy is threatened by the monster,' increasingly psychoanalysis displaces the source of that menace from physically traditional monsters to the *id* as *initially* uncontrollable force, or, in many cases, as in *film noir,* to a femininity or to an urban condition (or to a confluence of the two) figured as the repository of a-social or anti-social forces" (186). In its repetition of these anxieties, *Someone to Watch Over Me* encodes a certain filmic nostalgia no doubt, but the particular form of its oppositions between masculinity and femininity and urban and domestic spaces offers a map of contemporary displacements of class and urban conflict onto gender and, conversely, of gendered conflict onto social or community spaces.

22 One cannot help noticing that the cinematography that monumentalizes the objects and the space of Claire's in a strikingly intimidating way makes it look much like the inner chambers of the Tyrell Corporation in *Blade Runner.*

23 For a discussion of paranoia expressed as an alternation of point of view between subject and object of sight and aggression, an alternation that involves a character's relation to the space and to the objects it contains, see Polan, *Power and Paranoia,* esp. chap. 3, pp. 145ff.

24 This network can also subvert masculine authority, as when Ellie later mobilizes it, to Mike's chagrin, when she asks Lieutenant Garber's wife to convince her husband to put Mike on the day shift.

25 Perhaps the most colossal recent example of this move to contain women's rage and aggression is Sigourney Weaver's Ripley in *Aliens* (1986). If Ripley can undertake the film's final lethal confrontation against the alien mother, it is only after all the males have been disabled—the trend epitomized in the figure of Ash, who is literally cut in half, reduced to a torso—and it is only as a "mother" driven by her urge to protect her "adopted" child, Newt.

26 Yvonne Tasker characterizes Catherine's allure, and the threat she poses, as follows: "Here the deadly woman's danger is not only that posed by a serial killer, but that of a figure who does not respect boundaries." "Pussy Galore: Lesbian Images and Lesbian Desire in the Popular Cinema," in Diane Hamer and Belinda Budge, eds., *The Good, the Bad and the Gorgeous: Culture's Romance with Lesbianism* (London: Harper Collins/Pandora, 1994), p. 173.

27 We recall that *Cruising* spurred gay activists to call for a boycott, much as happened later

with lesbians and *Basic Instinct*. In their provocativeness, both films are admittedly politically risky. They seem to me, however, not so much homophobic as intent on targeting and aggravating homophobic fantasies that the spectator may harbor. Friedkin's tendency to provide images that bluntly address homophobic anxieties is also evident in *To Live and Die in L.A.* (1985). The political risks that such films run is related to the inability of their discourses (like any text's) to predict, determine, or stabilize the volatile fantasies which they may seek to stir up. On the other hand, Clare Watling supplies a different and provocative take on *Basic Instinct* and its place in the "positive images" debates: "It is a film which is in many ways in line with a long Hollywood tradition of deploying homosexual characters as signifiers of criminality. . . . However, as the film which kindled the contemporary debate around positive images it deserves some comment. Because what is different about *Basic Instinct* is how glamorous its lesbian characters are. It is of course a film that plays outrageously (in order to outrage) on its lesbian content, proving that Hollywood is only too happy to use lesbianism as subject-matter so long as it pays." "Fostering the Illusion," in Hamer and Budge, *The Good, the Bad and the Gorgeous*, p. 187.

28   Over the dead body of Jim Mackey, Frank antagonizes his co-investigator, Gruber, wondering aloud about the difference between them that has permitted Gruber to "steal [his] wife." Gruber replies that Frank "didn't treat her right," and that "if you want to kick somebody's ass about it, kick your own." Later, Frank will use the same metaphorics to describe his job-related depression: "This twenty-year thing, it's really kicking my ass."

29   In this respect, the initially all-male world of *Sea of Love* displays the tensions with which it is fraught, and these are tensions very much like those that Susan Jeffords analyzes in her account of Vietnam narratives in contemporary culture: "While sexual images must be foregrounded in order to act as constant reminders of the structuration of gender that reinforces the ideology of collectivity, they pose a constant risk of displaying the dependency of that collectivity on the very relation it denies—the association with women. . . . Because they are grounded in that which they deny, the narratives of masculine collectivity, trapped in the inevitability of their own logic, must constantly rework themselves. They can never completely achieve their separation from the feminine and so must constantly retell their relation to it." *The Remasculinization of America: Gender and the Vietnam War* (Bloomington: Indiana University Press, 1989), p. 72. Now, *Sea of Love* is self-conscious about this internal disturbance and its sources; its critical distance on Frank produces a space for analysis of the workings of these tensions.

30   For D. N. Rodowick, writing on domestic melodrama, this difficulty is central to the form of melodramatic negotiation of heterosexual relations; while the films can readily acknowledge the failure of secure and fixed gender identification, they "rarely acknowledge . . . the *impossibility* of this identification" (272). On this issue, Jacqueline Rose argues that "the unconscious constantly reveals the 'failure' of identity. Because there is no continuity in psychic life, so there is no stability of sexual identity, no position for women (or men) which is ever simply achieved." *Sexuality in the Field of Vision* (London: Verso, 1987), pp. 90–91.

31   Much of the credit for this must go to Richard Price's screenplay. Price's fiction, including *The Wanderers* (New York: Avon, 1974), *Bloodbrothers* (New York: Avon, 1976), and *Clockers* (Boston: Houghton Mifflin, 1992), treats masculinity and masculine sexuality as always embedded in social relations, always rooted in particular locations and communities. Price's men always confront their sexuality in specific social situations composed

of family, history, and community based in race, ethnicity, and geography, as well as of heterosexual relations.

32   Sherman is still married, and he is overweight; so he cannot compete with Frank on the singles market, but rather he establishes a relationship of comic complementarity.

33   The film introduces the suggestion that feminine independence automatically becomes dominance on the economic level as well through Sherman's comments later on when he has been interviewing a series of "dates": "I've seen eight women in two hours, and I bet every one of them makes more money than I do."

34   The question of dangerous, even lethal, sex must be related to AIDS anxiety, which is completely repressed on the explicit level in this film. In this context the references to asses in the running patter between men, and the overestimation of feminine lethal powers suggest a common reactionary ideology about AIDS, one which associates the threat of contagion with gay men, and with women—contrary to medical evidence which shows that HIV transmission from men to women is much more likely than the reverse—and which constitutes the defensive projections of male heterosexuality.

35   As Tasker analyzes it: "The investigation becomes bound-up in desire, as process which literally involves the shifting and questioning of assumed identities, as different kinds of transgressions are collapsed together. This is exactly the sort of narrative that *Basic Instinct* plays on through the relationship of Nick and Catherine, whose pursuit of each other is entangled in sexual desire. This kind of popular narrative exemplifies the processes by which identifications are forged and blurred within the cinema, generating an uncertainty that is both disturbing and, more importantly, pleasurable" (177–78).

36   For a discussion of the structure of identification, fraught as it is with aggression and linked to mimicry as the grounding of subjectivity, see Mikkel Borch-Jacobson, *The Freudian Subject* (Stanford, Calif.: Stanford University Press, 1988). Borch-Jacobson's description of the adversarial nature of specularity bears a striking resemblance to the structures at work in *Sea of Love*. "The subject either plays a part in the spectacle or is a spectator. . . . The dilemma is implacable, insurmountable. The lack of distinction between self and other—the mimesis—has to be acted out; yet no sooner is it represented to the subject in the specular mode than it is betrayed. At the very moment of the image in the mirror, the spectacle will have already opened up the space of adversity (note that I am not saying of alterity); hence the instantaneous rage that overcomes the child when she *sees* the other in *her* place. . . . And no doubt the other will be at that moment scarcely different from me myself (almost myself); but this self, myself, being specular, will already be an adverse, adversary self, and enemy (almost another)" (40).

37   Angela Galvin reads similar dynamics in structures of identification and in the therapeutic situation that the film represents. "But the film is less concerned with investigating the crime than it is with investigating the emasculation of the nineties man as revealed through the psyche of Nick, his psychotherapist (Beth Garner) and Catherine. . . . In these terms, the choice of the therapist-patient relationship as pivotal to the narrative is an interesting one. It acts to disclose a series of neuroses and psychoses which undermine the terms of difference between Nick and the two women, and between the two women and each other." "*Basic Instinct*: Damning Dykes," in Hamer and Budge, *The Good, the Bad and the Gorgeous*, p. 222.

38   In this regard, the film opens up a more radical logic than it can follow through on, and this may be why it closes down the question of sexual difference so raggedly and feebly in

the marriage. At times, the film seems to assert that identity is always a failure, and that this is its social nature. Joan Copjec has argued this point forcefully in "Cutting Up," in *Between Psychoanalysis and Feminism,* ed. Teresa Brennan (London: Routledge, 1989): "this failure, the very *impossibility* of representing the subject to the subject, is conceived as that which founds the subject's identity. *The failure of representation* produces rather than disrupts identity. That missing part which representation, in failing to inscribe, cuts off is the absence around which the subject weaves its fantasies, its self-image, not in imitation of any ideal vision, but in response to the very impossibility of ever making visible this missing point. We are constructed, then, not in conformity to social laws, but in response to our inability to conform to or see ourselves as defined by social limits" (241–42).

39 For a more extended analysis of this process, see chap. 6.

40 *Clint Eastwood: A Cultural Production* (Minneapolis: University of Minnesota Press, 1993), p. 138. This film's hero is, like Frank Keller or Nick Curran, "almost disabled by his recognition that the erotic and murderous desires of the killer he stalks are also his own" (122).

3 Combative Femininity

1 Two "asides" come to mind here. The first concerns the increasing ubiquity of Barbara Kruger's images and their imitators. By the mid-1980s various forms of publicity—from activist posters, to public service announcements about HIV in the subways, to product advertising—had either commissioned Kruger herself to produce images, or had appropriated her "signature" style: combining bold black and white images bordered in red with aggressive texts offering injunctions or admonitions. The cover of *Ms.* marks a moment of feminist re-appropriation of images whose popularity and marketability depended on their overtly feminist origin, even when they were manipulated in distinctly nonfeminist contexts. The second aside concerns the "marketability" of feminine rage in general. Overheated media attention to the Bobbitt case, in which an abused wife severed her husband's penis in retaliation, for example, consistently played the story as the latest turn in an escalating "battle of the sexes" and suggested that this event appealed to women's revenge fantasies in a general and predictable way. The public fantasy, whose authorship we might want to interrogate, that women share a desire to punish men by mutilating their sexual organs participates in ongoing confusions about the status of fantasy in our culture and, more specifically, about the status of aggressive fantasy in relation to struggles around sexual difference and gender equality.

2 In *Fatal Women: Lesbian Sexuality and the Mark of Aggression* (Princeton, N.J.: Princeton University Press, 1994), Lynda Hart also examines the contradictions within much critical response to the film: "First, spectators' responses to the film manifest the familiar denunciation, couched in aesthetic terms, of its lack of verisimilitude, and *at the same time,* the fear that its content is all too imitable" (73).

3 *Lost Angels: Psychoanalysis and Cinema* (New York: Routledge, 1995), p. 22.

4 In an earlier version of this argument, Lebeau suggests that this model must imagine both the feminine and the mass/youth spectator as marked by insufficient relationships to both the superego and the paternal function. "Daddy's Cinema: Femininity and Mass Spectatorship," *Screen,* Autumn 1992, p. 248.

5 To support this point, in "Daddy's Cinema" Lebeau cites Thomas Doherty's description of American International Pictures' "exploitation code drawn up in the mid 1960s," from

his book *Teenagers and Teenpics: The Juvenilisation of American Movies in the 1950s* (London: Unwin Hyman, 1988), p. 157. This code selects the nineteen-year-old male as the target to aim for in the quest for the largest audience, because, according to its logic, younger children "will watch anything that an older child will watch," and similarly, "a girl will watch anything a boy will watch," while there is no reversibility between the paired categories (253).

6 Jacqueline Rose, *The Haunting of Sylvia Plath* (Cambridge, Mass.: Harvard University Press, 1993), p. 158.

7 The intensity of debate around the issue of *Thelma and Louise*'s political responsibility is somewhat suspicious in ways that are related to Lebeau's analysis of a certain kind of critical authority applied to popular or "mass" cinema, which imagines that cinema dissolves political agency through the presentation of fantasies, "wishes" that might come to occupy the place of the spectator's "will" or "demand" ("Daddy's Cinema," p. 255).

8 Colin Mercer suggests that this is because pleasure, "more than any other notion (except perhaps those of taste or choice) . . . entails individual sovereignty. This is the 'unsaid' of pleasure, its presupposition when mobilized in any discourse (collective pleasures are always a bit tacky)." "A Poverty of Desire: Pleasure and Popular Politics," in Formations Collective, ed., *Formations of Pleasure* (London: Routledge & Kegan Paul, 1983), p. 96. See also Judith Butler, "The Force of Fantasy: Feminism, Mapplethorpe, and Discursive Excess," *Differences* 2, no. 2 (1990): "fantasy works to secure the illusion of a subject in place for it" (109).

9 Butler, "The Force of Fantasy," p. 111.

10 Lynda Hart reads the Texas matter somewhat differently. "The inarticulation of Louise's trauma is associated with consternation about the film's incoherent geography. . . . Just as Louise refuses to articulate the particulars of her past, she attempts to avoid literally traversing that history. . . . What Louise needs is an imaginary landscape, a map with another route to follow than the one preordained for her in the symbolic order. Thelma has to learn that reality is a ruse, a lure. But Louise already knows 'we don't live in that kind of world . . .' " (70).

11 Tom Conley has suggested to me that *Thelma and Louise* reads like a long commercial for Coors Light. Based on the Silver Bullet bar's centrality to the narrative progress, his point is well taken. But it leads to some questions about a competing image: Thelma's obsessive purchase of the tiny one-shot bottles of Wild Turkey to drink on the road. The cumulative effect of this manic accumulation of miniatures points to the excess and its pleasures that seem to drive Thelma and Louise. But where light beers have been sufficiently enough coded as feminine that their advertising now aggressively targets male consumers, Thelma's move to Wild Turkey in the film is clearly marked as a move toward a more traditionally masculine style and taste in drinking.

12 For further discussion of anxieties about violence and specific audiences, see chap. 5, "Tell the Right Story," which treats the dominant culture's fantasies about audiences of young African American males and assigns particular social and political obligations, as well as responsibilities for "realism," to films by African American filmmakers.

13 As Jacqueline Rose argues in *The Haunting of Sylvia Plath,* such fantasies or images involve a difficult and peculiar intersection of identifications with victim and perpetrator: "For being a victim does not stop you from identifying with the aggressor; being an aggressor does not stop you from identifying with the victim. To which we could add a formula

only deceptively tautological—that being a victim (or aggressor) does not stop you from identifying with the victim (or aggressor). Identification is something that has always to be constructed. Wherever it is that subjects find themselves historically, this will not produce one, unequivocal, identification as its logical effect" (210).

14   Lynda Hart sees this incident as part of the film's strategic play with lesbian suggestions: "the film titillates spectators with the possibility of desire between the women, then recuperates that desire by introducing male lovers at heightened moments" (76).

15   In *Spectacular Bodies: Gender, Genre and the Action Film* (New York: Routledge, 1993), Yvonne Tasker characterizes *Thelma and Louise* as a narrative of transformation, a "rites-of-passage" story, which may be "reminiscent of the narratives constructed around the male bodybuilder, whose physical transformation signals his changed status in the world," and of "the rites-of-passage narrative that situates women in relation to health or body culture," which also "defines the heroine's transformation through the body" (137).

16   The tremendously animated discussion surrounding *Thelma and Louise* suggests that I am not the only woman fascinated by driving and its myths. As the film's screenwriter, Callie Khouri, remarks: "I just got fed up with the passive role of women. They were never driving the story, because they were never driving the cars."

17   Some of these questions were suggested to me by Elissa Marder in a conversation during which I was groping for my point of departure with *Thelma and Louise*.

18   This seems to be a somewhat more interesting, because more expansive, approach to the question of the iconic use of butch and femme figures in popular culture than that advanced by Diane Hamer and Belinda Budge, who begin their volume *The Good, the Bad, and the Gorgeous* by asking: "why dominant culture—whose privileged discourse has always been heterosexuality—has become obsessed with homosexuality . . . constructed as a glamorous, rather than a despised identity" (6). "So little is now forbidden within a heterosexual landscape," they contend, "that new metaphors must constantly be sought out. Homosexuality serves as a new and (still) shocking arena for the reworking of stories of sex and love, romance and desire" (6–7). But images of lesbians must surely perform more ideological and representational work than the mere provision of newness, new stories, new metaphors. Surely, as well, we must take into account that lesbian images on screen interact in complex ways with a social context in which lesbian subjects and bodies may not profit, or may profit only unevenly from the "romance" with lesbianism that these authors find on the screen and in music culture. Later in this essay, the authors point to another possible source for the new attention to figures of lesbianism: "A . . . related possibility as to why homosexuality is in ascendancy may be the anxiety about gender currently at large within mainstream culture" (7). I would argue that such a claim makes more sense in the context of more general cultural anxieties about the relationship of visibility to identity.

19   These complexities disrupt any sense of the coherence of gender identity, foreground its performativity, in the sense that Judith Butler proposes when she suggests that identification be understood as "an enacted fantasy or incorporation." This enactment makes it clear, she argues, "that coherence is desired, wished for, idealized, and that this idealization is an effect of corporeal signification." *Gender Trouble: Feminism and the Subversion of Identity* (New York: Routledge, 1990), p. 136. But the very performativity at the heart of identification gives the lie to any dream of coherence since, as Butler continues, "such acts, gestures, enactments, generally construed, are performative in the sense that the

essence or identity that they otherwise purport to express are fabrications manufactured and sustained through corporeal signs and other discursive means" (136).

20　Yvonne Tasker cites certain textual elements that maintain the film's availability to what she calls "lesbian appropriations": "*Thelma and Louise* also draws on the cowgirl/cowboy image, a theme which emphasizes the particular white Southern culture within which the protagonists are located. Clearly, *Thelma and Louise* cannot be described as a 'lesbian film' in the same way as *Desert Hearts*. Yet in its focus on the developing central relationship between Thelma and Louise, its juxtaposition of C and W music styles with, for example, Marianne Faithfull's 'The Ballad of Lucy Jordan,' *Thelma and Louise* draws on a similar iconography. Both films draw on the kind of popular music that has been appropriated by lesbian audiences in other contexts. In this sense, *Thelma and Louise* is itself available to be appropriated as a lesbian film." Yvonne Tasker, "Pussy Galore: Lesbian Images and Lesbian Desire in the Popular Cinema," in *The Good, the Bad and the Gorgeous,* ed. Hamer and Budge, p. 182.

21　"*Thelma and Louise* and the Cultural Generation of the New Butch-Femme," in *Film Theory Goes to the Movies,* ed. Jim Collins, Hilary Radner, and Ava Preacher Collins (New York: Routledge, 1993), p. 133.

22　Griggers continues: "this social process of becoming lesbian is the crucial insight of *Thelma and Louise.*" "Thelma and Louise don't become butch because they're lesbians, they become lesbians because they've already become butch to survive. Lesbian identity is represented in this film as a social condition, rather than an 'innate' sexual orientation" (140).

23　*Making Things Perfectly Queer* (Minneapolis: University of Minnesota Press, 1993), pp. 3–4. Doty explains: "as such, the cultural 'queer space' recognizes the possibility that various and fluctuating queer positions might be occupied whenever anyone produces or responds to culture . . . because the queer operates within the nonqueer, as the nonqueer does within the queer (whether in reception, texts, or producers)" (3).

24　Doty's argument, then, would suggest that readings like the one Cathy Griggers offers as "aberrant" (134), and the ones Constance Penley cites for "Pee-wee's Playhouse," characterizing them as "camp," in "The Cabinet of Doctor Pee-wee: Consumerism and Sexual Terror," in Constance Penley and Sharon Willis, eds., *Male Trouble* (Minneapolis: University of Minnesota Press, 1993), pp. 133–39, and the one offered by Jonathan Goldberg in "Recalling Totalities: The Mirrored Stages of Arnold Schwarzenegger," *Differences* 4, no. 1 (1992): 172–204, are not really aberrant at all, but structurally central to any dominant or "preferred" readings.

25　Tamsin Wilton, ed., *Immortal Invisible: Lesbians and the Moving Image* (New York: Routledge, 1995), p. 3.

26　One of these is clearly *Butch Cassidy and the Sundance Kid.* By comparison to its male buddy film precursor, however, Thelma and Louise's image is not immediately memorialized as public, as news, the way that *Butch Cassidy* memorializes its heroes, framing their immobility on film stock that shades into sienna tones. Butch Cassidy and the Sundance Kid are frozen as figures of failed masculinity outstripped by the history whose image they become. Thelma and Louise, on the other hand, are suspended as the image of the unfinished.

27　In this regard, they may recall the national obsession with transformer toys that Susan

Willis analyzes in *A Primer for Daily Life* (New York: Routledge, 1991). Willis sees in this "vast array of toys whose singular purpose is to transform," "a fitting motto for late twentieth century capitalism." And that motto is, bluntly put: "Everything transforms but nothing changes" (36). Broadly speaking, these toys suggest a pleasure in pure and perpetual transformation. Willis locates a different manifestation of the consumer drive to transformation that is specifically related to sexual difference in feminine exercise culture. She describes the phenomenon of the aerobicized body as fashion in the following way. "The image of the workout woman articulates the fundamental contradiction between the desire for dramatic transformation shackled to the desire for gender identity, in a society where only one gender needs definition" (76).

28 Yvonne Tasker calls this phenomenon "musculinity," characterizing its effects as follows: " 'musculinity' indicates the way in which the signifiers of strength are not limited to the characters." "That is," she continues, "some of the qualities associated with masculinity are written over the muscular female body" (*Spectacular Bodies*, p. 149).

29 In this respect, the figure resembles what Ed Guerrero has termed African American "ghosts" in Hollywood texts. See *Framing Blackness* (Philadelphia: Temple University Press, 1993).

30 Paul Smith discusses "annoyance" with films that sketch the problematic nature of sexuality, only to "see fit to fall back upon that moment of self-congratulatory and secure repression. That annoyance is, of course, the origin of a critique of the movie; at the same time, even this ending and the disappointment it occasions leave imaginary residues—memories of the film, its images and its gestures that remain provocative, evocative, even problematical." *Clint Eastwood: A Cultural Production* (Minneapolis: University of Minnesota Press, 1993), pp. 139–40.

31 *Looking Awry* (Cambridge, Mass.: MIT Press, 1991), pp. 8, 11.

32 *Playing in the Dark: Whiteness and the Literary Imagination* (New York: Random House, 1993), pp. 12–13.

33 Gannett News Service, July 9, 1991: *Terminator 2* opened on Wednesday, July 3–July 4th weekend: "grossed $31.4 over the weekend, estimates Tri-Star Pictures." "The highest opening of 1991, surpassing *Robin Hood: Prince of Thieves* $26.5 million. It's also the second-biggest three-day opening ever: 1989's *Batman* is still champ ($42.7 million)." "The new action movie drew significant numbers of female moviegoers; 42 per cent of its opening-weekend audience were women," reports Tri-Star. " 'That's a very impressive number,' " says the *Hollywood Reporter*'s Martin Grove. "The standard action film has an audience composed of 70 percent to 80 percent men."

34 Susan Jeffords, "Can Masculinity Be Terminated?" in Steven Cohan and Ina Rae Hark, eds., *Screening the Male: Exploring Masculinities in Hollywood Cinema* (New York: Routledge, 1993), p. 246.

35 This would suggest that Jeffords's claim that repetition indicates obsession and "conservative" tendencies needs some modification of the sort that Paul Smith proposes in *Clint Eastwood: A Cultural Production*: "genre lives not by repetition alone; rather it subsists, as does the whole of Hollywood production, in a dialectic of repetition and difference" (20).

36 It is safe to say, in fact, that this film is built to be marketed on spectacular effects. The Carolco videocassette carries an advertisement designed to solicit one's desire to own a copy in the following terms: it shows a family rapt before the television screen, one

child enthusiastically asking: "How did they do that?" "See it again and again." But the equally powerful question operating at the subterranean level here concerns Sarah Connor's body: "How did she do that?"

37 This is the pleasure that Jonathan Goldberg identifies as central to *The Terminator*'s appeal: "The Terminator blasts the yuppie fuckers. As the relentless refusal of heterosexual imperatives, he embodies—or bears the image of—leather culture, displaying machismo with a difference" (189).

38 "Making Cyborgs, Making Humans," in *Film Theory Goes to the Movies*, p. 240. But Pyle also suggests that the earlier film's opposition was equally specious: "when the human opposition to the machine finally triumphs in *The Terminator*, the opposition between the human and cyborg begins to appear as the human projection it always was" (234).

39 Goldberg points to one knot that unravels almost automatically: "the refusal of the machine is, patently, an ideological lure: at the simplest level, sci-fi movies appeal through their special effects, the mark of their complicity with advanced technology. Need it be said that the star of *The Terminator* is the terminator? . . . this suggests that the pro-life aspect of the movie is also a ruse, a cover for the destructivity the movie celebrates . . ." (180).

40 "The quasi Oedipal path in which the son kills the father is doubled by the exterminating anti-paternal terminator; this doubling also is, in the present, a site of erotic identification, as fully as in that future in which Reese is the worshipful follower of John Connor. . . . Paths of cross-identification mark the relation between Reese and the machine he pursues" (182). See also Constance Penley's brilliant seminal essay on technophobia and oedipality in *The Terminator*, "Time Travel, Primal Scene, and the Critical Dystopia," in *Close Encounters*, ed. Constance Penley, Elisabeth Lyon, Lynn Spigel, and Janet Bergstrom (Minneapolis: University of Minnesota Press, 1991), pp. 63–80.

41 Goldberg underlines the ironies that bear on this image of the reconstituted family: "This film may believe it has reconstituted the family: but father is a cyborg, mother perhaps a lesbian, and the kid is part juvenile delinquent, part computer hacker, a bushytailed white version of the black computer technician that the movie abjects" (194).

42 As Forest Pyle notes, it is through the persistent opposition of "mechanical mimicry and genuine learning" that the film manages to reappropriate the T101 to the "human" side (232).

43 In this respect, Arnold Schwarzenegger's embodiment of the terminator contributes distinctly to this effect, if we read his body through its history in bodybuilding competitions. Goldberg explores the fantasmatic displacements of the phallus entailed in the contemplation of such a body: "the built body offers the spectacle of the made body, the artificial, 'different' body (becoming a statue is the favored trope in the bodybuilder's discourse) as a locus of Imaginary identifications. If, to return to our initial tautology, this (displaced) paternal body 'is' the phallus, it cannot simply secure the Symbolic" (175).

44 Goldberg reminds us that the police psychologist in *The Terminator* "characterizes terminator's mission as a 'retroactive abortion'" (180).

45 See Carol Stabile's essay, "Shooting the Mother: Fetal Photography and the Politics of Disappearance," *Camera Obscura*, January 1992, in which she tracks the shift that new imaging technologies have produced in representations of the "maternal environment" which the fetus inhabits, from a utopic to a dystopic space. Stabile describes this effect as an "ideological transformation of the female body from a benevolent maternal environment into an inhospitable wasteland, at war with the 'innocent person' within" (179).

For a detailed and comprehensive analysis of contemporary contest over the meaning of "motherhood," see Valerie Hartouni, "Containing Women: Reproductive Discourse in the 1980s," in *Technoculture,* ed. Constance Penley and Andrew Ross (Minneapolis: University of Minnesota Press, 1991), pp. 27-56. Hartouni sees as a central dividing line in these discourses a "distinction between social activities and meanings on the one hand, and 'biological processes' on the other," suggesting that we need to regard pregnancy as a "biosocial experience," and "motherhood as a historically specific set of social practices, an activity that is socially and politically constructed and conditioned by relations of power" (31). This is what new technologies for visualizing and intervening in reproduction might allow us to establish as a prevailing understanding. On the other hand, those very technologies may contribute to paranoias about the maternal body that lead to its discursive containment as a vehicle or incubator.

46   Among the details in *Alien 3* that play on anxieties about bodily invasion in the form of illness is, no doubt, Ripley's shaved head, in its resonance with the effects of chemotherapy on the body's surface. It would perhaps be fair to say that some of the film's force derives from its ability to produce details that perform within several interpretive circuits simultaneously, and often combining camp humor and its pleasures with terrifying allusions to collective anxieties about the proliferation of disease.

47   Neither the film itself, nor the framing discussions of it, has made anything of the butch-femme aesthetics that mark a subcultural influence and audience for some recent representations of women; revised versions of the butch and femme styles have emerged only in regard to the consumer fashion circuit.

48   This anxiety is reminiscent of the function of mimesis in 1950s science fiction, where the alien within, which the heroes struggle to discern, represents the threat of communism.

49   "The Body in Question," in *Black Popular Culture,* ed. Gina Dent (Seattle: Bay Press, 1993), p. 107.

50   See Kobena Mercer's argument about the politics of ambivalence in "Skin Head Sex Thing: Racial Difference and the Homoerotic Imaginary," in *Welcome to the Jungle* (New York: Routledge, 1994), pp. 189-204.

4   Do the Wrong Thing

1   Bailey describes the attitude these films share: "The hallmark of these 'New York' films is an almost ethnographic attitude towards the rest of the US, focusing with ironic fascination on middle-American popular culture, culture produced for the white working class outside the larger cities." This attitude, according to Bailey, is matched by a common tone of "deadpan mockery." But, he continues, "The ridicule that informs it is matched by nostalgia, and by a desire to make art out of the experience of popular culture." "Nigger/Lover: The Thin Sheen of Race in *Something Wild,*" *Screen* 29, no. 4 (1988): 29.

2   On this issue, see in particular Timothy Corrigan, *A Cinema Without Walls* (New Brunswick, N.J.: Rutgers University Press, 1991). In contemporary culture, Corrigan argues, "the auteur can be described according to the conditions of a cultural and commercial intersubjectivity, a social interaction distinct from intentional causality or textual transcendence" (104). In such a context, authorial "agency becomes a mode of enunciation that describes an active and monitored engagement with its own conditions as the subjective expresses itself through the socially symbolic" (104-5). In other words, the auteur

function now has as much to do with audience formation and critical reception as with subjective expressivity or textual inscription.

3 Citing Andreas Huyssen, Naremore exhibits a certain caution about the limitations of auteurism as well: "In the current climate, few people would doubt the value of asking: Who is writing? or Who is speaking? Continued skepticism about such questions not only forestalls important forms of historical inquiry; it also fails to engage with what Huyssen describes as 'the ideology of the subject (as male, white, middle-class),' and it forsakes the chance of 'developing alternative and different notions of subjectivity.' Partly for these reasons, the emphasis in critical writing on film and television has begun to shift from avant-garde practice to ideas of 'low culture' and popularity. At the same time, we've continued to be interested in historical subjects as producers and reproducers of culture." James Naremore, "Authorship and the Cultural Politics of Film Criticism," *Film Quarterly,* Fall 1990, p. 20.

4 Let me make it clear that I consider myself to be part of this target audience. Otherwise, I would not have experienced the film as I did, as a vicious assault, and as a parade of a particular social unconscious. To respond in this way, I clearly have to feel addressed by it, "taken in" by it, to the extent that I can read its intertextual references, that I share much of its grounding knowledge and aesthetic. In other words, it is only because I feel implicated in both the film's address and its discourse that I can read this way, and *react* to it to this way. However, such resistance also depends on a spectator's simultaneously having access to certain counterdiscourses that come into contradiction with the film's structures of visibility. For it is precisely on the ground of such counterdiscourses that one feels the most attacked by the film, if not by the culture at large.

5 "Something Really Wild," *Movieline,* September 1990, p. 32.

6 "Hunka Burnin' Love," *Village Voice,* August 20, 1990, p. 58.

7 In his subtle and attentive reading of *Wild at Heart*'s sound design, Michel Chion offers an interpretation of music that would seem at first to lead us to altogether different conclusions. "In the case of *Wild at Heart,"* he writes, "the force of sound relates to the good, non-destructive, vital power of love, and is an integral part of the thematic structure, stated from the outset by the very flamboyance of the credit sequence, just as a tonality is affirmed at the beginning of a symphony." *David Lynch,* trans. Robert Julian (London: British Film Institute, 1995), p. 133. However, given the association of ambient sound with the "good," with "love" in the context of the film's timelessness, the saturation effects that characterize the sound design could easily be associated with a certain preoedipal nostalgia for the amniotic realm.

8 In *Audio-Vision: Sound on Screen,* ed. and trans. Claudia Gorbman (New York: Columbia University Press, 1994), p. 155, Michel Chion credits Lynch with particularly resourceful uses of the special features of Dolby. For Chion, Dolby allows for the production of "music as spatiotemporal turntable" (81). "Dolby . . . creates a space with fluid borders, a sort of superscreen enveloping the screen—the superfield" (69). "What does a sound typically lead us to ask about space? Not 'Where is it?'—for the sound 'is' in the air we breathe or, if you will, as a perception it's in our head—but rather, 'Where does it come from?' The problem of localizing a sound therefore most often translates as the problem of locating its source" (69). Lynch's use of Dolby, then, would contribute substantially to the film's narrative and visual effects of scattering and dislocation.

9 In *David Lynch,* Chion makes a none too convincing case for this scene's status as a mistake or miscalculation: "One is left with the sense of a false, cynical cartoon, which the

rest of the film in no way confirms. It is an isolated case of a botched scene, poorly filmed and morally confused in its way of showing both the murder of a black man and Marietta's supposed orgasmic pleasure at the sight of Sailor blowing his top . . ." (132). Clearly, my own argument is that the rest of the film does, in fact, bear out the tendencies displayed in its opening sequence.

10 This series of structural effects produces a suspension of point of view that culminates in something like what Edward Branigan calls "excess vision." Excess vision occurs when we see not only what a character does see, but also what they would have seen had they been looking; "the passage from equilibrium to disequilibrium (homogeneity to heterogeneity)—so vital to narrative—is here stated in terms of the tension between two POV structures—what should have been seen . . . and what was instead seen . . . —leaving shots . . . intermediate between the two structures as a kind of excess vision, the emblem of a narrative violence which will be reinvested in the narrative to ensure its continuation." "The Point-of-View Shot," from *Point of View in the Cinema: A Theory of Narration and Subjectivity in Classical Film* (New York: Mouton, 1984), reprinted in Bill Nichols, ed., *Movies and Methods, II* (Berkeley: University of California Press, 1985), p. 685.

11 In this connection, it is worth remarking that Lynch's script is based on Barry Gifford's novel, *Wild at Heart: The Story of Sailor and Lula* (New York: Random House, 1990), a book that was reissued by Random House's Vintage Contemporaries series in time to coincide roughly with the U.S. opening of the film. Lynch has changed the novel in several significant ways, which in the film make those altered elements stand out all the more. Bob Ray Lemon's race is not made explicit in the novel; we assume he is white, like Sailor. Marietta is not the incarnation of eroticized sadism and oedipal rivalry that she is in the film, nor has she killed her husband. The character Santos, Marietta's accomplice in the murder of her husband does not exist in the book. Nor are there any particular references to either Elvis or *The Wizard of Oz*. Finally, and strikingly, the novel provides no happy ending, no marital plot resolution. Lynch's version of the narrative works to bring race into view, along with maternal violence and viciousness, for its own particular purposes. These elements, then, begin to appear as the particular obsessive fascinations of the Lynch version.

12 *New York Times,* August 17, 1990, p. C1.

13 "Czar of Bizarre," *Time,* October 1, 1990, p. 86.

14 "Review," *Nation,* September 17, 1990, p. 285.

15 "The Heart of the Cavern," *Sight and Sound,* November 1987, p. 101.

16 Here we might consider that Lynch's films, with their discomfiting attention to monumentalized objects, present a closer look at too many things, but that, by getting right into our faces with certain details, they fend off a closer look at other things, like violent assaults on women's bodies—literally or figuratively—or like a racial subtext.

17 The good witch who appears to Sailor at the end notwithstanding, this witch's ability to stand for the "good" mother, as her model in *The Wizard of Oz* does, is canceled by the fact that she is played by the same actress who plays Laura Palmer in "Twin Peaks." In the intertextuality that Lynch's texts depend upon, she is therefore already undone. A comic, campy witch, this figure appears as a hilariously disguised version of the deceptive, manipulative, sluttish Laura Palmer, who can present only a camp recitation of a discourse on "true love."

18 See Alice Jardine, *Gynesis* (Ithaca, N.Y.: Cornell University Press, 1985), pp. 231–33. Jardine characterizes much of postmodern U.S. fiction written by men as attacking the body of the mother, who is held responsible for the failure of the paternal function in culture.

19   My thanks to Leonard Green for helping me pose the problem in this way.

20   Michel Chion describes the film's sound design in the following terms. The soundtrack consists of "sound copulas, those low, sinister held notes which link up the different worlds edited in parallel . . . as well as the explosions of sound which accompany the closeups of cigarettes being lit and the depictions of fire." "These sound effects are meaningful," Chion continues, "because they contrast with other, more muffled and subtle passages bordering on the inaudible. One forgets that Dolby stereo expands the cinema's sound field towards not only the very large but also the very small, by allowing the use of effects close to silence" (133–34).

21   Two readings of *Blue Velvet* are interesting in this regard. See Peter Brunette and David Wills, *Screen/Play: Derrida and Film Theory* (Princeton, N.J.: Princeton University Press, 1989), pp. 139–71; and Lesley Stern, *Camera Obscura,* May 1992, pp. 77–90.

22   It is worth noting that the male body is never exhibited in the film. The telling symptom here is that the one time we see Sailor undress, he is made comical, as he climbs into bed in his black briefs and white socks. Sailor is primarily face, gaze, voice, and motion—not body. In this connection it is interesting that "Twin Peaks"'s Special Agent Cooper, another Lynch stand-in, is played by Kyle MacLachlan, Jeffrey of *Blue Velvet,* surely the most disembodied actor available. MacLachlan is the perfect "talking head," utterly without relation to his body, which is consistently cut out of frame, or coded as a sort of cross between a wardrobe and a vehicle.

23   There is more of the Lynch adolescent humor and intertextuality here. Various smirking allusions in "Twin Peaks" have connected women's genitals with fish. Later in *Wild at Heart,* Bobby Peru will make a similar joke, "One-eyed Jack's yearnin' to go a peepin' in the seafood store," a joke that makes the same connection and advertises for "Twin Peaks" in the bargain. "One-Eyed Jack's" is the name of the casino-cum-brothel where Laura Palmer has worked.

24   This economy might be connected to what Kaja Silverman argues for reflexive masochism: "reflexive masochism not only maps two very different desiring positions at the level of the unconscious, but fosters the production of two contrary images of self—the image of the one who pleasurably inflicts pain on behalf of the exalted standard which it purports to be, and that of the one who pleasurably suffers that pain. Consequently, within that libidinal economy the ego itself assumes the partial status of a tyrannical ideal." *Male Subjectivity at the Margins* (New York: Routledge, 1992), p. 325. This kind of masochism, Silverman stresses, entails the subject's occupying "the sadistic and masochistic positions *simultaneously,* rather than *in turn*" (324). In a discussion of action movies, Paul Smith suggests a connection between masochism, conservative pleasure, and the hysterical residues at work in action film narratives: "Male masochism is at first a way of not having to submit to the law, but equally importantly it turns out to be a way of not breaking (with) the law. Masochism might well bespeak a desire to be both sexes at once, but it depends upon the definitional parameters of masculinity and femininity that undergird our current cultural contexts. Male masochism might, finally, be seen as another way for the male subject to temporarily challenge his desire for the father and to subvert the phallic law, as ultimately another step in the way (one might even say the puerile way?) of guaranteeing the male subject as origin of the production of meanings." *Clint Eastwood: A Cultural Production* (Minneapolis: University of Minnesota Press, 1993), p. 166.

25   In *Men, Women, and Chain Saws: Gender in the Modern Horror Film* (Princeton, N.J.: Prince-

ton University Press, 1992), Carole Clover describes a version of this affective shock to the "witnessing body" as central to the functioning of slasher films: "At least one director, Alfred Hitchcock, explicitly located thrill in the equation victim=audience." Hitchcock, Clover points out, was self-conscious about this in filming the shower scene of *Psycho:* "Not just the body of Marion is to be ruptured, but also the body on the other side of the film and screen: our witnessing body." "Cinefantastic horror, in short," Clover contends, "succeeds in the production of sensation to precisely the degree that it succeeds in incorporating the spectators as 'feminine' and then violating that body—which recoils, shudders, cries out collectively . . ." (52–53). Lynch's work exploits a similar mechanism, I would argue, except that effects are coded as "borrowed" from the popular horror genre. The campy posture of Lynch's work, then, also helps to suppress the gendered subtext that Clover brings out, to suppress it, that is, by framing the whole process as a self-conscious rehearsal of effects that are appropriated "un-selfconsciously" by the spectators of the genre it pretends to quote rather than reproduce.

26 Because television requires a level of self-censorship, the series can suggest only the lines of a particular fantasy, but it cannot play it out completely. The suggestive glimpses, the narrative hints, then, are eroticized substitutes for the more fully visualized, "completed" fantasies that we find in Lynch's films. Part of the obsession with violence and disgust that characterizes *Wild at Heart* seems to function censoriously, as if the film were nervous about the pleasures of sexual fantasy. Television's demand for prior censorship relieves the text of the burden of guilt, so the images and scenes are less visually sadistic, more open to multiple investment on the part of spectators.

27 And, as Klawans argues, this operation depends in part on formal skill: "Sometimes, as with David Lynch, formal skill is all the artist provides. In either case, the presumed assault on bourgeois order is safely contained—in an art gallery, at a performing arts center, on the screen. The danger of the image is assumed; the image of danger is all that's demanded" (287).

28 Fred Pfeil makes a powerful argument about how consumerism functions to produce distinction in his *Another Tale to Tell* (London: Verso, 1990), p. 111. Pfeil describes this aspect of postmodern consumer taste as "the instantly self-cancelling nostalgia for the authenticity of the non-coded, non-commodified 'real.' " This position is coupled with a particular "attitude towards the commodification and fragmentation of the self," characterized by "horror and disgust towards those trapped in and defined by the endlessly proliferating codes, clichés and slogans of everyday life: a horror whose underlying anxiety [is] that even the subject him/herself feeling it is not 'free.' "

29 Of course, this effect was later enhanced when Lynch appeared on the series as a father figure, an agent who served as mentor to Cooper.

30 For a longer discussion of camp as a feature of a certain "taste culture" of distinction, see Andrew Ross, *No Respect: Intellectuals and Popular Culture* (New York: Routledge, 1989), p. 155. In a passage that cites *Blue Velvet* and *Eraserhead* as exemplary, Ross proposes: "Today, the most advanced forms of bad taste vanguardism are located in a loosely defined nexus of cultish interests that have grafted the most anti-social features of 'sick' humor on to an attenuated paranoia about the normality of the straight world."

31 For a reading of *Blue Velvet,* along with several other films, that seeks steadfastly to de-oedipalize them in favor of reading them as allegories of postmodern positions on cultural history, see Fredric Jameson, "Nostalgia for the Present," *South Atlantic Quarterly,*

Spring 1989, pp. 53–64. My reading is obliged to contradict Jameson's on several counts, not the least of which is that his article bypasses any account of the ways that these films write their allegories across the bodies of women.

5   Tell the Right Story

1   The entire quotation goes: "People who cannot escape thinking of themselves as white are poorly equipped, if equipped at all, to consider the meaning of black: people who know so little about themselves can face very little in another: and one dare hope for nothing from friends like these." James Baldwin, *The Devil Finds Work* (New York: Bantam Doubleday, 1990), p. 69.

2   bell hooks has explored the ways that popular culture constructs difference as consumable in *Black Looks: Race and Representation* (Boston: South End Press, 1992). See esp. chap. 2, "Eating the Other."

3   Wahneema Lubiano, "But Compared to What?: Reading Realism, Representation, and Essentialism in *School Daze, Do the Right Thing,* and the Spike Lee Discourse," in *Representing Black Men,* ed. Marcellus Blount and George P. Cunningham (New York: Routledge, 1996), p. 175.

4   Of course, it is interesting to ask about other representations of interracial couples in recent years—few and far between as they are. For my purposes here, I will stick with those that emerge in dramas, rather than comedies, which offer completely different opportunities for both fantasy and containment. Indeed, one could imagine an interesting study of the radically different representations of interracial desire that emerge in the various generic forms available. How, for instance, does the futurist science fiction framework of *Strange Days* (Kathryn Bigelow, 1995) help to structure its particular construction of the black heroine (Angela Bassett) as both subject and object of desire for the struggling white detective (Ralph Fiennes)? The most recent example of serious analytical treatment of cross-cultural exchanges in a number of arenas, including the erotic, would be John Sayles's *Lone Star* (1996). Significantly, some smaller independent films, two by African Americans, Carl Franklin's *One False Move* (1992) and Charles Burnett's *The Glass Shield* (1995), organize their narratives around complex and penetrating explorations of interracial bonding and sexual relations. Jonathan Kaplan's 1992 *Love Field,* which died at the box office, also critically explored the nuances of the relationship between an interracial pair on the road together in 1963 and the complex brutalities of the social context around them as it coupled a white Houston housewife obsessed with Jackie Kennedy and a younger, professional, black man returning to Philadelphia from family business in the South. In contrast to these complicated analytical explorations of the interracial couple in its particular, local, and historical context, the most spectacular treatment of the theme may have been *The Bodyguard* (Mick Jackson, 1992). One reader of these pages has remarked that "critical attention to interracial romance on screen seemed to get amazingly, effectively contained" by that film. If that is as true as it appears to be, one wonders if Whitney Houston's star figure did not somehow "cancel" serious attention to race. Or, did the film's patently fairy-tale structure—which allowed for ludicrous implausibilities, since it effectively maintained Houston as herself, and then paired her with a completely eviscerated, cardboard cutout of a white male (Kevin Costner)—foreclose any unironic speculation about the meanings of the romance? In other words, no one believed the

image for a minute. Finally, the film managed to offer one of the first representations of a successful professional black woman and then to present as the source of all evil in her life another black woman, her jealous sister. In its heavy-handed balance of "positive" image against "negative" image, the film finally deflected its interest and our own away from the couple it had posited as central.

5   As one of the most ironic and trenchantly critical of these directors, Mario Van Peebles, puts it: "We're looked upon as the cinematic equivalent of a track and field team." *New York Times Magazine,* July 14, 1991, p. 40.

6   "The Documentary Impulse in Contemporary African-American Film," in *Black Popular Culture,* ed. Gina Dent (Seattle: Bay Press, 1993), p. 58.

7   Jacquie Jones, "The New Ghetto Aesthetic," *Wide Angle,* July-October 1991, p. 33. Jones goes on to distinguish this phenomenon from a parallel in market success, that of rap music. "Some will argue that, like rap, these films present warped perceptions shaped in the space between disenfranchisement and escalating consumerism—that both are, at their core, violent, bitterly misogynistic and nonredemptive. But there is a profound dissimilarity between contemporary Black Hollywood and rap music: as a phenomenon, Black Hollywood is necessarily not of its own making" (33).

8   Jacquie Jones, "The Accusatory Space," *Black Popular Culture,* p. 95.

9   Lisa Kennedy, "The Body in Question," *Black Popular Culture,* p. 110.

10 "*Boyz N the Hood* and *Jungle Fever,*" *Black Popular Culture,* p. 125.

11 A recent example is *Newsweek,* August 30, 1993, which announces a special section on the black family across a cover photograph of a seven-year-old African American boy: "A World Without Fathers: The Struggle to Save the African-American Family."

12 "It's a Family Affair," *Black Popular Culture,* p. 307.

13 In the same vein, Lisa Kennedy criticizes this tendency for "the failure inherent in casting the collective over the individual or mistaking the individual vision for collective reality" ("The Body in Question," p. 110).

14 On these incidents, see Mike Davis, "Fortress Los Angeles," in *Variations on a Theme Park,* ed. Michael Sorkin (New York: Hill and Wang, 1992), p. 180, and Mark Reid, *Redefining Black Film* (Berkeley: University of California Press, 1993), pp. 133-34.

15 We might note that Lee seems to reproduce this "character" in other venues as well, from his media interviews, to his books, to his television commercials.

16 Examples include Giancarlo Esposito as the fraternity king in *School Daze,* then as Buggin' Out in *Do The Right Thing;* John Turturro and his brother in *Mo' Better Blues*—Italian-Americans standing in for Jewish characters. But in *Jungle Fever,* Turturro figures as the enlightened, progressive figure. This effect might be connected to Lee's ability to make the most of the ethnic and racial signifiers inscribed on the body.

17 *Differences* 2, no. 2 (1990): 106.

18 See "But Compared to What?"

19 This formulation of the tension comes from Isaac Julien's and Kobena Mercer's "Introduction: De Margin and De Centre," *Screen,* Autumn 1988, p. 4: "it has become apparent that what is at stake in the debates on 'black representation' is not primarily a dispute over realist or modernist principles, but a broader problematic in cultural politics shaped, as Paul Gilroy suggests, by the tension between representation as a practice of depiction and representation as a practice of delegation."

20 Having chosen the same title, "Skin Deep," for his review, Terrence Rafferty in the *New*

Yorker (June 17, 1991, pp. 99–101) advances much the same criticisms as Denby does. Describing the film's approach to its material as "stubbornly, and perversely, external," Rafferty argues that the movie "keeps swerving around its main characters' emotions as if they were land mines," as "just like that, the focus of *Jungle Fever* shifts from the lovers to their communities, from the private to the public, from the bedroom to the street" (99). He goes on, like Denby, to compare the film's rhetoric to that of talk shows (see p. 99).

21   Writing this, I am suddenly aware that I do not know what to call Paulie's store. I had been thinking of it as a candy store, which I think is an anachronistic name for that fading New York City institution, a neighborhood store that sells candy, newspapers, and tobacco products, but that also maintains a soda fountain and lunch counter.

22   "Spike Lee and the Fever in the Racial Jungle," *Film Theory Goes to the Movies*, ed. Jim Collins, Ava Preacher Collins, and Hilary Radner (New York: Routledge, 1993), p. 178.

23   These tracking shots amplify or enhance the overall strangeness that tracking may introduce into narrative and point-of-view structures, as Edward Branigan has suggested. "The subjective tracking shot . . . incorporates additional parameters—such as the angle and speed of the camera movement—which are part of the POV structure and thus may reinforce or undermine the structure as a whole. What, for instance, do we say of a subjective tracking shot which is moving 'too fast' for the character to keep up or where the character suddenly spurts out in front of the camera?" "The Point-of-View Shot," in Bill Nichols, ed., *Movies and Methods, II* (Berkeley: University of California Press, 1985), p. 676.

24   Michele Wallace argues in "*Boyz N the Hood* and *Jungle Fever*" that "visually, the racial difference between Sciorra and McKee is nil." *Black Popular Culture*, p. 130.

25   Mary Ann Doane has examined the ways that femininity makes "white" racial identity visible in her analysis of the interaction of epistemologies of racial and sexual difference in *Imitation of Life* (Douglas Sirk, 1959) in her book *Femmes Fatales* (New York: Routledge, 1991), where she writes, "What allows whiteness to be represented (unlike the case with blackness) is a certain conceptualization of sexual difference" (244).

26   See Abdul JanMohamed, "Sexuality on/of the Racial Border: Foucault, Wright, and the Articulation of 'Racialized Sexuality,'" *Discourses of Sexuality*, ed. Domna Stanton (Ann Arbor: University of Michigan Press, 1992), pp. 94–116.

27   In *Black Film/White Money*, Jesse Alergeron Rhines takes Lee to task for the ramifications of this representation of the family. "As displayed in *Jungle Fever*," Rhines writes, "the plight of the underclass is not an individual phenomenon. Unfortunately, again, Lee fails to present his viewers with a clear idea of why or how this underclass behavior came about. Is Gator, despite having been 'raised right,' a drug addict because his father was too overbearing and his mother too lenient? If so, is a dysfunctional family life also the reason the hundreds of others flock to the Taj Mahal? Or has Gator—like those hundreds of others—been unable to find a job paying a living wage? . . . Drug addiction is of epidemic proportions in *Jungle Fever*, yet Spike Lee never says why this is the case" (New Brunswick, N.J.: Rutgers University Press, 1996), p. 127.

28   James Baldwin develops a rhetorically forceful analysis of the weight of history in our collective political imaginary as it confronts race in this passage: "To overhaul a history, or to attempt to redeem it—which effort may or may not justify it—is not at all the same thing as the descent one must make in order to excavate a history. To be forced to excavate a history is, also, to repudiate the concept of history, and the vocabulary in which history is written; for the written history is, and must be, merely the vocabulary of power, and

power is history's most seductively attired false witness. And yet, the attempt, more, the necessity, to excavate a history, to find out the truth about oneself! is motivated by the need to have the power to force others to recognize your presence, your right to be here. The disputed passage will remain disputed so long as you do not have the authority of the right-of-way—so long, that is, as your passage can be disputed: the document promising safe passage can always be revoked. Power clears the passage, swiftly; but the paradox, here, is that power, rooted in history, is also the mockery and the repudiation of history. The power to define the other seals one's definition of oneself—who, then, in such a fearful mathematic . . . is trapped? Perhaps then, after all, we have no idea of what history is; or are in flight from the demon we have summoned. Perhaps history is not to be found in our mirrors, but in our repudiations: perhaps the other is ourselves." *Just Above My Head* (New York: Dell, 1990), pp. 480–81.

29   As Abdul JanMohamed describes this phenomenon: "Racialized sexuality refused or failed to develop a dense discursivity primarily because white patriarchy's sexual violation of the racial border—the master's rape of the female slave—was an 'open secret.' . . . This contradiction leads to the 'one drop of black blood' criterion, which simultaneously provides a means of denying miscegenation and augmenting the supply of slave labor" (104).

30   This scene may also allude, somewhat more obliquely, to director Martin Scorsese and to Lee's "interethnic" rivalry with him.

31   "The Multicultural Wars," *Black Popular Culture*, p. 193.

32   "Skin Deep," p. 76.

33   Dominant cultures notoriously have difficulty acknowledging themselves as objects of ethnographic scrutiny. bell hooks offers pointed anecdotal evidence of the processes governing this difficulty when she writes about how her white students often react to observations about "whiteness." "Usually, white students respond with naive amazement that black people critically assess white people from a standpoint where 'whiteness' is the privileged signifier. Their amazement that black people watch white people with a critical 'ethnographic' gaze is, itself, an expression of racism. . . . They have a deep emotional investment in 'sameness,' even as their actions reflect the primacy of whiteness as a sign informing who they are and how they think. . . . Even though the majority of these students politically consider themselves liberals and anti-racist, they too unwittingly invest in the sense of whiteness as mystery" (*Black Looks*, pp. 167–68).

34   As JanMohamed describes it, racialized sexuality works to preclude certain kinds of analysis: "Why does the sexual violation of the socio-political borders not call into question the validity and the enforcement of the entire racial border, including its civil and political demarcations? Why does the regular crossing of the racial border through racialized sexuality not enter the daylight of the discursivity along with other supposedly 'hidden' aspects of sexuality? And, finally, why does white racist society not produce racialized sexuality through the kind of 'dense discursivity' utilized in the production of white bourgeois sexuality?" (99).

35   Writing in the conservative journal *Commentary* ("Spike Lee Fever," August 1991, pp. 50–53), Richard Grenier holds out for the value of a completely private and subjective ethnography, which he uses to justify singling out the war-council scene for a special criticism of its inauthenticity. "Some black friends of mine in Washington, D.C., drove to white upper-middle-class Bethesda, Maryland, to see *Jungle Fever* during its opening weekend;

they found the house far from full . . . I made a point of seeing the movie at Washington's Union Station, which draws a preponderantly black audience . . . the reactions of the black audience were not only different from those of the largely white audience at Bethesda (as I later ascertained from my friends), at several points they did not even match the ones the movie seems to call for" (50). "The high point of the movie," he continues, "as far as the Union Station audience was concerned, is the 'war council' held by Drew and a group of her friends to discuss Flipper's adultery and the question of sex between the races as well as men generally. This is about the only place in the film where one encounters a variety of opinions. Some of the women, for different reasons, are more tolerant of Flipper's behavior than others. Well-dressed and economically middle-class, these women talk the way I'm told middle-class black women seldom talk, like streetwalkers (actually, like Spike Lee)" (52).

36   Lee is quoted in "Spiking a Fever," *Newsweek,* June 10, 1991, p. 46.

37   About this matter, Lee seems consistent. He recounts another incident of this "truth effect" in his interview with Barbara Grizzuti Harrison, which has been aggressively titled "Spike Lee Hates Your Cracker Ass," *Esquire,* October 1992: "we wanted Danny [Aiello] to say the word 'nigger' and he would not say it, and we all knew he had said the word many times. What finally got him to say it was when [the character named] Buggin' Out called him a fat guinea bastard. And something snapped in Danny, and he just vomited all this 'black cocksucker nigger motherfucker.' He didn't want to be perceived as being racist or prejudiced, and that's why he had trouble saying the word. We all knew he had said those words many times. Once he was hit with 'fat guinea bastard,' the floodgates started opening. You have all said the word many times" (135).

38   *Waiting to Exhale* (New York: Pocket Books, 1992).

39   In Toni Morrison, ed., *Race-ing Justice, En-gendering Power: Essays on Anita Hill, Clarence Thomas, and the Construction of Social Reality* (New York: Pantheon, 1992), p. 404.

40   "Mama's Baby, Papa's Maybe: An American Grammar Book," *Diacritics,* Summer 1987, p. 65.

41   Another perspective on the problem of "intersectionality" appears in an essay entitled "Watching the Miss America Pageant" by Gerald Early. Recalling his complex reactions to women's hair treatments in his youth, Early sets his reactions within the contradictory textures of what he calls "race pride," crystallized in black women's relationships to their hair: "the complex contradictions, the uneasy tentative negotiations of that which cannot be compromised yet can never be realized in this flawed world as an ideal . . . the epistemology of race pride for black American women so paradoxically symbolized by their straightened hair." *The Culture of Bruising* (Hopewell, N.J.: Ecco Press, 1994), p. 269. For a complex discussion of contemporary meanings and (mis)interpretations generated around black women's hair and beauty culture, see Deborah Grayson, "Is It Fake?" *Camera Obscura* 36 (special issue, "Black Women Spectators and Visual Culture," ed. Deborah Grayson), September 1995.

42   This formulation obviously cites the title of the famous anthology edited by Gloria T. Hull, Patricia Bell, Barbara Smith, and Mary Berry, *All the Women Are White, All the Blacks Are Men, But Some of Us Are Brave: A Black Feminist Anthology* (New York: Feminist Press, 1982).

43   For a provocative account of Houston's status as cultural icon, see Marla Shelton, "Whitney Is Everywoman?" *Camera Obscura,* September 1995.

6   Borrowed "Style"

1   Lisa Kennedy, "Natural Born Filmmaker," *Village Voice*, October 25, 1994, p. 32.

2   "Blood Lust Snicker Snicker in Wide Screen," Dennis Hopper interviews Quentin Tarantino, *Grand Street*, Summer 1994, p. 17.

3   And although Tarantino's films seem intently focused on the possibilities for humor associated with smearing, they may maintain this focus precisely to deflect attention from the ways that smearing is often directly connected to sexist- and racist-inflected violence, just as it is one means of eroticizing violence.

4   Sasha Torres has remarked on the suggestiveness of the Maxipad, connected as it is in form to diapers, and to the ways that advertising seeks to work on female anxieties about leakage, which is described just as it is in diaper commercials. This image connects gender confusion to the infantile.

5   A pulp serial novel and comic book female spy, Modesty Blaise emerged in the film of the same name, directed by Joseph Losey, in 1966. Thanks to Julie D'Acci for this information.

6   It may be worth remembering that popular legend about Elvis registers that he died while sitting on the toilet, reading.

7   I am grateful to Fred Pfeil for his shrewd comments on the oedipal-preoedipal oscillation that is discernible in this film, and perhaps in my own initial reading of it in "The Fathers Watch the Boys' Room," *Camera Obscura*, September-January 1993-94, pp. 41-73.

8   As Tarantino told *Sight and Sound*, "I've been a fan of John Travolta . . . forever. I think he's one of the best actors there is. . . . But I've been very sad about how he's been used . . . the movies he's been doing. . . . What is wrong with these directors? Why don't they see what they have—that if they just blew the dust off it. . . ? And then I realized that's not going to happen. John needed to work with somebody who would take him seriously and would look at him with the love he needed." *Sight and Sound*, May 1994, p. 10. If this story is not about redemption, it is not about anything. Moreover, it seems to offer the fantasy of a son redeeming a father who persists as a childhood memory to be restored.

9   For a fascinating account of Keitel's particular status, as an icon of a certain working-class white ethnic masculinity, of the significance of his relationship with Martin Scorsese to this icon, and of the 'zine culture fandom around him, see Clint Burnham, "Scattered Speculations on the Value of Harvey Keitel," in *Boys: Masculinities in Contemporary Culture*, ed. Paul Smith (Boulder, Colo.: Westview Press, 1996), pp. 113-29.

10   For a discussion of the fascination that popular culture held for Jean-Luc Godard, and the impact of this fascination on his auteurist principles, which at times seem quite coherent with Tarantino's cinematic practice in its self-conscious attention to authership, see James Naremore, "Authorship and the Cultural Politics of Film Criticism," *Film Quarterly*, Fall 1990, pp. 14-23.

11   Timothy Corrigan, *A Cinema Without Walls* (New Brunswick, N.J.: Rutgers University Press, 1991), p. 104.

12   Peter Biskind of *Premiere* is only one of many critics to incorporate this notion into the title of his article on Tarantino, "An *Auteur* Is Born," *Premiere*, November 1994, pp. 94-102. But there is also a certain national identity issue here, one that surfaced in much writing about Cannes. U.S. critics want to claim Tarantino as our auteur for export—an American answer to the New Wave, an American analysis of the American roots of that French film movement. See, for example, Richard Corliss, "Saturday Night Fever," *Time*, June 6, 1994, p. 7.

13 On Tarantino's status as a fan, his "resemblance" to Jean-Luc Godard, and his fascination with the New Wave director and his American imitator, Jim McBride, see Jeff Dawson, *Quentin Tarantino: The Cinema of Cool* (New York: Applause, 1995), pp. 33, 61, and 205 respectively.

14 Lisa Kennedy documents this effect in "Natural Born Filmmaker": "This afternoon Quentin is reconsidering his superfan persona. . . . 'There's been such a concentration on this film geek makes good. . . .' I look around his apartment and the evidence . . . is everywhere in sight. 'Oh, he's just a little encyclopedia,' he mocks. 'It makes me wonder if, when I'm with journalists, I'm playing a routine. A character' " (31).

15 My evidence that Coolidge is a directorial stand-in comes from the director's interview performances of his persona as both a fan and a punk. Now, Coolidge is certainly a punk; more important, he is the one character in *Pulp Fiction* who directly defies Marsellus's paternal authority. In a recent interview, the director characterizes Butch this way: "I wanted Butch to be a complete fucking asshole . . . I wanted him to be a bully and a jerk, except that when he's with his girlfriend Fabian he's a sweetheart" ("Pulp Instincts," *Sight and Sound,* May 1994, p. 10). This characterization is remarkably close to Tarantino's description of his own youthful aspirations to be a bully: "Did you ever hear that expression of, like, teachers sayings about some kid who starts trouble, 'Someday you're going to try that on the wrong guy'? Well, I just had this thing in my head: I wanted to be the wrong guy . . . so if it looked like a fight was going to come up, I would just hit the kid in the face and start taking him out right away. I became my own worst enemy, because then people would try to fuck with me, because I was one of the tough guys" (97).

16 In *Pulp Fiction* the radio and the CD player function to produce what Michel Chion calls "passive offscreen sound" and to provide the kinds of guarantees that he suggests. As opposed to "active offscreen sound," which raises questions like: "What is this? What is happening? . . . passive offscreen sound, on the other hand, is sound which creates an atmosphere that envelops and stabilizes the image, without in any way inspiring us to look elsewhere or to anticipate seeing its source. Passive offscreen sound does not contribute to the dynamics of editing and scene construction—rather the opposite, since it provides the ear a *stable place* . . . which permits the editing to move around even more freely in space, to include more close shots, and so on, without disorienting the spectator in space." *Audio-Vision: Sound on Screen,* ed. and trans. Claudia Gorbman (New York: Columbia University Press, 1994), p. 85.

17 This scene might remind us of the famous *intra*racial male rape scene in John Boorman's *Deliverance* (1972).

18 And consequently, it is worth considering how the film's apparently critical edge of suggested antiracism, which is built as much out of interviews with its author as out of its diegetic handling of racial material, is implicated with the racist discourse it seeks to dislodge or hold up for our examination. The smugly superior distance that the film provides on these "hillbilly" characters—for itself and for us—may be more than slightly akin to the concept of "white guilt" and its social functioning that Judith Butler describes in *Bodies That Matter: On the Discursive Limits of "Sex."* "For the question . . . is whether white guilt is itself the satisfaction of racist passion, whether the reliving of racism that white guilt constantly performs is not itself the very satisfaction of racism that white guilt ostensibly abhors . . . for white guilt . . . *requires* racism to sustain its sanctimonious posturing. . . . Rooted in the desire to be exempted from white racism, to produce oneself as

the exemption, this strategy virtually requires that the white community remain mired in racism; hatred is merely transferred outward, and thereby preserved, but it is not overcome" (New York: Routledge, 1993), p. 227, n. 14. The emphasis in Tarantino clearly lies more on the side of the will to exemption than on the posture of guilt, but the two seem deeply interrelated. The substitution of an acrimonious, ironic, and aggressive posture for a sanctimonious one hardly slips the social knot that ties together guilt and a desire to exempt oneself from racism.

19   Liz Lyon has reminded me that another character in the film is associated with a trunk: the Gimp. The Gimp, entirely clad in leather, his face masked in leather, is confined in a trunk by the two rednecks who rape Marsellus. We know nothing about this figure who has, effectively, neither a face, nor a gaze. He is left to watch Butch Coolidge, while the other two attack Marsellus, but his gaze is entirely impotent, since he is unable to communicate what he sees.

20   "What's transgressive in *Reservoir Dogs* is not the level of violence or the terrifying realism of bodies that bleed and bleed, but the way Tarantino lays bare the sadomasochistic dynamic between the film and the spectator. The masochistic (feminised) position of the audience is inscribed in Mr. Orange's bleeding body. Mr. Orange's pain and Mr. White's guilt at not being able to save him bind them together in a sadomasochistic relationship that supersedes Mr. White's code of professionalism and leads to his destruction and everyone else's as well. . . . Mr. Blonde, dancing around the frozen, fascinated cop (who is literally tied to his seat), changing rhythm mid-step, cracking a joke here, slicing off a bit of flesh there, is a stand-in for the director." Amy Taubin, "The Men's Room," *Sight and Sound,* December 1992, p. 5.

21   For a provocative argument on the ways that the effects of cutting contribute to a spectator's feelings of being threatened, see Lesley Stern, "Meditation on Violence," in *Kiss Me Deadly,* ed. Laleen Jayamanne (Sydney: Power Publications, 1995). Stern writes, "cutting carries threatening connotations. However, this is not all that cutting implies . . . editing is frequently combined with speed of filming (employing both resolute slowness and rapidity) to enact a compulsive drive" (255). Certainly, we might characterize Tarantino's films as performing a compulsive drive.

22   Jeff Dawson rightly warns of the error that I remain on the verge of making when he argues that *True Romance* is not Tarantino's film: "It is wrong to treat it as such and is a great injustice to Tony Scott, who not only has got the best out of the screenplay, but has also imbued Tarantino's story, his most overtly comedic so far (the climactic Mexican standoff, almost a direct repeat of *Reservoir Dogs,* is this time played for laughs) with a fairy tale, dream-like innocence—some achievement for a film that contains no small degree of violence" (99). Nonetheless, the elements of the screenplay that Scott retains clearly fit within the set of obsessions that I ascribe to Tarantino here. Scott himself describes the distinction between the film that Tarantino envisioned and the one he made as follows: "Quentin would have made a very different *True Romance*—tougher, edgy, less dreamlike, less self-conscious—but I stuck religiously to his script, as did the cast. Nobody wanted to alter anything, just reproduce what was on the page because it was so good" (vii).

23   According to Jeff Dawson's conversations with Tarantino, " 'It was Tony who turned him into Joel Silver,' adds Tarantino, who at the time of writing didn't move in such esteemed circles. Tarantino actually based Donowitz on his acting coach, Allen Garfield" (114).

24   Donowitz's film may recall Stone's *Platoon* (1985), especially through the references to

Vietnam veterans' enthusiastic reactions to the film. For an account of the dispute between Stone and Tarantino over the script that Tarantino originally produced for *Natural
Born Killers*, and which was so thoroughly rewritten that Tarantino would accept credit
only for "original story idea," see Dawson, pp. 122–38.

25   In "An Auteur Is Born," Biskind reconstructs a mediated dialogue between Tarantino and
Stone, where Tarantino quotes an exchange with Stone: "And he said, '*Reservoir Dogs* is a
very, very good movie, but it's a movie. I make films and you make movies.' . . . He meant
it in a kind of condescending way, but I was thinking about it later and realized he's
right. I don't want to make films. I like movies." Stone comments on the exchange: "I was
saying, Quentin, you're in your 20s. You're making movies about movies. I'm making
movies about the life that I've lived to my 40s. I've seen more violence than you've ever
seen in your life. I've been in Vietnam. I've been shot. If you want to talk about violence,
let's get real" (100).

26   In the original script, however, as Dawson also reports, Clarence was supposed to die of
his wound to the eye (107). Scott accounts for his change to the original story this way:
"as a romantic at heart, I fell in love with Clarence and Alabama and wanted to see them
fulfill their dream. Quentin had shattered that dream with Clarence's death. Though I
shot both endings, my weakness for romanticism let Clarence and Alabama live happily
ever after" (vii).

27   The cops who are coaching Eliot Blitzer in the sting operation aimed at incriminating Lee
Donowitz in *True Romance* threaten him that if he fails to cooperate he will go to prison
and come back "very understanding of his wife's needs," because he will "know what it's
like to be a woman." The problem, they laughingly agree, will be that "you'll wanna fuck
her in the ass because pussy won't be tight enough for you anymore." Several themes
seem to subtend each other mutually: a drive to "know what it's like to be a woman," and
an aggressive drive not to be treated like a "bitch," not to be feminized, but also to know
another man as a woman, to make him into a woman.

28   For a study that may help to set Tarantino's borrowings of "style" in a long history
of white appropriations of African American cultural forms, see Carol Clover's brilliant
essay, "Dancin' in the Rain," *Critical Inquiry*, Summer 1995, pp. 722–47. Clover explores
"the great irony" that "*Singin' in the Rain* itself enacts the kind of talent 'relocations' it
claims to deplore and correct" (723), and she studies this enactment through symptomatic moments. For Clover, this text's symptomatic moments may be characterized as "the
kind of symptom that, in the postmodern critical scheme, is readable as a sign of repressed anxieties that underwrite the text but are denied by it. . . . The moments I have
just enumerated in *Singin' in the Rain*," she writes, "seem to me just such 'memories' in
the framework of 'forgetting.' Glancingly but unmistakably, they suggest that *Singin' in
the Rain*'s concern with miscredit has a racial underside—that its real subject is not white
women's singing success, but black men's dancing bodies" (737).

29   This formulation owes much to John Michael, who pointed out that the process by which
Tarantino's work converts its fantasies about African American masculinity into iconic
representations involves a translation of "race" into linguistic and cultural expression.

30   Pam Grier is best known for *Coffy* (Jack Hill, 1973) and *Foxy Brown* (Jack Hill, 1974), two
films in which she takes on white-dominated drug gangs. In the latter, as described by Ed
Guerrero "after being tortured, then drugged and raped by two white sadists in a sequence
that pointedly evokes memories of the black woman's plight under slavery, replete with

the soundtrack of country banjo music and Foxy being lashed by a bullwhip, Foxy manages to escape and persuade a group of militant black brothers to join her fight. . . . In a concluding sequence that comically seems to overlap with the conventions of the horror movie. Foxy and her militant crew capture the film's chief white gangster and castrate him." *Framing Blackness* (Philadelphia: Temple University Press, 1993), p. 99. But *Coffy* may be the most immediately pertinent film for *Pulp Fiction*, since its avenger is a nurse, like Bonnie. For the characters in *Reservoir Dogs*, Pam Grier as cultural icon seems to condense sex and violence as both subject and object of sexualized violence, but all played out on a cartoonish scale; so the castrating bitch is something of a titillating joke. This may be a fair reading of *Foxy Brown*, but the transposition of that iconic figure into the context of Tarantino's film is another matter altogether, and it seems to depend on her complete dehistoricization.

31   This alibi function is consistent with many popular cultural representations of interracial relationships, where each partner's racial identity is imagined to be interrupted, realigned, exempted from its own category by virtue of the other partner's difference.

32   I am not, of course, attempting to speak to the range of pornographic objects addressed to heterosexual publics — especially in the diversified contemporary field, where couples-oriented films, among other subgenres, have emerged. For analyses of these new generic and spectator possibilities in relation to the history of pornographic viewing practices, see, for example, Linda Williams, *Hard Core: Power, Pleasure and the "Frenzy of the Visible"* (Berkeley: University of California Press, 1989) and Pamela Church Gibson and Roma Gibson, eds., *Dirty Looks: Women, Pornography, Power* (London: British Film Institute, 1993); Laura Kipnis, *Bound and Gagged: Pornography and the Politics of Fantasy in America* (New York: Grove Press, 1998); Constance Penley, "Crackers and Whackers: The White Trashing of Porn," in *White Trash: Race and Class in America*, ed. Matt Wray and Annalee Newtiz (New York: Routledge, 1997), pp. 89–112.

33   Paul Willeman, "Letter to John," *The Sexual Subject* (New York: Routledge, 1992), p. 174. I cite Willeman's essay, originally published in *Screen* in 1980, for specific reasons. While this analysis would not be accurate for a large segment of contemporary heterosexual-directed pornography, since its specific object is the pornography of its own contemporary moment, the 1970s, it is potentially all the more appropriate for the study of Tarantino's work. The moment of cinematic pornography's commercial success as a popular and more mainstream product in the United States is certainly the 1970s, the period of greatest fascination for Tarantino's films.

34   Manohla Dargis, "Who's Afraid of Red Yellow and Blonde?" *Artforum*, November 1992, p. 11.

35   Dargis contends that in *Pulp Fiction* "the scene is as much about the damage unleashed by boys-who-will-be-boys as a poke at male-female relations through the women who either enter stage right, or don't." "Pulp Instincts," *Sight and Sound*, May 1994, p. 8.

36   This title expresses Tarantino's chosen cinematic paternity. The graphic logo, a group of men in narrow-legged black suits, recalls the clothing of Godard's men in the early 1960s, and the basic plot of *Reservoir Dogs'* botched robbery is a homage to *Bande à part* (1964). Interestingly, Godard's criminal group included a central female character, played by Anna Karina. It is interesting to note that Uma Thurman's hair and her solo dance in *Pulp Fiction* directly cite Anna Karina in *Vivre sa vie* (Godard, 1963).

37   Jeff Dawson reports the following exchange between Oldman and Tony Scott as they dis-

cussed the possibility of working together: "he said, 'Tell me about my fucking character, what's my character?' " Scott recounts, "and I said, 'He's a white guy who thinks he's black and he's a pimp' " (114).

38   In this sense Tarantino's film may fit squarely within the lineage of *Singin' in the Rain* as Carol Clover analyzes it: "What *Singin' in the Rain* doesn't-but-does know is that the real art of the film musical is dance, that a crucial talent source for that art is African-American performance, and that, relative to its contribution, this talent source is undercredited and underpaid. It is admitting, in effect, that although there may be no fixed line between homage and theft in the world of the film musical, there are roughly zones, and even white people know what they are" (742).

39   "Tarantino's Mantra?" *Chicago Tribune,* Sunday, November 6, 1994, p. 2C. Boyd has clearly made a political decision not to cite the word "nigger," since his whole argument makes the point that the word is dramatically overused—overcited—in a variety of contexts, including rap music. In none of these, he argues, does its citation necessarily diffuse its force, and in no context can the word appear without in some sense reinforcing its whole history as a derogatory term. Boyd, then, is performing in accordance with the critique he spells out in his argument. After some consideration, I myself have decided that to use the word, which clashes and jars with the context of scholarly, analytic prose, is to assume that its "citation," far from diminishing its power, produces effects that remember the violence of its use and circulation in daily life speech.

40   Amy Taubin has analyzed the fascination with rap culture that emerges in *Reservoir Dogs* and has theorized what underlies it, specifically in connection to Tarantino's violence. "If the unconscious of the film is locked in competition with rap culture, it's also desperate to preserve screen violence as a white male privilege. It's the privilege of white male culture to destroy itself, rather than to be destroyed by the other. Violence is the only privilege these underclass men have. It's what allows them to believe that they're the oppressor and not the oppressed (not female, not black, not homosexual)." "The Men's Room," 5.

41   Consider, for example, the contemporary controversies around *Menace II Society.*

42   On the relationship of self-consciousness to African American vernacular styles and their consequent susceptibility to a variety of appropriations, see Kobena Mercer, *Welcome to the Jungle:* "It is this self-consciousness that underscores their ambivalence, and in turn marks them off as stylized signs of blackness. In jive-talk the very meanings of words are made uncertain and undecidable by self-conscious stylization which send signifiers slipping and sliding over signifieds: bad means good, superbad means better. Because of the way blackness is recognized in such strategems of creolizing intonation, inflection and accentuation, these practices of stylization can be said to exemplify 'modernist' interventions . . ." (New York: Routledge, 1994), p. 121.

43   And this holds, despite Samuel L. Jackson's claims to the contrary: " 'As Quentin said, he's trying to de-sensitize the word' . . . I say he's taken the word nigger and he's used it every possible way it could be used. He's used it as a descriptive, he's used it as a term of endearment, he's used it as a derogatory, he's used it as a generality. It's just a word that's used and it happens" (quoted in *Quentin Tarantino,* p. 117).

44   See "Pulp Instincts" for Tarantino's take on this: "Bruce has the look of a 50s actor. I can't think of any other star that has that look. He reminds me of Aldo Ray in Jacques Tourneur's *Nightfall"* (10). Meanwhile, Jackson shed his jheri curl wig for the film's publicity stills, increasing the effects of incoherence.

45 This effect may help to produce the intense attraction-repulsion that Tarantino exhibits toward Oliver Stone. In a kind of narcissistic rivalry, each director accuses the other of making his films into a screen for his own fantasies. Stone's work, of course, tends in the opposite direction from Tarantino's; rather than deny history, Stone affirms it, but in a context that monumentalizes his fantasies, projected on the screen of "History."

46 For an analysis of recent cult films that seem predicated on the idea that "history" has "already been laid to waste," see Corrigan, *A Cinema Without Walls*, pp. 88–91.

47 Paul Gilroy makes a detailed argument about the centrality of the African or black diaspora to Western culture, most particularly in the United States and England, in *The Black Atlantic: Modernity and Double Consciousness* (Cambridge, Mass.: Harvard University Press, 1993). For example, Gilroy contends: "The history of the black Atlantic . . . continually crisscrossed by the movements of black people—not only as commodities but engaged in various struggles towards emancipation, autonomy, citizenship—provides a means to re-examine the problems of nationality, location, identity, and historical memory. They all emerge from it with special clarity if we contrast the national, nationalistic, and ethnically absolute paradigms of cultural criticism to be found in England and America with those hidden expressions, both residual and emergent, that attempt to be global or outernational in nature" (16).

INDEX

Abelove, Henry, 225 n39
abortion debates, 119-21
accidental pairings by race, 158
aestheticization: of difference, 1-2, 10, 12, 22;
    of race, 153; of social conflict, 152-53; of
    violence in Lynch, 140-41
affirmative action, 160, 171
Aiello, Danny, 250 n37
Alexander, Elizabeth, 57, 228 n60, 228 n62,
    228 n63
Alien movies, 60, 232 n25, 113, 125; *Alien 3,*
    120-21, 125
"America's Most Wanted," 239-40 n6
anality, 86; and masculine anxiety, 86; in
    Tarantino, 194-95, 203; and violence in
    Tarantino, 189-92, 193, 199-200
Angelou, Maya, 187
Ansen, David, 39, 164
Aronowitz, Stanley, 61, 229 n5
Ashby, Hal, 201
audience, 39-40, 55, 126-27, 132, 183-84,
    197, 250 n35; for African American films,
    163; for Lynch, 155-56
auteur/auteurism, 22; and censorship, 152;
    and fandom, 133; and independent films,
    132-33; and race, 160-61; Tarantino as,
    196; and taste cultures, 22-23; theories of,
    133, 196-97, 241 n2, 242 n3

Bailey, Cameron, 131, 154, 241 n1
Baldwin, James, 29, 31, 51, 159, 246 n1, 248
    n28

banality, 6, 218 n12
Barkin, Ellen, 85
Basic Instinct, 21, 61, 63, 64, 68, 70, 83, 84, 88,
    89, 91, 95, 96
Bassett, Angela, 188, 246 n4
Batman, 219 n13, 239 n33
"battle of the sexes" in popular culture,
    99-100, 111
Baumgold, Julie, 109-10
Becker, Harold, 61
Bellour, Raymond, 221 n3
Berenger, Tom, 71
Bergstrom, Janet, 221 n3
Bersani, Leo, 225 n38
Bigelow, Kathryn, 188, 246 n4
Birth of a Nation, The, 188
Biskind, Peter, 251 n12, 252 n25
Black, Shane, 222 n11
black Hollywood, 160-61, 247 n7
black masculinity in film, 161-62; and Afri-
    can American women critics, 161-62; in
    Tarantino, 210-11. *See also* masculinity
Blade Runner, 104, 231 n17, 232 n22
blockbusters, 126; failed, 55-56, 57; vs. small
    productions, 7, 9, 27, 99
Blue Velvet, 131, 133, 134, 140, 142-43, 149,
    151, 245 n31
Bobbitt, John Wayne, 235 n1
body and body/mind split, 32-33; female
    hardbody, 109-10, 113, 116, 120, 239 n27;
    and gender theater, 116; as machine, 113,
    116-17, 122; male body as spectacle, 45-48,

body and body/mind split (*continued*)
113; and masquerade, 113, 116; mutilated
body, 42, 45–46, 56–57
bodybuilding, 109–10, 113, 116–17, 239 n27,
240 n43
Bodyguard, The, 188, 247 n4
Body Heat, 230 n8
Boorman, John, 252 n17
Borch-Jacobson, Mikkel, 234 n36
Boyd, Todd, 211, 213, 256 n39
Boyz N the Hood, 161
Bracco, Lorraine, 71
Branigan, Edward, 225 n36, 243 n10, 248 n23
Brophy, Philip, 32, 33
Brown, Georgia, 135, 137, 141
Brunette, Peter, 244 n21
Budge, Belinda, 237–38 n18
Burnett, Charles, 246 n4
Burnham, Clint, 251 n9
Busey, Gary, 224 n30
Butch Cassidy and the Sundance Kid, 105, 238
n26
butch/femme figures in popular culture, 109,
111, 121, 237 n18, 241 n46
Butler, Judith, 103, 106, 165–66, 211, 217 n1,
236 n8, 237 n19, 252 n18
Byrne, David, 131, 154

Cage, Nicholas, 136
Cameron, James, 113, 116, 120
Campbell, Virginia, 131, 134, 141–42, 143, 155
Canby, Vincent, 140, 41
Cannell, Barry, 227 n53
Carby, Hazel, 178, 186
Carlson, Margaret, 100, 101
Caughie, John, 38, 224 n26
Chion, Michael, 41, 139, 225 n34, 225 n36,
227 n52, 242 n7, 242 n8, 243 n9, 244 n20,
252 n16
Church, Pamela, 255 n32
Close, Glenn, 65
Clover, Carol, 14, 17, 220 n24, 245 n25,
254–55 n28, 256 n38
Coffy, 255 n30
Cohen, Philip, 34–35, 223 n20
coincidences and the historical moment,
6–7, 219 n13

Collins, Jim, 220–21 n29
Coming Home, 201
Conley, Tom, 236 n11
Copjec, Joan, 63, 83, 234 n38
"Cops" (TV show), 229–30 n6
Corliss, Richard, 140, 141, 165, 252 n12
Corrigan, Timothy, 7, 8, 196, 197, 214–15, 228
n58, 241 n2, 257 n46
Costner, Kevin, 247–48 n4
Crenshaw, Kimberlé, 185
Crooklyn, 174, 187
Cruising, 85, 89–90
Crying Game, The, 7, 9–13, 19
cultural dupes, 8–9
cultural studies, 58–59; debates, in 8–9
Curtis, Tony, 29

D'Acci, Julie, 251 n5
Dahl, John, 229 n1
Dargis, Manohla, 208, 256 n35
Dash, Julie, 181
Davidson, Jaye, 10–13, 219 n19, 219 n20,
219–20 n21
Davis, Geena, 221 n1, 222 n11
Davis, Mike, 247 n14
Dawson, Jeff, 252 n13, 253 n22, 253 n23, 254
n24, 254 n26, 256 n37
De Certeau, Michel, 218 n12
Deer Hunter, The, 194
Defiant Ones, The, 29
Deliverance, 252 n17
Demme, Jonathan, 131, 154
De Mornay, Rebecca, 80
Denby, David, 168, 178–79, 248 n20
De Palma, Brian, 84
Dern, Laura, 136, 143
desubjectivization/subjectivization, 66, 230
n12
Dickerson, Ernest, 171
Die Hard, 20, 27–30, 32–35, 36–58, 223 n19
Die Hard 2: Die Harder, 29, 33, 224 n22
Die Hard with a Vengeance, 29, 30–35, 48,
51–52, 221 n1, 222 n9
Disclosure, 68, 229 n1
displacement and social conflict, 2–3, 123–
25; of class and gender, 229 n5
Doane, Mary Ann, 248 n25

documentary effects, 160-61, 167-68, 180-81, 182, 184; "documentary impulse," 161

Doherty, Thomas, 235 n5

Donner, Richard, 27

Do the Right Thing, 132, 161, 163-67, 176, 219 n13

Doty, Alexander, 112, 238 n23, 238 n24

Double Indemnity, 230 n8

Douglas, Michael, 13, 65, 68, 83

Dressed to Kill, 84

Duvall, Robert, 14

Dyer, Richard, 224-25 n32, 226 n42

editing, 40-41, 44; crosscutting in Lynch, 148; and the cut in *The Crying Game,* 10-11, 15-16; parallel editing, 41-42, 79, 192; and threat to the spectator, 253 n21

Elvis, 193, 201, 208, 216, 251 n6

"ER" (TV show), 218 n7

erotic process, 113

Esposito, Giancarlo, 247 n16

Falling Down, 7, 9, 13-19, 67, 88

family: aberrant sexuality and family values, 184-85; African American families in the media, 162-63, 247 n11; and oedipalized social conflict, 157; and race, 78-82, 125-26; and violence, 69-70, 78, 118-19, 122

fantasy structures, 99, 100; collective fantasy, 20, 138, 157; in Lynch, 153; theories of, 103, 165-66; and violence, 105-6, 164-65

Fatal Attraction, 21, 60-61, 64, 65-71, 77, 78, 79, 96, 99, 101

fellatio, 11

feminine anxiety, 92, 96-97

feminism and feminist debates, 98-100, 127; African American women in, 186-87; feminism and rage, 70, 98-102, 104, 105-6; figuring in film, 69-70, 96-97, 98-100

Fenn, Sherilyn, 148

Ferrell, Tyra, 158, 169

Fiedler, Leslie, 222 n6

Fiennes, Ralph, 246 n4

Figgis, Mike, 229 n3

Final Analysis, 229 n1

Fincher, David, 113

Fleming, Victor, 139

48 HRS, 33

fourth look, 207-8

Foxy Brown, 255 n30

Franklin, Carl, 227 n51, 246 n4

French, Sean, 142

Friedkin, William, 85

Gabriel, John, 220 n23, 220 n25, 220 n28

Galvin, Angela, 234 n37

gaze, the, 45; paternal gaze in Tarantino, 194-95; reversibility of and gender anxiety, 90-92, 104; as a social phenomenon regarding race, 173-79; theories of, 46

gender: and AIDS, 120-21, 234 n34; and anality, 86, 87; and feminine anxiety, 92, 96-97; and feminism, 102; gender anxiety, 60-61, 83-84, 85-86, 88-89, 92, 96, 103; and homophobia, 94; and identification, 106; and lesbianism, 109-10, 112; and masculine anxiety, 67-68, 72-73, 76, 84-85, 86, 88; and reversibility of gaze, 90-92; and sexuality, 112-13; and other social differences, 20; and Vietnam war, 233 n29

gender theater, 20, 116

genre: action films, 27, 32-34, 37, 55, 57, 60, 105, 222 n5; buddy films, 28-40, 43-45, 53-54, 55, 60, 99, 105, 222 n5; disaster films, 39-40; film noir, 61-62, 72, 78, 83; horror, 32, 33-34; horror in *The Hand that Rocks the Cradle,* 79; hybrid, 21, 39, 60, 62, 64; melodrama, 60-61, 80, 233 n30; neo-noir, 62-64; N.Y. films, 131-32; police thrillers, 60-61, 72, 82-83; pornography, 207-8; road movies, 105, 115, 135, 153; westerns, 28, 39, 50, 105, 227 n50; women's pictures, 60

Gibson, Mel, 27, 113, 226 n44

Gifford, Barry, 243 n11

Giles, Jeff, 219 n20, 219-20 n21

Gilroy, Paul, 162-63, 217 n4, 220 n22, 247 n19, 257 n47

Giroux, Henry, 229 n5

Glass Shield, The, 246 n4

Glover, Danny, 28, 187
Godard, Jean-Luc, 209, 215, 251 n10, 252 n13
Goldberg, Jonathan, 116–17, 125, 238 n24, 240 n37, 240 n39, 240 n40, 240 n41, 240 n43, 240 n44
Goodman, Ellen, 99
Goodman, John, 61
Gramsci, Antonio, 3
Grand Canyon, 187
Green, Leonard, 244 n19
Grenier, Richard, 249 n35
Grier, Pam, 206, 208, 255 n30
Griffith, D. W., 188
Griffith, Melanie, 229 n2
Griggers, Cathy, 111, 114, 238 n22, 238 n24
Grove, Martin, 239 n33
Guerrero, Ed, 35, 55, 170, 172–73, 182, 228 n61, 239 n29, 255 n30
Gun Crazy, 105
Gunning, Tom, 230 n14

Hamer, Diane, 237 n18
Hamilton, Linda, 109, 113, 116, 126, 240 n36
Hand that Rocks the Cradle, The, 21, 60, 64, 70, 78–82, 95–96
Hanson, Curtis, 60
Harlin, Renny, 221 n1
Harrison, Barbara Grizzuti, 250 n37
Hart, Lynda, 109, 111, 230–31 n15, 235 n2, 236 n10, 237 n14
Hartouni, Valerie, 241 n45
Hawkins, Yusef, 177
High Noon, 50, 227 n50
Hill, George Roy, 105
Hill, Jack, 225 n30
Home of the Brave, 223 n13
"Homicide" (TV show), 218 n7, 218 n9
homoeroticism, 28–31, 41–42, 43–45, 93; anxiety about, 89, 90, 94; in Tarantino, 202–3; theories of, 222 n6
homoerotophobia, 94, 95
hooks, bell, 16, 172, 220 n26, 246 n2, 249–50 n33
Hopper, Dennis, 134, 195, 204, 212
Houston, Whitney, 188, 247 n4
How to Make an American Quilt, 187

Hudson, Ernie, 80
Hughes Brothers, 227 n51
Hurt, William, 230 n8
Huyssen, Andreas, 242 n2

Ice Cube, 161
Ice T, 57, 161
identification: and aggression, 2, 101–2, 106, 163; cross-gendered, 107–8; cross-racial, 210; in fantasy, 100–102, 105–6, 127, 165–66; and identity, 1, 127–28, 163, 166; and imitation, 100–103, 105–6, 163; as psychic process, 102–3; and sadomasochistic fantasy, 47; and sexual difference, 92–93, 106, 108; in spectatorship, 100–101, 103, 108, 163, 165; theories of, 106, 127, 234 n36, 236 n8, 236 n13
identity as visible sign, 173–78
identity politics, 6, 159–60, 188; African American women and national identity, 185–86, 216; and ambivalence, 2–3; and feminism, 124, 127
ignorance: passion of, 159; privilege of, 179, 249 n33
Illusions, 181
Internal Affairs, 229 n3

Jackson, Mick, 188, 247 n4
Jackson, Samuel L., 30, 174, 191, 214, 221 n1, 222 n11, 257 n43
Jameson, Fredric, 246 n31
JanMohamed, Abdul, 174, 249 n29, 249 n34
Jardine, Alice, 244 n18
Jarmusch, Jim, 131, 154
Jeffords, Susan, 32, 116, 233 n29, 239 n35
Joanou, Phil, 229 n1
Johnson, Richard, 99
Jones, Jacquie, 161–62, 247 n7
Julien, Isaac, 248 n19
Jungle Fever, 158, 160, 167, 168–87, 247 n16

Kaplan, Jonathan, 229 n4
Kasdan, Lawrence, 187, 230 n8
Kauffman, Stanley, 34, 104
Keitel, Harvey, 191, 195–96, 251 n9

Kennedy, Lisa, 124, 162, 196, 200, 211, 215, 247 n13, 252 n14
Khouri, Callie, 237 n16
Kipnis, Laura, 255 n32
Klawans, Stuart, 141, 151, 245 n27
Kline, Kevin, 187
"knowingness," 38
Kotto, Yaphet, 125
Kramer, Stanley, 29
Kroll, Jack, 164
Kruger, Barbara, 98, 235 n1

Ladd, Diane, 136
Last Boy Scout, The, 29, 33, 37, 42, 56, 221 n1, 226 n49
Last Seduction, The, 229 n1
law: and/of the family, 65, 71; and sadomasochistic fantasy, 47; and sexual difference, 33
Lebeau, Vicky, 101, 236 n4, 236 n5, 236 n7
Lee, Spike, 22-24, 132, 133, 158-87; as a character in film and media, 164-65; effect of real and racial identity in, 167-68, 179, 182-83; oedipal dramas in, 176, 187; as racial delegate, 167; reception of, 23, 158-69, 172, 178-80, 181-82
lesbianism: and gender, 109-10, 112; popular association with the female criminal, 111; visibility and invisibility of, 109-10
Lethal Weapon series, 20, 27, 28-30, 33-37, 45, 56, 113; Lethal Weapon 1, 28-30, 32, 33, 36, 39, 41-42, 44, 47, 51, 224 n30, 225 n37, 226 n47; Lethal Weapon 2, 35; Lethal Weapon 3, 27, 29-30, 33, 37, 221 n1
Levinson, Barry, 68, 229 n1
Levy, Michael, 56
Lewis, Joseph H., 105
Lonely Villa, The, 230 n14
Lone Star, 246 n4
Long Kiss Goodnight, The, 221 n1, 222 n11
Losey, Joseph, 251 n5
Lubiano, Wahneema, 159, 166-67
Lurie, John, 154
Lynch, David, 22-24, 131-57, 197; audience for, 155-56, 197; and hatred of women's bodies, 149-50; the "Lynch effect," 132-34,

140, 156; and the "oedipal thrall," 134-36, 156; primal scenes in, 134, 142-48; and punishment of audience, 151; reception of, 131-35, 137-38, 140-42, 143, 151, 155-57; and shock, 138, 151-52
Lyne, Adrian, 60
Lyon, Liz, 253 n19

MacLachlan, Kyle, 134, 155, 244 n22
MacMillan, Terry, 183
Madonna, 208
Marder, Elissa, 237 n17
marking, 4, 217-18 n5
masculinity: and African American women critics, 161-62; and AIDS, 120-21, 234 n34; and anality, 86, 87; and anxiety, 67-68, 72-73, 76, 84-85, 86, 88; black masculinity in film, 161-62; and the body as masquerade, 113-14; and homophobia, 94; and incompetence, 60-61, 64, 68, 76-78, 229 n2; and reversibility of gaze, 90-92; as spectacle, 45-46; in Tarantino, 210-11; and Vietnam War, 233 n29; white masculinity and crisis, 20, 31-32, 41, 46-47, 49, 53-55, 225 n35
masochism, 226 n47; male, 46-47
McBride, Jim, 252 n13
McDonnell, Mary, 187
McDowell, Jeanne, 164-65
McKee, Lonette, 171, 248 n24
McTiernan, John, 27, 30, 39
Medak, Peter, 229 n1
Menace II Society, 227 n51, 256 n41
Mercer, Colin, 236 n8
Mercer, Kobena, 2-3, 160, 241 n50, 247 n19, 256 n42
Merck, Mandy, 66
"Miami Vice" (TV Show), 224 n23
Michael, John, 255 n29
Miller, D. A., 231 n18, 232 n19
minority discourses and "the burden of representation," 23, 160, 167, 186
miscegenation, 37, 38-39, 82, 158-60, 168-70, 173-77, 181, 188
Mo' Better Blues, 247 n16
Modesty Blaise, 193
Modleski, Tania, 8, 29, 226 n47

Moorhouse, Jocelyn, 187
Morris, Meaghan, 218 n12, 219 n16
Morrison, Toni, 3–4, 115, 218 n10
Mulcahy, Russell, 55
multiculturalism, 13, 19–20, 51, 123, 160, 177,
    186, 216; theories of, 178, 227 n57

Naremore, James, 7, 132–33, 196, 242 n3, 252
    n10
Neale, Steve, 45–46, 225 n41
New Jack City, 161, 163
"NYPD Blue" (TV show), 218 n7, 218 n9

object: good object/bad object, 38, 48
oedipal structures: in Lee, 176, 187; in Lynch,
    134–35, 141–42, 157; in male-authored
    African American film, 162–63; in Taran-
    tino, 194–95, 198, 201–2, 204–7, 209, 251
    n7, 251 n8; in Terminator 2, 117–18
Oldman, Gary, 209
One False Move, 227 n51, 246 n4
overdetermination and coincidence, 58–59

Pacific Heights, 229 n2
Pacino, Al, 61, 85, 90
Pakula, Alan, 229 n1
Passenger 57, 57
Passion Fish, 187
Penley, Constance, 238 n24, 240 n40, 255
    n32
Penn, Christopher, 203
permissive realism, 34
Pfeil, Fred, 41, 45, 58, 221 n1, 223 n15, 224
    n22, 224 n24, 224 n31, 225 n35, 225 n37,
    245 n28, 251 n7
Platoon, 254 n24
Plummer, Amanda, 190
point of view, 38, 43–45, 66, 117, 122, 136–37,
    138, 146–47, 150, 169–70; and shot-
    reverse-shot, 43–45, 169–70; theories of,
    225 n36, 243 n10, 248 n23; and tracking
    shots, 171, 248 n23
Poitier, Sidney, 29
Polan, Dana, 232 n21, 232 n23
political correctness, 5, 102
Presumed Innocent, 229 n1, 229 n2

Price, Richard, 233 n31
primal scene in Lynch, 139, 142–48
professional-managerial class, 155–56, 225
    n31; and "taste culture," 156
projection, 102
public sphere, 7–9, 179, 186, 214; and pri-
    vatization, 7, 214; public opinion, 9,
    186
Pulp Fiction, 23, 136, 189–215
Pyle, Forest, 117, 240 n38, 240 n42

Queen Latifah, 183
"queer erotics," 112, 238 n23, 238 n24

race, 2–6, 13; biraciality, 12, 173; "black sur-
    rogacy," 115; cultural representations of,
    186–87; and gender, 173–74, 188; as ico-
    nicity, 4, 6, 23, 158–59, 174, 187; interracial
    bonding, 27–29, 125, 187–88; interracial
    couples, 158–60, 168–70, 173–88, 246 n4,
    250 n34; as local color and authenticity,
    23, 153–54, 161, 163, 167; metaphoricity of,
    4, 180; passion of ignorance about, 159;
    racialization, 186; and the unconscious,
    182–83; and violence in Lee, 163–67;
    and visibility, 170–71, 172–73, 177–78;
    and "whiteness" vs. "blackness," 3–4, 6,
    159–60, 170–71, 174–75, 177–78, 213, 248
    n25
racial epithets, 23–24, 189, 196, 199, 204, 207,
    209–14, 250 n37, 252 n18
Rafferty, Terrence, 179, 181–82, 223 n19, 248
    n20
rage: and feminism, 70, 98–102, 104, 105–
    6; as a mark of nondominant groups, 66;
    political implications of, 70, 78, 82, 231 n16
reaction shots, 38–39
reception: of action films, 55–57, 58; of Lee,
    158–69, 172, 178–80, 181–82; of Lynch,
    131–35, 137–38, 140–42, 143, 151, 155–57;
    of Tarantino, 191, 197, 207, 209; of Ter-
    minator 2, 115–16; of Thelma and Louise,
    98–101, 103–4, 109–10; theories of, 58; of
    Waiting to Exhale, 183–84
referentiality, theories of, 166–67
reproductive freedom, 119–21

Reservoir Dogs, 23, 189, 190–91, 193, 195, 201, 202, 203, 204, 206, 208, 209, 210, 211, 213
Rhames, Ving, 189
Rhines, Jesse Alergernon, 248 n27
Rich, B. Ruby, 62, 63–64, 92
Richardson, Miranda, 10, 12
Ricochet, 55–57
Roberts, Julia, 229 n2
Robin Hood: Prince of Thieves, 239 n33
Robson, Mark, 223 n13
Rodowick, D. N., 46, 72, 233 n30
Rogers, Mimi, 71
Romeo Is Bleeding, 229 n1
Rose, Jacqueline, 102, 110, 233 n30, 236 n13
Ross, Andrew, 219 n13, 245 n30
Rossellini, Isabella, 134, 143
Roth, Tim, 190, 191, 193
Ruben, Joseph, 229 n2
Rubinek, Saul, 201

sadomasochistic spectacle, 28, 45, 46–47, 200, 253 n20, 253 n21
Sayles, John, 154, 187, 246 n4
Schickel, Richard, 39, 99, 223 n19, 226 n48
Schlesinger, John, 229 n2
School Daze, 247 n16
Schroeder, Barbet, 229 n1
Schwarzenegger, Arnold, 118–19, 122, 240 n43
Sciorra, Annabella, 80, 158, 169, 248 n24
Scorsese, Martin, 249 n30, 251 n9
Scott, Ridley, 60, 104, 113, 231 n17
Scott, Tony, 189, 252–53 n22, 256 n37
Sea of Love, 21, 61, 64, 73, 83, 84–96
Sedgwick, Eve Kosofsky, 112
Shapiro, Laura, 101
shock: as cinematic effect, 134, 138–39, 151; theories of, 245 n25, 152
Shohat, Ella, 5, 218 n11
Silver, Joel, 56, 201
Silverman, Kaja, 46, 244 n24
Simon, John, 100, 223 n19
Single White Female, 229 n1
Sleeping with the Enemy, 229 n2
Smith, Paul, 7–8, 33, 95, 226 n45, 235 n40, 239 n30, 239 n35, 244 n24

Smith, Valerie, 161, 167
Snead, James, 4, 217–18 n5
Snipes, Wesley, 33, 57, 158, 169
Someone to Watch Over Me, 21, 60, 61, 64, 70–78, 96, 229 n5
Something Wild, 131
sound: sound track, 136, 139, 148, 150; and space, 41, 139, 225 n34, 242 n8; and speech, 41, 225 n34; theories of cinematic sound, 227 n52, 252 n16
special effects, 115, 116, 152–53
spectatorship, 2
Spillers, Hortense, 185
Stabile, Carol, 240 n45
Stanton, Harry Dean, 144
Stone, Oliver, 201, 215, 254 n24, 254 n25, 257 n45
Stone, Sharon, 83
Straight Outta Brooklyn, 161
Strange Days, 188, 246 n4

talk shows, 179, 181
Tarantino, Quentin, 22–24, 133, 136, 189–216; and African American popular culture, 211–16; anality in, 194–95, 203–4; the bathroom in, 189–93; black masculinity in, 210–11; cult audience, 214–15; as fanboy, 196–97; father's gaze in, 194–95, 196, 199, 203; feminine authority in, 206–7, 208; homoeroticism in, 202–4; id/superego figures in, 204; and nostalgia, 197–98, 215–16; oedipal in, 201–2, 204–6, 213, 215–16; pornographic pleasure in, 207, 255 n32; primal scenes in, 199–200; race in, 203–7, 209–16; racism in, 199, 200–201, 202; reception of, 191, 197, 207, 209; sadomasochistic spectacle in, 200, 253 n20; and television, 194–95, 198; and trash, 195; and violence, 212; violence and anality in, 189–92, 193, 199–200, 212
Tasker, Yvonne, 221–22 n4, 222 n5, 223 n14, 225 n35, 226 n49, 232 n26, 234 n36, 237 n15, 238 n20, 239 n28
Taubin, Amy, 253 n20, 256 n40
technology: and anxiety, 47–48, 68, 230 n14; and the body, 47–48; and the gaze, 50

television, 5, 9, 38, 49, 50, 159, 179, 194-95, 198, 218 n7, 218 n9; and censorship, 245 n26; and political correctness, 5
Terminator, The, 116, 117, 240 n38, 240 n39
Terminator 2, 21, 60, 99, 109, 113, 115-26
Thelma and Louise, 21, 60, 66, 98-115, 126, 221 n11, 227 n51
Thomas-Hill hearings, 98
Tightrope, 95
To Live and Die in L. A., 232-33 n27
Tololyan, Khachig, 227 n54
Torres, Sasha, 251 n4
trash: as an aesthetic category, 55; and cultural authority, 189, 191, 195; history as, 216
Travolta, John, 189, 195, 196, 251 n8
Trespass, 161
tributary media, 7-8
True Romance, 23, 189, 192, 193, 195, 201, 202, 204, 209, 213, 253-54 n22
Tuggle, Richard, 95
Turner, Kathleen, 230 n8
Turturro, John, 158, 169, 247 n16
"Twin Peaks" (TV show), 131, 144, 149, 151, 152, 155, 244 n22, 244 n23

Unlawful Entry, 239 n4

Van Peebles, Mario, 247 n5
Verhoeven, Paul, 61
Vietnam War, 35-36, 39, 49, 194-95; and masculine anxiety, 201, 215, 233 n29, 254 n24

visibility/arguability, 170
visuality and the unconscious, 170
violence and fantasy, 100-101, 105; and feminine violence, 99, 101, 105-7, 109-10, 115; and reproductive freedom, 119-21

Waiting to Exhale, 183, 188
Walken, Christopher, 194, 195, 201, 204
Wallace, Michele, 162, 184, 248 n24
Washington, Denzel, 56, 57
Watling, Claire, 232-33 n27
Wayans, Damon, 33, 37, 576, 228 n61
Weaver, Sigourney, 113, 125, 232 n25
Whitaker, Forest, 13, 183
Wiegman, Robyn, 55
Wild at Heart, 22, 131, 133-41
Wilder, Billy, 230 n8
Willemen, Paul, 207-8, 255 n33
Williams, Linda, 255 n32
Williams, Patricia, 218 n6
Willis, Bruce, 27, 33, 39, 45, 49, 56, 214, 226 n44
Willis, David, 244 n21
Willis, Susan, 239 n27
Wilton, Tamsin, 112
Wizard of Oz, The, 135, 139, 146-47, 157, 243 n11, 243 n17

youth culture, 101, 197, 209, 235 n4, 235 n5

Zabriskie, Grace, 144
Zinneman, Fred, 50
Žižek, Slavoj, 62-63, 115, 230 n12, 231 n17

Sharon Willis is Associate Professor of Visual and
Cultural Studies at the University of Rochester. She is
the author of *Marguerite Duras: Writing on the Body*
and co-editor (with Constance Penley) of *Male Trouble*.

Library of Congress Cataloging-in-Publication Data
Willis, Sharon.
High contrast : race and gender in contemporary
Hollywood film / by Sharon Willis.
Includes index.
ISBN 0-8223-2029-0 (cloth : alk. paper).
ISBN 0-8223-2041-X (pbk. : alk. paper)
1. Afro-Americans in motion pictures. 2. Sex role in
motion pictures. I. Title. PN1995.9.S47W56   1998
791.43'655—dc21   97-13147 CIP